The Scientific Analysis
of Personality and
Motivation

PERSONALITY AND PSYCHOPATHOLOGY
A Series of Monographs, Texts, and Treatises

David T. Lykken, Editor

1. The Anatomy of Achievement Motivation, *Heinz Heckhausen.* 1966°

2. Cues, Decisions, and Diagnoses: A Systems-Analytic Approach to the Diagnosis of Psychopathology, *Peter E. Nathan.* 1967°

3. Human Adaptation and Its Failures, *Leslie Phillips.* 1968°

4. Schizophrenia: Research and Theory, *William E. Broen, Jr.* 1968°

5. Fears and Phobias, *I. M. Marks.* 1969

6. Language of Emotion, *Joel R. Davitz.* 1969

7. Feelings and Emotions, *Magda Arnold.* 1970

8. Rhythms of Dialogue, *Joseph Jaffe* and *Stanley Feldstein.* 1970

9. Character Structure and Impulsiveness, *David Kipnis.* 1971

10. The Control of Aggression and Violence: Cognitive and Physiological Factors, *Jerome L. Singer* (Ed.). 1971

11. The Attraction Paradigm, *Donn Byrne.* 1971

12. Objective Personality Assessment: Changing Perspectives, *James N. Butcher* (Ed.). 1972

13. Schizophrenia and Genetics, *Irving I. Gottesman* and *James Shields,* 1972°

14. Imagery and Daydream Methods in Psychotherapy and Behavior Modification, *Jerome L. Singer.* 1974

15. Experimental Approaches to Psychopathology, *Mitchell L. Kietzman, Samuel Sutton;* and *Joseph Zubin* (Eds.). 1975

16. Coping and Defending: Processes of Self-Environment Organization, *Norma Haan.* 1977

17. The Scientific Analysis of Personality and Motivation, *R. B. Cattell* and *P. Kline.* 1977

°Titles initiated during the series editorship of Brendan Maher.

The Scientific Analysis of Personality and Motivation

R. B. CATTELL
Department of Psychology
University of Hawaii,
Hawaii.

and

P. KLINE
Washington Singer Laboratories,
Department of Psychology,
University of Exeter, Exeter, England.

1977

ACADEMIC PRESS   New York   San Francisco   London
A Subsidiary of Harcourt Brace Jovanovich, Publishers

ACADEMIC PRESS INC. (LONDON) LTD.
24/28 Oval Road,
London NW1

United States Edition published by
ACADEMIC PRESS INC.
111 Fifth Avenue
New York, New York 10003

Library of Congress Catalog Number 77–71812
ISBN: 0 12 164250–X

Printed in Great Britain by
Whitstable Litho Ltd., Whitstable, Kent

Preface

This book is a development of *Scientific Analysis of Personality*, written by the senior author, which, for over a decade, was widely available as a Penguin paperback and which has now been superseded by the present somewhat larger text. The present book has developed in several directions, has been brought up-to-date in relation to intervening advances, and has been adapted more to student use.

It is a fairly explicit policy in universities and colleges to adapt courses in a particular science to two distinct groups: (1) to professionally-oriented students, specializing in undergraduate and still more in postgraduate work in the given science; and (2) to students in other areas who want a glance over the given science as part of a liberal education. To understand how we have tried to cater for the second while aiming mainly at the first it is necessary to consider the state of the subject, as of this decade.

Personality is the natural core of psychological science, since the "process" areas—perception, memory, learning theory, physiological psychology—can only be effectively understood in relation to the unified organism. Considering the complexity of the subject, all areas have made remarkable progress in the last twenty years toward the standards of exact experiment, dependable laws, and quantitative formulae, which characterize the more mature sciences. But personality hung back until recently—regrettably so in view of its integrating function—because most writing for most students still dealt with the sometimes entertaining but invariably speculative and unproven "laws" of clinical and even literary approaches.

That so many texts on personality clung to these qualitative, clinical, disputable and disputed grand theories is not surprising in view of the greater discipline, e.g. in mathematics and experimental design, required by the newer movement. Nevertheless, around the middle of the century the serious study of personality "turned a corner" and began to put its concepts and laws in order on an experimental and quantitative basis. Through so doing it has already shown itself to be a more theoretically respectable science and one with a practical technology of dependable utility. But it has become more difficult, and professional psychology, at least, is no longer a convalescent home for refugees from the rigors of such subjects as chemistry, physics, medicine and engineering.

One result, however, is that the exposition of the subject, in this new adolescent phase, requires special concerns and skills. The present authors have had experience in clinical and educational areas, and have written with, we trust, some understanding of, say, Freudian and Jungian ideas, and their more recent formulations. At the same time both are scientifically committed to bivariate and multivariate quantitative experimental approaches, and have therefore tried to bring the historical background to the student illuminated by the sharper light of modern scientific developments. Continuity of certain broad concepts has been maintained, but with fairly extensive demolition and reconstruction. In particular we have sought to link up at the frontiers, on a basis of equal scientific discipline, with learning theory, genetics, perception, physiological psychology, statistics, and other domains.

Returning to the two types of program needed for students we must express grave doubts about the solution, now somewhat prevalent, of teaching scientific psychology to professionals, and humanistic psychology to those looking at the subject as part of a broad panoramic acquaintance with fields outside their own speciality. Whatever else the recent cult of so-called humanistic psychology may be, it is not psychology as developed as a science in the last fifty years. At its best it communicates shrewd and sympathetic acquaintance with human nature as formerly gained from the classics, e.g. from Plutarch's *Lives*, from literature, as in, say, Macbeth, and from such maxims as appear in La Rochefoucauld or Lord Chesterfield's letters to his son. To transpose the well-known comment of the French generals on the charge of the Light Brigade, "C'est magnifique, mais ce n'est pas la science." If specialists in other fields need a relatively brief but genuine acquaintance with what modern psychology is doing we would humbly suggest that a selection of chapters from the present book could be part of their reading.

Nevertheless, it is to the first type of student that this book is primarily directed, in its total organization, with the aim of laying a firm foundation for the education of a psychologist—be he teacher, clinician, industrial psychologist or researcher. With this intention we have not hesitated, for example, to use technical terms fairly freely (although these are always explained), and to encourage a critical evaluative attitude to popular theories. In particular, in going over the evidence for personality structure one finds that a couple of dimensions such as neuroticism and extraversion are absurdly few to cover the real complexity of human personality which factor analytic research reveals.

Consequently, the new unitary temperament and motivation traits require new, more technical terms, and these terms it is now reasonable to expect the professional student to learn.

When students read a book without benefit of a teacher to summarize —and perhaps even *with* his experienced help—it is very important that the authors provide at the end of each chapter such a perspective-giving summary, and this aid we have taken care to prepare carefully. A bibliography of sources has also been provided to help the reader. We anticipate that with guidance by the teacher to two or three readings beyond each chapter the student will gain a good overview of modern personality psychology, and we trust it will serve him well not only immediately but in assimilating more easily the directions of research advance likely to be active in the future.

January, 1977

RAYMOND B. CATTELL
PAUL KLINE

Contents

Acknowledgements

The writers would like to acknowledge the following publishers and authors for permission to quote passages and reprint tables and figures.

Penguin Books Ltd: from *The Scientific Analysis of Personality* (1965) Copyright (C) Raymond B Cattell
   Table 22, Examples of items from MAT, pp 196–197
   Diagram 38, The Adjustment Process Analysis Chart, p 275
   Diagram 11, Second-order factor structures and the relation of questionnaire and objective test factors, p 118
   Diagram 17, Subject's choice of interpretation, p 149
   Diagram 21, Fragment of a dynamic lattice, showing attitude subsidiation, sentiment structure, and ergic goals, p 186

University of Illinois Press: from *Objective Personality and Motivation Tests* by R. B. Cattell and F. W. Warburton,
   p 196, description of T factors.

Holt, Rhinehart and Winston: from *Motivation and Dynamic Structure* by R. B. Cattell and D. Child
   Table 2.11 p. 40
   Table 2.12 p 46
   Table 2.14 p 55
   Fig 3.6 p 83
   Table 9.6 p 222
   Table 10.1 p 241
IPAT, Champaign Illinois: From *Handbook to the 16 PF Test* (1970 Edit)
   Fig. 14.1 and 14.2 p 265 and p 267

Oxford University Press, New York: From *Explorations in Personality* by H. A. Murray
   p 144–5 List of 20 Needs
Clinical Psychological Pub. Co: From *Monograph 34 of J. Clinical Psychology*— clinical diagnosis by the objective—Analytic Personality Batteries by R. B. Cattell, L. R. Schmidt and A. Bjerstedt
   Table 55

Jossey-Bass Ltd, San Francisco: From *Personality and Mood by Questionnaire* by
R. B. Cattell

Table 4 p 51–52	First 15 normal questionnaire primaries
Table 6 p 57	Seven missing factors
Table 12 p 98	Primary traits in clinically deviant behaviour
Table 22 p 130	Secondary factors
Table 24 p 140	Pre-adult and adult second-order factor patterns
Table 26 p 199	Second-order state patterns
Table 27 p 200	Second-order change structures
Table 29 p 215–16	8 state factors by combined P and dR T technique
Table 62 p 441	Correlations of personality and intelligence with school grades
Table 66 p 453	Personality profiles for various occupational groups
Table 67 p 458–59	Characteristic profiles of principal abnormal syndrome groups

Routledge and Kegan Paul: From *Personality Structure and Measurement* by H. J.
Eysenck and S. B. G. Eysenck
   p 31 Descriptive list of Guilford Factors

Methuen and Co Ltd: From *The Energies of Men* by McDougall
   p 97–98 list of innate propensities

*British Psychological Society and Association of Teachers in Colleges and Depts of
Educ.* From *the Brit. J. Educ. Psychol.* 1972, 42, 137–151
   Personality and Academic Attainment by N. J. Entwistle Table 1 p 141

Chapter 1

The Scientific Investigation
of Personality

ETHICAL PROBLEMS

One end result of the scientific investigation of personality, if it is successful, will be the ability to predict precisely the apparent vagaries of human behaviour. It follows, of course, that if we can predict behavior then we can control it. This brings with it moral and philosophical problems which we shall mention briefly but which lie outside the scope of this book.

Thus, if we can control behaviour there arises the problem of who shall control it—a problem at least as old as Juvenal—*quis custodiet custodes ipsos*? Furthermore the old philosophical issue is raised of free will and determinism. Can there be free will, in any meaningful sense, if all our behaviour follows causal laws? Or will we arrive at the position of physics where the behaviour of matter can be predicted except at the level of individual particles where the rules break down and Heisenberg's indeterminacy principle has to be invoked? Yet another problem arises in the issue of personal responsibility and morality. This is particularly important in the field of law. After all to what extent may an individual be blamed if his actions are predictable in terms of his past experience and personality? Similar difficulties arise too in the field of changing behaviour for any purpose such as, an extreme instance, brain-washing, or psychotherapy, or advertising (where hopefully consumer behaviour is

1

changed) or ultimately indeed education itself. These last are practical modern examples of the problem first discussed in this paragraph. From this we can see that the scientific study of personality confronts us with acute moral, political, social and personal dilemmas. These, however, important as they are, are not the concern of our book. Our book is concerned with the scientific study of personality. In it we want to propound and explicate the most recent position, for, as we shall see, we are at the dawn of the era when we shall be able to predict behaviour and understand the enormous complexity of human personality.

SCIENTIFIC METHODOLOGY

To understand fully the scientific study of personality in its modern form we must set it in two related contexts. It has to be seen against the backcloth of scientific method as it applies in psychology and against the background of previous "pre-scientific" speculations about personality, and we must now briefly discuss both these topics.

Scientific Method. What is meant by scientific method has long been the debate of philosophers of science. It seems generally agreed however (e.g., Popper, 1959) that there are two essentials, one dependent on the other. First and most important is the falsifiability of hypotheses which turns on, and is bound up with, quantification of variables.

Thus scientific statements can be refuted. For example, if we say that smoking in adults is associated with early weaning, there are obvious ways in which this statement may be shown to be false. Thus if we find a group of smokers who were weaned later than a similar group of non-smokers, it is simply wrong. Note too that quantification is implicit in this hypothesis, even if not explicit. Thus it would be a very crude experiment if we simply compared two groups: non-smokers and smokers (including the man who had the odd cigarette after a meal and the man who chain-smoked 100 a day inhaling every puff to the full). Similarly there is no dividing line between early and late weaning. Now this example illustrates the problem of quantification with two variables, length of feeding in infancy and amount of tobacco smoked, which are relatively easy to quantify. However often in the study of human personality this is far from the case. Such terms as bravery, will-power, gullibility, are obviously difficult to measure. Much of our book will necessarily be concerned with just these problems of measurement.

From our illustration of a simple hypothesis relating weaning to smoking, we can see that quantification is involved in falsifiability. Of course many of our hypotheses in personality are far more complex than this and could not be tested at all without accurate quantification. For example if we say that adult dominance is related to parental dominance and the child's interactions with his family and peers, then without a precise measure of dominance the statement cannot be refuted. Falsifiability as a demand of scientific method refers strictly to *logical* rather than practical refutation. Thus if we *could* measure dominance, the statement would still be scientific even if we happened to have no test of dominance. However, if, in contrast, we were to argue that dominance was due to a need to dominate, this would not be scientific unless we postulated some external measure of this need. Thus we often find such circular, unscientific statements in theories postulating needs or instincts. Dominance depends on the need to dominate. The evidence for this need comes from the fact that people do dominate, but the need was postulated to explain the behaviour which is then taken as evidence for the need! Perfect circularity.

We may summarize this discussion of the scientific method by stating that in essence it demands that we state our hypotheses in such a way that they are open to refutation. This in turn with hypotheses of any complexity demands accurate quantification. This is the background of logic which we assume in the scientific study of personality as we discuss it in this book. We shall make no real attempt to justify this approach other than to say that in the natural sciences it is this method that has led to their large increase in knowledge and understanding. There is no *a priori* reason to think that a similar approach should not be successful in the study of human behaviour. Only when such methods have failed would we be justified in trying to argue as some have done (e.g. Allport, 1939) that scientific methodology is inappropriate.

As we indicated, the scientific investigation of personality may be understood only against the background of scientific methodology, which we have discussed, and against the "pre-scientific," in the chronological (not pejorative) sense, speculative findings of earlier workers. Since we have, previously, so stressed the importance of the scientific method, some readers may be wondering why we should bother at all with non-scientific speculations. There are a number of reasons for this. For example, some of the workers in the field of human personality have been among the most remarkable intellects of their time. Thus it would seem foolish to dismiss on the grounds of methodology alone the work of such as Freud, Jung or Kretschmer. The scientific method *ensures* the accuracy of what is found. It is possible that immensely insightful men can hit on the truth. Their insights then, like the insights of great writers, may be useful. Furthermore although their work lacks quantification it is based on observation. Thus in their clinical work, Freud and Jung had access to data which few others have bothered to study. Their attempts to understand personality are not purely speculation but rest on data (however tenuous the connection).

PRE-SCIENTIFIC WORK ON PERSONALITY

Philosophy and Literature
Much speculation, quasi-empirical statement, is contained in both philosophy and literature either implicitly or explicitly. Thus Plato, in the Phaedrus,

claims that the human mind resembles a chariot with two horses, one fiery and uncontrolled, the other docile, controlled by a rider—a dynamic tripartite view of human mental processing based on no data but common everyday observations. It represents an attempt by one of the outstanding minds of Europe to account for human behaviour. This is a philosophical example made especially interesting by its resemblance to the Freudian concept of mental provinces—ego, id and superego. Rousseau's Emile constitutes another important work of this type.

The great literary figures often embody implicit psychological hypotheses in their work and are valued for these insights. So many examples abound that all we can do is give a few illustrations although there can be no doubt that it would be a highly interesting exercise to try to uncover the most salient psychological assumptions of great authors. Thus Homer's Iliad is based on two assumptions (a) that a young man, Achilles, who feels he has been insulted, will stay sulking in his tent no matter what cost to his friends and (b) that when his best friend is killed, in revenge and in shame, he will emerge to fight more powerfully than ever. These two assumptions, it will be noticed, can be put to the test, although as far as we know they never have been. These are but two hypotheses from the earliest literary work in Europe. There are in the great sweep of events in both his epics naturally many more.

Shakespeare is a mine of testable hypotheses. In Julius Caesar we note the correlation of body type and personality—objecting to the personality of Cassius and finding it typical of thin men. In Macbeth guilt destroys sleep and leads to symbolic obsessional rituals—symptoms are given psychological meaning. In more modern writers we have to be more careful about considering their psychological assumptions for they may have been influenced by psychological theories. Thus Patrick White's fine novel, *The Tree of Man*, is a powerful exemplar of Jungian theory—especially the notion that true maturity emerges only as we allow ourselves to know our own racial or collective unconscious. To throw away the insights of these men seems foolish, as foolish indeed as to rely on them. We feel that they should be borne in mind as one possible way of conceptualizing the scientific, trustworthy evidence as it is collected, a view not altogether different from that put forward by Joynson (1974) who urges us to attend to common-sense intuitions about behaviour.

Organized Observation and Theory

This came into being with the development of psychiatry, really at the beginning of the nineteenth century. When Pinel cast off the chains from the lunatics of Paris, regarding them not as evil or possessed by devils but as ill and in need of treatment (the nature of which was then, as it still is, quite problematical), this ushered in the age of organized observation and theory. The main figures in this early period of psychiatry were Kraepelin, Charcot and Janet. These were noted for their accurate clinical descriptions and categorizations. Then came the psychoanalysts at the turn of the twentieth century and, writing for its first thirty or forty years, Freud, Jung and Adler are justly the most renowned of these observers and theorists. At this time, too, academic, university based psychology was coming into being and this produced personality theorists whose work may be properly described as pre-scientific in that it was innocent of measurement.

These then are the two stages in the pre-scientific study of personality. Actually both continue, for much clinical psychiatric personality theory has remained at this level—the work of Laing (1960), Berne (1968) and Szaz (1961) being of this kind.

However, gradually, from the turn of the century, the scientific study of psychology in general and personality in particular began to get under way. In the last decade, as the advent of powerful computers has made possible the use of highly complex, multivariate statistical techniques, great strides have been made in the scientific study of personality and it is these that form the main contents of our book.

In our earlier discussion of the scientific method, we noted that accurate quantification was a prime necessity for the precise testing of hypotheses—the essence of the scientific method. We also stressed that logical rather than practical refutability was important. This is true but in the actual procedure of science, in the study of personality, practical refutability becomes all important. This means that enormous efforts have had to be expended in the quantification of variables and, because of the complexity of the hypotheses, in the development of appropriate statistical techniques for analyzing our quantified results. As we said, the real value and impact of the modern scientific investigation of personality can only be seen against the backcloth of the two stages of personality study discussed above. This is because from the viewpoint of scientific method, these two stages are hopelessly flawed. We shall discuss briefly their faults and shortcomings below.

FLAWS IN THE LITERARY AND PHILOSOPHICAL METHOD

Tot homines quot sententiae, is the essence of the problem here. Even if the great writers contain some truths how are we to know whether they are correct or not. There is simply no way of choosing. Furthermore it is doubtful whether insight and speculation is sufficient to discover the lawful regularities underlying human behaviour. We may need, as in the sciences, special methods and techniques of investigation. After all, atomic nuclear theory is contra-intuitive as indeed is the fact of the roundness of the earth and its circling the sun. Thus there is no *a priori* reason, except that some writers of great genius do appear to have outstanding insight, to expect that this method would reveal facts of great value and there can be no certainty about the truth or falsity of their propositions.

Flaws in stage of clinical observation. As we indicated many of the great early figures in the study of personality worked in the psychiatric clinic. Their observations, therefore, were necessarily made on psychotic and neurotic patients. Although one good result of this was the realization that mentally well and mentally sick patients were not radically different from one another, to base statements about normals on observations of patients is logically inadmissible. Thus their work is flawed by *sampling error.* Before you can generalize from normals to neurotics you have to demonstrate that they are similar populations. The art or science of sampling was, of course, not developed at this time.

An argument sometimes used in defence of the study of the abnormal for reference back to the normal is that there you can see things writ large that would otherwise escape observation. Thus the obsessional neurotic may spend his day washing his hands to avoid contamination. This is a clear example of a trait that is found in many normal housewives who pride themselves on the cleanliness of their homes. However this assumes that it really is the case that the abnormal does exaggerate the normal. Recent studies of obsessionality however, do not support this common-sense intuitive view (e.g. Kline, 1969) and the study of the psychotic factor (Eysenck and Eysenck, 1968). Strictly, therefore, this problem of assumptions, is subsumed under our earlier paragraph as sampling error.

Sampling errors are sufficient on their own to invalidate findings. Even more serious was the *complete lack of quantification.* This is particularly important since the kind of hypotheses many of these workers discuss demands quantification. Thus, if anxiety is held to reflect Oedipal conflict, we must have measures of both these things. The statement more or less anxious is a crude form of quantification. Similarly the degree of Oedipal conflict, in Freudian theory, shows individual variation. Adequate tests of this theoretical statement demand, therefore, precise quantifications of anxiety and Oedipal conflict. Without these we can put no trust in the theory. Furthermore subjective ratings by psychiatrists are notoriously poor, not only in assessing anxiety but on almost any variables. Psychiatric judgements indeed as with interviews are simply unreliable (Beck, 1962). Thus then lack of quantification means that the statements themselves need verification and are likely to be faulty.

Yet another related fault of these studies is the nature of the data. In Freud's papers we are never told what observations Freud actually made. Instead we find an intertwining of speculation, inference, and observation. Further, as is well known, Freud only recalled later what patients had said to him, no written records were made at the time. Thus how reliable what little observation there was is quite unknown. The scientific method makes great play of the importance of replicable observations. Hence this is a great flaw in the psychoanalytic method, and in most of the clinical psychologies of this kind.

To summarize: these kinds of theory have extensive flaws from the scientific viewpoint of poor recording of data, no quantification and poor sampling. Inevitably because of these weaknesses there was no statistical analysis to demonstrate that their findings were not as might arise by chance.

As we look at the enumeration of the flaws of this period of personality study one point should begin to stand out. In reality it is little different from the frankly literary speculation of an avowedly unscientific kind. Other than that the authors claim that their work is based on observations there is a similar subjectivity. Support for this essential similarity comes from the fact that in psychoanalysis, for example, there are a large number of conflicting theorists: Freud, Jung, Adler, Anna Freud, Melanie Klein, Fairbairn, Fromm, Reich, Horney, Sullivan, Rank and the fantastic Sadger who claimed that some conflicts could be traced back to problems at the time of the formation of the zygote. These are only the main protagonists. This hardly gives us confidence in the reliability or validity of their claims.

AIM OF THE BOOK

Against this background of scientific method and the flawed procedures of pre-scientific attempts to conceptualize personality, the aim of our book emerges. It is to describe the findings of the modern scientific study of personality. This involves, of necessity, a study of the special methods which have had to be devised for such investigations so that we can judge their adequacy and an account of the results which they have yielded. However, we do not want to ignore the clinical findings of over half a century of often dedicated observations. As we said it could be the case that such brilliantly insightful investigators as Freud or Jung or Kretschmer *could* have stumbled on some truths. This is especially true of the psychoanalytic school who have concentrated their observations on data (free associations of patients) which most psychologists have entirely ignored. Thus it is our hope that the modern scientific procedures can develop their own sets of results which can sort out of the confused mass of speculations the dross from the gold. It would be absurd to expect that many of these early claims would be supported *in toto*. On the other hand it may well be that their claims can be suitably modified. Certainly it may well be the case that their insights will enable us better to conceptualize our empirical findings.

One further point remains: the scientific methods that we shall be describing are those that have been especially developed for or found particularly useful in the study of personality. Nevertheless these methods have tended to be developed separately from those in the mainstream of experimental psychology and very often the findings from the two branches of psychology have remained unaffected by each other. We shall also, where relevant, weave in this work especially in the field of learning where complementary results to those in the field of personality have long been known. We must now, in the next chapter, turn to a study of the scientific methods especially useful in the study of personality.

SUMMARY

1. The ethical, philosophical, social and moral problems implicated in the study of personality were briefly mentioned.
2. The essence of the scientific method was described with great emphasis being put on refutability of hypotheses and quantification.
3. Pre-scientific work on personality, which has gone on since the dawn of civilization, was discussed. Two stages were recognized:
   (a) the philosophical and literary, where the theories of great writers such as Plato and Shakespeare are to be found;
   (b) the observational, which includes the work of many famous clinicians such as Freud and McDougall.
4. The flaws in the approaches to the study of personality were scrutinized. Sampling, quantification and lack of replicable data were all discussed.
5. Finally, in the light of these points, the aim of the book was clarified—the description of personality, as it has emerged from its scientific study.

Chapter 2

Scientific Methods in the
Study of Personality

MULTIVARIATE AND UNIVARIATE METHODS

Cattell (1957 and 1965) has been amongst the foremost in stressing this basic
distinction in the methods of scientific psychology. The Univariate method,
developed mainly on the model of the physical sciences, for laboratory
studies of perception, learning and information processing, consists essentially of varying one variable and seeing how it affects some other variable.

9

Thus, for example, we can vary light intensity and see how this influences the legibility of print. This illustration shows two things of great importance about the univariate method. First it necessitates complete *control* over our variables: we must be able to vary light intensity as we wish, which may require complex instrumentation. In the second place, it is manifestly too simple. Thus, for example, some type-faces might be easier to read at certain intensities than others. Ideally we really need to be able to vary more than one variable at once. In fact Fisher (1936) has developed such methods and designs —analyses of variance—which allow more than one variable to be varied at once.

Analysis of Variance

These analyses of variance methods have become highly sophisticated, and details can be found in such books as Snedecor (1956) or Edwards (1968). Nevertheless although analyses of variance designs are obviously an improvement over simple univariate designs, they still demand control over the variables and the number of variables in the design is inevitably limited. If a large number is inserted the meaning of significant interactions is impossible to grasp. Thus if we found that there was a significant interaction effect of light intensity and type-face on legibility, the meaning is clear. If, however, there were an interaction effect of personality, apititude, interest, light intensity, heat, time of day, typeface, and sex of tester (a purely hypothetical research design!), the meaning would defeat even the most ingenious interpreter. Furthermore the practical difficulties of finding samples to suit an analysis of variance design of this complexity would be virtually insuperable. Certainly the time necessary to carry out such a design would be enormous and, in terms of results, totally ill spent.

We can thus summarize univariate methods and their related analysis of variance techniques as ones characterized by the need for controlling variables with great exactitude and by the necessity of varying only a small number of variables at once. These techniques have in the experimental branches of psychology yielded highly valuable results and they are capable of putting hypotheses to the test with great precision.

Cattell has described personality as our total behaviour, as being concerned with all we do both overtly and covertly (psychological responses) (Cattell, 1957). This is a definition which many writers find broadly agreeable: there is no doubt, anywhere, of the rich complexity and breadth of the term (e.g. Sanford, 1963). It is this breadth and complexity which makes the univariate methods we have discussed above, essentially unsuitable for the study of personality. For it would seem evident that the number of important variables is large. Thus what is required in the study of personality is a technique which can handle a huge number of variables. In addition the need to control variables rules out huge areas of experimentation in human behaviour, as a few examples make clear. In our hypothetical study of the legibility of type-faces we can have in our analysis of variance, with ease, say six levels of light intensity. But suppose that in our study of personality we are interested in the effects of bereavement or of chronic pain. It is patently obvious that we cannot as experimenters commandeer a sample of mothers and dividing them at random, kill off the children of one group but leave the others, or give one randomly selected group a serious, chronic and painful disease. Thus the laboratory study of much human behaviour has to make use of analogous procedures, which many psychologists certainly those of a clinical persuasion find feeble and unconvincing. Thus studies of stress may use electric shock (of a mild strength). This laboratory experiment shows not only the impossibility of control (killing children) but also the flaw, from the viewpoint of personality studies, of its inability to handle a large number of variables. Thus it should be apparent that the effect of bereavement will vary with attitudes towards the bereaved. Not all children are wanted by their parents and some are actively ill-treated. Now in the analysis of variance approach this variable of attitude to children is not measured. It is hoped that it will be equivalent in the two groups. Yet this randomization of the variable, even if successful, means only that we know nothing about its effects. This example seems to us to illustrate the need for techniques which can let variables vary as they truly do in the real (as distinct from laboratory) world and which can handle a very large number of variables.

Such techniques are available and are called by Cattell (1957, 1965) multivariate methods—by which he means mainly factor analysis. These are the methods which he contrasts with univariate procedures.

Multivariate Methods

At this point we ought to clarify our definition of univariate and multivariate methods especially since we have classified analysis of variance in the former group although it manifestly is multivariate since more than one variable is manipulated. First as Van de Geer (1971) points out in terms of statistical models there is no basic, real distinction between the various techniques of multivariate analysis and multivariate analysis of variance. This of course implies that the simplest univariate case where only one variable is manipulated is also the same (since here we also use analysis of variance). Our distinction is really not one of statistical models and mathematical assumptions. Rather it is one of practical usage. By this criterion univariate methods, as we have seen, demand control or manipulation of at the most a few variables. Multivariate methods, on the other hand, are those that can handle a very large number of variables and can use them as they occur in nature. We must now describe these multivariate methods although we shall concentrate on factor analysis since this has been the most widely used in the study of personality and has been developed especially for this purpose by Cattell and his colleagues.

THE DIFFERENT VARIETIES OF MULTIVARIATE ANALYSIS

Our purpose here is to allow us to see how factor analysis fits into the family of multivariate techniques and how, by virtue of what it can do, factor analysis is peculiarly suited to the particular problems arising in the study of personality. We shall not try to differentiate these methods in terms of their models but rather in terms of their practical utility. For a statistical summary of the relationships between these techniques readers are referred to Van De Geer (1971), Anderson (1966), Horst (1966), or Cattell (1966).

Multiple Correlation

This is a widely used multivariate technique. In this we maximize the correlation between a set of predictor variables and the criterion variable. In doing this we arrive at a set of optimum weightings for each of the predictors. These weightings (beta weights) indicate the importance of each variable in predicting the criterion. Thus in a simple example we might find a multiple correlation of 0.7 between academic success and personality, ability and motivation variables, as did Cattell and Butcher (1968). Examination of the beta weights indicates that while ability on its own is the best single predictor, personality and motivation measures are also important. Multiple correlation is a valuable technique in the applied fields of psychology. Thus in the area of personality, when we know what variables to measure (which we can only know after the kind of scientific investigations we shall be discussing in this book) multiple correlation is useful in determining their significance in say vocational success, academic performance, becoming neurotic or psychotic, wherever indeed we can set up some criterion to measure. In theoretical investigations too multiple correlation is valuable. Thus in a longitudinal study of child development, the beta weights could well indicate the salience of different variables. However as a technique for investigating personality it has two difficulties. First we must already know what variables we wish to investigate. Since there is no agreement among theorists of personality as to what the most important variables are this is a serious limitation of the technique. Chronologically, therefore, in the programmatic study of personality, multiple correlation comes in late. A perhaps more serious defect lies in the criterion variable. With this technique we regress a set of predictor variables on to *one* criterion variable. Now it does not take much imagination to see that in a complex area of investigation of any sort there is a severe problem in selecting just a single criterion variable. That is why multiple correlation is used in vocational and educational psychology where it is possible (although somewhat unsatisfactory) to set up a simple criterion. Academic success can be the mean score in public examinations, vocational success can be the size of yearly income or a supervisor's rating.

Canonical Analysis or Canonical Correlation

To overcome this last deficit, the single criterion, when obviously a set of criterion scores is far more accurate, the method of *canonical analysis* or *canonical correlation* has been developed by Hotelling (1936). Apart from the difference that correlations between sets of variables are computed, canonical correlation resembles multiple correlation. It is highly interesting to note that, as Anderson (1966) points out, there is much similarity between principal components, factor analysis and canonical correlation. Indeed if the canonical correlation between the set of principal components and the original variables is computed, there is a correspondence between the canonical correlations and the principal ones.

Discriminant Function Analysis

This is a multivariate procedure designed to investigate differences between two groups. This method could be valuable in the study of personality if we had *a priori* reasons for expecting personality differences between any two groups and were interested in the validation of assessment techniques for such differences. It would be possible by a series of "t" tests to examine such group differences one by one but this procedure ignores correlations between the variables and does not allow the relative power of each variable in determining group differences to be measured. This the discriminant function analysis does permit. However it must be noted here that, as indeed is the case with multiple correlations, results tend to fluctuate depending upon the particular sets of variables and the sample so much so that replication on other samples is a prerequisite of using the results of discriminant function and multiple correlation studies. Just as canonical correlation allowed multiple correlation with more than one criterion score, so has discriminant function analysis beeen developed for application to more than one group, especially by Rao (1952).

Other Related Methods

Two other related multivariate methods deserve brief mention although they have not been widely used. Lazarsfeld (1950) developed *latent class analysis* which is used for assigning subjects to groups on the basis of dichotomous data. This is a useful exploratory technique in the study of objective test data. *Configural analysis* (Cattell, 1949) classifies patterns of responses and is useful in clinical case studies.

Factor Analysis

We now turn to examine *factor-analysis*. Factor analysis was developed (by Spearman, 1927) especially for the purpose of investigating abilities. As a result of his studies of the phenomenon, observable in the sphere of abilities, that all human abilities are to some extent correlated together, Spearman hypothesized that there was a general ability factor, named "g", which would account for such intercorrelations. This hypothesis of the underlying structure of abilities was based on the factor analysis of the correlations between ability tests. Thurstone (1938), in the USA also applied different methods of factor analysis to human abilities and emerged with a different result. He emphasized not one general factor, g, but nine primary mental abilities. Continued work over the years in the factorial analysis of human ability and in the development of different methods of factor analysis has to some extent produced a compromise between these two discrepant findings in the field of abilities (Cattell, 1971). This example has been introduced for two reasons. First the method, despite the disagreement over results, was producing highly interesting findings in the field of abilities—results which when applied led to improved selection procedures (e.g. Cronbach, 1970). There was thus every hope that similar methods would prove equally useful in the personality field. This was certainly the rationale behind Cattell's vast research programme (Cattell, 1948). Secondly it illustrates the disagreement between factor analysts—an example of the plain fact that there are an infinity of possible factor analytic solutions to a given matrix of correlations. This last difficulty indeed has certainly caused many psychologists to view factor analysis with considerable suspicion.

Since factor analysis has been the multivariate technique of the greatest importance and widest use in the scientific study of psychology, we must now describe it. Our aim here is not to elaborate on the computational procedures or the mathematical linear models implicit in factor analysis. This has already been done and readers are referred to Harman (1964) or for a very simple version Child (1971) for such statistics. Rather we shall try to outline the logic of factor analysis, to discuss the problems involved in interpreting results and in rotating axes and to enable readers to grasp the results of factor analyses and see possible weaknesses and flaws when factorial studies are presented in the main corpus of the book.

DESCRIPTION AND LOGIC OF FACTOR ANALYSIS

Definition of a Factor

Our first concern must be to describe what factor analysis can do and what a factor essentially is. Eysenck (1953) has a description which seems generally applicable. Thus a factor "is a condensed statement of (linear) relationships obtaining between a set of variables ...". This description, in Eysenck's view, can be further amplified depending upon the particular use to which we put the factor analysis.

Three views were distinguished:

(i) The factors are descriptive. For example we may factorize the intercorrelations between 60 tests. Ten factors emerge which (condensed statements) fully account for all the variance. They may be uninterpretable, without rotation, but we could describe the data in terms of our ten factors—a more parsimonious *description* than one in terms of 60 variables. Needless to say this purely descriptive use plays little part in psychology.

(ii) The factors are suggestive of a hypothesis. For example if we find a general factor loading on all our linguistic tests but none of our mathematical tests, it suggests that linguistic ability or a linguistic factor may play a part in test performance. We should proceed then to test such a hypothesis further, with new data.

(iii) The factors support or disprove a hypothesis. Here from clinical evidence or *a priori* reasoning we might expect a factor to appear. We can then factor the appropriate data. Thus Kline (1968) hypothesized from Freudian theory that an obsessional factor would load on certain obsessional tests but not on the 16PF or EPI tests. This was confirmed by a factor analysis.

These last two uses of factor analysis, especially the hypothesis suggestive use are crucial in the study of personality.

We have seen the three possible uses of factor analysis, according to Eysenck, a view which is non-controversial. We must now elucidate further the nature of the factor itself—what is this condensed statement of linear relationships? There have been many different definitions of a factor. Royce indeed (1963) quotes the following descriptions: dimensions, determinants, functional unities, parameters and taxonomic categories. However we feel that Royce's own definition of a factor as a *construct operationally defined by its factor loadings*, manages to embrace, as it should, all the varied descriptions we have previously mentioned.

An example will clarify this definition, and illustrate, as it happens, the importance of factor analysis in the study of personality. Perhaps the most famous factor yet found is Spearman's "g" which as Cattell points out (1971) is truly comprised of gf, fluid ability, and gc, crystallized ability. Now "g" loads on Raven's Matrices, digit span, information, amount of education, job status. In other words g is a construct which is correlated with all these variables. Its identification as general ability is determined by these loadings. What other construct could we conceive that would thus correlate. Its identification can, of course, be tested in a number of ways, e.g. do doctors score more highly than plumbers? Do children selected as intelligent by their teachers score more highly than those not selected and so on? This example demonstrates why factors are so useful in the scientific study of psychology. Unlike intelligence which is vague in meaning and subjectively defined, this factor is rigorously, objectively defined by its factor loadings on specific variables. Because of this we can then develop tests and estimate their validity against this factor. Tests so developed are not measuring some factor which is arbitrary and conceived to the whim of the particular test constructor. This variable "g" is of known importance in varying occupations, academic success, and other criterion behaviours. To argue therefore that an intelligence test, which is highly loaded on g, merely measures some skill particular to the test is wrong—utterly and completely wrong.

Thus it is with all our factors. Even the most humble factor emerging from the most simple factorial analysis can be operationally defined. Thus then we regard factors as operationally defined constructs. One further point needs to be raised here before we further describe some other attributes of factor analysis. This is the problem of conceptualizing factors as causal agencies.

Factors as Causal Agencies

This causal implication of factors was certainly accepted by Thurstone (1947) and Spearman (1927). What is at issue here is really, again, the nature of factors. Thus "g" or general ability does not exist. As Burt (1940) points out we must not reify the factors. "g" is just a very neat way of conceptualizing a dimension which can simplify the complex mass of data relating to abilities. In some sense, perhaps, it is not incorrect to argue that "g" has causal implications. Thus we may ask why do Latin, Greek, maths and physics inter-correlate highly together (while sociology fails to do so). The answer lies in the fact that general ability is important for performance in these subjects but not so for sociology! Eysenck (1953) takes an example from medicine. If we were to factor analyze a group of symptoms we should perhaps find a factor loading on all the symptoms of tuberculosis, e.g. coughing, weight loss, sweating, etc. This factor might be said then to be causal. Thus from this we can see that factors can be causal, although they are not necessarily so.

To summarize our position so far we argue here that a factor is an operationally defined construct which can be a causal agency. Factor analysis itself can be used to describe data economically, to suggest hypotheses or to put them to the test.

However the status of factors as causal agencies because of its importance requires further discussion. So far we have adopted a moderate position and argued that while factors can be causal agencies, they are not necessarily so. However Cattell (1966) goes further. He argues that the mathematical model of factor analysis implies that factors are *determiners* and that if the factors are rotated to simple structure, there is a high probability that they have causal status. Thus then Cattell sees the attainment of simple structure as vital in the process of factor analysis. Since, too, there is a common and obvious objection to factor analysis as a statistical technique namely that there is no unique solution to a factor analysis but that there are an infinity of possibilities, it is obvious that we must now discuss simple structure in factor analysis.

SIMPLE STRUCTURE IN FACTOR ANALYSIS

In any factor analysis there is no *a priori* method determining the position of the factors (axes) relative to each other in factor space. To overcome this problem of the indeterminacy of the position of axes, Thurstone (1947) proposed that they be rotated to simple structure.

When we rotate, it is necessary to distinguish, in Cattell's (1966) view, rotation for a general scientific meaning from rotation for special psychological meaning. This latter can be useful, perhaps in the applied field, if the variables which form the data of the analysis are well known. However in most research, this is not the case, since we are there concerned with new knowledge. This distinction involves therefore on the one hand principles for the scientifically meaningful rotation and on the other principles for specific hypothesis testing.

Scientific Rotational Principles

(1) Simple structure and (2) Confactor rotation (Cattell, 1966). Thus Cattell has added a further principle to that advocated, as we saw, by Thurstone. Cattell's (1966) discussion of simple structure is so complete and makes the points so powerfully, that we make no apologies for summarizing his views. We shall summarize them under a number of heads.

Definition of Simple Structure

Simple structure was essentially defined by Thurstone as the attainment of factors with a few high loadings and many low loadings. The rationale of this is really a particular example of Occam's razor—the law of parsimony—namely that the simplest explanation (which fits the facts) is the best. Thus in a wide sample of variables we should expect any natural influence to effect only a few of them rather than all. This, of course, is only true if we really have sampled variables widely. Cattell and Gorsuch (1963) have shown that simple structure cannot be reached with data matrices of random numbers but only in real data where underlying influences may be assumed to be at work. Simple structure is best obtained by maximizing the hyperplane count— i.e. the number of zero loadings.

How is Simple Structure to be Reached?

The answer to this question is crucial to the argument, especially since Cattell claims that demonstrably $\frac{3}{4}$ of published factor analyses are nowhere near simple structure and that even slight modifications in the rotational resolution can lead to analyses that would be interpreted quite differently. Certainly Cattell claims that many of the apparently disparate findings of factor analysts in the field of personality are due to failures to reach simple structure (see chapters 5 and 6).

(i) Originally, as in Thurstone's pioneering work in the field of abilities (Thurstone, 1938) simple structure was obtained by eye. Trial and error rotations to likely looking positions, naturally tinged with subjective judgement, were carried out graphically. This procedure was lengthy and only approximated simple structure.

(ii) Many of the first computer programmes were orthogonal rather than oblique rotations. Since orthogonal rotations produce uncorrelated factors only in those cases (which are probably rare) where the underlying influences are unrelated can they attain simple structure. Cattell and Dickman (1962) have shown with a study of the behaviour of five balls that orthogonal rotation cannot reach simple structure. It must be remembered with this artificial example that the causal influences were known (from the laws of dynamics) so that the adequacy of the rotational procedures could be judged.

(iii) Thus we are reduced to using, in the search for simple structure, computer programmes for oblique rotations. Oblique factors are, of course, correlated. Cattell distinguishes two kinds of oblique rotational programme—the analytic and the topological.

Analytic Rotation Programmes

Analytic programmes generally seek to maximize the sum of the fourth power of the loadings over all factors at once a procedure which maximizes the dispersion of factor loadings. It arrives at simple structure (in these terms) when there is the largest possible number of either high or low loadings. However, as Cattell points out this is not maximizing the number of loadings in the hyperplane which is the real objective. In fact there is a correlation between analytic oblique solutions and those maximizing the hyperplane count of around 0.7. Although this seems quite high, any analytic solution can be remote from a simple structure obtained by other means and itself corresponding to a known meaning.

Topological Rotation Programmes

Cattell has developed two topological rotational programmes—Maxplane and Rotoplot. Maxplane which is entirely automatic (Cattell and Muerle, 1960) searches by trial and error until it has maximized the hyperplane count. It is topological in that it locates clusters of variables. Rotoplot (Cattell and Foster, 1963) enables the researcher to adjust by hand on the computer oscilloscope the last few rotations to simple structure without which final polish the finest results are impossible. In other words, it is possible to object that at this late stage we introduce subjectivity again. However this argument is rebutted because Cattell and his colleagues have developed a statistical test on the final position reached. Hence whether the programme is automatic or hand-adjusted becomes irrelevant. These evaluations of simple structure are important and they can be briefly mentioned below.

(i) It is demonstrated that any further attempts at rotation produce a drop on the hyperplane count.

(ii) A statistical test of simple structure is applied—Bargmann's (1953).

(iii) The percentage of variables in the hyperplane is counted. This should lie between 55 and 85%.

If these three criteria are obtained, the method by which the solution was reached is not important.

Although, perhaps, not all factor analysts would agree that simple structure is best attained by maximizing the hyperplane count, there is no question about the validity of the search for simple structure. If factor analysis is to be useful in the clarification of complex areas of research and in the isolation of causal agencies, the scientific aim of the methodology, then rotation to simple structure is essential. Cattell (1966) however proposes another principle for the scientific rotation of factors, confactor rotation, which we must discuss, although it is not widely accepted beyond Cattell's Illinois school.

Confactor Rotation

This procedure, in principle at least, was first proposed by Cattell in 1944. If factors are determiners then "certain relations will hold between factor loading patterns of such determiners in two experiments using the same variables in samples and situation where the determiners would operate with different magnitudes (variance contributions)" (Cattell, 1966). In effect this means that in two experiments we should expect the loadings on a factor to be proportional, i.e. multiplied by a constant variable. However this only holds for orthogonal rotations (which as we have seen are unlikely to be useful with most data). Thus although theoretically this is an ideal way to reach a replicable rotational solution, in practice it is not workable unless the absolute levels of variance are held constant in the two investigations and the proportionalities hold at all factor levels, not only at the first order. Cattell and Cattell (1955) indeed have developed a solution which carries out this confactor rotation at all factor levels. However in practice due to programming and computer difficulties there have been few researches in which confactor rotation has been used.

To summarize, therefore: if we assume that factors are determiners, then the search for simple structure is a logical procedure in terms of Occam's razor. From artificial examples there is no doubt that simple structure rotations do in fact yield genuine causal agencies and that they produce invariant results across researches. Maximizing the hyperplane count, which demands topological rather than analytic rotational procedures, produces simple structure with the greatest accuracy, as judged by a number of objective criteria. Cattell has also proposed confactor rotation which produces directly invariant results from different researches. However it has not been used to any extent. These then are the procedures necessary for the scientific use of factor analysis in the study of personality.

This methodology has implicit in it a faith in empiricism. To put it crudely, you throw everything in you can think of, compute a rotated factor analysis and seize on the factors as some kind of eternal verities (determiners). Now as we shall see the leading factorists have never done this. Any resulting factors have been investigated with great care, and much of this work forms the corpus of this book—for our real knowledge of personality depends on just these results.

SPECIFIC HYPOTHESIS TESTING

However, as we saw on p. 15, specific hypothesis testing is another important usage for factor analysis in the study of personality. This is important since by utilizing this method we can examine the value of some of the major personality theories—a procedure incidentally of which, so far, there are but few practical examples. Basically the method requires that:

(a) a set of factors and loadings be hypothesized either from theory or previous results

(b) that a factor analysis be computed and rotated as nearly as possible to the hypothesis, and

(c) that some test of goodness of fit of hypothesis and result be worked out.

These three stages each have their problem and we shall discuss these below.

The difficulty with the first stage if we are seeking to test theories lies in the precise statement of the factors and their loadings. Kline (1972) has reviewed, for example, much of the objective evidence relevant to Freudian theory. A major problem here when factor analytic studies are involved lies in the factorial hypothesis. Often it resolves itself merely as a matter of opinion, as to whether factors reflect the theory or not. This is clearly unsatisfactory for a science.

The difficulty at the second stage, fitting the rotation to the hypothesis is not, now, considerable. Hurley and Cattell (1962) have developed the Procrustes programme which attempts to match by the least squares fit, hypothesized with empirical factors, and this is not the only programme of this type. Finally, and this is a procedure that is rarely carried out, there is the problem of how close a fit two factorial solutions really are. Most investigators have been content to rely on subjective judgment. This is not as careless as it seems however, since, in view of the problem of developing an adequate set of hypothesized factors, it could be considered somewhat inappropriate to make a complex statistical comparison at a later stage.

Actually there is a nice logical point involved in the procedures for hypothesis testing by factor analysis which we have discussed above. Suppose that we get a good fit to our hypothesis using a Procrustes. This, however, may not be simple structure, as judged by a standard oblique rotation. How can we resolve this paradox? What this essentially means is that while the hypothesis is a viable way of conceptualizing the data, it is not the simplest. Hence if we follow the law of parsimony it is to be rejected. This means that the value of hypothesis testing factorial studies with programmes that try to fit results to some hypothetical structure is limited. It also means that there is no real distinction between our first two principles of scientific methodology and hypothesis testing. Indeed the best way to test a hypothesis is to seek simple structure *and then* see to what extent the two sets of factors match. If then we have a good fit, we can truly regard the theoretical position as having empirical support.

Conclusions about factor analysis as a multivariate technique in the study of personality

We have not attempted here to go into details concerning the use of factor analysis. We have tried to give an overall view of what it can do as a method. Here we have seen that by correct oblique rotational procedures, factor analysis can produce invariant factors which may be regarded as determiners, perhaps even causal agencies. This is a huge step forward for personality study because it enables us to define operationally the most important constructs in the personality sphere.

FACTOR-ANALYTIC DESIGNS

Before we leave the topic of factor analysis as one possible multivariate technique, useful for the investigation of personality, we must briefly point out that there is a variety of different factor analytic research designs (Cattell, 1952). Since each design has a particular application, it will be useful at this juncture to describe each design together with its field of application because, in this way, we shall be able to see the full scope of the technique.

R Technique

This is the common form of factor analysis. Here variables are factored and the resulting factors are common traits related to individual differences between people. Typical R factors are "g", general ability, and extraversion.

P Technique

Here we correlate the attributes within one person and hence factorization discovers unique traits.

Q Technique

Here we factor people rather than tests. Tests become subjects, subjects tests. The resulting factors loading on people, form groups and the Q technique is highly useful in the study of groups, e.g. criminals or schizophrenics where their attributes can often be revealed. However Cattell *et al.* (1968) regard Q analysis as "wide of the mark".

O Technique

Here we correlate the attributes of one person on two occasions and factor the resulting correlations. This O technique is useful in the study of how different stimulus situations affect personality and in personality changes during psychotherapy, for example.

T Technique

Here test-retest reliability coefficients are factored.

S Technique
Where the test responses of two persons on a series of occasions are correlated and factored and which is useful in the definition of social interaction. This is the last of these designs.

T and S technique, however, are rarely used.

From these descriptions it must be clear that factor analysis has a very broad field of application in research. Q analysis, it will be noted, can be used in the study of groups, or even types, despite its imperfections. Now there has been developed what is essentially another branch of multivariate analysis—for the isolation and recognition of groups, and we must briefly discuss this.

TYPE RECOGNITION

Cattell *et al.* (1966) have devoted great effort and ingenuity to the development of a method of multi-dimensional type classification. A special correlation coefficient is used, rp, the pattern similarity coefficient which takes into account in matching persons' profiles, shape, level and accentuation of shape. This matrix of rp is then searched by Taxonome for the identification of phenomenal and nuclear clusters. A further search of these clusters defines segregates. The power of this procedure has been shown in two empirical studies—one of Jane's Fighting Ships (Cattell, 1966) and in a further one with thoroughbred dogs (Cattell *et al.*, 1973) where the accuracy of the groups could be estimated against the facts in the case—and also in a study of cultures. Here it was interesting to note that the ten or so types of culture agreed with the intuitive historical classification used by Toynbee (Cattell, 1948). Taxonome seems the most highly developed multivariate procedure for the study of types or groups. However there are other less sophisticated methods of cluster analysis, e.g. McQueen J. B. (1966) which require less computing and allows very large samples of subjects to be used. Clearly in the study of personality, classification of people rather than variables is an important facility—and cluster analysis, even in a simple form, is therefore a valuable technique.

Finally mention should be made of the work of Guttman. Essentially, as Cattell (1966) points out, Guttman has been concerned with the study of order within data matrices. This has resulted according to Guttman (e.g. 1957) in even more parsimonious accounts of complex correlations than that yielded by factor analysis. Certain structures, such as the Radex (Guttman, 1954), the Simplex (Guttman, 1955) and the Circumplex (Guttman, 1966) seem particularly useful in these descriptions. However, as Cattell (1966) argues, there is a danger with structures of this sort that they do not reveal "the real world" but rather psychologists construct a world of test items and batteries to fit these models!—the virtual opposite of the scientific method.

These then are the multivariate methods useful in the scientific analysis of personality. Our description should enable us to see the possibilities they offer for investigation in this area. Certainly it is results culled from the use of these multivariate techniques that we shall discuss in the main body of this book.

SUMMARY

1. The differences between multivariate and univariate methods were discussed.
2. The different varieties of multivariate analysis and their use in the study of personality were examined.
3. Factor analysis was particularly singled out for more detailed discussion, because it has been extensively used, and attention was paid to the notion of simple structure and the claim that factors are causal agencies.
4. Various factor-analytic designs were discussed and finally a few other methods were mentioned suitable for the study of types.

Chapter 3

The Application of Factor Analysis to Personality

In Chapter 2 we discussed the various multivariate techniques and compared them favourably with the traditional bivariate procedures for the elucidation of the complex area of personality. We were there mainly concerned with the underlying logic especially of factor analysis because this is the statistical method above all others that has been used in the scientific study of personality.

TECHNICAL RULES FOR FACTOR ANALYSIS

In this chapter we shall begin our description and discussion of the results of these factor analytic studies. However before we can do this so that we can estimate the merits of the researches, we shall have to mention briefly some of the practical rules, that over the years, have become accepted by factor analysts. This is necessary because many published investigations fail always to comply with these procedures. Needless to say in most cases this is not due to ignorance or laziness. Sometimes it is simply impossible to sample as we wish, or we are not given time to administer all the tests that we really should. However in an imperfect world, some results are better than none. If we know and understand the reasons for the practical rules of factor analysis below, we shall be able to judge to what extent any results are flawed. We shall also avoid accepting results at face value or rejecting them entirely because of imperfect procedure. Some of these rules we have previously discussed in our section on simple structure and are highly technical in nature but the first two are crucial for understanding the differences in results obtained by different investigators.

Cattell (1973) lists the "eight required conditions in a factor analytic experiment to define unitary traits" thus:

1. Strategic choice of variables
2. Sampling of people
3. Decision of number of factors based on an objective test
4. Fixing communalities
5. Unique oblique rotational resolution
6. Test of significance of simple structure
7. Check on degree of invariance of pattern across research
8. Check on invariance of higher order structure.

Choice of Variables

We shall discuss the first two requirements in the most detail. The choice of variables is, as Cattell has always stressed, critical in factor analytic investigations. (Cattell, 1946, 1957, 1973). This point is most easily illustrated by example. If we were to give tests of vocabulary, spelling, grammar, verbal reasoning, French language, German language, and linguistics to a large sample of adolescent children, it is highly likely that general intelligence and verbal ability factors would emerge—Gc and V, as they are named (Cattell, 1971). Now such a battery of tests would yield a false picture of the sphere of abilities. Thus there is no chance of a mathematical or numerical factor emerging, simply because there is no test that could possibly load up on it. Thus such a study could not, by nature of the choice of variables, give us a clear picture of abilities. This we know because the groundwork in the areas of ability has been carried out by the pioneers of factor-analysis, Spearman, Thurstone, Burt and indeed by Cattell in his early work. Because the field is charted we know when we have failed to sample the variables adequately. How, then, are we to know in an uncharted field such as personality and motivation where there is little agreement either among theorists or empirical researchers? One answer to this question has been provided by Cattell (1948) who developed the concept of the *personality sphere*. This is a method of defining the field of personality and we shall describe it below when we discuss findings. What is now important is the recognition of the problem itself, of sampling the whole universe of variables.

General and Specific Factors

There is yet a further difficulty in mapping out the field of factors and in sampling variables. This arises from the notions of common and specific factors. It is generally accepted that test variance can be broken down into general factor variance + specific factor variance + error variance. The reliability of a test, indeed, is the sum of the general and specific factor variance. This is certainly a simplified model of test variance, which is not in all cases applicable (e.g. Lord and Novick, 1968 or Birnbaum, 1968) but which has a useful explanatory power (e.g. Guilford, 1956). This model has implicit in it for the study of personality, the view that one task for the scientific investigation of personality (or of any area) should be the isolation of general factors if we define a general factor as one loading on several variables and a specific factor as one loading on only one—the test itself. Thus a list of general factors will be a far more parsimonious account of the variance than the list of the variables loading on them. Intelligence, g, verbal ability, V, numerical ability, N, extraversion, neuroticism are all examples of general factors. Thus Cattell's factor B is composed of B intelligence + a specific factor (related to the type of items and the particular questions used) + error variance.

However this distinction between general and specific factors is not as clear as our examples make it seem. Suppose we consistently ask the same question again and again in a personality questionnaire but with different forms. We would soon produce a series of items loading on a common factor and indeed even a number of short tests. " Do you enjoy gay parties ? Are you the life and soul of a party ? If people want a lively time, do they ask you to a party ? Do you feel miserable on your own ? Do you like the noise and bustle of a crowd of people ? Do you enjoy spending an evening quietly on your own ?" and so on. Such a "general" factor is called by Cattell a bloated specific (Cattell, 1971). It can certainly be argued that Guilford's three dimensional model of abilities which yields 120 factors (Guilford, 1967) and for which a large number of relevant tests have been developed is an example of the construction of an edifice of bloated specifics with no referrents in the external, in the real world. Thus what we have to guard against in our factorial studies of personality is that the dimensions we reveal are truly common factors. Actually this can be done best by subjecting the emerging factors to further study rather than by attempting to monitor the variables we put into an analysis. For if we find that a factor discriminates among groups in a meaningful way or correlates with real life criteria, it is highly unlikely that it could be a bloated specific. It much more supports the notion we discussed earlier of a factor being a determinant or a causal agency.

From our discussion above it is clear that in our factorial studies of personality in the initial exploratory stages we must sample variables as widely as possible but avoid the dangers of bloating specifics by too zealous variable construction.

However once we have discovered some of the main dimensions of personality we need not sample so widely. Instead we can put in marker variables. An example that springs to mind concerns the Dynamic Personality Inventory

(Grygier, 1961). This inventory which purports to measure Freudian psychosexual development as well as other variables derived from psychoanalytic theory, seems to be useful in a variety of situations e.g. with criminals (Grygier, 1961) and with students in predicting academic performance (Hamilton, 1970). Examination of its item content and the theory of the test both suggest it should be relatively independent of standard personality questionnaires, e.g. the 16PF test (Cattell *et al.*, 1970) or the MMPI. However the necessary factor analysis of the test with known marker variables has not been carried out so that the factors emerging from the DPI cannot be located in factor space and hence properly identified. The difficulty is discussed in detail in chapter 5.

Marker variables are also necessary if instead of simply exploring the personality sphere we are testing hypotheses. Here, unless we have such markers to identify the factors, as it were, empirically, the test of the hypothesis becomes hopelessly subjective.

We may summarize this first requirement by arguing that in the exploratory stage it is necessary to sample variables as widely as possible being careful however not to bloat specifics. At the hypothesis testing stage or when some firm agreement has been reached we can cut down this large number of variables provided that some adequate marker variables are included in the analysis.

Choice of Subjects

The second of the requirements referred to the necessity for wide sampling of subjects. This problem is perhaps most easily seen and understood when we consider the phenomenon of the attenuation of correlations due to homogeneity. Thus, for example, if we sample open scholarship holders at Oxford and Cambridge (all of whom are of very high general ability) and correlate their IQ scores with academic performance the correlation will be slight. This is because, in effect, this group has been selected for intelligence, and there is little variance in IQ. Hence variance in academic performance must, of necessity, be due to other attributes e.g. personality or motivation. A factor analysis of the performance scores in this group would show a relatively small "g" factor. Vernon (1961), indeed, has cogently argued that some of the early differences between Thurstone's and Spearman's work, one factor or many, were *in part* due to such sampling differences. If however we were to study the determinants of academic performance throughout the whole population, we should undoubtedly find gf and gc as perhaps the most important factors.

In the sphere of personality as we hunt for the major dimensions it is, of course, by no means so easy to decide in what respect samples may be inadequate. This means that the factor analytic study of personality demands random sampling and checking with sub-samples to ensure that the personality structure has not changed. It would not be good enough, for example, to work only with students who, in terms of personality, as ability, do not represent a random sample of the population: students tend to be neurotic introverts. However in Great Britain, at least, while this overall claim is supported, there are faculty differences (Entwistle, 1972). It is also possible, especially if clinical claims about the importance of child rearing procedures are accurate, that there would be social class differences in personality. Thus sampling of people has to be comprehensive in factor analytic studies.

These strictures apply in the main to those studies aimed at delineating the personality sphere. Where, however, we are hypothesis testing, and hence have some theoretical knowledge of the variables involved, it may be in order to use a homogeneous sample. This is important to remember when estimating the worth of any experiment. Thus we cannot dismiss the results of an investigation simply because it used a homogeneous sample.

Finally before we leave the topic of subject sampling, we should briefly mention sample sizes. It is generally agreed that for an R analysis, factoring variables, the minimum number of subjects for a reliable (in the statistical sense) factor analysis is 200. This is in order to minimize the standard errors of the correlations—a particularly important requirement since the factor loadings aim to reproduce the original correlations. It is also generally agreed that the number of variables should not exceed half the number of subjects, (a parameter dictated by the matrix algebra). Thus large scale exploratory studies demand large samples. It is in order here to mention Q analysis (see p. 21). If we ignore, for the moment, the logical problem of the meaning of Q factors a major reason for the scarcity of Q analyses lies in these sampling necessities. Thus a very large number of variables needs to be administered to subjects, if the requirement of subject and variable size is to be met. This therefore limits its use except with small samples.

Other Rules

The six other requirements for scientifically valid factor analysis are, in the main, technical points aimed at obtaining simple structure. We shall not here go into the mathematical assumptions behind these canons (readers are referred to Cattell (1966) for such information) but shall simply comment here on those points which we have not previously mentioned in our section about simple structure.

How many of the principal components are rotated has an important effect on how well our solution approaches simple structure. De Young and Cattell (1973) indeed have shown both with real data and with plasmodes that underfactoring tends to produce second-order factors at the first order. A simple and effective method seems to be the Scree test (Cattell, 1966). With the exception of the necessity of fixing communalities by an iterative procedure taking into account the number of factors previously decided upon, we have discussed these other conditions. All of them are aimed at reaching simple structure and checking as objectively as possible, the replicability of the factors from study to study. We have nothing here to add to our previous discussion which made the logical point that if factors are underlying dimensions, then simple structure since it is the most elegant or parsimonious account of the data must yield a scientific description of the data (in terms of the law of parsimony).

Such then are the demands of good factorial investigations. Actually they could be simplified to three if we are prepared to forego the technical points of how to fulfil these demands. They are: (i) Sampling the universe of variables, (ii) Sampling the universe of subjects, and (iii) Finding the invariant simple structure. With these demands in mind we are now in a position to begin our studies of the application of factor analysis to personality. We shall begin by looking at the pioneering studies of Cattell which have extended over the last thirty years.

From our previous discussion, it must be clear that to attempt to map out the major dimensions of personality demands somehow that we have an adequate sample of personality variables. To select an adequate sample depends in turn on being able to define the *totality*. This concept of the total personality has been conceived in the work of Cattell, (and ultimately this may turn out to have been his major contribution) as the Personality Sphere. This we must now describe.

THE PERSONALITY SPHERE

Cattell (e.g. 1946, 1957) has argued that the only practicable source for the totality of personality traits is found in language. Thus over the years especially in languages with highly developed literatures, it is highly likely that every discernible aspect of behaviour has been verbalized. Allport and Odbert (1938) in their oft quoted classic study found 4,500 trait names in the English language and similar numbers are found in other modern languages. This personality sphere, the Language Personality Sphere, formed the basis of Cattell's factor-analytic approach to personality. Synonyms were removed, subjects were rated for the remaining traits and the intercorrelations were factored. These factors are the source traits of personality which Cattell, for precision and ease of assessment, now measures by means of questionnaires and objective tests. This overview of Cattell's work which we discuss in detail throughout this book has been included here so that we can discuss the adequacy of this concept of the language personality sphere for embracing the totality of personality and hence for the purposes, finally, of defining the major dimensions of personality.

First we certainly would argue that if there is no name for something it is difficult to say that it exists. Thus it is claimed that Eskimos can recognize or discriminate 17 kinds of snow whereas the British use only three classifications say hard, melting and dirty. Thus for us it is true to say that these Eskimo varieties do not exist. Similarly therefore if there are no words in this language, or any other, to describe a behaviour, this means that it has not been discriminated and hence does not exist for anybody. This is fine, as far as it goes. Certainly we would agree that the language sphere must cover personality as it has been observed. However it seems there may be a flaw at this point in the argument. Suppose some behaviour defies ordinary observational techniques. Thus ultra violet light has not been observed. However it can be meaningfully shown to exist. A similar argument applies to molecules and atoms. Not all the descriptions of colours and careful discriminations would lead to the establishment of ultra violet. These arguments, attractive as they appear, do not in fact destroy the validity of the language personality sphere as a basis for the scientific investigation of personality. On the contrary they enhance it! Thus originally nuclear particles were *hypothesized* from studies of the behaviours of substances. Now this is exactly analogous to the factorization of observed behaviour. The factors, especially at the higher order, are not observable. Indeed as we saw in our discussion of factors they are hypothetical constructs operationally defined. Factors indeed may be expected to reveal any such causal agencies as genes, or germs (medical symptoms). Similarly if we subjected the changes in response of different materials, sensitive to light of different wave lengths, to factor analysis we should undoubtedly uncover ultra violet and infra red factors. Thus it does seem reasonable to assume, as does Cattell, that the language personality sphere gives us a good picture of the totality of personality.

The next stage in Cattell's studies involved reducing the personality sphere to manageable proportions. The 4,500 trait names were reduced to 171 by eliminating synonyms, at least as judged by English scholars. These 171 *trait elements* were intercorrelated and 36 clusters of correlations were isolated—*surface traits*. Ten other surface traits were added to these, a few from a study of the abnormal literature in psychiatry and some that appeared in experiments over the years. These 46 surface traits are referred to by Cattell in his work as the *standard reduced personality sphere*. Thus Cattell argues that 46 surface traits embrace the whole personality sphere. Since surface traits are not convenient to work with compared with the underlying *source traits* we do not intend to set out the whole list, which is given in Cattell (1957) pp. 813–817. It will be noted that this reduced personality sphere of 46 variables was based upon ratings. Ratings, of course, are notoriously poor as a form of psychological measurement since they are likely to be unreliable both between different raters and even on different occasions with the same rater. Indeed ratings *may* reflect the rater rather than the subject being rated. Thus the spinster headmistress of a girls' school who rates an attractive student as flighty, with her head filled with undesirable thoughts, may be there reflecting her own problems rather than her student's characteristics. Since there are problems with ratings and since Cattell makes considerable use of them in his work we must now examine this problem, the nature of the raw data, in more detail.

THE THREE DATA BASES OF PSYCHOMETRY

Cattell uses three forms of data—L data based on real-life ratings, Q data based on questionnaires and self report inventories, and T data based on objective tests.

L Data

This life-record data reflects behaviour in the real, everyday situation. Ideally we should aim at behaviours which are objective facts and need only observation not rating. Examples of these might be: number of car accidents over a period of time, number of GCE "O" level passes, number of societies or clubs to which a person belongs. Actually even these apparently objective observations are not so clear as they first seem. Thus what do we mean by an automobile accident? Is hitting a family car and killing its occupants due to high speed driving, the same as being hit by this same fast driver? Are either of these the same as scraping the car against a wall when negotiating a narrow bend? It would certainly appear that, in terms of personality, these accidents are not similar. Even examination results whether reflected by marks or number of passes are not equivalent. Thus the rather dim girl who has domestic science, needlework, art, home economics, and human biology cannot be meaningfully compared with the blue-stocking who has passes in Greek, Latin, Chinese, applied mathematics and physics. The same difficulty arises in the case of clubs and societies. Thus the man who is a member only of a blue film club may not be similar to the one whose only membership is that of the local Methodists society. Only cynics would equate the two. This is not to deny the value of such objective data. It is merely to point out that even objective data has hidden within these quite complex problems of equivalence.

Generally however life records do not make use of such data mainly because they are difficult to obtain. Instead ratings, as we have indicated, are used. Before we turn to a discussion of ratings, however, we should consider a method of obtaining objective data which is coming into use recently partly because of the new generation of computers which can handle large amounts of data and partly because new statistical techniques have been developed which can handle them.

Dichotomized scores and content analysis. Our discussion of objective data in life records showed clearly that, despite appearances, it was flawed because it was crude—a difficulty caused by the fact that it is not possible to equate behaviours that are not identical. However a content analysis of all our information where it was reduced to dichotomous categories captures all the richness of the original material and yet allows reliable, objective scoring. This technique has proved highly successful in scoring Rorschach protocols (Holley, 1973), where, indeed, perfect discrimination had been obtained between schizophrenics and depressives. Hampson and Kline (1976) in a number of studies have used this technique extended into projective tests and L data interviews, and we shall illustrate the method with examples from these investigations.

In this work, we were trying to identify the psychological characteristics of groups of different offenders. In our interview data we obtained their opinions about crime, and recorded what they said about the seriousness of offences, among other things. The protocols for each individual were then subjected to content analysis and dichotomized scores. Here is an example of a subject's protocol "Sexual crimes are the worst of all. Sex criminals should be whipped, that would teach them". Interviewer "Do you think this for all sex crimes, or just some. I mean are some worse than others?" "Well, they're all bad, but with children especially, that's very bad ..." Examples of scoring categories derived from this are set out below.

Sexual crimes are worst of all	0	*1*
Sexual crimes deserve punishment by whipping	0	*1*
Sexual crimes with children, the worst	0	*1*

The next subject's protocol is scored in the same way, on variables idiosyncratic to him and on the others. Thus if he did not regard sex crimes as the worst, he would score 0, and so on. In this way it is possible to encapsulate all the data without losing any of the richness. The reliability of scoring this data between two scorers, working entirely independently was extremely high. In fact the few disagreements were clerical errors.

There are disadvantages with this technique. One major one is that it inevitably leads to a large number of variables. For normal R factor analysis this is serious since there are then more variables than subjects. For Q analysis, in the study of groups, this becomes a positive advantage but it must be recognized that this method is suitable only for Q analysis and multivariate methods such as Taxonome and cluster analysis (see p. 22). Another difficulty, we have found with this scoring technique is that many of the variables are poor discriminators, perhaps indeed only one subject will have scored in the positive mode. This leads to artificially high correlations between people, and a general factor in the Q analysis which is truly an artefact of the method. In practice we have been forced to use only variables with a fixed minimum number of responses at one pole. This can lead to difficulties in cross-validating results with new samples. A final problem resides in the entirely atheoretical nature of the data. Factors can be found which are difficult if not impossible to identify. We have attempted to overcome this problem by computing factor scores and then relating them to known marker variables.

G Index. Until the development of the G index of correlation (Holley and Guilford, 1964) such dichotomous scores would have presented some unpleasant correlational problems which would have rendered any subsequent factor analysis of dubious worth. Thus the tetrachoric correlation, r_{tet}, has a very large standard error (at least twice as large as for the comparative product-moment correlation), assumes that the two varieties are normally distributed, and is affected by how even is the split between the two poles—an uneven response split ensures that the correlation coefficient cannot reach unity. Phi, which makes no assumptions about distributions, is sometimes substituted for the tetrachoric coefficient. However Phi is affected both by the size of the item split and by the polarity. Holley (1973) has shown that if the polarity of the items is changed, e.g. John likes cricket 1 0 becomes John hates cricket 1 0, the Phi coefficients between the people vary. Since the polarity of items is naturally and rightly quite arbitrary, since the meaning is identical, this difficulty bodes ill for the use of ϕ in factor analyses. The G index of correlation is a coefficient which overcomes all these problems. Furthermore since it can be used in double-centred matrices, scores are automatically normalized and ipsatized—an essential for Q analysis and a feature which makes the Q factors equivalent to R factors (Holley, 1973, Burt, 1940), although this equivalence has been a matter of dispute (Cattell, 1966).

In fact the G index has been used with the Rorschach test (Holley, 1973) and the Meta Contrast technique (Holley, private communication) with great success. By success we mean that the groups being studied were discriminated with enormous clarity (validity coefficients of unity) so much so indeed that Holley concluding his review article on G methodology states in relation to the Rorschach that previous failures to validate the Rorschach were probably due to statistical defects rather than defects in the test. Our own studies with TAT, HTP and interview data also show good separation of offender and non-offender groups. From this we should like to propose that the G index of correlation is likely to be highly valuable in the analysis of objective L data. As yet, however, it has been little used.

Problems with ratings. Much of Cattell's L data, however (the life records, the first of his three data bases), come from ratings. Ratings of everyday real-life behaviour are beset with problems:

(i) Raters must, obviously, see their subjects for a long period of time.

(ii) The very fact of observation may affect the behaviour under observation. Thus as Beach (1956) points out, inexperienced lovers are put off by observation or the threat of observation, experienced ones find it adds a touch of piquance.

(iii) There is a halo effect, so that being rated high for one trait tends to make ratings on the other traits higher.

(iv) There is unreliability between raters and between occasions.

(v) Raters tend to use a scale differently some preferring the extremes, others never using them.

All these disadvantages reduce not only the reliability of ratings but of course their validity also. A further difficulty relates to our first objection that rating requires time. Thus time sampling is necessary. Yet the physical arrangements for time sampling compared with administering a battery of tests are formidable. How many schools for example would allow a rater into a child's class? To overcome these difficulties Cattell (1957) proposed methodological points for good rating which we must now briefly summarize.

Essentials of good rating (i) *Implicit time sampling*. The rater should see the subject in a wide variety of situations and hence roles. Ideally he should live with his subject (in the non sexual sense). This is a highly important aspect of good rating, and one which, for purely practical reasons, is often a major weakness in ratings. In many studies we have ratings by teachers or tutors Now, although these raters may have known their subjects for a long time it is usually only in a limited role—that of pupils. Thus, as many parents can attest, they may be seeing an untypical aspect of their subjects.

(ii) *Time*. The length of the observational period should be long—preferably a year, certainly not less than two or three months. This ensures that subjects are observed in a variety of extreme situations where deep emotional reactions can be seen. This need for a long period of observation underlines again the causes of failure in many rating situations, the interview being an outstanding example.

(iii) *Definition of behaviour*. The traits should be carefully defined and illustrated by a list of actual behaviours in different situations. Thus for example if we were trying to rate children for rudeness we would have in effect a check list such as swears at father or mother when asked to do something, gives V sign, deliberately ignores them when talking, and so on In this way there is less room for unreliability due to rater differences.

(iv) *Comparable sigmas*. Subjects should be ranked by paired comparisons and the ranks should be converted to standard scores by percentile tables. This eliminates rater differences.

(v) *Avoidance of role relations*. Peer ratings are probably the best even among children. As we have indicated role relations such as teacher/pupil, interviewer/interviewee obviously distort the picture. If we define behaviour by a specific check list as in (iii) above (e.g. Stott's Bristol adjustment guides, (Stott and Sykes, 1956)) intelligent children can be effective raters.

(vi) *Many raters*. Each subject should be judged by from 10-20 raters. This increases the reliability of the ratings, and the validity since each judge adds in some common factor variance—until the judges do not know the subjects well enough. This, therefore, limits the number of possible raters.

(vii) *Reduction of halo effect*. This is best done by defining the behaviour operationally as in (iii) above, by training the judges to be objective and by having some desirable traits rated high, others low by our choice of words. More important than these is the methodological point of having subjects rated for one trait at a time. If a few days elapse before rating the next trait, the halo effect is likely to be reduced.

(viii) *Comparable means for judges*. Since all judges cannot rate all subjects, either a small common sub-sample has to be provided so that the means for judges can be equated, or an artificial rating situation can be created, e.g. a play and the judges thus scaled.

(ix) *Independence of judgment*. Finally raters should do their job independently, without discussion.

These are ideals which obviously demand great resources and patience on the part of the researcher. These methods were used by Cattell in his collection of L data, and thus we must feel reasonably confident that many of the normal objections to ratings have been overcome.

Q Data

The second source of data, used by Cattell, consists of the responses to questionnaires and self report inventories. Cattell (1957) makes a distinction between Q and Q' data. If the responses to items have been shown to be correlated with actual behaviour, Cattell regards them as Q data. If, however, they merely remain the unverified introspections of subjects to questionnaire items they are regarded as Q' data, which are obviously less valid. For example there are problems of deliberate distortion, self-delusion, the fact that the means and standard deviations of scales are different for individuals and the difficulty that there can be no check on the accuracy of the response—introspections are simply private not public events. Since these objections are so serious we shall briefly discuss the means of overcoming them, although it must be pointed out that the best investigators use questionnaires as Q rather than Q' data which, at a stroke, removes these objections. An example will clarify the point. In the EPI (Eysenck and Eysenck, 1964) we find the item (No. 40 B) "Do you suffer from 'Nerves'?" If we were to regard this as Q' data, the following difficulties spring to mind: "What do you mean by 'nerves'?" "How nervous do you have to be before you can be said to suffer?" "I refuse to admit to nerves, only pooves suffer from them." (this with a trembling hand and sweaty brow). "I'll put nervous, then they'll see how ill I am." These then are the kinds of ideas influencing responses to such an item. Small wonder that as Q' data, such items have poor credibility. However as Q data, we can argue as does Eysenck in the manual to the test (Eysenck and Eysenck, 1964), that the truth of the assertion or the motivations behind the response of Yes to this item are not important. What has been demonstrated empirically is that those subjects who respond "Yes" to the item tend to be classified as neurotic compared with those who respond "No" at a highly significant level of probability. Hence it is a useful item in the N scale of the test. This approach to questionnaire items makes criticisms of items on grounds of wording or apparent relevance worthless. All that matters is the quality of the empirical support.

Distortions of Q data. As we mentioned at the beginning of the previous paragraph, there are some serious objections to questionnaire measurement, and we must discuss these at this point. *Deliberate distortion* can affect the validity of a person's responses, even where the test scores are Q data, i.e., as we saw, they are regarded as pieces of behaviour per se, not as veridical statements about the subject's behaviour. This is not in contradiction to our claims about the force of Q data. This is because the empirical support for items is obtained, as far as possible, from subjects who are not deliberately distorting their results. Thus if we give a test to a psychiatric patient seeking help or a person needing vocational guidance to help him choose his career, the chances are that such subjects will not deliberately distort the results. They want help, to distort is to make help difficult. In a research setting, too, where subjects are volunteers and are certain of the confidentiality of the results, deliberate distortion is rare (restricted to the inevitable group of psychopaths). Thus then since the results are gained with the test items operating under a fixed set of conditions (no deliberate distortion) to change those conditions may well change the results. This is why Eysenck's EPI, for example, contains a scale for picking out the deliberate distorter so that we can eliminate his results. Actually, of course, deliberate distortion is only likely to occur when the subject feels that the testing is not in his own interest. The primary example of this is in selection. This is what makes questionnaires, whether regarded as Q or Q' data of dubious use in selection procedure—the fact that they can be so easily distorted.

Social desirability. Deliberate distortion, then, can be avoided if we restrict the use of Q data to situations in which it is unlikely. Lack of self-knowledge, self delusion, is also an important weakness in questionnaires and can lower their validity considerably, although if we are careful in their construction and use our questionnaire responses as Q data, we can eliminate its influence. The most common form of self-delusion tends to create a response set known as social desirability (Edwards, 1957). This response set is the tendency to endorse an item depending on the degree of its social desirability. Thus Edwards (1957) found with MMPI items that there was a highly substantial correlation between how socially desirable judges rated an item to be and the percentage response it received.

Edwards concluded that much of the variance of questionnaire items simply reflected differences in social desirability. Edwards (1959), indeed, in an attempt to overcome this problem, developed the Edwards Personal Preference Schedule. This test uses forced choice items where subjects have to choose which of a pair of activities they prefer. Since each of these choices has been equated for social desirability, it is argued that social desirability cannot influence preference. Hence this serious form of test distortion is eliminated. However there is some evidence (Corah *et al.*, 1958) that the close relation of two test items which are obviously not identical in social desirability heightens the difference between them so that the test is still contaminated by its influence. Most test constructors consider that social desirability is an influence on test items which can be minimized in item writing. Thus if we choose items which have a split in responses that is roughly equal, it is difficult to see how they could be argued to be socially desirable. Furthermore without going to judges, we can easily see that some items are going to be thus affected and not use them. For example the item "I have revolting personal habits" is one that is inevitably going to be influenced by social desirability, and it would have to be entirely rephrased. Before leaving the topic of social desirability, one further point deserves to be made. If we are interested in a particular personality factor, say, ego strength, then social desirability is a contaminating influence to be eliminated as far as possible. If, however, we are interested in the whole personality sphere, then the tendency to respond in a socially desirable fashion becomes itself a worthy object of investigation, so that we should not necessarily wish to eliminate it, although we might restrain its influence to a particular set of items—a social desirability scale.

Acquiescence. Another common and pervasive response set which we must mention at this point is acquiescence—the tendency to agree with items regardless of their content. Since this response set was first discussed by Cronbach (1946, 1950) it has received an inordinate amount of study. We do not intend to discuss here any of this in detail—readers are referred to Wiggins (1968) for a full discussion. Suffice it to say that acquiescence has shown itself to be a contaminating feature of many of the MMPI scales and of the original F scale of the authoritarian personality, as has been discussed by Brown (1965). As was the case with the response set of social desirability, we have to be careful in always regarding acquiescence as a contaminating variable. Certainly if we are purporting to measure some other variable, we shall want to eliminate it but acquiescence as a personality trait is interesting per se. Indeed it can be argued that acquiescence should run through the F scale because it is part of the syndrome to be acquiescent. Thus in large scale studies of personality we may want some measure of this tendency, especially if we are trying to remove specific instrument factors (but see p. 41 for further discussion).

In constructing scales, it is usual to overcome this acquiescence difficulty by arranging items such that an equal number of items are keyed "Yes" and "No". This is therefore purely a matter of careful item writing. However in practice it is not easy to write items with equal conviction keyed in a particular way. It is certainly not good enough to insert the negative e.g. "I like gay parties" and "I do not like gay parties". Kline (1971) in the construction of his Ai3Q personality test, at the item trial stage, compared the percentage of responses to items keyed "yes" with the percentage to items keyed "no". Since there was no difference between these figures, it could not be argued that acquiescence had contaminated the items and he was content to use only five items (out of 30) keyed "no" in the final scale. Actually as some acute readers will have realized, balanced scales with equal numbers of items keyed "Yes" and "No" can ensure only that acquiescent individuals are not confounded with high scores on the variable, they do not eliminate its influences. Guilford (1959) claims that acquiescence occurs most frequently when items are ambiguous. Hence clear item writing goes a long way towards overcoming this difficulty.

Deliberate and unconscious distortion, then, are the two major difficulties with questionnaire data, which careful scale construction can do much to minimize. Certainly their importance is less if we regard such data as Q data rather than Q' data.

Trait-view theory. However it should be mentioned that recently Cattell (1973) has outlined an attempt to deal with motivational distortions of the kind discussed under the term response sets by a more general theory. This is necessary because in the case of social desirability for example the *ad hoc* correction is crude: in addition, far worse, it loses a substantial portion of the second-order anxiety factor.

Since social desirability has never appeared as a first or second order factor although personality scale scores do change when subjects try to make themselves more attractive a different model of social desirability effects is needed. This is given by *trait-view theory* which states that every distortion of perception and evaluation in Q and L data is to be understood as a product of the personality of the observer and his situation. Thus misperception (caused by social desirability) can be understood just as any other behaviour in terms of the specification equation. Dominance for example might lead a man to overestimate surgency when evaluating himself to his girl friend and anxiety to underestimate his intelligence at a university interview.

In fact it is possible to estimate motivational distortion if the tests are given on more than one occasion in different situations (e.g. selection and counselling) by partialling out personality, role and cognitive cliché factors, as demonstrated by Krug (1970). Here the 16PF was given in four different conditions—anonymity, job seeking, presenting an aesthetically ideal self and date seeking. In addition strength of interest in getting a job and interest in members of the opposite sex were assessed by T tests—role factors.

The results showed a clear role factor in both situations and that scores on every factor were affected. However the weights for the role factors were not more than the average for the general personality factors. Across all traits and all four instructional situations allowance for the perceptual effects of the other traits significantly raised the validity of the factor scores which was further increased by the addition of the role weights, thus partialling out motivational distortions.

Using trait-view theory research psychologists must establish mean shifts and weights for each trait by factoring the tests in those situations where the test is most commonly employed. In this way motivational distortion can be effectively eliminated.

T Data

The third source of data in Cattell's factor-analytic studies of personality arises from the administration of objective tests. An objective test is one where the purpose of the test is hidden from the subject, because the subject makes a behavioural response to a defined situation. In one sense therefore Q data are really T data for the fact of responding "yes" on an item is the salient point. However they differ from true T data because they depend on self-knowledge and, of course, their purpose is often quite clear to the subjects. Almost any task where we can find subject variance can be used as an objective test, provided that some kind of score can be estimated from it. Cattell and Warburton (1967) have collected a compendium of some 200 such objective tests which provide more than 800 variables. Many of these are as yet of unknown reliability and validity, although some of these have been published and are available to professional test users for practical purposes. Although we shall be discussing some of the published objective tests in later sections of this book and although we still have to devote some considerable space to examining the evidence for the validity of those objective tests which have provided data for Cattell's systematic work, it will be appropriate at this point to give examples from the compendium of some of Cattell's tests. Our examples will illustrate the ingenuity of Cattell and his colleagues in test construction and will also show the obvious difficulties relating to the validity of these measures.

Examples of objective tests.   (i) The slow line drawing test: Subjects have to draw a line as slowly as possible for a fixed length of time. The score is the length of the line. Notice how difficult to fake this test it is. We could make the line longer than it might otherwise be, by drawing faster, but would this be a good thing?

(ii) The fidgetometer: A chair is constructed with electrical contacts at various points which are closed by movement. The score is the amount of movement recorded over a fixed interval of time. Apart from the fact that subjects, in the main, failed to notice anything unusual about the chair, so that the question of faking never arises, to fake this test needs extreme confidence. I suppose if we were going for a job as a model, it would be wise to fidget as little as possible, otherwise it is not at all clear how best we might compose ourselves.

(iii) The balloon blowing test: Subjects are required to blow up a balloon as large as they can. The scores derived from this objective test are the size of the balloon on completion or the time until bursting. As is to be expected there is great variation in results, some balloons being limp and flaccid, others being rapidly burst.

Some of the tests are physiological and require a laboratory both for administration and analysis of results. Blood sugar counts, systolic and diastolic blood pressures, urine analyses, all are examples of physiological measures which may be utilized in the objective study of personality. Other tests, again of a physiological nature, require a psychological laboratory for their administration. Thus one such test measures the startle response of the pupil to a given stimulus (a loud revolver shot). Such measures cannot be deliberately distorted except by those who have brought their involuntary, autonomic nervous system responses under conscious control either through following the mystical procedures and practices of eastern religions or by the feedback procedures of the modern phenomenological psychologists of consciousness such as Ornstein (1975).

As we listed before in our definition of T data, Q data, as distinct from Q' data can be encapsulated within the category of objective tests. Thus it should not come as a surprise to find that some of Cattell's objective tests are in questionnaire form. Some of them require subjects to estimate how quickly they would learn novel activities, others enquire into their food preferences. Since these tests are often given in a large battery, it is possible within one session to administer the same test several times but with significant changes. A good example of this is the distraction test. Early on in the battery there occurs a test consisting of a number of simple addition sums—to be done within a fixed time. Later in the battery the same sums are given but they are set out amidst jokes. The score derived from this is the difference in score on the two occasions. Later on there is a test of memory for the jokes, which is another test of distractability. Readers must agree that this is a good example of ingenious objective test construction, hard to see through or distort yet simple to administer. Finally to show that complex apparatus is not always necessary we shall mention the hand-writing pressure test. The measure here is the number of legible carbon copies.

Validity of T tests. There are grave problems in demonstrating the reliability and validity of these tests. The vast majority of those in the Cattell and Warburton (1967) compendium are still even now in the experimental stage. However since the publication of that book, as Hundleby (1973) points out, some progress has been made in assembling special objective test batteries for clinical use and for use with children. However there still remains a large task of painstaking research into the tests. The problem is that since the tests have no face validity, that is, it is not evident what they might be measuring, we need scales with clear marker variables to tie them down. However since, as we shall see in later chapters where we also discuss the published objective tests, there is some evidence that T data does not overlap Q and L data, this is not a simple task.

Since there are these difficulties over validity with objective tests some readers may be wondering why we should bother with them at all. There are several reasons for this. Important in the argument for objective tests are the defects in questionnaires and life records. L data are difficult to obtain if they are to be of any value and Cattell was early on in his research programme forced to develop tests which could be administered in practical research. The faults with questionnaire data we have fully discussed and the fact that they can be so easily distorted makes them less than ideal for selection. Objective tests overcome all the problems and there can be little doubt that when they can be shown to be valid they are a superior form of testing to the older methods. Another advantage of objective tests is that a battery of them can consist of many different *types of test*. This effectively reduced what Cattell calls "instrument variance" i.e. variance due to the particular format and kind of tests, as a source of contamination of scores. In connection with their resistance to distortion it is clear that an ethical problem arises over deceiving subjects since many tests take place without the knowledge of the subject, as in the fidgetometer, or pretend to be what they are not. This is not yet a serious problem, but it could lead to considerable opposition to objective tests.

Projective tests as T tests. Just as questionnaire data in theory can be regarded as objective T data so does this category of objective tests cut across an older category of tests—projective tests. Projective tests usually take the form of ambiguous stimuli which subjects have to describe. Since they are ambiguous, often amorphous, it is generally considered that descriptions must reflect not the stimuli but the subject who projects his idiodynamics (Rosenzweig, 1959) his feelings and conflicts on to them, hence the term projective tests. Cattell, who prefers them named misperception tests, is prepared to use such tests provided that the responses are regarded as T data and not subjected to the arbitrary, if insightful, clinical interpretations which is normally the case.

Enough has now been said about the three data bases of Cattell's factor analytic approach to personality. We shall conclude this chapter by giving a brief overview of Cattell's approach. He defines the personality sphere by first determining its extent linguistically, from a dictionary search of words describing behaviour. He then uncovers the underlying dimensions or causal agencies by factor analysis, rotating to simple structure, and using three sources of data: life records which are criterion data, questionnaires and objective tests.

SUMMARY

1. The technical rules for carrying out reliable factor analyses were set out. The prime importance of wide sampling both of subjects and variables was demonstrated. The distinction between general and specific factors was also discussed.

2. The concept of the personality sphere and its importance to the factorial study of personality was discussed. Trait elements, surface traits and source traits were defined.

3. The three data bases of psychometry, L data, Q data and T data were discussed. The problem of ratings were outlined and a promising approach —G analysis—was described. Q and Q' data were discriminated and the various problems with these data were scrutinized. Motivational distortions and trait-view theory were examined. T data was the final subject of discussion. Examples of objective tests were given and special attention was paid to problems of validity.

Chapter 4

Principal Source Traits in
L and Q Media of Observation

INTRODUCTION

Since 1939, Cattell and his colleagues at the Illinois laboratory, having defined the personality sphere in terms of descriptive words from the dictionary, have rated, from ongoing behaviour, subjects for these traits and subjected the resulting correlations to factor analysis (L data). They have written batteries of questionnaire items and objective tests and with numerous different samples have factor-analyzed the results, ever seeking after simple structure (Q and T data). All the resulting factors have been subjected to

TABLE 4.1

Source Trait Index	Low-score description	High-score description
A	SIZIA Reserved, detached, critical, aloof, stiff	AFFECTIA Outgoing, warmhearted, easygoing, participating
B	LOW INTELLIGENCE Dull	HIGH INTELLIGENCE Bright
C	LOW EGO STRENGTH At mercy of feelings, emotionally less stable, easily upset, changeable	HIGHER EGO STRENGTH Emotionally stable, mature, faces reality, calm
E	SUBMISSIVENESS Humble, mild, easily led, docile, accommodating	DOMINANCE Assertive, aggressive, competitive, stubborn
F	DESURGENCY Sober, taciturn, serious	SURGENCY happy-go-lucky, gay, enthusiastic
G	WEAKER SUPEREGO STRENGTH Expedient, disregards rules	STRONGER SUPEREGO STRENGTH Conscientious, persistent, moralistic, staid
H	THRECTIA Shy, timid, threat-sensitive	PARMIA Venturesome, uninhibited, socially bold

I	HARRIA Tough-minded, self-reliant	PREMSIA Tender-minded, sensitive, clinging, overprotected
L	ALAXIA Trusting, accepting conditions	PROTENSION Suspicious, hard to fool
M	PRAXERNIA Practical, "down-to-earth", concerned	AUTIA Imaginative, bohemian, absent-minded
N	ARTLESSNESS Forthright, unpretentious, genuine, but socially clumsy	SHREWDNESS Astute, polished, socially aware
O	UNTROUBLED ADEQUACY Self-assured, placid, secure, complacent, serene	GUILT PRONENESS Apprehensive, self-reproaching, insecure, worrying, troubled
Q1	CONSERVATISM OF TEMPERAMENT Conservative, respecting traditional ideas	RADICALISM Experimenting, liberal, free-thinking
Q2	GROUP ADHERENCE Group-dependent, a "joiner" and sound follower	SELF-SUFFCIENCY Self-sufficient, resourceful, prefers own decisions
Q3	LOW SELF-SENTIMENT INTEGRATION Undisciplined, self conflict, follows own urges, careless of social rules	HIGHER STRENGTH OF SELF-SENTIMENT Controlled, exacting will power, socially precise, compulsive, following self-image
Q4	LOW ERGIC TENSION Relaxed, tranquil, torpid, unfrustrated, composed	HIGH ERGIC TENSION Tense, frustrated, driven, overwrought

further study to aid identification and we can now describe many of them in some detail with sound support from empirical evidence.

In this chapter we shall set out first the factors identified in both Q and L data, and then the Q factors only—i.e. those that for various reasons have not been identified in L data. We shall then in the next chapters proceed to a description of the major T factors. Our descriptions will be taken from the various detailed sources about the factors—Cattell (1957) for L factors, Cattell (1973) and Cattell *et al.* (1970) for Q factors and Cattell and Warburton (1967) for T factors.

ADULT PERSONALITY FACTORS FOUND IN Q AND L DATA

The personality dimensions above are based on factor analyses over the years, some using item inter-correlations, others using correlations between parcels of items. The personality test developed over these studies for the measurement of these factors is Cattell's 16PF test (Cattell *et al.*, 1970). The HSPQ is for High school children and the CPQ for younger children at the primary school. It should be noted that these eight studies have involved several thousands of subjects, the eighth indeed used almost 6,500 alone. Our descriptions of the factors are taken from Table 4 of Cattell (1973). Factor B, intelligence, is also included, as it is in the Cattell personality tests, although really an ability factor. The factors are in descending order of size. Fifteen have been regularly found.

The 16PF Factors

These are the fifteen factors regularly found in personality questionnaire testing up till the last edition of the 16PF test (Cattell *et al.* 1970). The missing letters, D, J, K and P reflect the fact that up till then these factors had not been identified in questionnaire data, although they had been found in the life records. Similarly the four Q factors reflect the fact that these have not been noted in L data but have been seen in questionnaire data. Some differences between L and Q data might reasonably be expected since it is logically possible that some factors are more easily observed through self reports than through objective ratings by others and vice versa. One interesting point relevant to this discussion is that P, J and K had been found in the Q data of adolescents.

Recently Cattell and Delhees (1973) with 225 undergraduates and De Voogd and Cattell (1973) in a replicative study with 240 undergraduates have managed to identify these missing factors together with some other questionnaire dimensions. Named by Cattell (1973) as the seven missing factors, they now form a new supplement to the 16PF test (Cattell and Marshall, 1973). These factors together with typical items are set out below, and are taken from Table 6 in Cattell (1973).

Seven Missing Factors

TABLE 4.2

D: Insecure Excitability

I bubble over with ideas of things I want to do next

  (a) Always
  (b) Often
  (c) Practically never

The people I want never seem very interested in me

  (a) True
  (b) Uncertain
  (c) False

J: Coasthenia *v* Zeppia

I enjoy getting a group together and leading them into some activity

  (a) True
  (b) Uncertain
  (c) False

People tell me I'm

  (a) Apt to be noisy
  (b) In between
  (c) Quiet and hard to understand

K: Mature Socialization *v* Boorishness

I prefer plays that are

  (a) Exciting
  (b) In between
  (c) On socially important themes

If I take up a new activity I like

  (a) To learn it as I go along
  (b) In between
  (c) To read a book on it by an expert

P: Sanguine Casualness

I rarely let my mind stray into fantasies and make-believe

  (a) True
  (b) Uncertain
  (c) False

I most enjoy talking with my friends about

  (a) Local events
  (b) In between
  (c) Great artists and pictures

TABLE 4.2 (*continued*)

Q5: Group Dedication with Sensed Inadequacy

I like a project into which I can throw all my energies

- (a) Yes
- (b) Perhaps
- (c) No

In a situation which puts sudden demands on me I feel

- (a) No good
- (b) In between
- (c) Confident of handling it

Q6: Social Panache

I am good at inventing a clever justification when I appear in the wrong

- (a) Yes
- (b) Perhaps
- (c) No

I have never been called a dashing and daring person

- (a) True
- (b) Uncertain
- (c) False

Q7: Explicit Self Expression

I am not concerned to express my ideas at public meetings

- (a) True
- (b) Uncertain
- (c) False

In many undertakings I am in I don't seem to get a definite idea of what to do next

- (a) Yes
- (b) Perhaps
- (c) No

If we include these seven factors we can now see that Cattell's factor analytic researches have yielded *15 personality factors in normal adults found in both L and Q data and 7 factors found only in Q data.* As we previously argued, these last seven factors may be Q factors simply because their variance in the rating field is small.

The Number of Factors

An obvious question in view of the basic methodology of Cattell's approach where he has attempted to embrace the whole personality sphere is whether or not these are the only factors. As a logical point until we could explain all the variance in all studies of personality or until we could use factors in prediction equations with almost perfect validity (which as yet we cannot do, but see p. 268 for a discussion of such work) it would be rash if not absurd to claim that these 22 factors were the only personality factors. However, we must make clear that it is likely that any other factors, in the sphere of normal adult personality, will be small because the factors necessarily emerge in descending order of magnitude. It is certain that, using factor analytic techniques no large factors could occur. However this does not mean that there are no further minor factors.

Nevertheless even if we admit there are some other factors, we have to avoid the danger of gratuitously enlarging what are little more than specific factors. As we pointed out in our general discussion of factor analysis there is no absolute distinction between general and specific factors and it is possible by repetition of items to bloat specifics into quasi group factors—manifestly what Guilford (1959) has done in his three faces of intellect model. Careful attention to correct sampling of the personality sphere should overcome this problem.

Another cogent and empirically-based reason for arguing for the presence of yet more than the 22 personality factors comes from the results with T data. Here around 20 factors have been found which seem to match not the first-order factors we have so far discussed but second-order factors. However, since T factors are by no means simple to interpret we shall leave our description and discussion of them until Chapter 8. Nevertheless the fact that there are apparently different T factors of personality makes it clear that we have not established a definitive list.

We must conclude from this discussion that it is likely that with research we shall uncover some further small personality factors although we must avoid the danger of constructing factors by item writing.

Now we must turn our attention to the personality factors among children and in abnormal, psychiatric populations. We shall then look at the higher order factors derived from the correlations among the primary factors. When we have thus stated what Cattell's personality factors are, we shall go into more detailed interpretations of them and examine their relevance to the various theoretical propositions about personality.

PERSONALITY FACTORS AMONG CHILDREN

As we have indicated in our study of Cattell's basic rationale and methodology in the previous chapter, the elucidation of the factors found in simple structure is an integral part of Cattell's work, the factors being the empirical basis of theory. It is therefore essential to study the development of the factors through childhood. Only when we can trace the life-history of a factor and see how it is affected or not by environmental events can we really hope to understand it. Hence Cattell has devoted considerable attention to factor analysis with samples of children.

Problems in the Personality Assessment of Children

There are great difficulties in attempting to measure personality variables among children and there are also problems in matching factors not only across studies but especially across ages where the tests from which the factors are derived may be different. Before we set out the factors we must, therefore, briefly discuss these difficulties otherwise we cannot properly appraise the value of this work and the claims of equivalence for factors.

Ratings. Cattell (1973) admits that no L data studies have ever been carried out with children which adequately meet the criteria for good ratings discussed on p. 34. This is hardly surprising when we recall that one of the criteria was that judgements are best made by peers and in addition careful training was required to concentrate on designated key behaviours. Perhaps it would be more accurate to say, certainly as regards children below about 12 years of age, that no adequate L data studies *could* be carried out—just because peer ratings by young children could be dubious.

Recent advances in telemetry however, may mean that we can get a good behavioural record of a wide sample of children's behaviour which can be rated later in the laboratory so that the outlook for L data studies with children is not entirely gloomy. Despite this Cattell (1957) was able to review a number of L data studies and it did not seem unlikely that the same factors were emerging from children's L studies as from adults. Cattell (1973) indeed, argues that A, B, C, E, F, G have been reliably identified in children's L studies. Nevertheless, the difficulties with ratings and the fact that none meet the ideals, mean that less reliance should be placed on L factors, than was the case with adults.

Questionnaires. For these reasons there has been emphasis on Q data with children. Immediate difficulties with questionnaires for children spring to mind. Reading ability and verbal comprehension may be limited. Response differences might imply cognitive rather than personality variance. Furthermore it is not certain how reliable children's self perceptions are, nor how valid. As psychoanalysis has shown, it is clear that adults' introspections are not accurate. We could suspect even greater inaccuracy (unless shown otherwise) among children. Furthermore children's interests and activities change so much with age that items suited say for a fifteen year old will not, as far as contents are concerned, be suited to a five year old. This problem of the comparability of items makes comparison across age groups difficult.

One possible way to match factors is to get samples of children of an age where without undue difficulty they can do two questionnaires. For example many eleven year olds are capable of completing the primary school CPQ without feeling the items to be too childish and the secondary school HSPQ without finding the items outside their experience. In fact it demands great skill in item writing to end up with items that tap the same traits satisfactorily for different age groups. For example, the sociability of the adolescent or ageing adult may well be reflected in his feelings about parties. This can, therefore, be reflected in items about parties. This is clearly different in the young primary school child who rarely, in Great Britain at least, organizes his own parties—they are arranged by parents. For the primary child parties are likely to represent birthdays, presents and food. Sociability has to be tapped in different ways altogether. Other considerations that make the production of equivalent items for different age groups difficult are the limits on vocabulary and attentional span of young children. Indeed at the 10-8 year old level it is permitted that the test be read aloud and lower than this reading aloud is required. At the youngest level, the questions are on tape and the psychologist records the answer himself.

Identification of Children's Factors at Different Ages

As we have stated, the adult factors are those in the 16PF and these have been the most studied. However there are in all five forms of the 16PF test for various age groups. They are the PSPQ (Pre-school personality Quiz) 4-6 years; the ESPQ (early school personality quiz) 6-8 years, CPQ (child's personality questionnaire) 8-12 years, HSPQ (high school personality questionnaire) 12-15 years and the adult 16PF test. Although less is known about the factors in the different versions (independent of internal evidence concerning correlations between factors) they are held to be the same and each has been subjected to considerable investigation. Thus each of the tests has been subjected to about 10 factor analyses and overlapping samples have made it possible to identify the factors in the children's versions as being essentially the same as those in the adult form. Despite this it has to be admitted that the tests for the lower age groups have not the same evidence for validity and are not so reliable as the 16PF and HSPQ versions.

Since identification of the factors depends to a large extent on studies with the adult form of the 16PF rather than with the children's factors, at this juncture we shall not go into the validity or reliability of the children's versions of these tests. These we shall discuss in later chapters concerned with the practical application of these findings in education, in the child guidance clinic and in occupational selection and vocational guidance. What we shall do now is to indicate which of the Cattell factors have been found at the different age levels. Cattell (1973) contains a full discussion of this work with references to the original papers.

From Table 4.3, which includes the latest adult factors in the 16PF supplement, it is clear that many of the adult source traits appear in children. Although there appear to be fewer factors among the younger age groups, it is possible (and only many years of research could resolve this problem) that this lack of factors reflects problems of writing suitable items rather than a real change. Support for this argument comes from the fact that N, for example,

TABLE 4.3

Showing Factors of Various Age Groups

Factor	PSQ	ESPQ	CPQ	HSPQ	16PF
A	*	*	*	*	*
B	*	*	*	*	*
C	*	*	*	*	*
D	*	*	*	*	*
E	?	*	*	*	*
F	*	*	*	*	*
G	?	*	*	*	*
H	?	*	*	*	*
I	*	*	*	*	*
J	*	*	*	*	*
K			?	?	*
L					*
M					*
N	*	*	*		*
O	*	*	*	*	*
P					*
Q1					*
Q2				*	*
Q3			*	*	*
Q4	*	*	*	*	*
Q5					*
Q6					*
Q7					*

has been found among adults and all age groups except the 12-15 year olds. It is highly unlikely that this source trait could occur among young children, disappear and then re-appear among adults. It would be far more plausible to argue that, as yet, items successfully tapping this trait for adolescents have not yet been written. When we remember that of these 23 factors, P, Q5, Q6 and Q7 have only very recently been found among adults, there is clearly a considerable similarity between source traits among children and adults in Q data. In examining this table two other facts need to be remembered. First there are life data equivalents for all the Q factors (other than those prefaced by Q) and secondly there are now no child factors that do not appear among adults, although D, J and K have only recently been found.

From this we think it fair to argue that as regards Q data Cattell seems to have established 23 source traits among normal adults most of which can be found in L data and most of which are found also among children although there is a possibility that among younger children there are fewer source traits. For a full discussion of just what these factors are and for the bearing they have upon theories of personality, we must turn to chapters 7 and 16.

ABNORMAL FACTORS

In the meanwhile before we can grasp the nature of these normal personality factors, it is necessary to turn to abnormal personality factors. As we have repeatedly stressed, the strength of Cattell's factor analytic approach lies in his attempts to embrace the whole personality sphere—all behaviour. However since the definition was based upon ratings of normals, there is the logical possibility that abnormal, psychiatric factors could have been missed. Indeed it is possible that abnormal factors are quite different. Since too the personality sphere was linguistically defined, if normal behavioural descriptions are inappropriate for abnormals, Cattell's methodology for the investigation of abnormal factors will have two weaknesses— sampling of people (the ratings were of normals) and sampling of variables (the trait elements were descriptive of normals). For all these reasons it is desirable to construct an abnormal personality sphere.

The Abnormal Personality Sphere
As Cattell (1973) points out, the fact of the logical possibility that personality factors among abnormals were different from those among normals would alone have made investigation of the abnormal sphere necessary. In addition however a mass of empirical work with abnormals with the 16PF test indicated that although the 16PF source traits would discriminate between different neurotic groups (results which we discuss in our chapter on the application of these findings to clinical psychology) and between such groups and normals, differentiation in the field of psychosis was unsatisfactory.

Over the years therefore Cattell and colleagues have attempted to delineate the abnormal personality sphere. For this three sources have been used:
  (a) descriptions of pathological behaviour from the psychiatric text books,
  (b) new items written by Cattell and colleagues as clinical work went on e.g. Cattell and Bjerstedt (1967) and
  (c) the MMPI item pool (Hathaway and McKinley, 1951) which was far the most important source.

The MMPI. The 566 items of the MMPI were selected by criterion keying i.e. if an item could discriminate one of nine criterion groups from the other and from normals, it was included in the item pool. The original form of the MMPI possessed in fact nine scales, each scale being comprised of items which discriminated the group relevant to the scale. Thus the score on the depression scale, for example, indicates the extent to which the subject resembles the depressive group. Actually the MMPI was always regarded by its authors as an item pool likely to be useful in the study of abnormal cases and Dahlstrom and Welsh (1960) in their MMPI handbook have collected over 200 scales, most constructed by criterion keying.

Criterion keying. Unfortunately this method of scale construction has several severe disadvantages. In particular, the same items can be in more than one scale. This obviously leads to artifactual correlations between the scales. Another problem is that much depends upon the reliability of the criterion groups. Since psychiatric diagnosis is notoriously unreliable (Beck, 1962) this is particularly serious with the MMPI. Nevertheless since this test is clearly useful in the study of abnormals it is obvious that its relationship to the source traits of the 16PF must be worked out. Furthermore since 200 scales can be formed from the MMPI items it is clear that they must represent a good description of critical abnormal behaviour—an ideal basis, therefore, for the abnormal personality sphere.

An even more severe disadvantage is the fact that a scale constructed by criterion keying is not nearly so useful for the study of personality as a factored scale. This is because criterion groups can differ in a wide variety of ways and a highly discriminating scale though useful practically may be theoretically valueless, since a collection of such discriminating differences may have no psychological meaning. Thus the MMPI and the Strong Interest test throw little light on the psychology of either psychiatric or occupational groups. This, of course, is even further reason to include the MMPI items in factor analysis with known personality dimensions.

The other two sources of the abnormal personality sphere require little comment. It is clearly a sensible technique to search the psychiatric literature for descriptions and this is analogous to the original dictionary search for normals. Similarly the technique of developing items as the first abnormal dimensions begin to emerge is also a standard technique although care must be taken not to thus create bloated specifics (see p. 27).

Problems with factoring the MMPI. Factoring the clinical scales of the MMPI is not a particularly satisfactory solution to the problem of the factors contained in it. This is because the method of scale construction by no means ensures unifactorial scales and in addition some items are scored in more than one scale. Furthermore there is little doubt that the response sets of social desirability and acquiescence affect some of the items which could provide a spurious general factor. (See chapter 3 pp. 36–39). Factor analyses of the MMPI clinical scales have been attempted despite these disadvantages.

Usually such studies show that there are but five dimensions underlying the MMPI clinical scales (e.g. Finney, 1961). Orme (1965) indeed has claimed that most of the MMPI variance can be accounted for by one factor—a factor of general emotionality which is similar to Cattell's second order factor of anxiety which we discuss below (see p. 59). Kline (1967), indeed factored the MMPI admittedly with a normal population and found two factors which correspond closely to Cattell's second-order factors of anxiety and exvia.

However the scale construction of the MMPI is such that the factoring of the clinical scales is unlikely to be useful. What is needed is the factoring of the item correlations. Until recently the factor analysis of a matrix of 566 item intercorrelations overloaded the storage capacity of computers. Furthermore the problems of obtaining satisfactory correlation coefficients for dichotomous variables which sometimes lead to the establishment of difficulty factors have made the interpretation of results problematic.

Cattell and Bolton (1969), however, have formed the items into parcels i.e. groups of factorially homogeneous items, and factored the correlations between these parcels and 16PF factors. Here it was found that all the 16PF personality factors (not including the seven new factors or B, intelligence) emerged together with five others which were interpreted as psychotic hypochondria, psychopathic behaviour, psychasthenia and religious interest. The fifth factor was not identified. This study of the MMPI then revealed four new abnormal factors.

These four new MMPI based source traits, together with items from the 16PF factors and items derived from a search of the psychiatric literature and those designed in the light of the emerging results were factored. Thus several depression factors had been found and items tapping these were included in the factor analysis. In this way 750 items were used to cover the whole pathological personality sphere. The result of this study was clear—twelve factors were needed to describe *this pathological personality sphere*. Thus based on five factorings and three sources of evidence, the CAQ *the clinical analysis questionnaire* has been developed which measures these twelve pathological factors plus the sixteen normal factors. The twelve pathological factors are set out in Table 4.4 (taken from Cattell, 1973).

Although we shall discuss the identification and nature of these factors more fully in a later chapter, it is interesting to note the factors related to depression. What this investigation makes clear is that there are several distinct kinds of depression and the attempt therefore in the MMPI to discriminate a depressive group with one scale is mistaken as is the simple diagnosis of depression, which is clearly heterogenous. This is sound evidence, if evidence were needed, of the superiority of factorial classification to atheoretical discrimination of criterion groups and tests constructed on such a basis are necessarily weak.

A summary of Cattell's basic position. At this juncture in our introductory overview of Cattell's work we have reached the point where we can say that:

TABLE 4.4

Primary Source Traits in Clinically Deviant Pathological Behaviour (Part II of CAQ)

Source-Trait Symbol	Low-Score Description (1–3)	High-Score Description (8–10)
Hd or D_1	LOW HYPOCHONDRIASIS Is happy, mind works well, does not find ill health frightening	HIGH HYPOCHONDRIASIS Shows overconcern with bodily functions, health, or disabilities
Sd or D_2	ZESTFULNESS Is contented about life and surroundings, has no death wishes	SUICIDAL DISGUST Is disgusted with life, harbours thoughts or acts of self-destruction
Bd or D_3	LOW BROODING DISCONTENT Avoids dangerous and adventurous undertakings, has little need for excitement	HIGH BROODING DISCONTENT Seeks excitement, is restless, takes risks, tries new things
Ad or D_4	LOW ANXIOUS DEPRESSION Is calm in emergency, confident about surroundings, poised	HIGH ANXIOUS DEPRESSION Has disturbing dreams, is clumsy in handling things, tense, easily upset
Fd or D_5	HIGH-ENERGY EUPHORIA Shows enthusiasm for work, is energetic, sleeps soundly	LOW ENERGY, FATIGUED DEPRESSION Has feelings of weariness, worries, lacks energy to cope
Gd or D_6	LOW GUILT AND RESENTMENT Is not troubled by guilt feelings, can sleep no matter what is left undone	HIGH GUILT AND RESENTMENT Has feelings of guilt, blames self for everything that goes wrong, is critical of self

	LOW	HIGH
Md or D_7	LOW BORED DEPRESSION Is relaxed, considerate, cheerful with people	HIGH BORED MISANTHROPIC DEPRESSION Avoids contact and involvement with people, seeks isolation, shows discomfort with people
Pa	LOW PARANOIA Is trusting, not bothered by jealousy or envy	HIGH PARANOIA Believes he is being persecuted, poisoned, controlled, spied on, mistreated
Pp	LOW PSYCHOPATHIC DEVIATION Avoids engagement in illegal acts or breaking rules, sensitive	HIGH PSYCHOPATHIC DEVIATION Has complacent attitude toward own or other's antisocial behaviour, is not hurt by criticism, likes crowds
Sc	LOW SCHIZOPHRENIA Makes realistic appraisals of self and others, shows emotional harmony and absence of regressive traits	HIGH SCHIZOPHRENIA Hears voices or sounds without apparent source outside self, retreats from reality, has uncontrolled and sudden impulses
As	LOW PSYCHASTHENIA Is not bothered by unwelcome thoughts and ideas or compulsive habits.	HIGH PSYCHASTHENIA Suffers insistent, repetitive ideas and impulses to perform certain acts
Ps	LOW GENERAL PSYCHOSIS Considers self good, dependable, and smart as most others	HIGH GENERAL PSYCHOSIS Has feelings of inferiority and unworthiness, timid, loses head easily

Note: The notation suggested for pathological factors uses two letters mnemonically related to the name (for example, Sd = suicidal disgust) to distinguish them from the normal factors, which use the alphabet by order of approximate variance: $A, B, C, \ldots, P, Q_1, Q_2,$ and so on.

(a) In the normal adult personality sphere, 23 factors have been found, of which 16 have been confirmed in L and Q data

(b) Within the abnormal adult personality sphere, 12 further factors have been identified, mainly in Q data.

(c) With various age groups of children, similar normal factors are found, although it is possible that among the younger groups there are fewer factors. Again our data is mainly Q data.

HIGHER-ORDER FACTORS

In the remainder of this chapter we must now discuss the yet more parsimonious accounts of personality that can be derived from higher-order factorizations, that is factors derived from the correlations between the first-order factors described in this chapter. When this is done we shall then have the framework of personality as revealed in the studies of Cattell and his colleagues at Illinois. What remains for later chapters is to examine the nature of the factors in detail, and to examine the factors resulting from objective tests, T data. At that point we will be ready to relate Cattell's system which is empirically based, to other empirically based systems which we shall also describe and to other clinically derived theories.

The Nature of Higher-Order Factors

As we pointed out in our discussion of factor analysis, if we are to use it properly for a scientific, parsimonious account, it is necessary to rotate to simple structure. Since, except in specific cases which are rather rare, simple structure necessitates oblique factors and since oblique factors are correlated, it is possible to extract second-order factors. These second-order factors are the factors accounting for the correlations between the first order factors. If, as we logically must, we rotate our second-orders to simple structure, we can factor the correlation between these and hence extract third-order factors. Theoretically we could go on until at least one factor alone accounted for the variance. Generally however high-order factorizations do not go beyond the third order. This is often because at this point the solution tends to be near the orthogonal position anyway—and perhaps only two factors emerge so that further factor extraction would not be useful. It is worth recalling before we discuss actual high-order personality factors that if we factor item intercorrelations the first-order factors load on items, and the second-order factors on first-order factors, while third-order factors load on second-order ones. Thus higher-order factors account for more variance than do primary or first-order factors and are thus more parsimonious. Note that higher-order factors can be tied down to items in that if, for example, items 1–20 load on factors 1 or 2 or 3, and a second order factor loads on these three factors, then it is automatically defined by items 1 to 20.

Since there is a considerable similarity between the normal adults' and children's primary factor patterns, it is highly likely that higher-order factors in these two domains will be the same. Nevertheless we shall consider the higher-order factors separately, as we did with the primaries. As was the case with the primary factors we shall rather boldly state the findings in this chapter. In a later chapter when we have fully discussed the primaries we shall try to justify their identification.

SECOND-ORDER FACTORS IN NORMAL ADULTS

Since, as we have seen, there is considerable identity between L and Q factors, and since far more research for reasons we have already discussed has been conducted with Q factors, for our present purpose of summary statement, the higher-order factors we shall list are those obtained from Q data. However similar second-order factors have been found in L data (Cattell, 1957) and the higher-order T factors will be considered later when we discuss objective tests.

Cattell (1973) has clearly summarized the position which is based on fourteen 16PF adult studies. Great efforts have been made particularly by Cattell and Nichols (1972) to match the higher-order factors emerging from the different studies.

Second order factors	*Description in terms of Primary factors*
1 Exvia	Sociable (A), surgent (F), adventurous (H), dependent (Q2)—i.e. Extraversion
2 Anxiety	Weak ego strength (C), timid (H), suspicious (L), guilt prone (O), low self-sentiment (Q3), tense (Q4)
3 Cortertia	Unsociable (A−), insensitive (I) shrewd (N)
4 Independence	Surgent (F), dominant (E), adventurous (H), unconcerned (M), suspicious (L)
5 Discreetness	Shrewd (N), sociable (A)
6 Subjectivity	Unconcerned (M), radical (Q1)
7 Intelligence	Intelligence (B)
8 Good upbringing	Superego (G), submissive (E−), desurgent (F), self-sentiment (Q3)

One point must be noted about these eight adult normal second-order factors. They have emerged from studies of the 16PF without the 16PF supplement of the seven missing factors. This is important because when we come to examine the second-order factors in childhood using the HSPQ and CPQ tests, these have different factors. Thus D and J are present but there is no N, for example. To some extent this will affect the second-order factors, although the difference may reflect problems of test construction and item writing rather than differences in the real world of personality.

TABLE 4.5

Agreement of Preadult and Adult Second-Order Patterns in Main Culture
(a) Factor-Pattern Loadings on Factors Common to All Ages

Factor	I Exvia				II Anxiety				III Cortertia			
	Adult	14 yr.	10 yr.	7 yr.	Adult	14 yr.	10 yr.	7 yr.	Adult	14 yr.	10 yr.	7 yr.
A	58	74	52	33	01	−21	−18	−18	−25	−30	−28	−75
B	00	01	37	23	−02	01	−09	−18	00	00	35	−36
C	07	05	32	09	−66	−71	−53	−02	10	14	−19	−00
E	07	−03	25	19	00	−10	45	23	01	44	−12	47
F	51	56	72	37	−03	03	09	07	01	02	14	43
G	06	03	−00	05	−03	15	−01	−03	01	−09	07	−11
H	50	51	72	36	−38	−60	−21	−09	−14	03	−29	−40
I	07	03	−31	10	00	04	08	03	−73	−62	−12	−43
O	−02	13	−06	−08	78	69	39	84	−06	−16	02	07
Q₄	00	01	−32	63	80	75	17	27	−05	01	62	00

Factor	IV Independence				VII Intelligence				VIII Good Upbringing			
	Adult	14 yr.	10 yr.	7 yr.	Adult	14 yr.	10 yr	7 yr.	Adult	14 yr.	10 yr.	7 yr.
A	01	06	10	02	00	01	23	07	-01	00	63	12
B	-01	-02	-01	02	67	63	39	72	-01	04	53	22
C	-01	04	-07	72	04	-05	-09	17	05	15	16	17
E	56	40	03	03	01	-06	22	16	-18	-02	-08	14
F	30	31	-01	46	02	07	39	-11	-27	-51	-04	07
G	-03	02	11	29	05	10	-03	15	67	64	99	59
H	34	31	00	37	-02	-02	-07	00	-00	-00	16	07
I	-03	-05	-13	18	01	-04	14	14	02	08	39	14
O	-05	-01	02	-08	-04	00	06	-20	03	07	21	-08
Q₄	10	05	14	-04	09	02	14	07	-02	-03	-28	-24

(b) Congruences (diagonals)

Age	Factors					
	I	II	III	IV	VII	VIII
Adult with 14	98	96	81	97	97	92
Adult with 10	84	73	21	15	50	66
Adult with 7	67	71	58	36	91	65
14 with 10	80	73	09	18	59	61
14 with 7	63	64	67	49	82	64
10 with 7	50	68	23	-20	51	86

SECOND-ORDER FACTORS AMONG CHILDREN

There has been less work with children partly because the various scales were developed later. However Cattell (1973) contains second-order factors for adolescent children based upon seven independent researchers and around 5,000 subjects.

Adolescent Factors (HSPQ)
1   Exvia
2   Anxiety
3   Cortertia
4   Independence
5 ⎫
   ⎬ Not found
6 ⎭
7   Intelligence
8   Good upbringing

These adolescent second-order factors are highly interesting because of the very good match to the adult pattern. Thus 5 and 6 are missing because the salient primaries for these factors N and Q1 are not measured in the HSPQ. Conversely primaries D, excitability and J coasthenia—independence—(not in the 16PF) fit into the appropriate second order factors. Thus D loads on anxiety, and J on the low pole of exvia. The difference in values of loading between the adult and adolescent second-order factors are not large, and there is no indication that these differences are significant. At this juncture therefore, we shall not comment upon them. In summary we can say that adolescent second-order factors do closely resemble those of adults and we may feel confident that when the adult 16PF with the supplementary factors is subjected to second-order analysis and if satisfactory items for the HSPQ can be found, the factors will be clearly identical.

Factors Among Younger Children
Since the PSPQ has never been subjected to second-order analysis, we cannot, obviously, make any statement about second-order factors among children below six year's of age. In the case of the two tests for 6 to 11 year olds, the CPQ and the ESPQ, there are so far only two second-order analyses. Since Cattell (1973) admits in the case of the CPQ that the results are far from reliable they need to be treated with caution. This is even more the case with the ESPQ and with these young children we must, therefore, regard the results as tentative. Table 4.5 shows eight second order factors at four ages. The loadings are mean values from studies. This is taken from Table 24 in Cattell (1973, p. 140).

When in our next chapters we come to discuss the nature and identification of these Cattell factors, we shall look more closely at the adequacy of some of the studies. Nevertheless it does appear that normal personality from child-hood upwards can be described in terms of six common second-order factors, exvia, anxiety (by far the most important), cortertia, independence, intelli-gence and good upbringing. We can be more confident about the adult and adolescent factors than we can about the childhood secondaries. All our second-order results so far discussed are based, it must be stressed, on the original 16 factors of the 16PF test. It does not include the seven most recent primary factors.

SECOND-ORDER ADULT FACTORS BASED ON 23 PRIMARIES

We shall now turn before we examine the abnormal second-order factors to second-order factors in the normal adult sphere, when we use all 23 of Cattell's factors. We did not include these before because there is only one study so far (Cattell, 1973c) using 275 young subjects. The results were highly satis-factory because the previous eight secondaries were confirmed and four more were found. Possible identifications are: 9 humanistic involvement, with loadings on Q2 and K, 10 tough stolidity with loading on F, D- and Q5-, 11 a genetic component involving F and J, and 12 may be a hypomanic security pattern. These identifications are entirely tentative since we have no other source of evidence about these factors than their loadings. Thus we have no information, even as regards high and low scorers, a method which often checks factor identification quite efficiently.

Another important finding in this study was that some of the new primaries loaded on the original eight secondaries, thus supporting their validity. For example factor D, excitability, loaded on the exvia factor, as would be expec-ted. In summary although much more research both on the actual factor pattern of the secondary factors underlying all the primary factors is required, we also need to study the nature of the secondaries, especially the new ones, in other ways. Nevertheless it does appear that we shall find twelve second-order factors among normal adults.

HIGHER-ORDER ABNORMAL FACTORS

Abnormal factors, as we have already fully discussed, have been established as embracing the 16PF factors plus twelve others derived from the MMPI, a search of the psychiatric literature and the construction of items, especially depression items, based on results. All the factors are measured by the CAQ which has been in one tentative study (Cattell, 1973) subjected to second-order analysis with a large sample of normal and pathological subjects.

Table 4.6 shows the second-order factors in the abnormal domain. This table is taken from Cattell (1973) p. 130.

TABLE 4.6

Secondaries Spanning 28 Normal and Pathological Primaries

Primary	I	II	III	IV	V	VI	Secondary VII	VIII	XIII	XIV	XV	12	h^2
A	35	−26	−18	44	10								35
B							64						41
C		−65										−41	56
E				34							24		52
F	21			33								−40	48
G							32	43		−30			51
H	35	−20		35	−45	−41							48
I			−39		−46	−08				−30			38
L				38				37					37
M			04	03		34							24
N		33			50		34		26				43
O		30			−42		34			25			45
Q_1	−31			17		59							69
Q_2	−73												58
Q_3		−35				−14		22					18

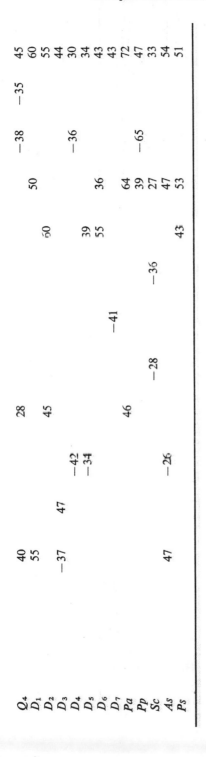

The following correlation values (× 100) appear in the table, arranged by the source-trait rows listed at the left (Q4, D1, D2, D3, D4, D5, D6, D7, Pa, Pp, Sc, As, Ps):

Q4	40, 55, −37, 47
D1	47
D2	−42, −34
D3	28, 45, 46, −28, −26
D4	−41, −36
D5	60, 39, 55, 43
D6	50, 36, 64, 39, 27, 47, 53
D7	−38, −36, −65
Pa	−35
Pp	
Sc	
As	
Ps	45, 60, 55, 44, 30, 34, 43, 43, 72, 47, 33, 54, 51

Some comments upon this table are desirable. First the eight normal secondaries which run through the 16PF test among normals appear. Factor 14 appears to be the psychosis factor, similar to the P of Eysenck (see p. 81). However its relation to the primary psychosis factor P needs to be worked out in further research. Factor 13 is a depression factor. This is interesting because it shows that some depressions are psychotic rather than depressive in origin. Factor 15 is hard to identify but might be associated with inhibition.

Thus at the second-order of analysis we find eight or twelve factors among normals and three extra pathological factors among abnormals. Among children the second-order pattern resembles that of adults but there seem to be fewer factors especially among the younger age groups. It must be noted that except among normal adults (and to a less extent older adolescents) these findings must be regarded as tentative.

THIRD-ORDER FACTORS

Finally before we begin our minute examination and description of these Cattell factors first- and second-order, we should briefly mention higher-order factors. Obviously, if the second-order factors are oblique, it is possible to factor the correlations between them and emerge with third-order factors. There are some problems here at this stage of the art which make results somewhat tentative. An appreciable difficulty is the resolution of simple structure when there are but few variables in the analysis. As we pointed out in our section on factor analysis, simple structure is best attained by utilizing the hyperplane count, but this requires a large number of variables to form "hyperplane stuff".

One study of these third-order factors was published in the handbook to the 16PF test (Cattell *et al.*, 1970). However Nichols (1973) has recently summarized eight careful studies among adults and adolescents. Labelling of the five factors is derived from item content although such face validity is a notoriously poor method of identifying factors or scales. However they have been called strength of contact, maladaptation, readiness and antisocial unconcern, a fifth factor cannot be named. Until scales have been developed for these third-order factors so that criterion relations can be studied little can be said about them.

Before leaving this question of higher-order factors, it should be mentioned that Warburton (1966) factored some data of Gorsuch and Cattell (1967) to the fourth-order using promax oblique rotations. He finally emerged with two factors adjustment and morality. However these findings are to be accepted only with the greatest caution.

Such then is the picture of personality as seen by Cattell who has attempted to embrace the whole personality sphere, normal and abnormal.

SUMMARY OF FACTORS

Adult normal: 16 + 7 primaries, 8 + 4 second-order factors and 5 third-order factors

Adult Pathological: 16 + 12 primaries, and 8 + 3 second-order factors

Child factors: a basically similar picture to that of adults but with fewer factors at the earlier age levels

These factors at the primary level are found in L and Q data (other than seven Q factors only).

Six tests have been devised: PSQ, ESPQ, CPQ, HSPQ, 16PF and the CAQ.

SUMMARY

1. The 23 factors emerging from L and Q data among normal adults were listed. This includes the most recently discovered seven factors.
2. The problems involved in the assessment of personality among children were discussed as they affected both ratings and questionnaires. However the factors found among children of different ages were listed.
3. Attention was then paid to the special abnormal or pathological personality sphere. The three sources of abnormal items were examined and the difficulties involved in the construction and factor analysis of the MMPI were discussed. The abnormal personality factors were then listed.
4. Higher-order factors were then introduced into the picture. First the second-order factors among normal adults were listed, then those among adolescents and finally those among younger children at various ages. All these were based upon the original sixteen primary factors.
5. A more tentative list of normal adult second-order factors was set out based upon the full set of 23 primaries.
6. Then second-order abnormal factors were set out, and finally third-order factors were listed among normals.

Chapter 5

The Evaluation of some Alternative Resolutions of Personality Structure

INTRODUCTION: EVALUATORY PRINCIPLES FOR FACTOR ANALYSES

At the stage of clinical observation and the inevitable subjectivity of its data it was not surprising that there were substantial differences in the structural conceptions of personality. Multivariate experimenters, however, were hopeful that their newer methods would be more objective and lead to precise, universal concepts. This has only partly been realized and onlookers seeing the hotly and sometimes bitterly contested issues have often felt disillusioned, overlooking the fact that the multivariate differences are far smaller and more negotiable than those of the clinicians.

Readers below the level of the postgraduate specializing in factor analytic research cannot be expected to possess the technical knowledge to arrive on their own at a decision on these issues. However they can be introduced to the most important relevant theories and methodological points in the argument. It is with these that this chapter will be concerned.

First we must distinguish between two issues: *differences about the actual form of the structure reached by multivariate research* and *differences of interpretation of agreed forms*. For example, Eysenck and Cattell differ on the theoretical interpretation of the first two second-order factors, Cattell considering QI to be exvia-invia, a dimension of social inhibition, and Eysenck claiming it to be a factor of general inhibition labelled by him as extraversion-introversion. The dispute is similar concerning QII. In this case Cattell claims that it is a factor of anxiety which is not necessarily pathological while Eysenck considers it to be Neuroticism. Apart from Cattell's criticism of the roughness of definition of these factors (since Eysenck through underfactoring reaches second-order factors without first obtaining the first orders), there is little difference in the structures or in the scales to measure them. On the other hand there are differences among other workers even in the simple *description* of the number and nature of the factors, (but see Chapter 7 for a full discussion).

Differences in Personality Structure

For this (the first of our two issues) three main explanations are possible.

(a) It could be the case that differences in description are real: these workers have sampled different populations and cultures with actual differences in structure.

(b) It could be the case that these researchers are making different and incompatible uses of the factor analytic method which would necessarily yield different concepts.

(c) It could be the case that they are using the same method but with such gross departures from its proper execution that all of them deviate in various degrees and directions from the true solution.

True differences. As we have discussed in various chapters (7 and 15) the main personality structures persist across populations differing in age, sex and national culture although it is fair to say that there are substantial differences of emphasis between various cultures, e.g. Britain, the USA and Italy (see the work of Warburton who found the British more inviant than their American counterparts, Warburton *et al.*, 1963). The factor of Dominance (E) provides another example of cultural variation which is probably genuine. Nevertheless such research makes it clear that relatively few differences in results can be attributed to our first possible explanation.

Incompatible methods. The discrepancies due to the second cause, if properly understood need create no more concern than those previously discussed. Some investigators utilize the method known as principal components and components except where they are rotated should not properly be called factors. The factor pattern has only mathematical not psychological meaning. Another difference is between orthogonal and oblique factors. Guilford (and originally Eysenck) retained orthogonality for their factors and did not, therefore, rotate them to an oblique position. It has been shown, however, (e.g. Cattell, 1973) that the factors of Guilford and Cattell are about equal in number (14-16) and occupy the same factor space (but see Chapter 6 for a full discussion). The final agreement fails, however, although some factors align closely, for the simple Euclidean reason that if line A is at 70° to line B, another line which is at 90° to line B cannot ever align with A. It implies nothing derogatory to either investigation that they do not provide the same result. The difference has to be looked for at the level of principle. Here the arguments of Cattell (1966), Thurstone (1947) and lately Eysenck (1967) against the artificiality of orthogonal primary factors are rapidly being accepted by technical workers in the field. However it must be noted that two well-known researchers in the sphere of ability and personality continue to utilize orthogonal systems which will not fit with the others, these two being Guilford (1967) and Vernon (1961).

Inadequate technical execution. Nevertheless, despite all this discussion the major source of differences among factor analytic results seems to lie in our third cause—the inadequate technical execution of the multivariate technique. This problem is not peculiar to factor analysis but occurs in areas (of all sciences) where many complex methods and instruments are used. An example of this might be the early attempts of Schiaparelli to draw maps of the canals on Mars utilizing simple optical telescopes. De Young (1972), Vaughan (1974) and Cattell (1973) have drawn attention to what they refer to as the basic requirements of a technically satisfactory factor analysis, and these have been discussed in the opening section of Chapter 3. Thus it is sufficient to set them out at this point.

Requirements for factor analysis:
    (a) strategic choice of variables,
    (b) sampling of subjects,
    (c) objective tests for number of factors,
    (d) iteration of communalities,
    (e) maximizing of simple structure in oblique rotation,
    (f) Bargmann (1953) test of simple structure,
    (g) invariance of primary factor pattern across researches, and
    (h) invariance of higher order structure.

These are the eight necessary conditions for a satisfactory factor analysis yet, as Cattell (1973) points out, many claims are made for factor analytic solutions in the personality field based upon one or two studies only, studies which omit at least one of these conditions. Indeed Vaughan (1974) has shown that more than half of the published studies in this area are invalidated by missing out two or more of these requirements although they are quoted by the statistically illiterate as confirming this or that alternative to the dimensions and structure elaborated by Cattell and his colleagues which are based upon programatic convergent researches which meet in full the technical requirements above. We refer, of course, here to the work of Barton (1973), Dielman and Cattell (1974), Eber, in his development of the 16PF test, Horn, (Cattel *et al.*, 1970) for his work with the MAT, Nesselroade (Cattell and Nesselroade, 1973) to mention but a few of Cattell's apparently indefatigable colleagues.

It could also be argued that it is misleading to use the term "factor analysis" to describe the methods of some of these researchers. For factor analysis was defined originally as a particular mathematical, analytic device and as stated in our first two possible causes of difference, it can provide different results when it is used in a scientifically simple-minded fashion. Indeed, as we have argued in the third chapter of our book, since the early days of Spearman and Thurstone factor analysis has developed so that it becomes part of a wide spectrum of multivariate methods. These form one half of research design (the other half being the classical bivariate experimental method) a point of view which has been rigorously and extensively argued in *The Handbook of Multivariate Experimental Psychology* (Cattell, 1966) which as Macaulay's schoolboy his Ovid, every advanced student in psychology should know well.

There all sorts of experimental conditions, techniques and sub-designs such as P, Q and dR analyses (examples of which are discussed later in the book) and other flexible developments out of factor analysis have been described. The term factor analysis is therefore inappropriate for both the narrow, rigid use of an old statistical device on the one hand and the more extensive multi-faceted use of factor analytic and other multivariate techniques on the other. Indeed a substantial part of the alleged disagreement among factor analysts, as seen by some students of personality research (e.g. Mischel, 1968), comes from this failure to recognize that quite different usages are being made of the original factor analytic procedure ranging from the mechanical to the flexible use of multivariate experimental techniques designed to test in some cases hypotheses and models of psychological action as such.

Broader use of factor analyses. When we come to examine this broader use of factor analysis where the results may be used to create a model or even a theory of personality structure and development it is clear that there is really no conflict between the factor systems of Edwards (1959) and Jackson (1967) and the work of Cattell and his colleagues such as Barton (1973) or Dielman (Cattell and Dielman, 1974). Here the difference lies in the choice of variables for both Edwards and Jackson attempt to investigate the motivational variables of Murray (whose work is discussed in chapter 9 on motivation) while Cattell has concentrated, as we have seen, on the temperamental traits of the personality sphere. Actually as we point out in the relevant chapter this work by Edwards and Jackson has its own specific problems stemming from the use of questionnaires in the motivational field and a clinical *a priori* analysis of the relevant variables. In addition a recent study by Nesselroade and Bates (1975) indicated that there is considerable overlap between the 16PF and Jackson's PRF at the higher-order level.

As to the problem of the differing numbers of factors in different work much of the confusion can be resolved by the technical advances that have been made in the mathematics of factor analysis as set out for example in Harman (1964) or more recently by Tatsuoka (1971). Thus Tucker (1955), Kaiser (1958) and Guttman (1954) have all devised statistical tests to decide on the number of significant factors in addition to the use of the maximum likelihood method. When these are applied to the factor analytic results, as Cattell (1973) showed, much of the confusion disappears since it always turns out that about 16–28 factors best fit the data. This is in strong contrast with, for example, the three factors of Eysenck and the ten of Comrey. Furthermore a recent study of the combined scales of Cattell, Eysenck and Comrey (Barton, 1973) (which we discuss later in this chapter) not only confirmed that the number of factors was greater than that claimed by Comrey but also demonstrated that Comrey's rotations were so far from simple structure that they were compounded of first and second order factors.

With regard to theoretical differences in the interpretation of findings alternative theories must be carefully examined until the critical experimental checks have been made. Hence we shall deal with such points of theory in the next chapter. However on questions of sheer description of factors and decisions on such technical issues as the number of significant factors and the attainment of simple structure we shall not inundate the reader with all technical details (although we shall refer him to the appropriate sources for further reading if he so wishes) and Chapter 3 will be found useful. Consequently we shall not list all the factors that all investigators have claimed to find. Instead in the survey of factorial studies of personality which follows this introductory section we take a stratified sample of the work. This embraces researches by Barton, Dielman, Eysenck, Eber, Comrey, Guilford, Nesselroade, Horn, Delhees, Scheier, Porter, Schmidt, De Young, Vaughan and others who have made a significant contribution. In a survey of this kind the authors have had to use their judgement and technical expertise both in sampling the research and in evaluating its worth on the technical criteria that we have discussed above. We must emphasize that this is not intended to be a complete list of all factor-analytic personality studies, most of which would be worthless anyway because of technical failings.

The actual factors discovered by the main workers and their research basis appear in this chapter. The evaluation of their work and the integration of the findings against the criteria above appears in Chapter 6.

THE WORK OF EYSENCK

Factors

The first set of personality factors that we shall discuss is that of Eysenck, who (e.g. 1967) has postulated three factors to account for the majority of personality variance. These are extraversion, neuroticism and psychoticism. Each of these factors may be regarded as a syndrome of traits or behaviours. Thus extraversion consists of sociability, friendliness, chattiness, craving for excitement, rashness, impulsiveness, optimism, cheerfulness, activity, spontaneity. Falstaff, Pistol and the rugby club hero are typical extraverts. Introversion, on the other hand, is the opposite of this. Neuroticism is characterized by worrying, moodiness, tenseness and nerviness often with physical symptoms such as sweating if anxious, blushing or feeling faint. Psychoticism, which is a more recently discovered factor which has not been so extensively studied as the others is more difficult to define except abstractly as "predisposition to psychotic breakdown" (Eysenck and Eysenck, 1968a). Generally it seems to involve feelings of persecution, a certain irrational mysticism, and a liking for powerful sensations.

Theoretical Background
As was the case with Cattell, Eysenck has done far more than establish a number of personality factors and develop tests to measure them although this is one of his achievements. In addition he (e.g. Eysenck, 1967) has tied the factor analytic findings into a complex psychological theory. To put his factors into some sort of context we can briefly summarize this theory by saying that extraversion is linked to the arousability of the central nervous system and to ease of conditionability. Neuroticism, on the other hand, is linked to the lability of the autonomic nervous system. Since the properties of our nervous system are obviously in part dependent on genetic factors as is to be expected there is a large genetic component in the heritability of extraversion and neuroticism. The psychological implications of this theory are wide-ranging and embrace, just to give a few examples, academic performance, smoking, cancer and crime. We have introduced some of the ramifications of this theory as a background to our brief description of the factors and their derivation. However the nature of the factors and the status of its concomitant theory, are discussed at various relevant points throughout the book.

Empirical Basis of Eysenck's Work
As was the case with Cattell the original study in which Eysenck identified extraversion and neuroticism (E and N) used ratings—but of abnormal subjects (Eysenck, 1944). In this investigation a sample of 700 neurotic soldiers was selected from a parent population of 1,000, to exclude, as far as possible those suffering from organic illness, brain damage or other physical complaints. Thus the first point to note about this study is that it is an abnormal sample. Thirty-nine rating scales were used to assess the patients, filled in by psychiatrists, and the resulting scores were correlated and subjected to factor analysis. Two orthogonal factors emerged E and N. N was "characterized by items such as badly organized personality, abnormal before illness,

little energy, narrow interests . . .' (Eysenck, 1970). The E factor opposed the typical personality traits of the hysteric to the traits typical of the dysthymic, for example, conversion symptoms and sex anomalies on the extravert pole, depression, obsessional traits and apathy at the introvert pole.

As a follow up of this early work in the *Dimensions of Personality* (Eysenck, 1947) Eysenck showed that these two factors were normally distributed among 1,000 male and 1,000 female neurotics. Thus the second point to note about this investigation is that with only 39 rating scales (and some of these clearly concerned with abnormal behaviour) Eysenck has by no means covered the whole personality sphere. In the light of our previous discussion about the importance of sampling both variables and subjects as widely as possible if we want to ensure that our factors are not highly restricted in nature, it is pertinent to question this study as a basis for a two factor theory.

Theoretical Basis of Eysenck's Work
However here we must take into account an important difference between Cattell and Eysenck. Cattell, as we have seen, regards the work of the early personality theorists as possibly insightful but certainly an imperfect observational basis to form hypotheses. Consequently Cattell's factor analytic researches have been entirely atheoretical. Only when we know what factors actually do emerge is Cattell prepared to try to interpret them in the light of previous theorizing. What he has to say, indeed, forms a large part of the later sections of this book. Eysenck, on the other hand, while agreeing that clinical observations and intuitive methods of analyzing them are unsatisfactory in fact used the theories of Jung and McDougall, together with some early statistical studies of personality as a basis on which to select his rating scales. Thus Eysenck's approach is not atheoretical but is a use of factor analysis to test hypotheses, a perfectly justifiable use (see p. 15) but one beset with the problem of deciding whether or not the results confirm them. *Jung*. To make an adequate judgement of this study by Eysenck (1944) it is necessary to discuss briefly both the theoretical formulations of Jung and McDougall and the early statistical studies. Jung most explicitly formulated his views on personality in *Psychological Types*, (Jung, 1923). Here we find that the extravert is described as a person who values the outer rather than the inner world. This means that he seeks power, prestige, popularity and social approval. He is sociable, cheerful, active, lively, likes new experiences and wears his heart on his sleeve. The extravert if he finds himself in difficulty likes to talk it over. The introvert is the opposite of all this. For him the inner world of feeling is important. In Jungian theory these are true types in that we should expect from the descriptions a bimodal distribution of the various personality traits. Actually Jung's personality classification is more complex than this basic attitudinal distinction between introversion and extraversion because in addition there are four functions of thinking, feeling, sensation and intuition. This therefore gives us an eight-fold classification

because in each person one of these functions is of primary importance. Thus one person will be an introverted thinker (Bertrand Russell perhaps) another an extraverted sensationalist. An example of this breed would be the president (by virtue of his post) of that rapidly growing organization for the preservation of real ale.

As regards mental illness Jung firmly linked extraversion with hysteria and introversion with psychasthenia, now, judging from Janet's description (Janet, 1903), a syndrome categorized as anxiety and depression. Furthermore, as pointed out by Eysenck (1970) Jung emphasized that introversion was not connected with neurosis. From this brief summary of Jung's personality theory it seems a reasonable claim that if we are to put this theory to the test we should expect to find among neurotics two distinct types separated out on an introversion-extraversion factor. Among normals we should expect a bimodally distributed extraversion factor and an independent neuroticism factor. Strictly speaking we should also expect to find sub factors of introspection, sensation, etc, within the extraversion factor. Eysenck's (1944) investigation, therefore, does seem a reasonable test of Jung's personality theory as it finds application in mental illness.

McDougall. McDougall (1926) in his *Outline of Abnormal Psychology* seems to have essentially presented the Jungian typology and thus to this extent Eysenck's investigation supports also McDougall's work. However it should be pointed out that this aspect of McDougall's work is not the core of his theorizing since McDougall was more concerned with the dynamics of behaviour where he postulated a large number of innate drives or instincts. Indeed it is only fair to point out that for Jung also this is an unimportant part of his work, almost a trivial one, in that for Jung the essential is understanding and getting into contact with the racial or collective unconscious, a concept that even the most inventive of psychologists would find it difficult to quantify. The conditional mood of the verb is not accidental because to our knowledge there has been no attempt to measure it.

Early statistical studies. These then are the theories that led Eysenck to select the 39 scales that seemed most relevant for an abnormal sample to factors of extraversion and neuroticism. However he took into account a number of earlier factor analytic studies of personality mainly carried out under the influence of Spearman in London. We shall mention these briefly, although they are important in the history of the scientific study of personality as pioneering ventures. Their results, however, should not be taken too seriously since, because factor analysis as a technique was not then highly developed and because the computational labours were so great that only small data matrices could be used, they have severe technical limitations (in terms of our evaluatory principles). Some readers may object at this juncture in the argument that if there were such technical limitations to factor analysis at this time how could it be the case that such great strides were made in the field of ability. However there can be no doubt that the field of abilities is far less complex than that of personality and the pioneering work of Thurstone and Spearman has been shown by modern techniques (Cattell, 1971) to be approximately accurate.

Heyman and Wiersma rated a large number of biographies and claimed from the number of overlapping traits in each individual that there were three personality dimensions underlying these traits—emotionality, activity and the dominance of primary or secondary function. They then proceeded to put this hypothesis to the test by having more than two thousand individuals rated by their family doctors. Eysenck (1970) has argued that their simple statistical analyses revealed factors that are in essence his neuroticism and extraversion. The bipolar primary and secondary function dimension corresponds to extraversion, emotionality to neuroticism in terms of their descriptions.

Webb (1915) subjected ratings of personality traits among a sample of students and schoolboys to factor analysis using Spearman's method of tetrad differences. He extracted a general g factor and another independent factor which he considered to be will and which he labelled w. This factor loaded on ratings for persistence conscientiousness and trust. Eysenck (1970) cites a number of reanalyses of Webb's data as different computational procedures became available and these support the notion of w as being the inverse of emotionality, a claim put forward by Burt (1939) who as early as 1915, had reported a factor of emotionality although with few details of the experimental procedures. Actually Burt (1937) conducted a Q factor analysis (in which people rather than variables are correlated) of ratings of eleven of McDougall's instincts with eleven problem children as well as a more normal R analysis of variables. Although these samples are far too small a factor of emotionality was extracted. In a later study Burt (1948) repeated this work on a sample of more adequate size and claimed to find essentially this same factor of emotionality together with a factor of emotional inhibition.

These were the main empirical studies, none of them wholly satisfactory, which led Eysenck to postulate that it was likely that two factors were supremely important in the personality sphere, extraversion and neuroticism. We have described these studies albeit briefly because we want to point out that they form a far from satisfactory basis for formulating hypotheses of any kind. Almost all of them utilize far too few subjects. In none of them is simple structure reached. In none of them are there marker variables for the identification of factors. For Eysenck to identify N and E within these studies was little more than inspired guessing.

If then the previous empirical studies were an insecure foundation for further research, the theoretical basis seems even weaker. For all his intellectual power and profundity of curious learning not even the most ardent admirers of Jung could claim that his work was rooted in sound observation. All the powerful criticisms that Eysenck has cogently aimed at the work of Freud (Eysenck, 1953) apply even more strongly to Jung although in fairness it must be admitted that the extravert-introvert portion of the theory is testable. Nevertheless it is curious that since the aim of Eysenck has been to put clinical psychology onto a scientific basis (Eysenck, 1961) that he should have bothered with these Jungian concepts at all. We should also be clear that it cannot be the case that Eysenck felt that this aspect of Jungian theory was correct and deserved careful confirmation since strictly speaking this rating study (Eysenck, 1944) does not test the theory in that it misses out the functional side—feeling, sensation, intuition and thinking.

From this it is clear that his first study of abnormals was not soundly based and although it appears that there was a factor of neuroticism, with this restricted sample and variables we could feel no confidence in making generalizations about the results. However since this early study there has accumulated a formidable number of studies relevant to these factors.

Further Confirmatory Studies of E and N

As we consider the nature of Eysenck's factors and compare them with those in other systems we shall examine this body of research—in later chapters of the book. At this point it is sufficient to say that once neuroticism and extraversion had been identified in ratings, questionnaires were developed to measure them with greater ease and reliability, just as was the case with the research of Cattell. Indeed it was this development of questionnaires which could be quickly applied in the practical and the research setting that has led over the years to the accumulation of knowledge about these factors.

Eysenck's Personality Tests. The main tests were: *The Maudsley Medical Questionnaire* (MMQ) which measured neuroticism using items embedded among questions about subject's health. *The Maudsley Personality Inventory* (MPI) measured both neuroticism and extraversion and had a lie scale to pick out the person who was attempting to create a good impression. This was an adult test but a junior version was developed for use with children down to around the age of nine. Later the *Eysenck Personality Inventory* (EPI) was constructed which, like the MPI, measures extraversion and neuroticism. Again junior versions for children were constructed and a special test for use with subjects of low intelligence—*The Eysenck-Withers Personality Inventory*. Since the construction of the EPI (Eysenck and Eysenck, 1964) questionnaire research with normals and abnormals (e.g. Eysenck and Eysenck, 1968) has revealed a third factor of Psychoticism, P. For studies of this personality factor Eysenck and his colleagues have taken to using the *PEN* which as its name suggests measures all three factors and combine the EPI E and N items with the new P items. However this test has not been at the present time published. Recently (Eysenck and Eysenck, 1976) a new test has been developed the Eysenck Personality Questionnaire, measuring E, N and P.

Since these tests are obviously similar to each other a brief discussion of the development of each is necessary. Otherwise we are presented with the logical problem that if the MPI is so unsatisfactory that a new test had to be developed, the EPI, we cannot really be expected to place much credence on results with the earlier test. On the other hand if the MPI was satisfactory the obvious question as to the necessity for a further test comes to mind. In addition since the tests measure the same variables we must be assured that they are correlated together. If they are the need for the new test again becomes questionable. If they are not the validity of the EPI becomes suspect.

The MMQ. The MMQ (Eysenck, 1952) showed itself able to differentiate between normal and neurotic subjects and the items loaded on some common factor, as revealed by item analysis although this did not, of course, indicate what this common factor was. However the difficulty with the MMQ was that the scale was not suitable for use with normal subjects mainly because both the keyed N items and the medical items in which they were embedded were not really relevant to normal non-psychiatric subjects. This was because like the MPI the items had been originally chosen with a psychiatric population in mind and the MMQ items read like the presenting symptoms of typical neurotic outpatients. Now the fact that the MMQ is not suitable for use with normals is a serious limitation for its use in the theoretical study of personality where some of the most useful data consist of the differences in scores of different groups of subjects. As a result of this deficiency Eysenck decided (Eysenck and Eysenck, 1969) to construct a questionnaire suited to more general use and capable of measuring the second factor found in the ratings—extraversion.

The MPI. This then was the rationale for the construction of the MPI which is fully described by Eysenck (1956) in an Italian journal which we have not been able to see. However, fortunately there is a good summary of this paper in Eysenck and Eysenck (1969), on which our account is based. 261 items were written which included the MMQ items, since these appeared to measure the putative N factor, and items from the Guilford scales (Guilford and Zimmerman, 1949). The Guilford scales which we discuss later in this chapter (see p. 84) were themselves constructed after extensive factor analysis and they appeared to measure neuroticism (Guilford's C) and extraversion (Guilford's R). The Guilford scales were not used in their original form for a number of reasons: the items were American, an obvious problem for use with British subjects, the scales were long and repetitive, a failing which British subjects abjure, being less docile in this respect than their American counterparts; possible sex differences had been ignored by Guilford in the construction of the scales; Eysenck also felt (Eysenck and Eysenck, 1969) that some of the items did not load highly on the scales of which they were supposed to form a part, although no supporting evidence for this impression is given and, finally, it was by no means clear from examination of the item content that the scales really were unitary concepts. This battery of items was administered to a mainly middle class sample of 200 male and 200 female subjects.

The data from this investigation were subjected to a series of highly detailed statistical analyses in which the relations of the Guilford scales to the Eysenck items and to each other were all examined. In addition separate item analyses for all the scales were conducted separately for each sex so that the adequacy of the individual items could be assessed. As a result of this work Eysenck selected 48 items from the battery and as a further check subjected the tetrachoric correlations between them to a rotated factor analysis. Two factors emerged and each of the 48 items loaded highly on one of them. From the correlations with the Guilford scales as well as inspection of the item content it was not unreasonable to regard these two factors as neuroticism and extraversion. Although the factor loadings for the items were impressive it must be realized that there must be more variance than either extraversion or neuroticism in these items. Thus the communalities for the items in a two factor solution are inevitably far short of unity. An item which loads 0.7 on E and 0.0 on N has a communality of only 0.49 so that more than half the variance is unexplained. Yet by any psychometric standards this is a good item. Nevertheless this test construction exercise is a sound basis for any test and these 48 items with their clear loadings on E or N were duly incorporated into a published test—the MPI.

The EPI. The considerable mass of research findings with the MPI will be examined later as we consider the nature of extraversion and neuroticism. We must now look at the basis of the EPI. Since, as we have seen, the MPI appears to be a soundly constructed test and since the research findings with it showed no obvious limitations, the raison d'etre for a new test is of some interest. In the manual to the EPI (Eysenck and Eysenck, 1964) it is claimed that the EPI "is sufficiently similar to the MPI and correlates sufficiently highly with it to make it almost certain that the experimental findings reported for the older instrument will also apply to the newer . . . ." Indeed in the manual the EPI is simply referred to as an improved version of the MPI. In fact so certain are Eysenck and Eysenck that the MPI and the EPI are identical that they discuss (1969) in a chapter on the validity of the MPI results with the EPI. The EPI, then, is a version of the MPI improved in the following ways. The EPI has two parallel forms, a useful feature where we wish to retest without the interference of memory. The EPI items have been simplified to make them more suited to subjects with but moderate standards of literacy. The low correlation in the MPI between E and N has been eliminated by more careful item selection, choosing only those that loaded on one factor. The EPI contains a lie scale for eliminating subjects showing a tendency to endorse the items in a socially desirable fashion. Finally it is a more reliable test than the MPI probably because of the increased simplicity of the items. Guilford (1959) argues that where ambiguity of item, either in content or in difficult wording, occurs we find both response sets and unreliability (though to different items since response sets can raise reliability).

These claims that the EPI is an improved version of the MPI come from a series of studies conducted with the items in both tests analysed together. A total of 30,000 subjects was used in all these studies and there is little doubt that the EPI and MPI measure substantially the same variables. The improvements although not considerable probably make it sensible to use the EPI rather than the MPI except where longitudinal studies have already first used the older test.

So far these tests have concerned themselves with the two variables that Eysenck has long claimed to be the most important in personality. Recently however he has introduced a third variable, psychoticism, P, orthogonal to both E and N. Eysenck and Eysenck (1968a) argue that up till this date psychoticism, defined as a correlated set of behaviours indicative of a predisposition to psychotic breakdown and continuously distributed in the normal population, has been neglected in the literature. Despite this a number of investigations have supported the existence of this third factor (e.g. Eysenck, 1956) although objective, experimental objective tests of personality of arguable validity (which we discuss in a later chapter) were used.

The P factor. However Eysenck and Eysenck (1968a, 1968b) have carried out two investigations in which the questionnaire measurement and definition of the P factor was attempted. The two researches represent a replicated or cross-validated study. In the 1968b investigation 106 items consisting of the EPI E and N items and items written to measure the putative P, and to be independent of E and N, were administered to a sample of 821 women and 512 men. A factor analysis of the item intercorrelations revealed three factors, similar for both sexes, the familiar E and N and a further factor loading on the P items. P was correlated 0.3 with N. Now it must be stressed that a factorial study of this design can reveal that a general factor runs through a set of items and that this factor is independent of E and N. However this description would fit equally verbal ability or intelligence hence its identification as psychoticism must depend on item content or face validity which is not, in the absence of other evidence, acceptable. In the 1968 study two samples were used. The first consisted of 500 males and 500 females in employment, which while not a random sample nevertheless constitutes a welcome addition to the endless chain of student samples, while the second comprised 700 male and 700 female students. The intercorrelations, separate for sexes, were subjected to a principal components analysis and a Promax oblique rotation (Hendrickson and White, 1964).

The results of this second study were largely in accord with the research we have discussed above. Three factors emerged from the oblique rotation with similarity indices of 0.9 and beyond for the two sexes. Similarly there was good agreement between the "random" and the student samples. As to the independence of the psychoticism factor, it was uncorrelated with extraversion but as in the first study there was a moderate correlation with neuroticism. This varied in the four groups from 0.3 to 0.45. Finally examination of the 20 P items shows clearly that they are saturated with P and are independent of E and largely of N—a confirmation of the correlation which we have already noted. From all this evidence it seems clear that Eysenck has demonstrated the existence of another factor underlying a set of personality items which is distinct from extraversion and moderately related to neuroticism. The 20 items which measure this factor, the P scale of the PEN inventory, are reliable—coefficients ranging from 0.81 to 0.66.

We have now seen in this chapter the theoretical and empirical basis of Eysenck's three personality factors. All that now remains for us to do is to give a brief description of each of these factors, a description indeed that will serve as an excellent concluding summary for this section on Eysenck's factors.

The extravert is cheerful, sociable, craves excitement and is optimistic. The introvert is the opposite of this. The neurotic is anxious, tense and moody while the psychotic (from the P items) feels persecuted, depressed and fails to get on well with people.

THE WORK OF GUILFORD

Guilford was one of the earliest workers in the factor analysis of personality, the first paper appearing in 1934 (Guilford and Guilford, 1934). In this an attempt was made to study extraversion by writing items that appeared to be representative of the typical Jungian description and administering them to a large number of subjects. In fact more than 900 students completed the 36 item personality scale and the item intercorrelations were subjected to factor analysis. Four factors emerged which were labelled social introversion, emotionality, impulsivity and interest in self. This investigation was replicated with a further sample of 300 subjects. Here (Guilford and Guilford, 1936) the tetrachoric correlations between the items were subjected to a centroid factor analysis, a method which approximates the principal components solution but with considerably less computation. From this analysis five factors emerged: social introversion (S), emotionality (E), masculinity (M), rhathymia (R) or freedom from care, and, finally, thinking introversion (T) or reflectiveness. There were other factors in this analysis but these could not be identified and the last two factors, R and T were only tentatively labelled.

These first two studies constitute the empirical basis, amplified by later work, of the Guilford scales and factors and because of their importance several points must be noted. In the first place the identification of factors is simply in terms of the content of the items loading on the factors. As we have previously argued this shows only that there is a common factor running through the items. It does not show what this factor is and reference to item content is no more than face-validity which can be notoriously misleading in the case of personality tests. Another important point to note is the fact that some of these scales have substantial correlations with each other, in the order of 0.4. Where we have correlated factors it is always possible to extract second- or even higher-order factors and this should be done both for the sake of parsimony and because the resultant higher-order factors can often prove useful in the identification of the primaries.

S, E, and M, it will be remembered, were confidently identified in the 1936 study whereas R and T were somewhat tentative. Guilford and Guilford (1939a) carried out a further study of these last two factors in which a 30 item personality scale was administered to 1,000 students and a centroid analysis of the item intercorrelations was again conducted. Of the nine factors emerging, S, R, and T were again identified together with two new ones depression (D), the largest of these factors, and alertness (A). The others could not be interpreted. In a further study (Guilford and Guilford, 1939b) nervousness (N) and general drive (GD) emerged—yet two more factors.

Guilford's Tests

Based upon these early studies Guilford developed two personality tests to provide measures of his factors. These were the Inventory of Factors STDCR (Guilford, 1940) and the Guilford-Martin Inventory of Factors GAMIN (Guilford and Martin, 1943). It will be noticed that these two tests contain two further factors identified in the same way as the others. These are cycloid disposition (C) and inferiority feelings (I). In their early forms little evidence was offered for validity other than the fact that the items loaded on the scales which were reliable. Furthermore the normative groups were clearly too small to be satisfactory. In addition the scales in each of the tests were highly intercorrelated some even to the extent of 0.8. However in 1949 Guilford and Zimmerman in response to the demand for a single test more easy to administer than the two previous ones but capable of giving a comprehensive picture of personality combined the GAMIN, STDCR and the Guilford-Martin Personnel Inventory (which had been developed by item rather than factor analysis, Guilford and Martin, 1943) into a single test—the Guilford-Zimmerman Temperament Survey (GZTS). This GZTS which consisted of 300 items of the yes/no variety contained three factors not previously mentioned—Objectivity (O), friendliness (F) and personal relations (P).

As we can see from this brief survey of the work on which the Guilford factors are based, as research progressed and new factors were found, so they tended to be added into the tests. Indeed it is difficult to form a definitive list although, as Eysenck (Eysenck and Eysenck, 1969) points out the list of factors and their descriptions given in Guilford and Zimmerman (1956) is probably as good a list as any. These factors and their descriptions which we quote below are, it must be remembered, correlated and the second-order factors which Guilford has ignored are of interest. These will be discussed in later chapters when we come to discuss the nature of these Guilford factors. We should also remember that, compared with Cattell and Eysenck's factors there is considerably less external evidence of validity. The main factors are as described in Guilford and Zimmerman (1956).

TABLE 5.1

Guilford's Main Personality Factors

G.	*General activity:* Energetic, rapid-moving, rapid-working person, who likes action and may sometimes be impulsive.
A.	*Ascendance:* The person who upholds his rights and defends himself in face-to-face contacts; who does not mind being conspicuous, in fact may enjoy it; who through social initiative gravitates to positions of leadership; who is not fearful of social contacts; who is not inclined to keep his thoughts to himself. There is little to indicate that "submission" accurately describes the negative pole, as was formerly believed.
M.	*Masculinity vs. feminity:* Has masculine interests, vocational and avocational; not emotionally excitable or expressive; not easily aroused to fear or disgust; somewhat lacking in sympathy.
I.	*Confidence vs. inferiority feelings:* Feels accepted by others, confident, and adequate; socially poised; satisfied with his lot; not self-centred.
N.	*Calmness, composure vs. nervousness:* Calm and relaxed rather than nervous and jumpy; not restless, easily fatigued, or irritated; can concentrate on the matter at hand.
S.	*Sociability:* Likes social activity and contacts, formal or informal; likes positions of social leadership; has social poise, not shy, bashful, or seclusive.
T.	*Reflectiveness:* Given to meditative and reflective thinking; dreamer, philosophically inclined; has curiosity about and questioning attitude towards behaviour of self and others.
D.	*Depression:* Emotionally and physically depressed rather than cheerful; given to worry and anxiety and to perseverating.
C_1.	*Emotionality:* Emotions easily aroused and perseverating, yet shallow and childish; daydreamer. (Not identical with Factor C.)
R.	*Restraint vs. rhathymia:* Self restrained and self controlled; serious minded rather than happy-go-lucky; not cheerfully irresponsible.
O.	*Objectivity:* Takes an objective, realistic view of things; alert to his environment and can forget himself; not beset with suspicions.
Ag.	*Agreeable:* Low-scoring individual is easily aroused to hostility; resists control by others; has contempt for others; and may be aroused to aggressive action. High-scoring person is friendly and compliant.
Co.	*Co-operativeness, tolerance:* Low-scoring person is given to critical fault-finding generally; has little confidence or trust in others; self-centred and self pitying.

From this survey of Guilford's work on personality, there can be no doubt that he is one of the most original workers in the field. Indeed, as we saw his factors formed the basis of Eysenck's first studies of extraversion. It is disappointing therefore that Guilford has never followed the work up in the way that Eysenck and Cattell have done and related the factors to a wide variety of other psychological variables. This lack of external reference has made convincing identification of the Guilford factors difficult since we are too dependent on item loadings on factors and on the relationships with other factor-analytic tests.

THE WORK OF COMREY

We must now discuss the programme of research carried out by Comrey and his colleagues, beginning in 1961 (Comrey, 1961) and still in progress, aided by the publication of the Comrey Personality Scales (Comrey, 1970). Our reason for including this work is that the relation of these factors to some of those which we have already described has been investigated and in addition the research has some interesting itemetric innovations. Perhaps we should also take into account the fact that Comrey, as Demaree (1972) points out, regards his factors as the major areas of the adult personality domain (Comrey, 1970).

Itemetric Innovations
The two technical itemetric innovations which make Comrey's research of special interest are his use of parcels of items rather than individual items in the correlation matrix from which the factors are extracted and his use of seven point rather than the more usual two or three point response scales. Comrey employs factor analysis to develop groups of homogeneous items called factored homogeneous item dimensions (FHIDs). These FHIDs are used in place of items to form the basic unit variables of the correlation matrix. Factors are then extracted which load on the FHIDs and the factor scales consist of the FHIDs which load on a particular factor. The advantage of this method lies in the unreliability of the responses to individual items. Thus because, as the Spearman Brown formula shows, reliability increases with length the FHIDs inevitably provide a more reliable basis for the correlations. In addition to this the usual correlation coefficients for dichotomous items, the tetrachoric correlation and the phi coefficient, are affected by the size of the response split and have large standard errors, disadvantages when the correlations are to be factored. All this the FHIDs avoid.

The use of a seven point response scale (nine points in some of the early studies) was designed to eliminate the response set of acquiescence (see p. 38) and the frequent irritation that many subjects feel, especially educated ones, on being required to respond to a highly complex question with an absolute yes or no. These then are the advantages in the technical innovations of Comrey's work.

Although we shall discuss these points more fully in later chapters when we come to examine the nature of the Comrey factors, at this juncture we need to be aware of two counter arguments. To use groups of items is not to escape altogether from the bogey of item unreliability. The second point, made by Cattell (1973) is that the FHIDs are by virtue of their construction very short primary factor scales. If this is the case, of course, Comrey's resulting factors are in reality second order factors.

We have discussed these itemetric points concerning the work of Comrey because in other respects its relatively small scale (most of the researches are with student samples of three or four hundred subjects) and the lack of any normative data about the factors, as exemplified in the manual to the test, render it less noteworthy. Indeed, as we have fully discussed in our chapter on the notion of the personality sphere, it is all too easy for researchers to construct items and find factors running through them. What these factors are, if no attention is paid to marker variables or to sampling the personality sphere, is of course problematic and there is always the possibility of bloating specific factors into apparent common factors. The factors in Comrey's work are set out below.

Comrey's Factors
     T,   trust vs defensiveness
     O,   orderliness vs lack of compulsion
     C,   social conformity vs rebelliousness
     A,   activity vs lack of energy
     S,   emotional stability vs neuroticism
     E,   extraversion vs introversion
     M, masculinity vs femininity
     P,   empathy vs egocentrism
In addition to these eight personality factors there are two scales concerned with the validity of the responses.

THE WORK OF GRYGIER

The next and final set of factors that we want to discuss at this stage of our book are those of Grygier, incorporated in the Dynamic Personality Inventory (Grygier, 1961). This test represents one of the few attempts to combine factor analytic methodology and psychoanalytic theory, other than a few one off scales which we shall consider where appropriate.

The Original KPPS
Although a highly original scale the DPI is based on an earlier factor analytic test, the Krout Personal Preference Scale (KPPS). This KPPS (Krout and Krout, 1954) attempts to assess which Freudian psychosexual developmental level subjects have reached. Freudian psychosexual theory, it will be remembered, postulates (Freud, 1905) that subjects may become fixated at the oral, anal or phallic stages of development and that the adult personality pattern is related to such fixation. Later analysts have extended the theory somewhat and Krout and Krout put a modern version of the theory to the

test by including the following ten levels in their personality inventory: infantile passive, prenatal, oral sucking, oral sadistic, anal retentive, anal expulsive, narcissistic, feminine, masculine, into-familial, sublimation and social sublimation. Each scale, in the final version of the test, consisted of ten items which were of an unusual kind being either words or phrases to which subjects had to respond "like", "fairly interested" or "dislike". The curious flavour of this test which the DPI possesses in full is best illustrated by a few items: a seat near the wall, eating soft boiled eggs, chewing on celery, swatting flies, archery and wearing boots. Although this scale was not originally constructed by means of factor analysis, partly because work was first begun with it in the thirties, Krout and Krout (1954) present a table of scale intercorrelations which suggests that there is considerable independence between them. Stagner *et al.* (1955) subjected the inter item correlations of a selection of the KPPS items (three per scale) to an oblique (Quartimax) factor analysis. Ten factors emerged which fitted to some extent the factors supposed to be measured by the items. This result suggests that a reliable factor structure may underlie these items particularly when we bear in mind the difficulty of defining factors in terms of only three items.

In summary we should like to argue that the KPPS by virtue of its interesting theoretical rationale, its highly individual item form and the promising factor analysis of Stagner *et al.*, (1955) could well encapsulate personality factors not measured by the atheoretical studies which we have so far discussed. This was certainly the view of Grygier (1961) who proceeded to develop this test into a new instrument, through factor analyses and investigations of specific sub groups. As we have previously indicated this test is the Dynamic Personality Inventory.

The DPI

According to the temporary manual to the DPI (Grygier, 1961) the test measures the tendencies, sublimations, reaction-formations and defence mechanisms associated with the various patterns of psychosexual development. For this Freudian theory was regarded as a stimulus rather than a rigid orthodoxy which had to be followed. As might be expected this has resulted in 33 scales which are of high reliability—around 0.8. Factor analysis of the item correlations was used in the scale construction so that unlike its ancestral KPPS the DPI is a true factored test. The items are similar in form to those in the KPPS and consist of 325 words or phrases to which subjects have to indicate like or dislike. Again a sample of the items gives the curious flavour of the test which leads us to feel that even if it does not measure what it purports to measure it could well be measuring useful personality factors omitted in more ordinary tests—a possibility to be discussed in chapter 6. The following items, although not in the DPI give an accurate impression of its bizarre nature which appeals to subjects doing the test: using scent,

TABLE 5.2

Variables in the DPI

H	Hypocrisy: self-satisfaction with own moral standards, lack of insight.
Wp	Passivity: liking for comfort, warmth and mild sensual impression.
Ws	Seclusion and introspection as a defence against social anxiety.
O	Orality: interest in food; liking for sweet creamy food.
Oa	Oral aggression: pleasure in biting and crunching, liking for strong drinks and savoury foods: suggestion of free floating aggression and anxiety about its control.
Od	Oral dependence, especially on parents and parental substitutes.
Om	Need for freedom of movement and emotional independence; a reaction formation against oral dependence.
Ov	Verbal aggression: verbally and/or intellectually aggressive behaviour.
Oi	Impulsiveness, changeability, spontaneity, reactive speed, emotional expressiveness.
Ou	Unconventionality of outlook.
Ah	Hoarding behaviour: anxious possessiveness, stubborn, clinging persistence.
Ad	Attention to details: orderliness, conscientiousness and perfectionism.
Ac	Conservatism, rigidity and tendency to stick to routine.
Aa	Submissiveness to authority and order.
As	Anal sadism: emphasis on strong authority, cruel laws and discipline.
Ai	Insularity: reserve and mistrust, social and racial prejudice.
P	Interest in objects of phallic symbol significance.
Pn	Narcissism: concern with clothes and appearance: sensuous enjoyment of luxury.
Pe	Exhibitionism: conscious enjoyment of attention and admiration.
Pa	Active Icarus complex: psycho-physical drive, drive for achievement.
Ph	Fascination by height, space and distance: aspirations at the fantasy level.
Pf	Fascination by fire, winds, storms and explosions: vivid imagination.
Pi	Icarian exploits: interest in active exploration, a love of adventure.
S	Sexuality: conscious acceptance of sexual impulses.
Ti	Enjoyment of tactile impressions, interest in handicrafts and creative manipulation of objects.
Ci	Creative, intellectual and artistic interests.
M	Masculine sexual identification, masculine interests, attitudes and roles.
F	Feminine sexual identification, or feminine interests, attitudes and roles.
MF	Tendency to seek roles regardless of their sexual identification.
Sa	Interest in social activities.
C	Interest in children, need to give affection.
EP	Ego-defensive persistence: tendency to act with renewed effort in the face of difficulties.
Ei	Initiative, self-reliance and a tendency to plan, manage and organize.

flogging, that floating feeling, firework displays, chewing pens, warm fur-lined shoes, the leaning tower of Pisa. The 33 scales and brief descriptions are given above.

From this description of the DPI scales it must be clear that they purport to measure variables very different from those in the factored scales that we have so far discussed. The pertinent question therefore concerns their factorial nature and it is to this that we shall now turn.

As Sells (1972) pointed out, the original test manual to the DPI (Grygier, 1961) made grandiose but unsubstantiated claims concerning the validity of these scales, claims indeed which would have made the DPI probably the finest test ever constructed. However a new manual has been published which allows us to evaluate, to some extent at least, their quality.

Grygier (1970) with reference to the factor analysis of the item intercorrelations still fails to give all the necessary details. Thus he shows the item loadings for two factors Wp and Ws which were obtained from a 45 degree rotation of a centroid analysis. Now it is impossible to tell from this information how closely this approaches simple structure. Nor do we know how much variance these factors account for or the loadings of these items on other factors. Indeed we are not even told the sample size on which the original correlations were based, nor the constitution of the sample nor the type of correlation used. All these omissions mean that we are unable to estimate the true worth of the factor loadings. In addition to this we are not given any information about the 31 scales except the somewhat cryptic note that they were developed in the same way and that the results were similar. From this we must conclude that the factor structure among the items remains to be elucidated. Certainly it fails to meet satisfactorily the criteria laid down in section 1 of this chapter.

Another approach to the study of the DPI lies in correlating the scale rather than the item scores, a procedure which makes more assumptions about item homogeneity than is desirable in an exploratory study. Grygier quotes correlations between the scales in the latest manual but with only small samples of students (N = 50). Since with 33 scales the number of correlations is large it is difficult to grasp these results which clearly demand a factor analysis to make them comprehensible, although the small sample size would render such an analysis of little value. However the correlation matrix gives the impression that some sensible factors could emerge from it. A disadvantage with this approach lies in the fact that any resulting factors are hard to identify except in terms of the DPI. Since one point in conducting the analysis would be to elucidate the scales it is clear the procedure is circular and that marker variables of some kind or other must be included in the analysis. This means in effect that a more valuable procedure would be to correlate and factor analyze the DPI and other test scores.

Grygier (1970) is able to cite only one reference of this kind—the work of Carey who studied 64 compulsive gamblers. Carey (1969) found correlations between various of the 16PF scales and the EPI which suggested that a factor analysis would reveal an interesting factor structure, although the sheer number of possible correlations makes interpretation without a factor analysis difficult. Unfortunately no factor analysis was reported presumably due to the small size of the sample.

Kline (1968) subjected the DPI to a Varimax orthogonal factor analysis in a study involving 70 students. Although the sample size and the orthogonal rotation are technical shortcomings eleven factors emerged. The majority of these made little sense either in terms of Freudian theory or identification in terms of the scales although a clear anal or obsessional factor emerged and factors of masculine and feminine interests. This analysis was repeated by Stringer (1970) on a much larger sample. Here again these factors were difficult to identify and there was little evidence that they were relevant to Freudian psychosexual variables.

At this point readers may be wondering why we are discussing this test at all since there seems to be little evidence either for its validity or for any kind of clear factor structure. However the studies with architectural and university students by Stringer (1967) and Hamilton (1970) show that whatever it is that the scales are measuring (and it is almost certainly, except for the anal scales, not Freudian psychosexual variables) it is highly useful in the prediction of academic success and in the differentiation of different types of student. Furthermore some of the evidence quoted by Grygier (1970) in the test manual indicates that the DPI is useful in the study of criminals. All this suggests that the DPI scales are measuring personality factors implicated in a wide range of behaviours. Furthermore the work of Carey which we have discussed suggests that these factors are to some extent independent of the 16PF factors and the factorial studies of Kline and Stringer indicate that a number of factors do run through the test, rather than just one or two perhaps pseudo second order factors. On these grounds, therefore, we would argue that the DPI factors do seem both useful and different from those in other factored tests. What is now urgently required is that a series of factorial studies are carried out on adequate samples, with modern rotational procedures and with marker variables from the main personality tests and even perhaps in view of the variables from motivational tests (see chapters 9 and 10). Certainly the kind of studies so far reviewed where the internal factorial structure of the scales has been examined are unsatisfactory without markers. Actually Kline (1971) as a validity study of his own test of the anal character, Ai3Q, factored the DPI with it. Here it was found that Ai3Q loaded highly on the anal factor which supports the validity both of the anal scales of the DPI and the anal questionnaire.

In conclusion we should like to argue that there is some reason to think that the DPI scales are measuring factors largely untouched by the majority of the personality tests. Certainly there is no anal factor in the 16PF or EPI. The DPI indeed is a test in search of a factor analysis.

THE MMPI

The MMPI is the most widely used personality test in the world (3291 references in the most recent edition of Buros (1972)). However we have already reviewed the factors within this 566 item pool (in Chapter 3 p. 53–55) since it was the main data base of the pathological personality sphere.

Although this test has proved useful to practical clinicians in that more than 200 scales have been developed from it, as we have shown, there is little psychological meaning inherent in such criterion-keyed scales. From the point of view of the definition of the personality sphere, we shall merely repeat the factors that we have already listed in the previous chapter: psychotic hypochondria, psychopathic behaviour, psychasthenia, religious interest and one factor which has not been identified.

In this chapter we have scrutinized 57 different factors and the research on which they were based. In the next chapter we shall evaluate the status of these factors many of which have been claimed as possible alternatives to the factors discussed in Chapter 4. This will be done in the light of studies especially designed to illuminate the relationship between these factors and those of Cattell and taking into account the evaluative criteria proposed in the early part of this chapter.

SUMMARY

1. Since there are a huge number of factorial findings in personality which would be hopelessly confusing if taken at their face-value, some evaluatory principles were proposed which enable us to estimate the status of the findings.
2. Sometimes these observed differences can reflect true personality differences: sometimes they are due to incompatible methods and more frequently to inadequate technical execution against the requirements of good factor analyses (set out in Chapter 3).
3. However the work of some of the leading researchers was described and their findings set out. First we looked at the background and empirical basis of Eysenck's three factor system—E, N and P.
4. The work of Guilford was described and his factors were listed.
5. Comrey's work was examined, especial attention being paid to his itemetric innovations.
6. The work of Grygier was then examined because it did seem possible that his factors did not overlap those of Cattell.
7. Finally the MMPI was briefly mentioned, although the factors in this test had been described in Chapter 4.

Chapter 6

Some Probable Integration of
Divergent Results

RATIONALE FOR COMPARING FACTORS

In the beginning of Chapter 5 we outlined the principles for evaluating different results obtained in the factor analysis of personality. While some differences could be real (for example between different cultural groups— say Africa and India), others would be accounted for by incompatible uses of multivariate techniques and in other cases by technically poor factorial resolutions resulting in failure to obtain simple structure. Indeed, as we discussed in Chapter 3, the eight criteria by which it is possible to evaluate the technical quality of factorial analyses are not often met in published researches. All these points can contribute to differences in obtained factor structures and they will have to be considered in evaluating all the factors we have listed in Chapters 4 and 5.

In our section on evaluatory principles we also argued that some differences were not in the factorial structure itself but in the interpretation of the factors and these will also be examined in our integration of divergent results. Here it must be noted that usually this type of discrepancy cannot be resolved by factor analysis alone. Rather we have to look at further criterion studies of the factors themselves often in the clinical or educational application.

Finally, it must be realized that the solution of the problem of different factors is not speculative or philosophical (however ingeniously such arguments can be contrived). Instead it is empirical and technical. It depends, in the main, on the common factorization of the different factors utilizing adequate samples and methods, and ensuring simple structure. This is the only way to resolve the first problem of divergent factor structures. Similarly interpretation of factors depends on empirical findings although we have also to argue from the factor loadings—a more subjective procedure.

Consequently in the following sections of this chapter we are going to examine the critical factorial investigations linking up the divergent factors in Chapters 4 and 5 in the light of our evaluatory principles and the technical criteria which we have previously discussed. This scrutiny will enable us to integrate the apparently discrepant findings and thus arrive at the most important components of personality and hence those most worthy of study.

COMPARISON OF EYSENCK, GUILFORD AND CATTELL

The first investigation which we are going to examine is that of Eysenck and Eysenck (1969) who in a large scale research factored together the Eysenck, Guilford and Cattell scales. Thus at one swoop the three most important factor analytic systems were compared. This is clearly a significant study and one which is of the kind precisely suited to answering the questions most pertinent to this book

Ideally in the study of personality tests we should study the intercorrelations of items rather than scales. This is because the items which have been *a priori* grouped into scales may not be truly homogeneous and thus the factor analysis of the scales is itself distorted. In addition there is a high degree of subjectivity in forming such scales. On the other hand the factor analysis of items demands enormous matrices and item responses are unreliable. As Cattell (1973) points out, there are considerable difficulties in reaching simple structure in the intercorrelations of items. In addition to this, since the factor pattern of item loadings can vary from population to population, the factors appear unstable. To overcome these problems Cattell (1973) advocates item parcelling where groups of homogeneous but not necessarily factor homogeneous items are factored. With this technique similar factors, and the same number, but with clearer loadings, are found to those in item factoring. With this problem in mind—factoring items or scales—it is pleasing to see that Eysenck and Eysenck (1969) did both. We shall examine first the results of the factoring of the scales.

Items in the Eysenck, Guilford and Cattell Scales

Eysenck's scales were represented by 48 Extraversion and 48 Neuroticism items from the EPI; 18 lie scale items were also used. On the basis of the factoring of the EPI items reported earlier in the book (Eysenck and Eysenck, 1969) these E and N items were grouped into 10 subscales: mood swings, sociability, jocularity, impulsiveness, sleeplessness, inferiority feelings, liveliness, nervousness, irritability, sensitivity, plus two lie scales and an acquiescence scale.

Cattell's 15 scales (factor B was omitted) were represented by 99 items selected by Cattell as the ones most salient to the factors. Guilford's thirteen scales were represented by 109 items selected as best by Guilford.

Scale Factor Analysis

The test battery of all these scales was administered to a mainly student sample of 600 males and 600 females. The correlations between the scales were subjected to an oblique rotated factor analysis (Promax, Hendrickson and White (1964)) separately for each sex.

Ten first order factors were extracted both for the women and the men. In both cases, according to the authors, two large factors accounted for the greatest portion of the variance and these were unambiguously extraversion and neuroticism. "The other factors are mainly doublets and perhaps of no great psychological interest." This was specifically stated of the male results but there was considerable similarity between the male and female results. However at the higher-order factor stage there were differences between the sexes. The females gave rise to three second-order factors. Two of these are claimed to be clearly extraversion and neuroticism while the third is considered to be an artefact—probably acquiescence in that it loaded on the acquiescence scales derived from the Guilford and Cattell scales but not on the Eysenck acquiescence score. In the case of the males at the second-order four factors emerged. Eysenck and Eysenck (1969) identify the first two as extraversion and neuroticism while the third factor seems related to the lie scale and the fourth, with loadings on cyclothymia superego strength, premsia and lack of rhathymia, is hard to identify. At the third order the ubiquitous extraversion and neuroticism emerge. No explanation is offered by the authors of the difference between the male and female solutions nor for the fact that N and E are in one group second-order factors but third-order factors among the males.

Although full discussion and comment on the results of this factor analysis are best delayed until we can include also the results of the study of items in these scales (see p. 97) a few points can be made now. As they stand these results would appear to support the claim, put forward, as we have seen, by Eysenck, that personality variance is best accounted for in terms of two factors (ignoring the later P which did not enter into this study). Obviously if Cattell and Guilford were correct we should expect 13 primary Guilford factors and 15 primary Cattell factors. The ten factor results could not have been interpreted this way. Furthermore it is not possible to impugn the investigation on the grounds that given the number of variables the subjects were too few in number. Nor can it be said that the items did not represent the scales since they were chosen by the original authors of the scales.

However, two points need to be considered before accepting the failure of the Guilford and Cattell scales. First there is the possibility that the Promax rotations did not reach simple structure or indeed anywhere near it. Although Hendrickson and White (1964) have shown that in some cases Promax can reach a known simple structure there seems little doubt, as pointed out by Cattell (1973), that usually Promax is inferior to topological solutions—a particular disadvantage being that it starts off from the orthogonal Varimax position. Furthermore against the other criteria of Chapter 5, there were serious deficiencies which we discuss on p. 99.

There may also be another very different influence at work in these results. This lies in the unequal number of scales (and ultimately of items) in the analysis relevant to the different factors. Thus Eysenck expected E and N to emerge at the first order and there were five scales relevant to each of these factors, comprising 48 items per factor. If, however, the Cattell and Guilford primary factors were to emerge they would have to load each on one factor alone which would be certain to be of limited variance in that each Cattell factor comprised only 6 or 7 items and each Guilford factor had eight items. Given that in any scale there is, as well as true factor variance, specific and error variance there was little hope from the number of items used that the Cattell and Guilford primary scales could emerge with clarity.

However we must now turn, for a complete evaluation of this investigation, to the second part the study of the intercorrelations of the items.

Investigation of the Items in the Three Scales
This is clearly a part of the research crucial to the argument running through this book. For if the items in the scales form factors different from those claimed by their authors, these claims must be refuted. The statistical analysis was similar for all the scales and was carried out using the same samples as the previous section of the research—600 males and 600 females. A principal components analysis (with unities in the diagonal) of the product-moment correlations between the items was computed, followed by an oblique (Promax) rotation. Higher-order factors were also extracted. Eysenck and Eysenck (1969) were aware of the dangers of under-factoring (which we have discussed on p. 29 and which are particularly relevant here) and their computer programme was set to rotate 20 factors. Although this was less than the number of factors with roots greater than one, which is a common criterion for including factors in rotation (e.g. Guttman, 1954) and is probably less than the number that would be suggested by the scree test (Cattell 1966), on theoretical grounds it should be more than sufficient since two factors are

claimed to underly the EPI, 15 16PF and 13, the Guilford items. This statistical analysis was computed for each test and for each sex separately—six analyses in all. Finally a technique was evolved to examine the factors common to all the tests together. We shall first turn our attention to the EPI.

Factors in the EPI items. The following factors emerged from the EPI items: sociability, impulsiveness, mood swings, sleeplessness, jocularity, carefreeness, nervousness, and sensitivity. For these factors there was considerable agreement between the sexes. Three factors were hard to identify, being different for the males and females—tentatively labelled as absent-mindedness, quickwittedness, and social shyness. There were 7 second-order factors for both males and females, although only the first two or three have many items with loadings beyond 0.3 and there is not a good match between the sexes. The first factor for men is a neuroticism factor which, however, splits into three among the females. The second factor for both sexes is extraversion but the other factors are hard to identify, although factor 4 (male) is a separate neuroticism factor. At the third order there were two large factors virtually identical across the sexes—neuroticism and extraversion. In the male sample there was a small extra extraversion factor which Eysenck is unable to account for.

We shall discuss these results more fully when we have examined the factors in the other two scales. Nevertheless it is clear from this analysis that E and N are higher-order factors and that in the EPI there are a number of primary factors. However the status of these primary factors is quite different from that of the Cattell factors. As the handbook to the 16PF test indicates there is a huge amount of evidence showing that the primary factors can discriminate different occupational and psychiatric groups and that they relate to external criteria in a psychologically meaningful way. These Eysenck primary factors, on the other hand, consist, some of them, in collections of items, differing only in phraseology. Thus, for example, "Jocularity" loads on three items only: "Do you like practical jokes?", "Do you like playing pranks on others?" and "Do you hate being with a crowd who play jokes on one another?". This is the most extreme example of what Cattell would regard as a bloated specific factor but it must be remembered that none of the other factors, even if they load on a more diverse range of items than this one, has any external referent. The identification is simply in terms of their item loadings. Technical problems especially those relating to reaching simple structure again make the interpretation of these results somewhat dubious.

Factors in the Cattell items. From the first-order analysis 20 factors were put into the Promax rotation ten of which showed some agreement between males and females. Even these ten were difficult to name from the nature of the items loading on them so that there is little point in listing them all. The first three were: physical activity, sensitivity and jocularity. One thing however is quite clear—the items did not fall into the fifteen scales of the

16PF test. None of the factors corresponded to any of these but were made up from items purporting to load on different factors. At the second order there were 8 male and 7 female factors. There was so little agreement between these that Eysenck and Eysenck (1969) were not only unable to label them but they do not even bother to present them. Instead they set out the third-order factors of which there were three factors highly similar in both males and females. The first was clearly identified as neuroticism, the second as extraversion and the third was tentatively labelled as "... another kind of extraversion factor, perhaps more concerned with *socialisation* than sociability."

At their face value these results confirm again the importance of the higher-order factors of extraversion and neuroticism and throw considerable doubt on the stability and hence value of the Cattell primary factors although we must remember that there were few items to mark them. These results will be more fully discussed when we have examined the Guilford scales.

Factors in the Guilford items. Of the 20 factors rotated 12 had a reasonable match between the sexes. These factors were identified by Eysenck and Eysenck with some confidence and were considered to be consonant with the factors postulated by Guilford. Thus the factors were: sociability (S), moodiness (mixed C and D), carefreeness (Rhathymia), sleeplessness (mixed N and D), dominance (no real correspondence here), optimism and compassion, factors with no equivalents in the Guilford system, inferiority (I), nervousness (M and N), ascendancy (Guilford's ascendancy and Lack of Inferiority), introspectiveness (T) and activity (G). Thus, of these twelve replicable factors, 5 resembled the postulated Guilford factors and 4 were a meaningful mixture of two factors. Thus these results support the Guilford primary factors to a far greater extent than was the case with the Cattell primary factors.

Eysenck and Eysenck (1969) do not present the second-order factors but go straight to the third order. Here there were two clear factors in both sexes—the ubiquitous neuroticism and extraversion. In addition among the women there was a small third factor which was not interpreted, loading on only three items. Once again the higher-order analysis supports the concepts of neuroticism and extraversion.

Combined analysis of the three scales. Ideally the best and simplest method would have been to have put all the items together and to have factored the intercorrelations as was done with the individual scales. However this would have overstretched the computing facilities then available and the following substitute procedure was adopted. A matrix was constructed consisting of the correlations between the factors within the questionnaires and across the questionnaires. This was done separately for the sexes and separately for first- second- and third-order factors. These matrices were then factored following the same procedures as were used in the study of the individual scales. It is to be noted that the factors in this matrix are those found empirically in this investigation and not the putative factors hypothesized by the test constructors.

As is to be expected, the results strongly confirm the previous findings. At the third-order there were two large factors replicable across the sexes and identified from the items loading on them as extraversion and neuroticism. There was a third factor among the males made up of Cattell items which was not interpreted by Eysenck and Eysenck (1969). Among the females there was a third factor made up of Cattell items and a fourth made up from Guilford items. While it is possible that both these third factors and the fourth factor are related to item format this is not convincing since such items would tend to load on all the Cattell and all the Guilford items. Without further study these factors cannot be identified. Nevertheless there can be no doubt concerning the identification of the first two factors. It is also noteworthy that the correlation between these was extremely low in both cases—0.19 and 0.08 so that it is probably fair to argue that they are uncorrelated although the significance of correlations so far from the original observations cannot be estimated. Further support for their independence comes from the fact that no items loaded highly on both factors.

In summary this investigation by Eysenck and Eysenck (1969) seems to show that personality variance is most reliably accounted for in terms of two independent third-order factors extraversion and neuroticism. The attempts to describe personality in terms of a larger number of primary factors were not found to be useful because none of the Cattell primary factors emerged and only a few of the Guilford factors could be clearly identified.

Problems with the research. However in all the studies there appeared to be some technical flaws in the statistical analysis if it is considered against the rules advocated by Cattell (1973) and fully discussed in this book on p. 25. The weakest point would appear to lie in the Promax rotation which may not have reached simple structure (for which there was no statistical check) although it is at least an oblique solution. From the viewpoint of the sampling of variables and subjects the only serious objection lies in the small number of items representing the Cattell and Guilford factors although this should not have produced the complete failure to reproduce the factors that was actually found.

In addition to these problems with the Promax rotation and the small number of items it is clear that this study is deficient in a number of other essentials. Thus there was no test for the number of factors rotated although theoretically 20 factors should not lead to underfactoring. Unities rather than communalities were inserted in the diagonals and no check was made of the hyperplane count so that it is not possible to estimate how closely the Promax rotation approaches simple structure. Again there was no statistical check for simple structure and no attempt was made to check congruence with other research.

All this has led Cattell (1972, 1973) to throw doubt on these results of Eysenck and Eysenck (1969). While it is true to say that there are no gross technical flaws there are as we have seen inadequacies at most essential points of the research. Whether these are enough to produce the distortions of results claimed by Cattell is, of course, a matter of opinion although we would expect some deviation from hypotheses due to these departures from the ideal. Thus our view of this research is that it confirms the importance of Neuroticism and Extraversion which most factor analysts have postulated. It supports also the claim that Guilford's primary factors are better regarded as oblique than orthogonal. However, at the level where it could have been most important—the primary factor level—the findings need replication in researches where the technical deficiencies (the effect of which is likely to be most prominent at just this level) are eliminated.

This research has been discussed at length because it is undoubtedly an important investigation. Furthermore, the results have been taken as definite disproof of the value of Cattell's and to a lesser extent Guilford's primary scales. Thus, not unexpectedly, we find this claim in the concluding pages of the report (Eysenck and Eysenck, 1969). However at this point in our argument we need to consider further evidence.

FURTHER EVIDENCE ON THE PRIMARY FACTORS

Our reasons for examining this investigation by Eysenck and Eysenck (1969) were to elucidate the relationships between the three sets of factors. In doing this however we have been forced by the results into a consideration of whether the Cattell factors are reproduceable from his items at all. We shall now deal briefly with this question before returning to combined studies of different personality scales. Actually this is an old problem and Levonian (1961) pointed out that the 16PF items did not form homogeneous scales. Howarth and Browne (1971a and 1971b) conducted factor analyses of the 16PF items and failed to replicate the factors but as Cattell (1973) points out, these investigations were also riddled with technical deficiencies of which the most serious was the failure to use an oblique rotation other than a hand solution. This with a large number of variables is almost certainly defective and subjective. Furthermore there was no hyperplane count, no attempt to test the significance of simple structure, and no test for the number of factors rotated. It is to be noted that an obsolete edition of the 16PF test was used.

However Cattell (1973) has fully reported two studies which meet the technical criteria for adequate factor analysis and which both compare inter-correlations of items and item parcels, i.e. small groups of items as particularly advocated by Comrey (1970). These investigations (Cattell, 1973b; Cattell and Vaughan, 1973) using two samples of 780 adults and 250 students show that with either items or item parcels the items do load on the hypothesized Cattell factors to a statistically significant degree. However the intercorrelations of the items in the scales were small—in other words there was low homogeneity. Guilford (1975) has attempted to account for the different factors in the Eysenck,

Cattell and Guilford tests in terms of levels of psychological complexity: the various factors representing different levels of such complexity.

Digression on Test Homogeneity

The relationship of test homogeneity to test validity is frequently misunderstood. Despite the claims of many elementary textbooks, what is required of a good test is high reliability in terms of test-retest reliability rather than homogeneity. If we take the example of multiple correlation the point becomes obvious. Thus the maximum multiple correlation between a battery of tests and a criterion is obtained where the correlation between each test and the criterion is maximized and the correlations between the tests themselves minimized. Thus, for example, if two tests correlate perfectly with each other the addition of the second test to the battery would add nothing to any information we could obtain from the first test. The same is true if we consider a questionnaire as a battery of items which should correlate with the factor being measured. Thus the ideal is tests which are composed of items which have high correlations with the factors but low intercorrelations among themselves. This is a type of test which is exceedingly hard to construct since, in practice, when we have managed to write items that do correlate with a factor, there is a natural tendency to construct other similar ones.

There is a further obvious common-sense advantage to a test that is not highly homogeneous—it can reflect a wider variety of behaviour. From this it is clear that test homogeneity is not necessarily an index of validity. Now it is true that a valid test can be homogeneous, although, from our arguments above, it is likely that its validity could be improved if new items were added which lowered homogeneity (provided that they were loaded on the relevant factor). On the other hand low homogeneity is no guarantee of a valid test, far from it. Indeed in this sense the elementary textbooks are correct since a perfectly invalid test made up of a random assortment of items would have an exceedingly low coefficient of homogeneity. From this then we can see that there is nothing essentially antithetic in the claim made by Cattell and his colleagues in these studies that the 16PF factors emerge clearly from their items although there are low intercorrelations between these items. Indeed this low homogeneity, in the light of the high factor loadings, is a positive advantage. Perhaps a final word of warning is appropriate here. The emphasis in test construction on homogeneity has led in some tests to the construction of items that are little more than paraphrases of each other. This, of course, leads to the danger of bloated specifics and there is no doubt, as we saw from some of the EPI factors that emerged in the Eysenck and Eysenck (1969) study, that the EPI can be criticized on this score.

Factor Structure Within the 16PF

We can now return to the original subject of this discussion—the factor structure within the 16PF test. The two investigations (Cattell, 1973b and

Cattell and Vaughan, 1974) both showed a clear replicable factor structure as hypothesized by Cattell. Only one of the 16 factors was not well defined (although this was better than that of many studies purporting to refute the Cattell factors and replace them with others)—Q1 radicalism. Thus it would appear that where there are no serious technical shortcomings so that simple structure can be reached it is false to argue that the Cattell primary factors do not emerge. On this reinstatement of the 16 PF factors it is again pertinent to examine their relation with other factors in different systems. In this review of the evidence we shall examine only those studies which reach or approach the standards of technical excellence advocated in our previous discussions.

Distinctions Between First- and Second-Order Factors: Pseudo Secondaries

In relating the Cattell factors and other factor systems together an important distinction needs to be made. Considered in relation to the Cattell system, Eysenck's E, N and P and Comrey's 8 factors are really second-order factors, not primaries, while Guilford's factors are primary factors, as are Cattell's. Cattell (1973) has argued that if too few factors are rotated the factors take up their position close to that of the real second-order factors. However they are not the real second-order factors because they contain variance due to factors that have not been extracted. Hence under-factoring as in the EPI according to this argument, leads to the formation of pseudo-secondary factors. These secondary factors have been called grounded secondaries because their loadings are in terms of the items rather than first-order factors.

However examination of the Eysenck and Eysenck (1969) study reveals that N and E were genuine higher-order factors in that 20 factors were rotated, although it is the case that the other higher-order factors were rejected. This distinction between the scales (whether their factors are primaries or secondaries and pseudosecondaries) is important in considering bridging studies because different questions need to be asked. In the case of the secondaries it is reasonable to investigate what has happened to their primaries. In the case of the primaries it is necessary to investigate how they differ from the primaries postulated by Cattell.

In Chapter 5 we mentioned that recently Eysenck has developed measures for a new factor of psychoticism. However, as we saw in Chapter 4, Delhees and Cattell (1971) and De Voogt (1973) have shown in the abnormal sphere that there are two "psychoticism" second-order factors among the abnormal primaries—measured in the Clinical Analysis Questionnaire (see Chapter 13 for further discussion of this test). One is a *general psychoticism factor* to which P is a first-order approximation, while the other is a general depression factor running through six of the seven depression factors. Thus, Eysenck's P is another pseudo second-order factor.

GUILFORD FACTORS

We shall now examine the Guilford factors. We saw in a previous chapter how Guilford has postulated 13 orthogonal personality factors. Apart from the improbability (*a priori*) of personality factors being orthogonal, the obvious question at issue is to what extent do these factors overlap with the Cattell factors, especially if they are rotated to an oblique position. We should not expect particularly good agreement with the Eysenck and Comrey second-order factors, except at the second-order. Thus the critical evidence we need is a rotation of Guilford and Cattell items together, preferably with a check on simple structure. Fortunately this has been carried out by Cattell and Gibbons (1968).

In this investigation 14 of the 16 PF factors and 15 of the Guilford factors were studied using 424 items parcelled into 68 personality variables plus a variable for sex. These items were administered to 302 undergraduate students roughly divided for sex. The intercorrelations of the item parcels were subjected to a principal components analysis and the number of factors to be rotated was decided by the scree test (Cattell, 1966). 18 factors were rotated with communalities in the diagonals. Two different rotational procedures were carried out. First a Varimax orthogonal rotation was computed which however failed to reach simple structure by Bargmann's (1953) test and in consequence a topological Maxplane oblique rotation, followed by the hand adjusted Rotoplot was carried out. This showed the typical climb to a maximum hyperplane count and reached significant simple structure by the Bargmann test, although the hyperplane count was not so high as that for the 16PF alone.

This description of the method indicates clearly that this study by Cattell and Gibbons (1968) overcomes the technical deficiencies of the Eysenck and Eysenck (1969) investigation. Of the 18 factors two were written off as "formless residuals" and one was regarded as an interest—motivation factor —an interest in arts. Of the true personality factors only one of the 16PF factors failed to emerge as predicted from the theory of the test—Q4, ergic tension, although C was to some extent confused with O. The Guilford factors present a different picture however, as is inevitable since orthogonality has been abandoned for simple structure. Three of the Guilford factors were clear but perfectly aligned with Cattell equivalents: thus M, masculinity, seems identical with Cattell's I, tough-mindedness, N, calmness, is identical with O, guilt proneness, and S, sociability, to H, adventurousness. Four Guilford factors—G, general activity, R, restraint, T, reflectiveness, and E, (from the G.Z.T.S., optimism and even-mood) split each into two Cattell factors. Thus it may be argued of these that they are composite scales. Finally, D, depression, P, tolerance, O, objectivity, F, lack of hostility and N, calmness, loaded all on one Cattell factor—O, guilt proneness, one of the central factors in the second-order factor of anxiety.

Since an important measure of the goodness of fit of sets of factors lies in the match of their second-order factors, these were extracted from an analysis of the correlations between the primaries. From the scree test 9 factors were put into a Maxplane and rotoplot rotation, which attained a hyperplane count of 63.5%. Cattell and Gibbons (1968) argue that there is sound general agreement with other studies although the first factor of exvia is weak in that it loads Cattell factors A, E, F, H and Q2 as it normally does but has substantial loadings on G, O and Q1. Factor two is an excellent anxiety pattern with perhaps rather small loadings on O while factors 3 and 4 are typical of cortertia and independence. Thus this second-order pattern supports the identification of the primaries and suggests that the rotation of O and Q4 is not ideal.

What bearing, then, does this investigation have on our question as to the identity of the Cattell and Guilford primary factors? It seems to us that it provides a definitive answer. As is to be expected on theoretical grounds (that Cattell has sampled the personality sphere and that orthogonal rotation as in the Guilford scale construction is unlikely to attain simple structure) when simple structure is obtained the Guilford factors align themselves with the Cattell factors although most of them load on more than one factor. There is no factor in the Guilford scales that could not be assessed by a combination of the Cattell factors. Thus we can say on the basis of this technically excellent study, especially as regards the reaching of simple structure, that the Guilford factors represent factors resulting from orthogonal rotation and non-simple structure. Their existence, far from impugning the claims of the Cattell factors to embrace the major variance of the personality sphere, in fact confirms them. This means that there is no reason to examine the relations of any of our other factorial systems with the Guilford factors.

The second-order analysis should be briefly discussed. All that we wish to say at this juncture, where our discussion is of primary factors, is that it confirms strongly what the Eysenck and Eysenck (1969) investigation also confirmed, namely the importance of two second-order factors exvia or extraversion and neuroticism or anxiety, (for a discussion of the differences between these two last factors see p. 121), as well as the fact that there are other smaller but replicable second-order factors.

Since we can now abandon the Guilford factors, and while our discussion still turns around primary factors, it might be considered apposite to discuss the factors in the Dynamic Personality Inventory (Grygier, 1961). However, this test is so far outside the mainstream of psychometrics and there has been so little research with it that discussion is best left until the end of the chapter, as an interesting footnote that will be useful in a later examination of the relevance of these factorial results to personality theory (p. 323 *et seq.*). Our next task must be to examine the relation of the Comrey factors to the Cattell factors. Comrey, it will be remembered being distinguished for his use of FHID's (factored homogeneous item dimensions) and his identification of 8 factors.

COMREY'S FACTORS

We have argued in relation to the Eysenck factors that they are pseudo second-order factors due to underfactoring although in the joint research with the Cattell and Guilford scales they emerged as genuine higher-order factors. Cattell (1973) has argued in relation to the Comrey scales that these too are second-order factors but ones which have arisen from Comrey's use of factored homogeneous item dimensions (FHID's) rather than single items as the basic unit of analysis.

Comrey and Duffy (1968) carried out an investigation into the factorial structure of their FHID's, the EPI scales and the Cattell 16PF factors, where the basis of the analysis was scales and FHID's rather than items. Using a sample of 272 undergraduates and subjecting the principal components analysis to an oblique rotation adjusted subjectively by hand, they rotated different numbers of factors in various solutions. There can be little doubt that the results strongly support the claim that these Comrey factors are really second-order rather than primaries. Thus there was a clear extraversion or exvia factor which loaded on three of the 16PF markers for this factor— F, H and Q2, Eysenck's E scale and Comrey's seclusiveness, social poise and lack of social activities. Similarly there was a clear anxiety factor which loaded on Comrey's inadequacy, pessimism and paranoia, Eysenck's N scale and the 16PF anxiety markers, C, L, O and Q4. From this alone it is clear that two of Comrey's factors are simply the two largest second-order factors in the primary scales of Cattell. Comrey's other factors do not seem a particularly close fit to the other Cattell second-order factors. However we must remember here the technical deficiencies of Comrey's work the failure to define the personality sphere and thus sample it fully, the reliance on face validity in the construction of the FHID's, the failure to reach or test for simple structure. All these faults could account for the fact that only the largest second-order factors have been found.

Barton (1973) in a study of the Comrey scales together with the EPI and the 16PF but utilizing all the technical advances which we have discussed found a very considerable overlap between the Comrey factors and the Cattell second-order factors. Thus we may summarize our position on the Comrey factors by arguing that essentially they are the Cattell second-order factors, but are hopelessly garbled versions due to the total failure (on account of hand rotation) to reach simple structure.

From this discussion we may conclude that the Guilford factors are essentially similar to the primaries of the 16PF and that when rotated to simple structure they are composite factors although some align themselves exactly with one Cattell factor. The Comrey factors on the other hand seem to be second-order factors probably by virtue of their construction. There is no doubt that the main second-order factors of exvia and anxiety run through this test and the other factors resemble, but less closely due to rotational confusion, the other second-order Q factors. This means that when we come in later sections of the book to consider the theoretical implications of the factor analysis of personality we shall not need to consider separately the Guilford or Comrey factors except as empirical support for the Cattell factors of which they are imprecise variants.

SECOND-ORDER SIMILARITY OF FACTOR PATTERN

Many of the studies which we have examined in this chapter in relation to the Guilford and Comrey factors have also included as variables the Eysenck factors. All the results show quite unequivocally that Eysenck's extraversion is identical with Cattell's exvia and that Eysenck's N is identical with Cattell's anxiety. Even the research most hostile to the Cattell system (Eysenck and Eysenck, 1969) found agreement among the higher order factors. What was in dispute was the value of the primary factors which in that research appeared unstable and, of course, the interpretation of the second-orders, referred to in Chapter 5 as interpretative problems of agreed forms and structures.

Apart from the powerful evidence presented by these factor analyses that the Eysenck factors and the Cattell second-order factors are the same there is extensive correlational evidence in support. Thus Kline (1967b) working with both the 16PF and the EPI in Ghana found high correlations between E and N scores on both tests. Indeed, considering the reliability of both tests in this population the correlation could not well have been higher. Again, therefore, as was the case with the Guilford and the Comrey scales, it is clear that the work of Eysenck has not added new factors into the personality sphere as defined by Cattell. Of course this does not diminish the value of the work of Eysenck whose investigations of the psychological correlates of these factors and his interesting theorizing have led to new insights into personality. These are discussed in later sections of this book (see p. 336).

DPI FACTORS

We must now discuss the DPI, which seems to measure variables and hence factors far removed from those we have so far examined. As we indicated in our discussion of this test, despite the claims made in the manual there is little published evidence relevant to its factor structure or indeed to the nature of any of the factors measured by it. Kline (1968a) carried out a factorial study of the validity of this test (which we described on p. 90) and only one factor, an anal or obsessional factor, emerged with any clarity. The sample size here was small and the rotation was an orthogonal Varimax so these results must be treated with caution. However, this anal factor does give us a clue to the nature of the DPI factors since its highest loading was on a test of the anal character or obsessional traits—Ai3Q (Kline, 1971). The factor loadings of Ai3Q with the 16PF and the EPI are known since a Varimax analysis of these three tests was carried out with a sample of Ghanian students (Kline, 1968b), after it had first been shown that all tests were valid in Ghana (Kline, 1967b, 1969). In this study it was found that the anal test loaded on C−, G and Q4 id pressure. It was entirely unrelated to neuroticism or extraversion. How accurately this obsessional trait factor was located in factor space is hard to estimate. Thus this study was not technically sound, in that factors with eigen values greater than 1, were rotated. No check was made that simple structure was reached, although the Promax oblique analysis was so like the Varimax that interpretation of it would not have differed, and there was no attempt to match the factors with those in other studies except subjectively. On the other hand there can be little doubt that the rotation was psychologically sound in that the main Cattell second-order factors emerged clearly. Carey's (Grygier, 1970) investigation where correlations are presented with the Cattell factors again suggests that there is some overlap with the DPI but that there is also a good deal of independent variance in the tests. Unfortunately there are no further studies elucidating this problem so that the DPI to a large extent remains a factorial mystery.

Recently, however, Kline and Hampson (Hampson and Kline, 1976) have made a detailed psychological examination of the personal characteristics of a small group of abnormal offenders and controls. Since the primary objective of the study was to isolate groups of offenders discriminated in terms of their personality patterns Q factor analysis and Taxonome were utilized on a large number of variables derived from projective and psychometric tests including the DPI, the 16PF and the EPI. Although a total of only 24 subjects was used (ideal for Q analyses) in view of the potential importance of the results an R analysis of the data was also carried out thus identifying the factors in the DPI. Obviously at the outset it must be realized that any results are tentative in view of the size of the sample and the fact that a Promax oblique analysis rather than a topological programme was used in rotation. However, since the factorial structure of the 16PF and the EPI are known, some check on the psychological meaningfulness of the results is automatically built in. Thus, if we fail to obtain even the large second-order factors of anxiety and exvia, it is clear that the study is ruined by technical faults. On the other hand, if we find that these factors emerge clearly it will be worth looking at the other factors—although we must bear in mind that such technical faults as there are will affect the smaller factors most.

Kline and Hampson extracted 12 factors from the matrix and rotated this number being decided by the criterion of eigen values greater than one which agreed with the scree test. The claim that the DPI is measuring variance untapped in other personality tests was supported. Thus the clear N factor had no loadings on DPI variables, quite an achievement in view of the ubiquity of this factor in personality tests. No clear E factor emerged. Instead,

E loaded on two factors, one a factor of discipline and control linked to conservatism, freedom from sensation seeking and low intelligence, the other a factor of feminine identification and pleasure in tactile sensations. The other factors which loaded on DPI scales did not load on the 16PF or EPI variables which supports the independence of the DPI from these tests. Of course the reason that the DPI scales are unrelated to EPI and 16PF scales could be because they are measuring variables outside the personality sphere—more in the field of drives and interests. As yet this possibility cannot be discussed further because the necessary correlational and factor analytic work with appropriate interest marker variables has not been done. Another important possibility lies in the nature of the DPI factors themselves. Thus they may be little more than bloated specifics. However, in view of the promising correlations of some of the DPI variables with academic success and choice of field of study in the work of Hamilton (1970) and Stringer (1967) which we have discussed in the previous chapter, this is unlikely since bloated specifics would not be expected to correlate with any external criteria. Consequently we should like to conclude our discussion of the DPI by arguing that although there is a dearth of sound evidence, what little there is suggests that it may be measuring factors, perhaps small, which are distinct from those in the Cattell test. More research must be carried out with this test.

CONCLUSIONS

Our study of the relationships between the different personality factors proposed by different investigators has led us ineluctably to one conclusion. If we regard factor analysis as a method for uncovering the dimensions, in this case of personality, then the factors claimed by Cattell to embrace the normal and abnormal personality sphere have been essentially duplicated by other investigators. The primary factors of Guilford were shown to overlap or align themselves with the Cattell factors when simple rather than orthogonal structure was obtained. Comrey and Eysenck, it was shown, for different reasons, had arrived at second-order rather than primary factors. Eysenck's three factors were obviously highly similar to three of Cattell's and Comrey's showed considerable overlap when simple structure was obtained. With all these there was no disagreement that there were two large second-order factors exvia or introversion and neuroticism and anxiety. Finally the DPI (Grygier, 1961) does indeed seem to measure factors untapped by the Cattell primary factors. Whether this is due to the fact that the factors really belong to the field of interests rather than personality or are just bloated specifics is not clear. These factors deserve further investigation. Nevertheless as regards the identification of dimensions or causal agencies in the field of personality it is clear that the abnormal and normal factors proposed by

Cattell embrace the field at present. The factors in other systems add nothing new to these. Thus in the next chapter we shall describe the nature of these Cattell factors as they have been revealed by psychological research.

SUMMARY

1. The evaluatory principles discussed in Chapter 5 were applied to the various divergent factors listed in that chapter. Various studies where the different factors were put into the same analysis were scrutinized.
2. First we looked at joint researches of the Cattell, Eysenck and Guilford factors. It was shown that the Eysenck and Eysenck (1969) research did not, as its authors claimed, demonstrate the instability of the Cattell primary factors. Rather technically adequate research revealed that the Eysenck factors were pseudo-secondaries due largely to under-factoring.
3. The Guilford factors were truly primary factors but insistence on ortho gonal rotation resulted in failure to reach simple structure. Technically sound research indicated that the Guilford factors overlapped those of Cattell.
4. The Comrey factors were again pseudo-second orders due partly to inefficient, subjective, hand rotation and partly to the use of FHID's
5. The DPI factors did appear to differ from those of Cattell. However there was no adequate research to locate them within the personality sphere and it could be the case that they were really motivational factors.
6. It was concluded that the factor analytic picture of personality drawn by Cattell from L and Q data and described in Chapter 4 still remains the clearest, although there are genuine differences of interpretation between Cattell and Eysenck which will be discussed as we examine the psychological nature of the factors in later chapters of the book.

Chapter 7

Description of the Factors Found in Q and L Data

INTRODUCTION

From the last three chapters it is clear that the application of factor analysis to personality has yielded around 20 primary personality factors and a smaller number of second-order factors to which we have referred, mainly by name or letter. However the point of applying factor analysis in the scientific study of personality, as we have discussed, was to establish on the basis of sound empirical evidence what really were the most important dimensions: to replace clinical intuition by sound replicable observation. Now that these dimensions have been established it is obviously necessary to look at them closely. This is the task of the present chapter.

To do this we shall be forced to summarize an enormous amount of research carried out at the University of Illinois and at other laboratories over the last thirty years. This prodigious volume of work means that we shall be unable to reference every statement that we make about each factor other than in a general way (e.g. to the appropriate test manual). Our aim is to bring out the psychological reality behind the mathematical abstractions of the factors, for, as we shall see in later chapters of this book, tests based on these factors have already proved highly useful in applied psychology and they can be expected to become even more useful in the future, if used intelligently. Our descriptions of these factors are culled from four sources, the Handbook to the 16PF test (Cattell *et al.*, 1970), Cattell's *Personality and Mood by Questionnaire* (1973), *The Scientific Analysis of Personality* (Cattell, 1965) and to a less extent Cattell (1957). Finally, before we begin our description, readers should note that as we descend the alphabet so the variance contributed by any factor becomes smaller. Each factor has a bipolar description and we shall follow the custom of beginning with the low score.

DESCRIPTION AND PSYCHOLOGICAL MEANING OF FACTORS

A: Sizia (reserved, detached) *v.* Affectia (warm-hearted, outgoing). It is highly satisfactory that this should be the largest of the primary factors since it closely resembles a personality pattern that has long been distinguished in clinical psychology—the schizothymia *v.* cyclothymia of Kretschmer (1925). The psychological meaningfulness of this factor supports the utility of the factor analytic method. Kretschmer, it will be remembered, claimed that there was a characteristic physique and temperament for schizophrenics (schizothymia) and for manic-depressives (cyclothmia) and that less extreme temperaments and physiques could be observed in the normal population. In support of Kretschmer's claims there is a tendency for the positive pole to be associated with the pyknic (fat and rounded) body-build.

The psychological meaning of the factor becomes clear when we note that high scorers are typically found among salesmen, business executives, priests and social workers whereas low scorers tend to become natural scientists. Indeed creative people generally, artists, musicians, writers are all low scorers. Also, according to expectation, high scorers receive more promotion than low scorers—they are easy to get on with. Cattell (1973) has argued rather convincingly that this factor is more than sociability or gregariousness. Rather the high scorer shows, easily expresses and controls his emotions while the low scorer has a rigid emotional inhibition. The typical sceptical, critical, aloof behaviour of the sizic person reflects the low rewards such behaviour brings in human relationships. This is why the sizic turns to the orderly, inhuman world of science, logic and ideas. Newton and Milton are famous exemplars of low A, while Falstaff would undoubtedly be at the opposite pole.

B: Intelligence. This is not a personality factor so we shall not describe it here other than to say that it is moderately associated with having more intellectual interest, showing better judgements and perseverance. It is included in the 16PF test so that we have an ability measure for adding in to the personality measures for multiple correlation.

C: Dissatisfied emotionality *v.* Ego strength (easily upset, emotional *v.* stable, calm and unruffled). This factor resembles (hence the name) the concept of ego strength to be found in Freudian theory. Thus the high scorer is able to avoid emotional difficulties or problems through careful planning and foresight and is able to face problems rationally when they do occur. Ego strength is high in pilots, nurses, athletes, administrators and airline hostesses but low in accountants, professors, artists and clerks. From this we can see that where the ability to deal with crises and problems is useful high ego strength is found.

However it is the clinical associations which truly confirm this factor as the ego strength of Freud. Thus virtually all forms of pathology show statistically significant low C. This of course supports psychoanalytic theory (Freud, 1940) where it is claimed that neurosis is the result of low ego strength in the battle with superego and id. Again supportive of the identification (in Western society at least) is the increase in this factor on marriage and with church participation. Lenin, Bismarck and Washington may be regarded as typical high scorers, Nero, Hamlet and Dylan Thomas as low.

D: Excitability. This factor was demonstrated in ratings and in Q data among children. It has recently been shown to occur in adults and is one of the seven missing factors (see p. 47). This factor, related to problems of conduct rather than personality disorders, increases until early adolescence and then decreases. This is why it does not appear in the adult version of the 16PF and why until recently it was one of the missing primaries in the questionnaire realm. As is to be expected the D+ pupil does not fit easily into the school routine and is the typical hyper-active child whose concentration span is seemingly nonexistent, the bane of teachers. Cattell (1973) stresses that this factor should not be confused with emotionality or instability. It is a cognitive excitability, a restlessness perhaps encouraged by families where the active child becomes the centre of attention. The Duke of Wellington and Archimedes are claimed to be low on this factor, Alexander the Great and Hitler high. However there are likely to be few eminent high scoring individuals since there is a negative correlation between this factor and many forms of achievement.

E: Submissiveness *v*. Dominance. The psychological meaning of this factor is close to what is usually understood by the terms dominant and submissive. Dominance may be seen in group behaviour such as heckling and badgering and in a general tendency not to follow rules. At school there tends to be a negative correlation with dominance and achievement perhaps because rules are there so important. The correlation, however, becomes positive at the college level. This factor tends to be low in the helping professions but is high in creative groups such as writers and artists. Indeed there is a positive correlation with creativity. This factor is affected by environmental events— lowered by long illness but raised by promotion, leaving home and psychotherapy. Cattell is careful to distinguish it from the self-assertion erg (see p. 180) which is the drive. E is the extent to which an individual has the confidence to put himself forward against opposition and this is why it is affected by such experiences as success and failure. Clearly from this description E is an important factor in any innovative work (hence the relation to creativity). Gallileo is a fine example of the E+ individual as is Freud who fought the scientific establishment for many years. Low E individuals are Ghandi and Buddha.

F: Desurgency *v*. Surgency (silent, full of cares, reflective and incommunicative *v*. talkative, cheerful, happy-go-lucky, quick and alert). Optimistic, cheerful, confident, bubbling with enthusiasm, this is the surgent individual. The desurgent on the other hand should not be confused with the depressed: rather he is sober and cautious. It is not surprising therefore that Factor F plays a large part in the second-order factor exvia. Surgency is high in psychopaths and delinquents (optimistic enough to think that they won't be caught) but low in neurotics, alcoholics and in physical illness.

Cattell (1973) has argued that there is a central environmental factor involved in surgency—the weight of experience. Thus the desurgent person, prudent, sober and cautious has been made so by his experiences. This is why there is a steady decrease in surgency scores with age (note the phrase grave old men and the Roman concept of *gravitas*) and it accounts for the correlations of steady work habits, achievement and creativity with the negative pole, desurgency. Although life experiences are important with this factor, heritability studies indicate a genetic component of irrepressibility and the ability to forget punishment. This last is very important in the light of Eysenck's (1967) linking conditionability to extraversion, in which F is an important component. According to this formulation the extravert takes longer to condition than the introvert and conditioned responses extinguish more quickly in the absence of reinforcement than they do among introverts. This would, of course, account for the noted ability to forget punishment. In addition Eysenck (1964) has linked high extraversion to criminality, a claim which fits the observed relationship of F with delinquency.

G: Superego (self-indulgent, slack, undependable *v*. disciplined, ordered, dominated by a sense of duty). This factor resembles the everyday concept of conscience and the psychoanalytic formulation of the superego. As is to be expected from this description the high G individual tends to reject loose sexual morals, acquires social responsibilities early, works hard as a student, drinks little or nothing and in marriage is devoted to the home. In short, a somewhat priggish person. G correlates positively with achievement and is the best single predictor of it of all the personality factors. G is low in homosexuals, psychopaths and criminals.

Cattell (1973) argues that the findings which we have summarized above match this factor with the Freudian superego. However, certain anomalies, such as the fact that academics and journalists have low superego scores (although they certainly show persistence) demand explanation. This is done by claiming that these exceptions are drawn from a subculture where there is fashionable revolt against contemporary moral standards—a revolt more verbal than actual. Certainly the Bloomsbury set illustrate this well since it appears that they daringly went three to a bed only to sit up reading and sipping Bengers food. Others, however, have taken their orgies more seriously.

A perhaps more important point in relation to factor G and the Freudian superego needs to be made. Freud (1933) linked anxiety to superego activity whereas in normals and children a strong superego reduces anxiety (Cattell and Gorsuch, 1965). Possibly among patients whose ego is weak (Freud's sample) superego activity may produce anxiety but Freud's generalization appears to be wrong. Although we shall discuss in a later chapter (16) the relation of factor analytic results to some of the important personality theories, we must point out here how neatly this finding that superego reduces rather than increases anxiety illustrates the value of the factor analytic method in personality research. For here we see how it has supported and *clarified* the theories in a way that clinical observation over more than 50 years had failed to do. In fairness to clinical methods, however, it should be stated here that Mowrer (1950) made precisely this point—that neurotics felt guilty because they *were* guilty, i.e. they had transcended their social mores because their superego was not sufficiently strong.

H: Threctia *v.* Parmia (shy, retiring, restrained, careful *v.* adventurous, active, responsive, friendly and impulsive). This factor is hypothesized as representing at the low pole the predominance of the sympathetic component of the autonomic nervous system and at the positive pole of the parasympathetic. The high H person is usually seen as pushful and brash, a man with many social contacts—the typical salesman. In fact high H is found in salesmen, competitive athletes and practising psychologists. It is low in priests and ministers and farmers. The psychopath is high on this factor as is the gang delinquent; the alcoholic and obsessional neurotic are low. The hypothesis linking factor H to the autonomic nervous system is supported by its correlations with large PGR and heart rate reaction to the cold-pressor test (Cattell *et al.*, 1970).

I: Harria *v.* Premsia (cynical, self-reliant, pragmatic, tough minded *v.* sensitive, gentle, insecure, intuitive, tender-minded). Factor I has a history older than that of extraversion and was discussed by William James. Eysenck (1954) in his studies of political attitudes isolated this factor. Indeed much to the discomfort of both fascists and communists he declared that this was what they had in common—they were both high on the tough-minded factor. Developmentally I is interesting in that it has a large variance among young children. At adolescence there is a steep decrease in its strength which then slowly rises throughout life. This reflects the phenomenon of student politics where tender minded attitudes (at least until very recent years) were prominent. Gradually, however, leading left wing figures veer right until at senescence they are respected props of the right wing establishment. Tender mindedness is associated with lax discipline at home, permissiveness regarding the expression of aggression and control by reason rather than punishment—the typical trendy, Hampstead, intellectual household (detached of course). It is found in artists, clergymen, professors and social workers. Low I is found among physicists, engineers, policemen and airline pilots.

L: Alaxia *v*. Protension (trusting, pliant, understanding, tolerant *v*. jealous, dogmatic, suspicious, irritable). This factor was difficult to locate in ratings but was defined by terms such as suspicious, self-sufficient and jealous. It appeared more clearly in Q data and is considered to be the result of using the defence mechanism of projection. The L+ individual tends to come from a home which gives him confidence and makes him feel superior. This factor is high in artists and some creative scientists although generally scientists are low, as are musicians. Clinically, criminals, neurotics, homosexuals and drug addicts score above the norm on this factor. In brief, Alaxia resembles the Freudian formulation of projection resulting from the projection of inner tension and being characterized by a moody, self-willed suspiciousness.

M: Praxernia *v*. Autia (practical, conventional, prosaic, down to earth *v*. unconventional, interested in art and ideas, imaginative, fanciful and en-thused). This factor is sometimes known aptly as bohemianism. As is to be expected from this description, M is very high in artists and moderately high in editors and clinical psychologists and very low in concrete occupations such as mining, geology and the police. This factor is related to accident proneness (presumably high-scorers are wrapped up in higher thoughts as they ram the car in front) and is higher in Italy, Brazil and Mexico than Britain or Australia. It is hypothesized by Cattell that Praxernia reflects concern with the inner life (hence the name autia) at the expense of the demands of the real world. This accounts for the increase in M after an unhappy love affair or failure to achieve promotion or even going to college instead of taking a job. Typical high M individuals are hippies and the Douanier Rousseau.

N: Natural forthrightness *v*. shrewdness (naive, unpretentious, spontaneous, lacking self-insight *v*. astute, worldly, polished, insightful, smart). N shows a small increase throughout life and is found high in occupations such as psychologist or manager where dealing with people is important although, interestingly enough, it is low in priests. Perhaps the nature of this factor is best illustrated by a list of people with high scores: Casanova, Mrs. Simpson, Lloyd George, Metternich and Voltaire. Those low in N include Diogenes, Kropotkin and Joan of Arc. From this we can see that N is involved with worldly cynicism and a trusting faith in the goodness of the world. Candide is perhaps a perfect example of a low N individual. Cattell (1973) cautiously hypothesizes that this factor may be developed by a selfish home background where the child is rapidly forced to fend for himself in competition with others.

O: Guilt proneness (self-confident, resilient, placid *v*. worrying, depressed, hypochondriacal, brooding). This factor plays a major part in the second-order factor of anxiety and is almost always found to be high in clinical pathology, e.g. alcoholics, criminals, homosexuals, manic-depressives and heart patients, just as C, ego strength, is almost always low. It is high in those who have few friends and are critical of group life and standards. They cry easily. This guilt proneness is not a liability to sudden pangs of guilt but a generalized feeling of inadequacy and loneliness which, however, can respond to success in life. Christ and Buddha (indeed most religious leaders) would be high on this factor while low scorers would include Genghis Khan, Stalin and many effective and ruthless administrators. The Indian Civil Service under the Raj must have been manned by those low on this factor.

We now come to factors Q1 to Q4 of the 16PF test, factors which appear only in Q data but have not been found in ratings. This failure to discover the factors in L data should be borne in mind when we discuss their meaning.

Q1: Conservatism *v.* Radicalism (respecting established ideas and traditions *v.* liberal, free thinking and experimental). This is a factor that has appeared in the work of a number of researchers—Thurstone and Chave (1929), Guilford, whose factor T is similar and Eysenck (1954) in his study of political attitudes. This was the factor that distinguishes the Fascist (conservative) from the Communist (radical), both as we have mentioned above in our discussion of factor I, being toughminded. To what extent Q1 is related to the authoritarian personality of Adorno (Adorno *et al.*, 1950) and Rokeach's (1960) dogmatism scale is not clear, although both these are probably factorially complex.

One of the problems with this factor is that the items loading on it show considerable instability with different samples so that the same items are not effective with middle aged men and young women students (Burdsall and Vaughan, 1973). Q1 loads most highly on items involving social, political and religious attitudes. Cattell (1973) regards the factor as a bloated specific combined with a tendency to try the new. Typical radicals are Shaw, the Huxleys, Marx and Napoleon while at the opposite pole are Churchill, Queen Victoria and most Popes.

Q2: Group Dependency *v.* Self Sufficiency (a joiner and a follower *v.* resourceful and preferring own decisions). This factor is an important component in the second-order factor of exvia and in the past it has been obscured by the then vague concept of introversion. This trait seems important in creativity in that it is high in occupations such as research scientists, creative writers and artists but low in nuns, nurses, cooks and footballers. Clinically, Q2 is high among conversion hysterics, inadequate personalities and schizophrenics of all kinds. Newton and Copernicus were high on Q2, Marilyn Monroe low.

Q3: Strength of self-sentiment (uncontrolled, lax, careless of social rules *v.* controlled, compulsive, following self-image). McDougall (1932) made much of the concept of self-sentiment in his work on personality. It seems to represent the clarity of self-image which an individual possesses and the strength of his adherence to it. It should not be confused with factor G, the superego, which is partly irrational and unconscious. Q3 is concerned with social reputation and self-image, moral values can become associated with it. For example a fervent churchgoer may have integrated into his conscious self concept abstinence of both drink and sex. If then Q3 reflects the clarity and importance of the self-image, it accounts for the observation that it is upset and reduced during adolescence but that it builds up steadily in early maturity as the individual finds his place in society. This reduction in adolescence relates well to the notion of loss of identity (Erickson, 1950). Q3, although high in paranoids, is low in criminals and gang delinquents, attempted suicides and neurotics.

Q4: Ergic tension (relaxed, tranquil, composed *v.* tense, frustrated, driven and fretful). Cattell (1957) has argued that this factor of ergic tension is the amount of undischarged instinctual energy. This makes it similar to the Freudian concept of the id and to McDougall's total instinctual energy. Certainly the fact that frustrations and deprivations increase with the factor, e.g. poor performance at school or work, bereavements or unhappy love affairs, supports the identification. So do the clinical findings that alcoholics, homosexuals, exhibitionists and all neurotic syndromes are high on Q4.

This description of Q4 concludes our exposition of the most researched primary factors in the Cattell system. These are the 16 factors measured in the 16PF test, and as our discussion shows, there is a considerable body of knowledge built up over the years concerning each of them. Our descriptions are not intended to be full resumées of all this information: our aim has been to give sufficient to grasp the nature of these factors. We must stress that all the statements made about the factors are based upon empirical research other than the cautious theoretical explanations of the factors and the illustrations of eminent figures from history and literature. From all this we hope it is possible to see the rich patterns of behaviour subsumed by these factors, as rich indeed as the work of the most imaginative writers (hence our literary examples) but unlike this fiction, patterns supported by rigorous and replicable data and data analysis. On reading these pictures it is surely hard to argue that these factors are mere mathematical abstractions.

However as we showed in our chapter describing the results and methods of Cattell and his colleagues in addition to the 16 factors measured by his personality test, 7 further factors have been found by more accurate rotation to simple structure in the normal adult domain as well as a number of pathological factors identified by careful item factorings of the MMPI. These we must now describe although our descriptions will be less full and rich than was the case with the earlier factors simply because less is known about them. Actually one of the 7 missing factors has been described in the previous section: being known at the child level, a good deal of information had been accumulated about it. We refer, of course, to Factor D, excitability.

SIX MISSING PRIMARIES IN THE NORMAL PERSONALITY SPHERE

J: Zeppia *v.* Coasthenia (zestful, likes group action *v.* individualistic, internally restrained and reflective). This factor which is found in the HSPQ resembles Q2, self-sufficiency, although it is clearly factorially distinct.

Zeppia is important in the second-order exvia factor and at the high pole it has been called the Hamlet factor while the low scorer is typified by full blooded vigorous rugby club group identification.

K: Boorishness *v*. mature socialization. This factor seems an accurate reflection of the classical idea of a gentleman—polished, kind and cultured, careful not to trample on other people's sensitivities. It does not seem to be simply a measure of years of education.

P: Sanguine casualness. The P plus individual is unambitious, self-assured, modest, casual and able to cope. This factor loads on the second-order independence which brings out well the flavour of this factor.

These factors have been found in ratings. The next three to be discussed have been found only in Q data.

Q5: Group dedication with sensed inadequacy. All we can say here is that the high scorer on this factor devotes himself to groups but thinks that other people think (echoes of Knots) that he is not successful.

Q6: Social panache. This factor is like the clinical concept of paranoia. The Q6-individual feels persecuted by society.

Q7: Explicit self expression. The high scorer on this factor likes drama and bohemian conversation, the heady discourse of avant garde ideas, at least as old as Aristotle.

PRIMARY FACTORS IN THE ABNORMAL SPHERE

D Factors

D1: Hypochondriasis. As the name suggests this factor is typified by concern over bodily health and is highest in psychotic depressives.

D2: Suicidal disgust. A depression factor related to feelings of the worthlessness of life, aggression against self and others and suicidal thought.

D3: Brooding discontent or ennui. Central here is the desire for something exciting to happen, perhaps the factor that stimulates some men to great deeds in war. It is high in psychopaths and is the least depressive of the D factors.

D4: Anxious depression. A combination of anxiety and depression typified by tenseness, being easily upset and clumsiness. Curiously it is not related to the second-order factor anxiety.

D5: Low energy, fatigued depression. This factor is distinguished by tiredness, weariness and insufficient sleep combined with some anxiety. It could be the result of conflict, anxiety and overwork.

D6: Guilt and resentment with depression. This is the tendency, central to depression, to self blame and groundless guilt. It is accompanied by some sleeplessness and agitation and is highest in alcoholics and neurotic depressives.

D7: Bored depression. The salient feature of this factor is withdrawal from people and a feeling of the pointlessness of life. It is high in schizophrenics as well as depressives.

These are the seven depressive factors that we discussed in the abnormal personality sphere. The fact that they form so many separate factors indicates the problems of those tests which attempt to measure depression with one scale formed by item analysis using depressives as a criterion group. Clearly any such scale would be a virtually random mixture of these 7 components and therefore of little value other than for practical screening. We now come to the five factors that were found in the items factoring of the MMPI.

Pa: paranoid tendency. The typical paranoid factor characterized by beliefs that one is being poisoned, persecuted, controlled and spied on and hence that everyone is untrustworthy.

Pp: psychopathic deviation. This factor closely follows the syndrome of psychopathy—immunity to criticism, amorality, little need for sleep and enjoyment of conflict.

Sc: Schizophrenia. Again this factor mirrors the typical schizophrenic symptoms of all types other than the paranoid who combines a high score on this factor and Pa. Central to Sc are irrational impulses, fancies, hallucinations and disorientation.

As: Psychasthenia. This is the typical obsessive symptom factor, characterized by compulsive ideas and anxieties as well as practical rituals.

Ps: General psychosis and maladapted disintegration. This is the best single factor in discriminating normals from psychotics although, contrary to expectation, it has little relevance to poor reality contact and emotional irrationality usually considered typical of psychosis. Instead this Ps factor loads on the inability to cope and feelings of unworthiness and inferiority.

It was suggested in our previous discussion of these abnormal factors that the P, psychosis, factor of Eysenck, is probably a second-order factor that runs through these abnormal factors of Cattell. If, however, this turns out to be the case the position and status of this Ps factor will be anomalous and it will demand further investigation.

These, then, are the factors that have been discovered by the application of factor analysis to the normal and abnormal personality sphere. Again our description of these pathological primaries, some of which follow closely the clinical descriptions of some of the major nosological categories, indicates how wrong it is to regard factors simply as mathematical entities or abstractions. These patterns, on the contrary, are richly descriptive. However, as the case of the 7 depression factors indicates, the factorial description goes beyond, where the data warrant, what even the keenest clinicians had been able to glimpse by unaided observation.

SECOND-ORDER FACTORS

These primary factors are oblique and factor analysis of their correlations has revealed a number of second-order factors which we must now describe. Two of these—exvia and anxiety—are particularly important since not only have they a long history, being delineated before the advent of factor analysis, but in addition there is considerable agreement between factor analysts as to their importance, although the names given to these factors do not entirely correspond. Eysenck in a vast array of publications (e.g. Eysenck, 1970; Eysenck, 1967) has explored the psychological associations of both these factors and attempted to develop a theoretical explanation to account for them. In this section all we shall try to do is to give them an adequate description so that we can see their essential nature. The relevance of such factors to theories of personality is discussed in a later chapter of this book. Again as was the case with the primary factors we cannot reference every assertion made about these second order factors. However, much of the material can be found in the Eysenck publications mentioned above and in the work of Cattell and his colleagues to which we have already referred.

Exvia–Invia: Cattell is happy to accept that this factor is identical psychologically to the second-order extraversion–introversion. He prefers the name exvia simply because, by popular usage, the term "extraversion" has degenerated to a meaningless ragbag. Roughly a third of the variance of primary factors A, F and H and around half of the variance of Q2 is accounted for by exvia. The exviant individual is thus sociable, warmhearted, good-natured, cheerful, frank, alert, impulsive, responsive, carefree, the genial clubman who keeps the bar happy. Exvia is related to good academic performance in the early years of school but later at the secondary level and at college the inviant person does better—not surprising since, as our description of the exviant shows, careful scholarship is hardly likely to be appealing.

This concept was fully recognized by Jung (1923) who, nevertheless, regarded extraverts and introverts as types—whereas in factor analytic terms exvia is a dimension. The theoretical import of extraversion or exvia to personality is discussed in Chapter 16.

Anxiety: Although the empirical studies which we examined in the previous chapter—Barton (1973), Eysenck and Eysenck (1969)—indicate clearly that there is considerable agreement between Cattell's anxiety, and Eysenck's neuroticism, the fact that all three use different terms for the factors is highly confusing. Add to this the problem that the Cattell studies yield more second-order factors than do Eysenck's and the difficulties of interpretation appear perhaps unsurmountable without much further work.

Nevertheless as we argued in the previous chapter many of the differences in this second-order factor can be attributable to technical shortcomings, especially rotation to simple structure and under-factoring, while the differences in nomenclature are simply misleading. Thus the term "neuroticism" is inappropriate because, as many studies have shown, neurotics differ significantly from normals on more factors than this second-order anxiety factor (e.g., Cattell and Scheier, 1961). This is not to deny the importance of this anxiety factor in neuroticism. In terms of primaries anxiety is defined by $C-$, $Q3-$, O and H so that the anxious individual is easily perturbed, worrying, emotional when frustrated, lax, uncontrolled, depressed, moody, hypochondriacal, shy, embittered and of restricted interests. A complex problem with this second-order factor of anxiety, lies in distinguishing between anxiety as a state and as a personality trait. Barton (1973) has developed a set of questionnaire items which are capable of making this discrimination, as has Spielberger (1972). Cattell (1973) argues that the balance of evidence supports this anxiety factor as being a trait rather than a state factor. However this whole problem will be discussed further in Chapter 11.

There are so many researches reporting psychological associations with anxiety that to discuss them all here would be an overwhelming task. Some of this material will be dealt with in Chapters 13 and 14.

These are the two main second-order factors which from our descriptions are clear and well recognized syndromes in psychology. These are certainly the factors most implicated in the theoretical formulations about personality and most relevant to theories of personality developed without the aid of factor analysis. We shall now examine the six other smaller second-order factors.

Cortertia–pathemia: The pathemic individual is warm, sentimental, likes art and drama and lives in his more melancholic emotions. The cortertic person is alert and realistic, with his feelings under control, an essentially practical individual. This factor may be similar to the T factor, cortertia, U.I.22 (which is discussed on p. 149).

Pathemia is related to neuroticism and depression and tends to be associated with chronic illness, while cortertia is associated with success in all practical occupations, heavy drinking and stability of marriage. Its primary factor loadings are chiefly A, I and M.

Independence v. subduedness: This factor loads strongly on E and H, on F and moderately on L, M and Q2 so that it can be seen that it overlaps with exvia on three factors—F, H and Q2. Although there is undoubted similarity with exvia it must be noted that exvia aligns with T factor U.I.32 (see p. 151) whereas independence seems more to resemble U.I.19. The independent person is assertive, unconventional, active, responsive, cheerful and alert. High independence is associated with nonconformity, making social contacts, drinking and the need for little sleep. It is a refusal to be tamed by experience.

Discreetness v. naturalness: This factor is largely N, shrewdness, A and Q7, and it loads on few other primaries. From this we can say that the high scorer on this factor is calculating, smart, ambitious, cool, objective and avant garde. It could be an exploitative use of social skills.

Prodigal subjective idealism v. Detached realism: This factor loads mainly on autia, radicalism and self sufficiency. It is therefore an idealistic, imaginative interest in subjective goals in contrast to the pragmatic acceptance of reality, a distinction summed up in the title of a book on education: "Education: what it is and what it ought to be."

Intelligence: This factor emerges at the second-order since it is really a second-stratum factor inserted for convenience into the 16PF test. However, it will not be discussed since it is an ability rather than a personality factor.

Good upbringing: This factor has a considerable variance contribution to the primaries so that its true rank may be higher than its present position. It loads highly on superego, G, self-sentiment, low surgency and low dominance so that a sensible interpretation would be that it is the result of training in morals and manners—good upbringing or, in psychoanalytic terms, a superego personality pattern. Cross cultural studies suggest that there is a Protestant/Catholic difference in these scores, Catholic countries being lower. This fits in well with the intuitive argument that confession produces lower feelings of guilt and hence may have considerable value in the maintenance of mental health.

HIGHER ORDER FACTORS

In Chapter 4 we listed some third- and fourth-order factors obtained by Nichols (1973) and Warburton (1968). However we can add nothing here to the description of these factors which have not been subjected to further study. In addition their factor loadings and the accuracy of the rotation are not fully established. We shall simply for completeness name these factors.

Third-Orders are strength of contact, maladaptation, readiness, anti-social unconcern and one unnamed factor.

Fourth-Orders are adjustment and morality.

In the next chapter we shall examine objective tests and the factors based on them.

SUMMARY

1. A description of the primary factors in the personality sphere aimed to exemplify their psychological meaning and richness (but based on empirical data, not rhetoric) was given for each factor.
2. The same procedure was adopted for the abnormal, second-order and higher-order factors.

Chapter 8

Personality Structure as Expressed in Objective Tests

THE RELATION OF OBJECTIVE TESTS TO STRUCTURAL THEORY ACROSS MEDIA

Most of the personality source traits based on correlational investigations so far discussed have been in the media of observation we call L data (life behaviour, usually rated) and Q data (questionnaire self assessment), though occasional reference has been made to T data—objective tests, including laboratory measures—on which we shall now concentrate.

It is wise in psychological discussion always to keep these media of data observation in mind, for they have different properties. And although Cattell and others have argued in the "theory of indifference of media" that the same personality structures will eventually be located through all, yet this' same theory recognizes there will be superficial distortions through *instrument factors* peculiar to each. The distortions in questionnaires, for example, are well known through the work of Edwards, Wiggins, Messick and others (see p. 38 for a discussion of these problems) and this is why Cattell and his co-workers have for thirty years worked to develop objective tests, free of the major "desirability" and "self-illusion" distortions in questionnaires. In the last resort, however, there might also be some instrument factors in objective tests, e.g. ability intrusions, and that is why the best assessment requires discovery of what is common through all media. This goal is expressed in general terms in Campbell and Fiske's (1959) *multi-method-multi-trait* approach and with more structure in Cattell's *equalization of instrument factor* method.

In terms of making psychology a science, there is a more important reason than accuracy of testing the individual for this creative effort which has issued in nearly 500 different types of objective test in Cattell and Warburton's *Compendium* (1967). It is that psychology, like all social sciences, gets caught in the flux of history. In chemistry and physics the melting point of sodium or the position of red in wave lengths in the spectrum remain the same. But in psychology the terms in rating (witness the change of "naughty" from Elizabethan times to the present) alter, and in questionnaires, "Do you like to go often to the movies?" is a variable which changed its meaning with the advent of TV. Laboratory behavioural measures and other T data, on the other hand, come nearer to providing the same variables from country to country and era to era. Thus one important aim of the T data approach is to obtain the "footprint" of any temperament or ability trait as it were in bronze rather than the ooze of L and Q data. The given source trait is thus caught in a pattern of loadings of variables which change little and can be reliably used in different populations and times to identify and measure the trait. Incidentally, this permits us also to recognize historical and cultural change in personality patterns without confusing it with instability due to variables as such.

Our purpose here is to look at the methods and the findings from quantitative research with objective tests. The same initial principle holds as in L and Q data: that if research is to proceed without bias from past clinical and other theories, it must take a complete "personality sphere" of variables, i.e. a set of behaviour variables varied to the utmost. This was substantially achieved as the Compendium of objective tests (1967) will show, though the student must remember that the ability modality was as far as possible excluded, since the new domain of personality is the goal. (However, that robust factor, fluid general intelligence, g_f, constantly turned up among the personality factors!) Just as in the L and Q researches, so here the factoring was carried out at different ages and across different national cultures (notably Japanese, Anglo-Saxon, and Austrian) and used both cross-sectional (R technique) and developmental growth (differential R technique) checks on the functional unity of the source traits found.

THE ESSENTIAL NATURE OF OBJECTIVE TESTS

The essence of an objective test is that the tested individual consents to respond with actual behaviour to some miniature life situation put before him. His response is measured in ways of which he is unaware so that faking (though not sabotage) is ruled out.

At the outset we must recognize that the line between objective and questionnaire measures is not always obvious. Some psychologists call questionnaires objective because different scorers applying the same key to the answer sheet get the same result (unlike, for instance, a Rorschach or some projection tests, where, despite rules, different psychologists will disagree). The term *conspective* (looking together) has been designed to recognize mere objectivity of scoring, to distinguish it clearly conceptually from the more important property of being *objective* as a test situation.

However, in response to the constant and insistent demand to make tests group administrable, such workers in this area as Baggaley, Barton, Cattell, Damarin, Dielman, Eysenck, Hundleby, Gruen, Pawlik, Scheier, Sweney, Tatro and others have converted individual tests to group administrable forms. These are generally pencil and paper, sometimes with group administrable sound tapes, and may, therefore, seem like questionnaires.

In any case even the questionnaire itself can in the last resort be used as an objective test if we take the response as a piece of behaviour and not necessarily as a true statement *about* behaviour. This last has already been mentioned under questionnaires, where the data were categorized as Q' data if the responses to items were believed. Thus if subjects reply that they enjoy noisy parties to a questionnaire item and we take this to be the case we are treating the data as Q' data. However if we take their response "yes" as simply an item of behaviour and only attribute its meaning from its factor loadings then we are treating it as Q data and it becomes far more objective than in our first example. However there is something unsatisfactory about this latter solution in that we still believe subjects understood the items and were answering in good faith. It is impossible to hold for example that there could be much indicative of personality in the responses to items of subjects who filled in the questionnaire blindfold, at random, or of subjects who understood nothing of the language of the questions. Nevertheless although even in Q data we have to make some assumptions about the mental interiors of the subject, the distinction from Q' data is both real and useful. Thus although it has been shown that neurotics do not in fact sleep worse than normals it is a discriminating response to answer "no" to the item "Do you sleep well?" Thus in keying this item "yes" Eysenck in the EPI is treating the response as Q data. On the other hand he does believe that this is how they feel, i.e. it is Q' data. Nevertheless the fact that questionnaire data can be treated as Q data in some sense removes its absolute distinction from objective test data when we remember that an objective test was defined as one whose purport was hidden from the subject and which could be objectively scored.

An expansion of the above definition of an objective test is given by Hundleby (1973) who writes "An objective test is a procedure for obtaining an individual difference score based on responses to a specific set of stimuli, or sequences of stimuli such that either the correct implication of the response in question is unknown to the subject or the nature of the response is such that the subject cannot readily modify his response in some desired direction". This description makes it clear that Q data are essentially objective test devices, although in fact Q data are much more frequently obtained from questionnaires. This definition should also make it clear that almost any task that can lead to an objective score and in which individual differences are found can be regarded as an objective test. This, therefore, raises the problem, which we shall discuss later, of how one goes about test construction in this area when there are an infinity of possibilities. There is a further important feature of this definition which must be clarified before any discussion of objective tests becomes worthwhile. This concerns the meaning of the phrase the "correct implication".

As Kelly (1955) has stressed, even if subjects are not let in on the secrets of a psychological experiment they will form their own hypotheses about its meaning. Indeed even if they are told, such is the dismal record of subject deception in psychology, they may still well form different opinions of their own. Now this is a particularly pertinent point in relation to objective tests which, as we have seen, are especially designed so that subjects will not be able to see through them. Thus the objective test situation is precisely that one where subjects are likely to form their own hypotheses, since they are clearly being tested. Since it has been convincingly shown by experiment (see Vernon, 1964, for a good account of this work) that with projective tests how the subject sees the test situation affects the results, the fact that the subjects of objective tests may form their own and perhaps different (even with the same subject on different occasions) hypotheses of their purport may adversely affect the validity of these tests. An example may make this clear. Let us take objective test T 145, balloon blowing. According to Cattell and Warburton (1967) the theory of this test is that it is expected that timid inhibited persons (high on factor UI.17, timid distrust or inhibition) will be less successful at the arduous task of having to blow up balloons, especially because there is a drastic penalty for over-enthusiasm. The subject is actually asked to blow up a balloon as far as he can and is then given thirty seconds to do it. After a thirty second rest he is given another balloon. A subject who sees the tests as a measure of lung-power despite his dislike of bursting balloons may yet do his utmost to burst them—in no sense therefore is this test, for this particular individual, a measure of UI.17. Another subject, on the other hand, may construe the task as a measure of courage and, determined to prove himself, burst the balloon. In this instance we may get two similar scores but they would hardly be reflective of common personality characteristics. To what extent such different "projections" or perceptions change the meaning of a test can be determined only by the correlations. Tests are rejected if correlations with the factor trait fail.

Hundleby (1973) admits that strong or irrelevant sets could distort the scores of tests. However he claims that in practice the effect of such sets seems to be minimal, that steps should be taken to minimize this damage during test construction and that generally the manifest purpose of the test is a sufficient guide line for the subject. Certainly it is true that if we can demonstrate that the objective test loads on a replicable factor of known validity then these problems of meaning for different subjects are to a large extent irrelevant. However it is to be noted that one justification for objective tests is that they are likely to be better measures than questionnaires or ratings which are spoiled by special and typical distortions such as response sets, although they do, as we have seen, load on clear and replicable factors. Thus it could be that our objective tests will load on factors but still carry a degree of error variance due to the problems we have been discussing. Certainly it would appear that the best precaution is to develop manifest purposes for the tests which are entirely convincing although even here distortion could enter the picture, depending upon subjects' self concepts. It seems that Kelly's objections are not answerable and that we have to be highly pragmatic and use an objective test if it yields satisfactory loadings.

THE SUB-CLASSIFICATION OF OBJECTIVE TESTS

Several systems of classification have been proposed. Hundleby (1973) classifies personality measures of all kinds into eight separate domains. This classificatory system is worthy of note because it brings out some other important features of objective tests which need to be taken into account when we come to assess the personality factors derived from them. These domains are: self-description (e.g. Q data), ratings and reports from others (e.g. case histories and Cattell's L data), life history, morphology (as in Kretschmer (1925)), expressive movement (e.g. writing), simulated real life situations, physiological variables, motor-perceptual and performance measures. This last domain is highly important in the development of objective tests and such measures are referred to by many writers, Cronbach (1970) for example, as performance tests.

As we suggested above, this classification system is useful as it highlights two important points about objective testing. First if we attempt to measure a factor using tests from different domains, we may find that tests from the same domain tend to cluster together. This is due to what Fiske (1971) has referred to as "method" variance and Cattell and Digman (1964), in perturbation theory, as instrument factor intrusion into variance. Now since each domain has its own instrument variance, it is clear that any kind of personality measurement which relies exclusively on tests from one domain must inevitably be distorted by such instrument variance. Such a criticism, of course, is particularly relevant to most personality measurement which as we have seen in previous chapters has relied almost exclusively on personality questionnaires. However if we design a battery of objective tests from as many domains as possible, since the biasing characteristics of each domain should be different, the effects of this instrument variance will be reduced to a minimum. Furthermore, if we combine T, Q and even L data, as suggested at the opening of this chapter, the distortion of instrument variance can be minimized.

So-called "projective tests" are, of course, a sub-category within objective tests. Before the broader varieties of objective tests were introduced they were virtually the only ones used. (The Rorschach alone has more than 4,000 references in the latest edition of Buros (1972)!) In using this device among others in motivation measurement (see Chapter 9) Cattell distinguished between true projection (Freud) and naive projection (misunderstanding through one's own limitations of perception). Although, as Semeonoff (1973) points out, the strict definition of a projective test is difficult, the common features to most is some kind of ambiguity of stimulus. The term "projective" does not any longer refer to the Freudian defence mechanism of projection, rather it implies that in some vague and unspecified manner subjects read into these test stimuli their own problems and conflicts, described by Rosenzweig (1954) as their idiodynamics. The academic objections to projective tests concern their notorious unreliability (Eysenck, 1959) and the lack of evidence for their validity. Within this classificatory system, however, projective tests fall clearly into the final category of performance tests. Hundleby (1973), indeed, argues that there is no reason why projective tests should not be included among objective tests provided that the meaning of the test responses remains hidden from the subject, that the administration of the test is standardized and that the test scoring becomes objective cutting out subjective interpretation by the examiner. When we come to look at objective tests some of the more famous projective tests will be discussed in the light of this classificatory system.

Given the definition of an objective test proposed by Hundleby (1973)—a procedure for obtaining individual difference scores which can be objectively scored and of which the purpose is hidden from the subject—we now come upon the problem of objective test construction. From the definition it would appear that there are few constraints on development of such devices as is largely true of personality questionnaire items. However, as we have seen, the concept of the personality sphere enabled us to sample it and cover it fully with a reasonable number of items. In the case of objective tests there was no one theoretical practicable way of specifying the personality sphere of sub-tests although all the workers in this field had such a concept in mind as the tests were developed over the years.

In practice, to develop as comprehensive a battery of tests as possible, the following procedures were adopted. First, every effort was made to produce a diverse range of tests. Whenever an investigator saw an example of behaviour which seemed to reflect personality differences he attempted to capture it in an objective test device. A deliberate attempt was made to cover the constructs already isolated in Q and L data.

Cattell and Warburton (1967) made the task of covering a personality sphere by objective tests somewhat easier by constructing a taxonomy of objective tests which took account of the following dimensions: (i) instructions, (ii) situation or material, (iii) mode of response, and (iv) mode of scoring response.

The first six parameters of the first two dimensions (instruction and situation) were reacting or not reacting, restricted v. unrestricted response, inventive v. selective answer, single v. repetitive response, ordered v. unordered responses, and homogeneous v. patterned. In fact ten polar dimensions were proposed which permitted 2^{10} (1024) types of test. In addition to this, six parameters were recognized in scoring responses of which three will be mentioned here: objective v. distortable, overt v. physiological and normative v. ipsative. The value of this taxonomy lies in the fact that it enables investigators to locate any test which they have developed relative to other tests. In this way it is possible to see which tests have insufficient numbers and the personality sphere of tests should be covered. This taxonomy of objective tests enables us to locate objective tests relative to other objective tests and is ideal for the objective test constructor. Hundleby's categorization of personality measures into eight domains on the other hand enables us to locate objective tests relative to all other personality tests. In fact we find that the last four domains, expressive movement, simulated real life situations, physiological variables and motor-perceptual and performance tests, are the categories which most completely embrace the field of objective tests. The examples of objective test devices either actual or possible, suggested by Hundleby (1973) as typifying these domains, make it clear that, as mentioned above, the last domain of performance tests is the most important for objective personality tests. Furthermore it emphasizes the necessity over and above this categorization for the taxonomy of Cattell and Warburton (1967)

Expressive movement (as studied by Allport and Vernon, 1933, in a pioneering investigation) has always looked so promising as an index of personality yet has yielded so little. In everyday life expressive movements are held to be important indicators of personality. The hearty laugh, the shifty gaze, the vicelike handshake, the bouncing walk, the cross legged sitting position, the list is endless, peaked, if that is the right word, by hand writing. This last has been elevated into a pseudo science—graphology. From our definition of personality as the sum total of behaviour, such expressive movements as those we have mentioned above should reflect personality differences. However the problem with them is from the viewpoint of psychological measurement that they are influenced by other variables which may blur the detection of the personality differences. Graphology demonstrates this point clearly. Thus even if writing reflects personality, it is also likely to be influenced by such variables as how we were taught to write, how we were encouraged to write by all the various teachers we may have chanced to encounter at school, by our parents (did they encourage italic writing for example?), or by the kind of pens and paper we first used which would affect the reinforcement we received for our efforts at writing, by the need to write in our job, by the need to write clearly and so on. Furthermore differences in writing are relatively small so that we are working with a scale that is highly sensitive to errrors in measurement and thus it is hardly surprising that graphology has failed so far to deliver the goods. We are forced to agree with Hundleby (1973) when he argues that some measures of expressive movement may tap a small amount of personality variance but that to rely on these alone in personality measurement would be woefully inadequate.

The simulated real life situation came into prominence mainly as a result of its use for officer selection both here and in America. Getting a band of men across a roaring torrent with no bridge and without getting wet, was the kind of simulated task given to officers (who were then chosen for administrative work in the Admiralty!). This test is by no means an objective personality test if it involves rating the men for leadership, resourcefulness or courage. However if the score is the time taken before abandoning the task, or the number of different methods attempted, for example, then it is an objective test. However the difficulty of establishing the validity of such measures together with the inevitably time consuming nature of such tests, not to say expense, means that very few objective tests fall into this category. Nevertheless it is useful to know that the possibility of developing such situational measures is there and it is to be hoped that, as occupational psychology develops, in large organizations at least some work will be done in this area of psychological testing.

Physiological indices of personality have been investigated over the years but, as Hundleby (1973) stresses, as yet no reliable test of accepted validity has yet been developed. Eysenck (1967) in the "Biological Basis of Personality" has linked extraversion to the concept of central nervous system arousal and neuroticism to the lability of the autonomic nervous system. Thus we should expect the relevant physiological measures to function as indices of personality and thus as objective tests. Examples of such tests might be heart rate, GSR or EEG activity. However empirical work in this area has yielded somewhat confused results and at present they are not suitable for practical personality assessment although they are essential for fundamental research into the nature of the various personality factors which have been so far isolated. It is likely that in the future some highly reliable and valid physiological indices will be developed although their practical use is probably limited on account of the need for laboratory facilities.

From this discussion of the tests from these three domains it is clear that in practice not many practicable objective personality tests fall into these categories. We must now turn to the last of these domains that of motor-perceptual and performance tests which, as we indicated supplies most of the objective personality tests which have so far proved themselves useful. This also brings us back to the classification system of Cattell and Warburton (1967) where objective tests (in effect tests in this domain) were classified in terms of various situation and response parameters.

ILLUSTRATION OF PRINCIPLES IN OBJECTIVE TEST INVENTION

The great difficulty in the area of objective personality tests lies in the enormous numbers of possible tests and the deliberate (by definition) lack of face validity so that factor identification is made especially problematic. In face of this the research strategy adopted over the years, as discussed by Cattell (1975), has been to start research without prejudice, in other words to use factor analysis as a mapping device which means, as we have elaborated in our introductory chapter on the scientific use of multivariate methods, that we must cover as best we can the universe of variables—the personality sphere. In addition the research strategy necessitated that simple structure be sought so that the resulting factors might be regarded as causal agencies (see p. 16). Since simple structure depends on the hyperplane count which in turn depends on having a large number of variables to act as hyperplane stuff and since the concept of the personality sphere demands a large number of variables, large numbers of tests had to be used which inevitably means (for subjects have to agree to be tested) brief tests had to be used of around five minutes duration.

Factors emerging from the application of this research strategy have to be identified by hypothesizing their nature then inventing tests which will measure them better and putting these into a new factor analysis. This spiral approach of inductive and deductive convergence has resulted over the years in the establishment of a number of replicable and identified (in terms of objective tests) factors. Indeed 20 factors and their second-orders have now been identified although, as Cattell (1975) points out, little attempt was made to relate them to L or Q factors, mainly because the task of establishing these factors, of developing tests to support their identity was more than large enough.

One weakness of this research strategy has been the necessity to develop short tests so that a wide variety of measures can be given in, say, a six hour testing session. These, being short, were inevitably of low reliability so that many of the correlations were small. Correcting these for attenuation due to unreliability in estimating their validities has seemed to the opponents of factor analysis statistically dubious. In the early studies the factor loadings were consequently low, in the region of 0.3, which again was a source of contention among critics (e.g. Mischel, 1968) but of course lengthening of the tests which show promise, as in the final version of the Schuerger HSOA (High School Objective Analytic) battery, has produced concept validities of between 0.8 and 0.9 (Schuerger and Cattell, 1971).

With tests of little face validity the identification of factors is particularly difficult. Identification rests finally on the loading pattern on a given population sample. This means that there must be a careful and precise list of variables and a properly indexed list of factors, where both variables and samples are described. Cattell and Warburton (1967) listed all objective tests that had been used in correlational studies and all resulting factors, even when these could not be properly identified and gave to both test variables and factors a master index number. Variables were allotted a master index number, factors a universal index number. Even at that time there were more than 400 tests but since a test consists of a fixed situation and set of instructions for responding and since such responses may be scored in more than one way (e.g. speed, errors, number of adjectives) the actual number of variables is far greater. In the Compendium, Cattell and Warburton (1967) list 2366, and it is these that form the real basis for factor identification. One important feature of these test variables complicates identification and must be carefully noted. It has been found that trivial changes in instructions, particularly those that affect the motivation of the subjects, can produce changes in factor loadings. Thus if the variable is pulse change under shock, the strength of shock needs to be specified. These details are given in the compendium of objective tests by Cattell and Warburton (1967).

Instrument factors may, of course, appear as readily in objective tests as elsewhere, but they may be distinguished from factors of genuine importance by their low correlations with external criteria and other non-objective test variables—indices of life criterion validity which are of particular importance in T factors.

Clearly with 412 tests and more than 2,000 variables, all we can do here is give some indication of the kinds of tests that have been developed over the years. To ensure that we discuss only tests that have shown themselves useful rather than flights of psychologists' fantasy we shall illustrate the nature of objective tests from those loading on the most important variables in the objective test domain. In addition we shall describe briefly some of the published examples of objective tests which are therefore available for practical use in psychology in contradistinction to the vast majority of objective tests which are still suitable only for research purposes.

T42 Mazes. We begin with this test because it has the distinction of having over a number of researches the largest loading on the biggest objective test factor UI.16—Assertive ego. This test consists of four mazes which subjects have to run through with a pencil without touching the sides. Fifteen seconds are allowed for each of these pencil mazes. Subjects are encouraged to work as fast as possible because they are told that they are scored on how far they get as well as on accuracy. A large number of variables may be extracted from this simple test procedure. Thus, for example, test performance can be measured in terms of absolute speed and accuracy (perhaps discriminating with children), accuracy relative to speed, sheer distance covered in a given time and relative speed on difficult tasks (the mazes are differentially difficult). In fact MI 379, speed and accuracy, is the high loading variable on factor

UI.16 although accuracy, fast speed on difficult relative to easy mazes and low excess of performance over aspiration also load on this factor. Actually these loadings alone, especially the last, have reasonable face validity for a factor of narcissistic ego. This mazes test (T 42) is a good illustration of how an objective test can yield a large number of powerful variables and yet be quick and easy to administer even to large groups.

T45 Line-Length Judgement. In this test pairs of lines are presented to the subject who has to decide whether one is the longer or whether they are the same length. A few of the lines are easily discriminable but most lie on the threshold of certainty-uncertainty so that since the test is scored according to the number of items attempted and since the task is "overlearned" for almost all members of any group it should measure natural temperamental speed and again narcissistic ego. As with the last test, this is an easily administered objective test device.

T314 Heartogram. This is an example of a physiological measure which is not suitable for group administration and needs a physiological laboratory. The variable which loads on UI.16 and also on UI.21, Exuberance, is increase in heart rate after startle. Heart rate might be expected to relate to the lability of the autonomic nervous system (reflected in Eysenck's N factor) and there is some evidence that this is the case (see Gale, 1973). This objective test is a good example of the physiological variables that can be used in the objective test analysis of personality.

Measures Involving Tastes and Values

The tests so far have been either physiological measures or simple tasks of judgement or drawing. However, even looking at the tests loading on UI.16 we can see great diversity. Thus we find: highbrow tastes, masculinity of interests, slow reaction time variables involving the Cursive Minature situations, reading backwards and acceptance of aphorisms. *The highbrow tastes test* tries to compare informed good taste with poor ignorant and uneducated taste in the field of recreation, arts, furnishing, music, dress and drama (not the full list). Examples are a preference for canasta, bridge or poker, and a choice of ballet, a musical or a Western. As Cattell and Warburton (1967) point out, the regular finding that this test loads on UI.16 suggests that vanity and competitiveness are the roots of highbrow tastes in the American samples used by Cattell. However the status of the intellectual is so different in France and the European continent that it is unlikely that this interpretation would be sustained in that culture, i.e. this test might not thus load in Europe. *Masculinity of interests* is measured by a personal satisfaction check list which requires subjects to state their degree of satisfaction with their achievements in a variety of fields, e.g. clothes, cars, academic or intellectual. It is thus an example of an objective test questionnaire. This test however differs from the traditional questionnaire in that it is difficult for any subject to guess how he is to be scored.

Peculiarities of Reaction Time. The reaction time apparatus is the standard experimental psychological set-up where the subject is faced by an array of buttons which he has to press in response to a series of stimuli visual and auditory. The personality behaviour is brought out by comparing responses under different instructions and conditions. The promise of such an approach was first shown by Shakow's work with schizophrenics. A variety of scores is obtained from this test of which the main ones are speed of simple reaction time, ratio of regularly warned to irregularly warned reaction time, ratio of time on complex to time on simple reactions, the number of "false" reactions to the wrong stimulus and the number of failures to comply with instructions.

The cursive minature situations test. This is a complex test to describe. The first suggestion of promise here came from the work on introversion-extraversion by McDougall using the old "spot-dotting" test (Culpin and Smith, 1930). A moving tape presents an onslaught of situations to which the subject has to react. It might be thought of as a card game or a chess game with a standard opponent. Subjects are told that it is the dividing pathways test. Five rules are then laid down: every horizontal line crossed scores one point; each upright line crossed scores four points; slanting lines must never be crossed; if there are groups of lines so close that in the time the rules cannot be obeyed, the group may be encircled; if the paths divide you must use only one track. Scores derived from this situation include number of slanting lines crossed, number of times circles are used, total score according to the rules and proportion of correct decisions.

Reading backwards. This test as the name suggests, compares the time a subject takes to read a story in the normal way with the time taken to read it backwards. .ksat siht ta llew od ot detcepxe eb ton dluow elpoep digiR

Reaction to Social Pressures on Attitudes. In several forms a subtle use has been made of what appear as ordinary attitude tests, which would normally be measures of interests and dynamics (Chapter 9) rather than personality. Here, however, a set of attitudes is checked and then the opinions of (a) authorities or (b) the majority are fed back to the subject and, at a retesting, the *shift* of attitudes is measured. Another test gives him new information on the social issues involved in the attitudes to see how much he will adapt.

Instability and Inconsistency of Attitudes. Two theories tried early, in the work of Cattell and Gruen (1948), were (i) that high general emotionality (ego weakness) will show itself in instability of a wide range of attitudes in retest after an hour, and (ii) that logical inconsistency of attitudes—an emotional dissonance, such as was later investigated by Festinger in the form of cognitive dissonance—will also be a measure of neuroticism and ego weakness. The first was confirmed by Rhea Stagner (1955) and the second by Cattell (1943). In the inconsistency or dissonance test, parts of logically correct syllogisms are presented in a large and random set of attitudes. In the fluctuation test the same attitudes are readministered, each reversed in direction and somewhat disguised. The latter test is also used to get a measure of *tendency to extreme responses* and of *tendency to agree with the authority* (set to give "yes" answers).

Other group objective tests which may *appear* like verbal attitude or inventory tests are the willingness to check more grossly and uncompromisingly stated aphorisms as true and the test which happens to measure the exvia factor (core of the popular but vague extraversion concept), and which asks for acceptance of unqualified statements versus more carefully "hedged" statements. The same is true of the "agreement with the majority" test of exvia.

There is no space here to describe further the rich variety of behavioural conceptions involved in these tests and psychology as yet lacks a sufficiency of terms for indicating classes of them, though the above analysis of dimensions of test construction by Warburton will help. Beginning with the aim simply of being as broad as possible the designs advanced, through some twenty successive factorizations, moving by a co-ordinated use of marker tests toward tests designed to check the theories emerging in the stable source traits. The best way to get a feeling for this scientific progression is to see the actual tests in the Cattell-Warburton Compendium (1967), but the titles in Table 8.1 may give some idea.

TABLE 8.1

Sample Titles from the Four Hundred Objective Test Devices so far Designed

---

Willingness to play practical jokes;
readiness to make an early decision while dark adaptation is proceeding;
amplitude of voice under normal relative to delayed feedback conditions;
awareness of social etiquette;
basal metabolic rate;
cidetic imagery;
cancellation of letters (a vigilance task) compared under two conditions;
readiness to imitate animal sounds;
critical flicker fusion frequency;
speed of arousal of negative after-images;
preference for crayoning own rather than provided drawings;
frequency of hand tremor in a decision situation;
amount of laughter at jokes;
pupil dilation after startle;
more fidgeting while waiting as measured by the fidgetometer;
    (a specially constructed chair with electrical contacts to record move-
    ment—a modern version of an invention by Galton)
speed of design copying;
height of tower block construction (six year olds);
care in following detailed instructions;
accuracy of gestalt completion;
distance covered in a brass finger maze, with and without shock.

Incidentally, among these 400 objective tests designed primarily for definite source trait measures, the authors have included also many former known objective tests, such as the Rorschach and Szondi tests.

Before coming to the systematic setting out of the source traits found in objective tests we shall digress briefly to discuss results of these older and therefore more widely tried types of test not designed for any specific theoretically checked dimension.

SOME SPECIAL TYPES OF TEST: RORSCHACH, HUMOUR, MUSIC AND ART PREFERENCE

The tests of a projective nature, and those dealing with humour, music, defense mechanisms generally and other somewhat unusual approaches which we shall discuss in this section come close in some ways to being dynamic, motivational measures, rather than general personality measures. As pointed out in chapter 10, where motivation and dynamic structure are analyzed, the difference is that the former deal with *particular* drive strengths, attitude strengths, defenses and complexes, whereas the general personality factors, where they occur in motivational manifestations, have to do with the *general quality* of the dynamic interests, such as their stability, *average* strength, and degree of integration or general susceptibility to inhibition.

The Rorschach (Rorschach, 1921) stands as an historical landmark on its own, whereas the use of projection in Murray's TAT (Murray, 1938) and in the MAT of Sweney (Cattell, Horn and Sweney, 1970) and others springs initially from Freudian concepts. So also does Cattell's development of the humour test (Cattell and Luborsky, 1952), though it checks the Freudian categories by factor analytic experiment. The music preference test, which Saunders and Cattell developed (Cattell and Saunders, 1954) is as blind in its search for empirical associations to categories as is the Rorschach.

In view of the quite severe criticisms of the Rorschach by no less eminent psychometrists than Thurstone, Vernon and Cronbach, it must today be regarded more as evidence of the need psychologists feel for objective test devices than of the satisfactory meeting of such a need. In the Cattell-Warburton Compendium it is pointed out that the objective tests can be open-ended as well as multiple-choice (i.e. fully conspective) and that a list of spontaneous answers can be set up which, if used by any subject, can be scored the same by all psychologists. As Holtzman (1968) for example has pointed out, the objection to Rorschach as an objective test is not in its open-ended response form, but precisely what its protagonists would consider its most important feature—its ability to provide data fit for rich subjective interpretation, by the psychologist who likes this kind of crystal ball test. Since projective tests were originally developed because they could provide such rich clinical data, it is indeed open to question whether one should lightly abandon such interpretation. The misunderstanding which creates this dilemma is the failure to distinguish between general personality dimensions and specific motivational and interest strength measures. Do we want to use the Rorschach (or any other test) to reveal specific interests, in which case response and interpretation should be free, or to measure the magnitude of certain general personality and temperament dimensions, where testing needs to be conspective? In regard to the latter we may simply look at the listing and appraisal of the test in the Cattell-Warburton Compendium. It appears among the 400 T tests as T 283, with a statement that despite Thurstone's factoring (which showed largely one factor only) the loadings of various Rorschach responses on the primary personality factors remain unknown. It points out the evidence of low validities as summarized by Vernon (1964) and Eysenck (1959) and warns that the word "projective" is here being used in a vague way, since the psychoanalytic view that subjects project their own conflicts and feelings into ambiguous stimuli (dynamic projection) had certainly not been developed at that stage. (It got into test design for the first time simultaneously in Cattell's (1938) Projection Tests and Murray's (1938, but used before) Thematic Apperception Test.) Rorschach hoped that the inkblots would be useful in psychiatric diagnosis in ways yet to be discovered. As indicated, the vast number of references in Duros (1972) showing that the Rorschach test has been and still is widely used in the clinic both in research and practice (albeit less than was once the case) is not argument for its scientific standing. Eysenck (1959), in his review of this test, argued that there was no sound evidence for its validity. Cattell and Warburton, on the other hand, are prepared to let the Rorschach take its chances along with the other 400 objective test devices. Subjects are undoubtedly likely to perceive the unstructured inkblots according to their cognitive style, their modes of interpreting the world and their perceptual habits, and if so, it is possible that certain measures from it will correlate sufficiently with the general personality factors in these behavioural measures. Incidentally, as with other tests, it is possible that, although subjects may not be aware of precisely how responses are scored, social desirability could affect them. Few subjects would admit, for example, that an inkblot resembled a gang rape of their mother.

On this theoretical basis a large number of variables are derived from the same test, just as with the various MI markers from the same T tests in the Cattell-Warburton objective tests listed in Table 8.1. Thus we find: total number of responses, number of human responses, number of human detail responses, number of anatomy responses, number of animal responses, number of sharp form-colour responses, number of unsharp form-colour responses, and so on. In this way the Rorschach has been reduced to an entirely objective test device. A similar procedure can be adopted with any projective test if it appears likely that strong individual differences will emerge. It must be noted, however, that as yet none of these Rorschach variables has loaded on any of the largest T factors. This however, at the present stage of research, should not be taken to mean that the Rorschach test is not a useful personality measure even in objective form. Holley (1973), as we have fully discussed in Chapter 3 (p. 33), separated depressive schizophrenics and controls using objective, dichotomous variables from the Rorschach test analysed by means of the G index and factor-analysis. Kline and Hampson (1976) have also found G technique useful in the study of criminals with other projective tests.

This question of projective tests actually forms a basis for discussing another important problem—the nature of the defence mechanism of projection—a problem which strongly affects our view of projective tests in relation to the whole field of objective personality tests. If we really think that subjects do project their conflict and feelings into the perception of ambiguous stimuli then in the construction of objective tests of the motivation side of personality we shall concentrate considerable effort on to the development of indices from projective tests. Actually Cattell and his colleagues have built up some important evidence on this point as they have developed objective T tests, though all but the defence mechanism aspects are handled in Chapters 9 and 10 on motivation. Not only is this work important from the practical research viewpoint of test development but also from the more theoretical view of personality and behaviour because in Freudian theory projection is an important defence mechanism. Indeed in psychoanalytic theory the understanding of personality demands insight into the mechanisms of defence.

In Freudian theory projection was the defence mechanism (an unconscious process) by which emotions and feelings which an individual could not tolerate often because they aroused guilt were imputed to others. Paranoia was a case in point because in Freudian theory the persecutory delusions which characterize this illness are thought to be projections. Thus "I love him" becomes by reaction-formation "I hate him" which by projection becomes "he hates me". However, Anna Freud has given us a categorical review of all the defence mechanisms, of which projection is but one (A. Freud, 1946). The purpose of the defence mechanisms is to support the ego in the dynamic conflict of ego, superego and id. Other defences are *reaction formation* where our conscious thoughts and feelings are the opposite of the unconscious ones, as in our example above, *fantasy, rationalization*, defined as finding good reasons for what we want to do, *denial* and *repression* where the emotion of feeling is pushed into the oblivion of our unconscious. All these mechanisms are regarded in Freudian theory as less adequate than normal ego control, though widely employed. For they do not allow any expression of the forbidden impulses and hence they have to be in continual use. It should be noted that sublimation is a term used to describe successful defence mechanism where the forbidden impulse is allowed expression but in an altered form (Fenichel, 1945). Thus, for example, the great artist may sublimate his Oedipal conflicts in his work—Hamlet or the brothers Karamazov are usually taken as examples of this (Freud, 1928). This is mentioned here because it exemplifies the importance of the defences which in the case of sublimation are seen as the basis of civilized (as distinct from savage) life. The arts, the sciences, all the apparatus of civilization, are defences.

From the standpoint of the multivariate experimentalist in personality and motivation the first question about the defence mechanisms is whether they correspond in number and nature with this clinical picture initially obtained. Are they truly independent and distinct from trait-processes? Are there just seven of them, or can others be detected? Factor analytic study of a wide variety of perceptual and reasoning processes by Wenig (1952) in his master's dissertation and Cattell and Wenig (1952) showed that most of these mechanisms had a clear functional unity and that rationalization, fantasy and autism (believing what one wants to believe) were distinct defences such that any individual is likely to use one more than the other. Thus one man may tend to favour autism so that his opinions and feelings seem objectively contrary to fact. Another may prefer rationalization, a method often found amongst highly intelligent people, so that actions are justified by a torrent of words, as Shakespeare noted "Methinks the lady doth protest too much". Most important, however, from the viewpoint of our discussion of the place of projective tests in the realm of objective test devices, was the finding by Cattell and Wenig (1952) that there are two kinds of projection—true projection and naive projection.

True projection was as the psychoanalysts had described: the attribution to others of feelings and motives that were unacceptable. Naive projection occurs where a person (e.g. a child, inevitably inexperienced) interprets the behaviour of others in terms of his own personal and limited motivation system just as anyone interprets new worlds in terms of that with which he is familiar. Since there is this distinction it is obviously wrong to interpret projective tests, as is usually done, in terms of true projection alone. What Wenig (1952) showed was that the interpretation of pictures always involves some degree of misperception, defined as the departure from a given norm (the zero point for scoring), the result of the various defences acting together. Diagram 8.1 makes this point clearly (17, p. 149 Cattell, 1965).

With this theoretical insight we can see that standard projective test interpretations as in the TAT hopelessly confuse the different mental mechanisms. For example, a child might select response 4, from his personal experience, thus exhibiting naive projection. True projection of an unacceptable sex drive might lead to response 3. To show how the same drive can lead to different responses when different defences are used we can take dominance: true projection would lead to response 1, rationalization might produce 2. However, 2 could be the result of a strong need for security. All these illustrations demonstrate how quite different feelings and emotions can determine the same responses. Indeed this ambiguity not only means that the interpretation of projective tests by clinical intuitive methods depends largely on the skill of the tester and is unlikely to be valid, but in addition it renders the term projective

Fig. 8.1   Subject's choice of interpretation (from Cattell, 1965, p. 14)
1. As a life guard, he is in charge of the beach and is enjoying being "master of all he surveys".
2. The swimmers feel secure in having such a confident person in charge.
3. He cannot keep his attention on the swimmers because he finds it hard to take his eyes off the shapely girls.
4. He feels insecure on the high tower and is wondering how firm it is.

inappropriate. Projection is but one component of the response and they should be called misperception tests.

Our discussion illustrates the way round this multidetermination of responses which can nullify standard projective testing technique. By using projective test pictures and forced choice responses selected so that different defences will lead to the endorsement of different responses we can go beyond brilliant intuition in the study of defences and in the interpretation of such tests. In this way these TAT-like pictures, if we think that they yield rich data, can be used as objective test devices.

In conclusion, then, we can see from this discussion that it is hardly surprising that the study of projective tests as scored and interpreted in the traditional way has almost always failed to demonstrate their validity. This lack of validity was almost certainly due to the low reliability inherent in subjective scoring and implicit in the nature of the tests themselves. Wenig's work however has shown that if regarded as misperception tests and supplied with responses so constructed that the different defences are not confounded and inter-scorer reliability is made perfect, such tests can give valuable information in both personality and motivation. Used thus, misperception tests are an important group of objective personality tests.

Mention should be made here of work on percept-genetics which has been carried out in the Universities of Lund and Oslo since the early fifties. Subjects are shown stimuli at gradually increasing speeds tachistoscopically until they can give a full description. The development of the percept is thought to reflect personality development at a very basic level for each individual (Kragh, 1955). Although we cannot discuss the full ramification of this work (but see Kragh and Smith, 1970) various defence mechanisms have been observed and a special defence mechanism test, consisting of slides shown through the tachistoscope, has been developed—the Defence Mechanism Test (fully described in Kline, 1973c). These findings fully support the reservations we have made above about simple interpretation of projective tests.

Now, as we stated previously, we shall briefly scrutinize two tests which have been developed from clinical, dynamically oriented theory and which are hard to classify—the *Humour Test of Personality* and the *Musical Preference Test of Personality*.

The Humour Test of Personality (Cattell and Tollefson, 1966) This test has two parallel forms. In one, each item consists of a pair of jokes and subjects are required to choose the funnier. In the other form jokes are rated on a two-point scale. This test has been developed by Cattell and his associates from the empirical studies of humour carried out by Cattell and Luborsky, (1947, 1952), (see also Luborsky and Cattell, 1947). The employment of wit and humour in the study of personality springs from the Freudian theory of humour (Freud, 1905b) where it is claimed that the joke allows us to express impulses that are normally repressed. Thus, for example, in the guise of wit, we are able to say highly aggressive things about individuals that would otherwise be impossible. According to this theory it is not surprising that so many of the jokes endemic in Western culture are concerned with sex and aggression. The explosiveness of laughter is supposed to be an index of how strongly in any individual the impulse in the joke is repressed. Certainly all readers must have noted in their own experience how there is usually one person who finds a joke excruciatingly funny far beyond all others in the group. This is because (in Freudian theory) the joke touches on a critical problem for him. The intellectual side of the joke, the clever pun, the play on words, was for Freud a bribe for the superego, which distracted the "censor" from his usual vigilance. Thus the individual enjoying the joke can pretend that he is a connoisseur of verbal skills. Freud in his theory of art regarded the formal side of art in much the same way. The composition, the skill of the brushwork or the wonderful colour were bribes to allow the artist (and thus, vicariously, the viewer) to express the forbidden content. This then is the theoretical rationale for attempting to use humour in the assessment of personality.

Cattell and Luborsky however found that there were severe problems in the study of humour. First, psychiatrists found it difficult to classify jokes according to the repressed impulses or drives with which they were supposed to be concerned. Psychiatrists disagreed and even when they agreed jokes purportedly having the same element of, say, sadism were not equally liked by the same individual who might find only one funny. It was therefore found necessary to correlate liking for jokes to ascertain empirically the underlying dimensions. Ten clusters of intercorrelations were identified: debonair sexual uninhibitedness, good natured play, tough self-composure, gruesomeness, hostile derogation, resignation, cold realism, ponderous humour, whimsical retort, and mistreatment humour. Jokes loading on these variables are included in the Humour test of Personality.

The manual to the test makes it clear that the Humour test must still be regarded as fit for research only because there is insufficient evidence for its concrete validity against life performances. Thus the main evidence for validity comes from correlations with the 16PF test but no specific figures or sample sizes are given in the manual. Again the test/retest reliabilities are low, well below 0.7, which is regarded by many psychometrists (e.g. Cronbach, 1970) as the minimum necessary if the test is to be used with individuals as distinct from research use with groups. On the other hand studies with the test make it clear that extraverts tend to like jokes that are hearty, socially uninhibited and with sexual content. Introverts on the whole prefer dry, cautious and acid jokes. Some concrete validities of an important kind now exist. Thus Egbert and Meeland (Egbert *et al.*, 1954) found that among soldiers in the Korean war, those who were considered by their companions to be good men to have around, reliable in danger and active in attack, could be distinguished from the rest by certain scores on the Humour test. This strongly supports the view that the test does measure useful personality dimensions although it is not clear exactly what these dimensions are.

Another obvious advantage with this test is that it is difficult to fake and Cattell (e.g. 1957) has always claimed that subjects have enjoyed doing it. One of the factors measured is general intelligence (an intelligence test hidden as appreciation of humour) and a practical advantage of this is that high level business executives, for example, who resist the idea of doing an ordinary intelligence test, can be measured. The second author here, however, working with students in Great Britain has found that this test has provoked more resistance than the standard personality questionnaire, such as the 16PF test. Our view of this objective personality test is that it is highly interesting but that the dimensions underlying these jokes need considerable further research before they can be reliably identified.

The Music Preference Test of Personality (Cattell and Eber, 1954) In this test subjects have to state preferences for different pieces of music played on a piano. The pieces represent most tastes in music—romantic, popular, jazz etc. The rationale of this test is perhaps best described as literary and folk wisdom. Plato was convinced that music had profound effects on behaviour and personality and in the "Republic" even went so far as to lay down the precise effects of the different modes. For Shakespeare music was the food of love and in modern times the Music Research Foundation of America devotes itself to the study of the therapeutic effects of music, as has Juliet Alvin in the United Kingdom. To put these ideas to empirical tests, therefore, Cattell and his colleagues looked at the musical preferences of patients suffering from different kinds of mental disturbance.

Eleven personality factors are found to underly the preferences for the 100 items of the Music Preference Test, factors which by no means correspond to technical schools or periods of music but to some probably more fundamental temperamental differences in the toleration of rhythms and speeds and in the liking for different kinds of emotional stimulation. In respect of this interpretation all readers who take any pleasure in music must be aware of the powerful emotional effect that their favourite pieces have on them: few lovers of classical music, for example, fail to be moved by Dido's lament at the conclusion of Purcell's Dido and Aeneas.

In the manual to the test only eight of these factors have been sufficiently identified to be labelled even tentatively. The factors are: adjustment, self-centredness, tough sociability, introspectiveness, anxiety and concern, eccentricity and, finally, tenacity. Evidence for the concrete validity and the psychological meaning of these has been slow to come in, because many psychometrists view this form of testing with a great deal of scepticism. However, Michel and others have shown that normals can be distinguished from mental hospital patients on these variables and that there were significant differences between schizophrenics, paranoids and manic depressives. Again as was the case with the Humour test this evidence suggests that important personality dimensions are being measured by this test but the nature of these factors needs considerable further elucidation. Kline (1974) carried out a small-scale study of the Music test correlating the factors with those in the EPI (see p. 78) and the DPI (see p. 87). This gave some support for the validity of factors 4 and 5, tough sociability and introspectiveness, but it is possible that the rather low reliability of the scales lowered the correlations. In conclusion, as with the majority of objective test devices, there is a need for much more research into the nature of the factors.

Related to this approach is the measurement of temperament through differences in taste in art. When the Romans said "There is no accounting for tastes" they meant by reason, but temperament explains what reason cannot. Both Eysenck and Cattell have factored out choices and they agree at least that the extraversion-introversion factor can be found in the correlations and that the extravert prefers bright colours and strong effects whereas pictures preferred by introverts are quieter and more subtle.

THE PRINCIPAL GENERAL PERSONALITY SOURCE TRAITS FOUND

All the above discussion of the nature of objective tests as such is an indispensable preamble to understanding the underlying personality source traits found by correlation of measures of hundreds of these behaviours on typical population samples.

Practically all the evidence in this field springs from two laboratories well equipped for the complex procedure needed and resides in about 100 publications by Cattell and colleagues at Illinois and Eysenck and colleagues in London. Additionally, there are factor studies on much the same tests by Schuerger at Cleveland University, Hundleby at Guelph, Connor at New York, Pawlik at Hamburg, Gibb at the Australian National University and Damarin at Ohio University. The methods by the Illinois group, as in the publications of Baggaley, Burdsal, Barton, De Young, Dielman, Gruen, Horn, Klein, Knapp, Meeland, Nesselroade, Saunders, Schmidt, Sweney and Vaughan, have covered more factors than those studied by the London group, though Eysenck's extraversion, neuroticism and psychoticism factors were simultaneously found among the 20, as exvia, regression and tensidia, and indexed as UI.32, 23 and 25 below. Both groups have sought and found important concrete validities in clinical diagnoses and the Illinois group has pursued predictions also in occupations and in educational achievement.

The main objective in indexing these factors by *universal index*—UI—numbers has been to avoid entanglement in premature theoretical crystallizations. A UI number is given to *the loading pattern on test performances* as such, once it is sufficiently replicated (by three or more researches). Then different psychologists can try their theories on the pattern, confident, despite different names, that they are referring to the same thing. Meanwhile the discoverers of these new patterns—for only a few have been glimpsed before by the unaided clinical eye—have given names to them, just as discoverers of, say, new elements in chemistry have exercised their right to name them. These names, as pointed out in examples below, are based on the best theoretical interpretation possible at this time, and, like the name oxygen (acid producer) *may* prove later to be wrongly conceived. The mixed reception, from welcoming to ignoring, given to these labels does not spring from that risk. It springs from xenophobia and leads to the persisting use of existing familiar terms—sociable, altruistic, suspicious, creative, fluent, etc. Unfortunately the new factors never correspond to such single variables, being patterns, and, still more unfortunately, popular terms mean all things to all men. (One study on the altruistic trait treats it as conscientious, another as kindness and another as intelligence!) Consequently, it is important in a scientific study of personality to get to know the technical terms for the well established source traits, as below, and to use them correctly in research and applied psychology.

As in L and Q data the factors have been indexed in order of diminishing size but as numbers instead of letters. The relation of the A through Q_6 series in L-Q data and UI.16 through UI.36 in T data is discussed in the next section. The assignment of descriptive and interpretive names is based initially on *content*, i.e. on an attempt to deduce, as a construct, what could be common to the shared performances and absent from the non-shared behaviours in a given case. With wider use of the objective batteries, the label is also directed by concrete validations found in the field, e.g. Knapp's finding that in the military, high UI.16 individuals far more frequently demand attention by visits to the sick-bay (Knapp, 1961). It will be noted that the interpretation problem here is decidedly more of an intellectual challenge than in the L-Q media where the items are some guide to the meaning. Thus if we have a factor loading on questionnaire items such as "I cannot sleep", "I worry all the time", "I feel anxious often for no reason," "I cannot help brooding over things", and so on, it is a reasonable hypothesis (which needs further proof) that the factor is one concerned with anxiety. A factor which loads on greater preference for weak smells, more care in following instructions and greater tendency to agree is by no means so clear. In fact this is UI.36, strong self-sentiment. Thus we can see that when factors have been tentatively identified from their objective test loadings, further research into their nature, e.g. following up high and low scorers, correlating scores with scales of known validity is essential. Since this concrete validation has not yet been fully carried out with many of these factors, we intend here only to discuss the largest ones (about which more is known) in any detail.

First we list the 21 factors as set out in Cattell and Warburton (1967).

TABLE 8.2

Primary Objective Personality Test Factors

U.I. 16	Narcissistic Ego	*v.* Secure, Disciplined Unassertiveness
U.I. 17	Inhibition-Timidity	*v.* Trustingness
U.I. 18	Manic Smartness	*v.* Passiveness
U.I. 19	Independence	*v.* Subduedness
U.I. 20	Comention (Herd Conformity)	*v.* Objectivity
U.I. 21	Exuberance	*v.* Suppressibility
U.I. 22	Cortertia (Cortical Alertness)	*v.* Pathemia
U.I. 23	Mobilization of Energy	*v.* Regression
U.I. 24	Anxiety	*v.* Adjustment
U.I. 25	Realism	*v.* Tensinflexia (Psychotic Tendency)
U.I. 26	Narcistic Self-Sentiment	*v.* Homespunness
U.I. 27	Sceptical Apathy	*v.* Involvement
U.I. 28	Super Ego Asthenia	*v.* Rough Assurance
U.I. 29	Wholehearted Responsiveness	*v.* Lack of Will
U.I. 30	Stolidness	*v.* Dissofrustance

(Continued)

Table 8.2—*cont.*

U.I. 31	Wariness	*v.* Impulsive Variability
U.I. 32	Exvia (Extraversion)	*v.* Invia (Introversion)
U.I. 33	Dismay (Pessimism)	*v.* Sanguine Poise
U.I. 34	Inconautia (Impracticalness)	*v.* Practicalness
U.I. 35	Stolparsomnia (Somnolence)	*v.* Excitation
U.I. 36	Self-Sentiment	*v.* Weak Self-Sentiment

Immediately one point stands out about this list—the fact that the two largest second-order Q factors appear at the first order in objective tests UI.24, anxiety, and UI.32, exvia.

UI.16 Assertive ego. As Cattell (1975) shows, over the years this factor has been reliably described by five marker variables: speed of letter comparison, greater number of objects seen (in unstructured drawings), fast line length judgement, higher numerical ability and more hidden objects seen. In that these variables are the highest loadings on UI.16 it can be fairly said that this factor illustrates well the problem of identifying objective test factors. It could be that this is an ability factor because several of its variables load on the general speed factor g_s (Cattell, 1971). However some of these are concerned with natural tempo, with social behaviour such as number of acquaintances, and with accuracy in mazes. UI.16 is interpreted as a factor expressing competitive striving for excellence in any performance rather than as a speed factor. The relations to life criteria of this factor have been studied and include low proneness to neuroticism, high achievement in school and outside (if the effects of intelligence are discounted) insistence on individual attention (in group situation) so that the factor resembles that of ego strength, although Cattell (1975) admits that these manifestations could be interpreted as over-compensation or narcisism. Thus the title of Assertive Ego rather than ego-strength has been adopted for this factor. It is noteworthy that this should be the largest and most influential of the T personality factors in the light of psychoanalytic theory which, of course, has always placed great emphasis on the concept of ego and ego strength.

As was mentioned, the index figures for these T factors were in order of factor size. However, because of the difficulties of sampling the personality sphere with objective tests, some of the factors which were large in the original studies have since been shown to be less important. UI.17, general inhibition, is of this kind and we shall not discuss it at this point. Instead we shall look at UI.18, Hypomanic Tendency, which itself is not as large as was originally thought.

UI.18, Hypomanic Tendency. Here the highest loading variables are higher ratio of final to initial performance in backward writing, fewer objects seen in unstructured drawings, more cheating, higher total score in the Cursive Minature situation (for description see p. 136), less numerical ability and faster speed of line length judgement. These are the objective test loadings which strongly suggest the kind of behaviour where everything is done as fast as possible. In addition, with children at least there are loadings on the Q factors, O, guilt proneness, F, surgency, and A, affectothymia (see pp. 112–118, for descriptions of these). Although the T variables suggest the manic nature of this factor and the Q variables have a similar implication of the cycloid temperament (to use Kretschmer's terminology) the best evidence for the identification of this factor comes from a clinical study of an abnormal population in a mental hospital. In this the psychiatric ratings for manic behaviour loaded on this factor (Tatro, 1967).

UI.19 Independence. High loading T variables on this factor are greater pessimism over doing good, higher personal than institutional values, fewer questionnable reading preferences, fewer friends recalled, more confidence in untried skills and less criticism of self. In addition Q factors E, dominance and I, tough mindedness, load on this factor. This factor would appear to be similar to the concept of field independence much studied by Witkin (1962). However it is clear that this field independence is more narrow than UI.19 which is a general temperamental independence. Nature–nurture studies have revealed that UI.19 is both substantially inherited and sex linked, being higher in boys. The fact that it is related in criterion studies with low proneness to neuroticism, creativity and leadership together with the Q loadings supports the identification of this T factor as independence.

UI.20 Comention (herd conformity) v. Objectivity (abcultion). High loading variables on this factor include tendency to agree with generalizations, measured in a variety of ways, being female, and respecting authority. From this it could be regarded as a factor of "acceptance of social and ethical values" or as a "dog and cat" factor (Cattell and Warburton, 1967) since high scorers show a dog-like emotional expressiveness, impulsivity and group dependence. Central to this factor seems to be a readiness to accept the culture and its demands.

UI.21 Exuberance v. suppressibility. Faster tempo of reading of interesting material, higher fluency on topics. less acceptance of unqualified statements, better immediate memory, these are the highest loading variables on this factor. As Cattell (1975) argues, it could well be that UI.21 is related to the ability factor g_r, fluency, (Cattell, 1971) although as was the case with UI.16 it appears to be picking up a different part of the variance. Interpretation of whether the factor represents high vitality of output or low inhibition of expression is difficult, and the description of exuberance is the most apt.

UI.22 Cortertia, cortical alertness. This factor seems to be one of alertness perhaps related to the individual's base level of cortical arousal or activation. It loads highly on speed on all kinds of reaction time tests, high critical flicker fusion frequency and much fidgeting action on the fidgetometer.

UI.23, capacity to mobilize v. regression. This is an important factor clinically so we must first examine the high loading marker variables: higher ratio of accuracy to speed in letter cancellation, more accuracy in spatial judgment (where the point at which lines cross has to be estimated), less rigidity in backward writing test, and faster ideomotor speed (based on coding tests). This factor has also been isolated by Eysenck (1947) who regarded it as the neuroticism factor. However since Cattell had isolated no fewer than six other T factors which statistically discriminate neurotics equally well it was clear that it must be a factor that is a *component* in neurosis, which Cattell has identified from the loadings we give above as *regression*. UI.23 is seen most clearly in mixed normal and clinical groups although it is reliably found among normals alone. Not only is this regression factor associated with neurosis but it is linked to poor school performance, to a clinical diagnosis of psychosis, to debility and poor resistance to stress.

If we think carefully about the requirements on subjects of the objective tests loading on this factor it is possible to see why it has been identified as regression. Thus the tests are not just manifestations of skills (which would make this factor an ability factor). Rather they test the capacity to apply the skills which subjects possess. Thus all subjects *can* write backwards but only some can bring their capacities together to actually do it. Scheier (Cattell and Scheier, 1961) has shown that in the face of practical difficulties this source trait tends to rise. In other words faced with a severe challenge people respond well. Perhaps therefore old fashioned harsh regimes in education and even in clinical treatment based on popular lore were not entirely foolish! There can be no doubt that much further research into this regression factor needs to be carried out.

UI.24 Anxiety v. Adjustment. This is clearly a most important factor, since as we showed in previous chapters, Anxiety in Q and L data is agreed to be, together with exvia or extraversion, the most important personality dimension, although at the second-order. The highest T tests loading on UI.24 are: more common frailties admitted, greater susceptibility to annoyance, higher rigidity and more restrained book preferences. These loadings may not appear particularly convincing. However, in addition Q factors O (guilt proneness), Q4 (high ergic tension) H − (timidity), Q3 − (low self-sentiment), G − (low superego strength) F (surgency) and C − (ego weakness) all load on it which makes its identification as the anxiety factor certain. It is interesting to note that unlike depression which as we saw turned out to have seven component factors (see p. 57) anxiety has remained a general factor. Further evidence as to the true identity of this factor as anxiety may be found in the fact that certain individual physiological indices load on it such as high kesteroid secretion and low GSR. There can be little doubt, therefore, that UI.24 is the trait anxiety factor. The value of this factor together with other T factors in the clinical study and treatment of psychiatric patients will be discussed in Chapter 13.

UI.25 Realism v. Tensidia. This factor has not only turned up in the research of Cattell and his colleagues but is also found in the work of Eysenck (Eysenck,

S.B.G. 1956) who isolated it in her doctoral dissertation. The high loadings on this factor are: higher respect for authority, fewer personal (relative to institutional) values, greater pessimism over doing good and greater accuracy in the Gottschaldt figures. By themselves these loadings would not enable us to label this factor with any confidence. However as Cattell and Warburton point out, although it resembles the psychoticism factor of Eysenck it has also a high negative correlation with anxiety (but psychotics are typically average on anxiety). Cattell (1975) argues that it is wrong to conceive of UI.25 alone as psychoticism because neurotics are also deviant on this factor, as Schmidt has convincingly shown (1972).

We shall not further discuss here UI factors 26-31 because their associations and relations have not been extensively worked out and as was the case with UI.25 it is difficult to identify these factors in terms of their objective test loadings alone. Instead we shall turn to UI.32, Exvia *v.* Invia or extraversion *v.* introversion. Further details of the factors we have omitted may by found in Hundleby, Pawlik and Cattell (1965).

UI.32 Exvia v. Invia (extraversion *v.* introversion). The objective tests loading on UI.32 are: more common frailties admitted, faster speed of line length judgement, less acceptance of unqualified statements, lower severity of judgement, faster speed of tapping and more agreement with the majority. These T tests are not particularly convincing as variables loading an exvia factor although there is nothing about them that would contraindicate such an identification. However this factor loads up on the exvia Q variables, F (surgency), H (adventurousness), Q3 − (low self-sentiment), A, cyclothymia and J − (zeppia) so that there can be no doubt that the factor UI.32 is identical to the Q factor of exvia.

Here we encounter an interesting problem. Extraversion has, since the time of Jung been a most important variable in the study of temperament, a claim reinforced by the empirical work with Q factors of almost all researchers, as we saw in Chapters 4 and 5. However, in terms of mean variance among objective T factors it is seventeenth. This is a paradox which cannot be fully explained at present although when we consider the second-order T factors some light will be thrown on the problem.

The T tests which we have shown loading on this factor are those that have been replicated across cultures. However in the USA more fluency about people's characteristics, more objects found in unstructured drawings, more self-confidence in untried performances and more rapid alternating perspective with the neckar cube all load on this factor suggesting strongly that the exviant individual is more carefree, confident, openly aggressive, fluent, sociable and less inhibited than the norm. This picture, of course, strongly confirms that originating from L and Q data. The fact that UI.32 is separate from UI.17 runs counter to the argument that exvia represents at the inviant pole some kind of general inhibition. If this were the case UI.32 could hardly be discriminated from that factor. Rather it appears that it is a factor of social inhibition springing from both genetic determinants (for H is the most inherited of the component factors) and from environmental influences such as early experiences in social interactions. This could certainly account for cross-cultural findings of Warburton *et al.* (1963) that British students (like Japanese students; see Tsujioka and Cattell, 1965) were less exviant than their American contemporaries.

Before leaving UI.32 we should discuss briefly the point that applies also to UI.24 Anxiety, namely that these factors are second-order Q factors but first-order T factors. The reason for this difference in stratum seems to be a question of size. The questionnaire items, being simple "yes" "no" items measure less than the relatively broad T tests. Thus the items correlate together to form factors that are individually measured by the T tests. Diagram 8.2 clarifies this point.

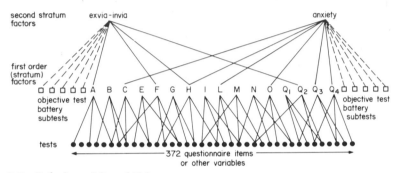
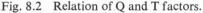

Fig. 8.2   Relation of Q and T factors.

With UI.32 we shall leave our description of the T factors. For more detailed descriptions the references already cited should be consulted. In summary we would argue that our understanding of T factors is less than is the case with L and Q factors because of the problems associated with the identification of factors from objective test loadings, tests which have little face validity and because there has been far less use of objective tests in the practical situation so that criterion relations of the factors are not known. Furthermore there remains the difficulty of the relation of T, Q and L factors although in the case of exvia and anxiety, as we have seen, there is some firm information.

SOME OTHER RELATIONS OF T DATA SOURCE TRAITS

Early studies of the relationship between T and Q factors showed no consistent results mainly because the notion of instrument factors and the resulting perturbation of results had not been fully worked out. However, as far back as 1955 the relation of exvia and anxiety with UI.24 and 32 had been discovered, by the correlations cited above, a finding which has been replicated since. As the names indicate, UI.22, cortertia, aligns with the second-order Q factor of that name (Q 111) and UI.19 aligns with second-order Q4, independence. It does not take brilliant perspicacity to see that all the T factors thus related to Q factors align with second-order factors; in other words: could it be that T factors are second orders in the Q–L medium? Cattell (1975) points out the obvious objection to this solution of the problem, namely that far more T factors have been found than second-order Q factors, and there is reason to think, as we have argued throughout this book, that our coverage of the Q domain is complete (so that few new factors are likely to be found) whereas our coverage of the T domain is not so comprehensive. As the matter stands new research is needed where special attention is paid to the influence of instrument factors. Nevertheless, what evidence there is still supports the claim that essentially L, Q and T factors are the same and that personality factors can be measured equally in any of the three media.

In our discussion of UI.24 and 32 we have already argued that they align with second-order factors because objective tests are more broad measuring instruments than questionnaire items. However Cattell (1975) makes the point that another possibility, particular to psychology, could account for this finding, namely that second-order factors are influences acting upon first orders. In *spiral action theory* it is assumed that the first orders generate the second order. Simple structure can be found only because a subset of primaries has this power of interaction. This is clearly seen with Q1, exvia, where high A causes exviants to seek company, which increases their social skills (N). This social success produces dominance (E) while the H makes him thick-skinned enough to ignore the inevitable rebuffs of such behaviour. With Anxiety a similar process could occur not unlike the Freudian concept of neurosis where weak ego strength (C−) makes the individual more susceptible to anxiety stemming from tension (Q4) and guilt (O), to translate psychoanalytic theory into Cattell factors. If this formulation be true then some T factors at least could be the measures of these interactions of primary factors.

Since all this rotational evidence clearly points to first-order, p imary, T data factors having moderate but significant correlations with one another, higher order structures among them are open to investigation. Some three independent studies looking for the secondaries among these primaries already exist. Any interpretation at present has to rest on content, because little is yet known about them in terms of criterion relations. Accordingly we shall simply list their names together with the names of the primaries loading on each. Obviously in view of the uncertainties about the theoretical interpretations of the primary factors themselves identification of the secondary factors must be highly tentative.

Finally, mention must be made of a study by Pawlik and Cattell (1964) who subjected a battery of objective tests to third-order factor analysis. Three samples were used, two consisting of 86 undergraduates each, the third of 315 Navy submarine school candidates. Factors UI.16-36 were included in this research, and the second-order factors were subjected to two oblique

TABLE 8.3

Nature of Second-Order Objective Test Factors: Average Loadings in Five Studies

F(T)I Tied Socialization or Superego Development v. Absence of Cultural Introjection

First-Order Factor (In direction of loading)	Loading
U.I. 20+, Comention	+.36
U.I. 1−, Low Intelligence	−.34
U.I. 25+, Careful Realism	+.33
U.I. 35+, Long-Circuited Dynamics	+.44*
U.I. 28+, Rigid Superego	+.21
U.I. 19−, Subduedness or Resignation	−.20
U.I. 32−, Exvia or Extraversion	−.19

F(T)III Temperamental Ardor v. Low Dynamic Involvement, with Sublimatory Capacity

First-Order Factor (In direction of loading)	Loading
U.I. 21+, Exuberance or Energetic Spontaneity	+.31
U.I. 1−, Low Intelligence	−.28
U.I. 20+, Comention	+.27
U.I. 19+, Promethean Will	+.21

F(T)II Expansive Ego v. History of Difficulty in Emotional Problem-Solving

First-Order Factor (In direction of loading)	Loading
U.I. 16+, Harric Assertiveness	+.34
U.I. 23−, Neurotic Regressive Debility	−.29
U.I. 1+, Intelligence	+.28
U.I. 19+, Promethean Will	+.23
U.I. 36+, Self-Sentiment Development	+.29*
U.I. 18−, Naive Self-Obliviousness	−.15

F(T)IV Educated Self-Consciousness v. Inexplicitness and Unrealism of Self-Sentiment

First-Order Factor (In direction of loading)	Loading
U.I. 22+, Corticalertia	+.31
U.I. 18+, Shrewdness	+.28
U.I. 36+, Self-Sentiment Development	+.51*
U.I. 25−, Imaginative Tension, Eager Subjectivity	−.17

	Loading
U.I. 30−, Nervous Responsiveness	−.16
U.I. 25−, Low Adaptation Energy	−.15
U.I. 33+, Dourness	+.20*

F(T)VI Narcistic Development v. Responsiveness to Environmental Disciplines

First-Order Factor (In direction of loading)	Loading
U.I. 26+, Narcistic Self-Will	+.33
U.I. 27+, Apathy-Fatigue, Lack of Keen Involvement	+.30
U.I. 34+, Autia, Bohemian Non-Conformity	+.51*

	Loading
U.I. 27−, Keen Involvement	−.19

F(T)V History of Inhibiting, Restraining Environment-Possibly, Bound Anxiety

First-Order Factor (In direction of loading)	Loading
U.I. 17+, Inhibition	+.35
U.I. 23+, High Mobilization	+.18
U.I. 31+, Wary Realism	+.15

F(T)VII Tension to Achieve or Controlled Drive Tension Level

First-Order Factor (In direction of loading)	Loading
U.I. 24+, High general Level of Free Anxiety	+.40
U.I. 18+, Shrewdness	+.23
U.I. 30−, Nervous Responsiveness	−.19
U.I. 25−, Imaginative Tension	−.18
U.I. 19+, Promethean Will	+.16
U.I. 33+, Dourness	+.21*

* This variable (first-order factor) appeared in only one study and thus has not been replicated.

rotated factor analyses—Oblimax (Pinzka and Saunders, 1954) and Maxplane, which we have discussed earlier (see p. 18). In fact three factors emerged: *immature self centered temperament*, loading on temperamental ardor, low self consciousness and narcissistic development. *Restrained acceptance of social norms* loaded on tied socialization, low self-consciousness and history of restraining environment. *High self-assertion* loaded most highly on expansive ego and tension to achieve. The two rotations varied on this factor and the one above is the preferred Maxplane solution. Although at three removes from the original correlations between tests of only partly known validity, as Pawlik and Cattell (1964) point out, there is a striking similarity between this solution and the Freudian description of ego, superego and id. Nevertheless, as Cattell (1975) admits, equally cogent arguments could be adduced for these factors being social or physiological rather than psychological influences, i.e. they may be correlations among personality factors produced for example by common social status selection, and so on. Indeed, until more is known about the status of objective tests and first-order T factors, identification of higher order factors is simply speculation.

SUMMARY AND CONCLUSIONS

1. Objective tests are defined as those in which the subject responds to a defined (and "portable") situation in an agreed general manner without knowing what is being evaluated from the response.
2. Such tests may or may not be *conspective*, i.e. scorable by a multiple choice, etc., key as opposed to open-ended, which test style is sometimes mistakenly called objective. Objective tests are classifiable along some seven dimensions, according to situation, instruction, kind of response, and manner of scoring.
3. A number of objective tests have appeared along projective lines, e.g. the Rorschach, in humour, music and art taste responses, etc., apart from the main line of development in the 400 tests defined by the Cattell-Warburton Compendium, centering on source trait factors analytically discovered and defined.
4. Among the projective sub-class, which includes both true and naive projection, one must distinguish between attempts to measure particular interests and dynamic attachments, which here we study in Chapter 9 as motivation measurement, and the testing of general personality factor domain. Such a test as the Rorschach may straddle these, but in the latter domain is far less valid than the HSOA and other batteries directly targeted on the source trait factors.
5. The importance of the T data approach is not merely in less fakability or distortion than Q and L data, but in providing a firm set of experimentally replicable, exact tests in terms of which the pattern can be held. These patterns are also probably less susceptible to change with time and culture than are verbal ratings or life behaviour questionnaire items.
6. Some twenty primary source traits and six secondaries have been established to date, with UI numbers from 16 to 36. Two have been firmly and two more hypothetically identified with second order factors in Q–L

data, and on the principle of indifference of medium, it is expected that the existing identifications across Q and L primaries and secondaries will be extended increasingly to T data traits.

7. The T data source traits have been shown to hold across different age groups, from 6 to 60, with some change of expression, and across at least three national cultures (Japan, USA, Austria).

8. Theoretical interpretations of the factor are shown by tentative new names, based partly on deductive reasoning from the variables showing high, low and negative loadings on each and partly on concrete validation against real life behaviour in clinical, educational and occupational domains. Although at least ten of the factors, such as anxiety (UI.24), ego strength (UI.16), regression (UI.23) and extraversion (UI.32) have well formed theories around them, research psychologists are challenged today by some ten others, each of which is an "established unitary trait in search of a theory".

9. In this connection, since the personality sphere strategy has been followed, it is highly unlikely that any major unitary trait structure in man has escaped the net taken across the L, Q and T media. Consequently the arbitrary invention of traits by taking a word out of the dictionary (as in "authoritarian personality") or from a locus in physiology (as in impulsivity) is an obsolete procedure. Any broad unitary personality trait suspected from physiological or sociological causes should be recognizable in the extensive analyses of behaviour per se already made and organized in these primary traits. On the other hand, many smaller factors in more specialized behaviour undoubtedly await factorial search.

10. The next important phase in general personality research and practice is the more extensive relating of the T data source traits to everyday life performances. This will result for applied psychology, in specification equations for various clinical, educational and social predictions (see Chapters 13-16) and in personality theory in enrichment of understanding of the nature, origins and life course of the source traits.

Psychologists have been slow in moving to these possibilities primarily because of the greater time and skill required to use T data batteries than questionnaires. With the construction of relatively streamlined batteries, as in the OA (Objective Analytic) battery by Schuerger, now published by IPAT, and the Clinical OA batteries of Hundleby in Canada and Schmidt in Germany, it is no longer necessary for the psychologist to put together results from numerous articles. Wider use, as in other human inventions, such as the first steam engine or jet plane, is bound to lead to improvement of the rather cumbersome batteries of the sixties for practical use. Already normal age curves and nature-nurture ratios have been worked out for the principal factors on the new batteries, and perhaps with further standardizations and computer scoring, these batteries will serve many clinical and industrial psychological purposes.

Chapter 9

Motivation: the Objective Measurement of the Components

DYNAMICS AND TEMPERAMENT

So far in this book our discussion of personality has centred on the investigation of temperament and the measurement of temperamental traits by objective, multivariate experimental approaches. As we saw from our opening chapter on the meaning of personality, these temperamental traits are concerned with *how* a person does what he does, his general style and tempo. It is these traits, source traits, that the factor analysis of personality has revealed through ratings, questionnaires and objective tests, which we have described in the last chapter. However it is possible to conceive of dynamic traits concerned with *why* a person does what he does and much of clinical psychology in the last generation was concerned with just this. Such traits would be related to individual differences of this kind: some people marry frequently, others not at all; some devote their lives to work, others are innocent of employment. Certainly there will be temperamental differences between these groups but, it would seem obvious, there must be motivational differences also.

This question of why is fundamental to a full understanding of human behaviour, although it may not be essential for practical psychological purposes. Thus sometimes it is sufficient to know that x is the case (e.g. that pressing the accelerator speeds up the car) without knowing why. However it is noteworthy even in this simple example that knowing why is helpful should something go wrong. Similarly, practical occupational and educational psychologists have been able to make useful predictions in the field of educational guidance and achievement using tests of temperament and ability only. For example, it is useful to know that the introverted student is likely to be more academically successful than the extraverted and we can use this relatively solid finding. However, we do not thereby know why the introverted student works harder, reads more and is less easily bored. If we did it might be possible to help the client who presents himself for counselling with work difficulties.

In any case, it must be noted that the predictions of behaviour based on personality and ability alone are far from perfect and thus there is every reason to hope that, could we add in dynamic motivational traits, we could improve prediction, a hope indeed fully born out by research (e.g. Cattell and Butcher, 1968). Indeed it could be argued that the success of much of the research into academic and occupational success where only temperament and ability have been measured is due to the fact that in our Western, achievement oriented, society motivation is relatively constant. Certainly some of the disparity in performance between the social classes could be due to such motivational differences, as many sociologists (e.g. Gordon, 1970) have argued, although without the evidence of reliable and valid measurement. The study of personality therefore clearly demands and embraces the study of motivation, and this kind of prediction at which we ultimately aim can be succinctly summarized by equation 9-1.

$$a_j = b_{ja}A_i + b_{jt}T_i + b_{ja}D_i \tag{9-1}$$

where the act, response or performance a_j for person i is a weighted combination of his ability traits, A, his temperament traits, T, his dynamic, motivational traits, D. The weights—behavioural indices, as we have called them above—will have to be experimentally found and, as the subscript j shows, will be peculiar to each act.

There is another interesting feature of motivation and this is that it affects our performance in ways that are often disconcerting. For example, many of us must have had the experience of being interviewed for jobs. If we do not really want the post we can often perform well at the interview answering questions easily and not making silly mistakes, but our performance when we really do want it can be much worse and so being strongly motivated can disrupt performance. Similarly, if a task demands great effort, poor motivation will adversely affect performance. This is particularly true of adults who in a research situation in which they have no interest or involvement may perform poorly on tests of ability or aptitude.

All these examples illustrate (what common-sense regards as obvious) that motivation is an important area of human psychology and that until we can understand the dynamics of human behaviour we cannot be said to understand human behaviour or personality at all. Just as, in our opening chapter, we justified the necessity for the introduction of the scientific method into the study of the temperamental side of personality because most current theories of temperament were literary, philosophical or pre-scientific, being based on clinical observation rather than precise measurement, so it is with the dynamics of personality.

PRE-SCIENTIFIC THEORIES OF MOTIVATION

Literary and philosophical theories of motivation are of little interest for the scientific study of personality although, of course, they are very numerous and sometimes fascinating in themselves. As Stafford-Clark (1963) points out, one of the more long lasting of these theories has been that of demonic possession which claims that much of the bizarre (indeed typically mad) behaviour of the schizophrenic is due to possession by the Devil. This theory, almost universal until the end of the 18th century, appears not yet to have died out in Great Britain since in the summer of 1974 in the trial of a person accused of criminal offences, which had been committed while he was apparently mad, a clergyman was brought forward who claimed to have exorcised his devil. However in the 19th century, especially in France, psychiatry began to advance under the influence of Charcot and Janet into the second clinical or pre-scientific stage and motivational theories of this type were then produced, and these together with later but allied theories, as regards scientific development, have dominated the field of motivation. Those who have discussed motivation include Adler, Bleuler, Jung, Freud, McDougall and Murray. More recently, apparently scientific theorists, ethologists such as Tinbergen and Lorenz, and Hull and Skinner have dealt with human motivation. Yet none of these has established that necessity of the scientific endeavour—a sound set of measuring instruments.

The same arguments that in the case of temperamental traits demonstrated the necessity, from the point of view of scientific study, for the use of multivariate statistics in general, in contrast to the classical univariate experiments of traditional experimental psychology, apply with respect to motivation. Many of the problems are similar, especially that of establishing what might be called the "motivational sphere" (equivalent to the "personality sphere"), i.e. the problem of knowing what variables to sample. This is where the various theories, even though they are founded upon insufficient evidence, might have proved helpful but this, unfortunately, is not really the case, partly because they are so diverse and partly because they are not conceptually precise.

Thus for example, Freud (1940) postulated, towards the end of his life, a two factor theory of motivation—man impelled by Eros and Thanatos, the life and death instincts. These are not amenable to the scientific test because it is not possible to refute them, to conceive of evidence that would disconfirm them. Furthermore the whole notion of instincts is of dubious value because of its inherent circularity. Thus to take aggression as an example, it is argued (e.g. Lorenz, 1966) that there must be an aggressive instinct because man is aggressive and the evidence for an aggressive instinct is aggression. In other words the evidence that led to the proposal of the instinct is also used to support it. Such circular arguments are obviously not very convincing. Indeed they can lead, as they virtually did in the case of Murray (1938) to the postulation of almost as many instincts as there are behaviours. McDougall (1932) also multiplied to some 15 "propensities", though several of these have stood up to factor analytic investigation. Jung's work (e.g. Jung, 1940) which claims that motivation wells from the racial or collective unconscious is as difficult as Freud's to put to the test and, as is the case with Thanatos and Eros, no tests that even purport to measure it have been developed. Adler (1927) on the other hand did propose as a basic human drive "the upward striving for superiority" and this has been measured by a number of investigators, notably McClelland (1961), work which we shall discuss later in this book. Murray (1938) who attempted to found what was virtually a new subject—personology—postulated 20 basic needs. In an important way his work differed from all that we have so far mentioned in that there was a considerable data base, of which the TAT is the most celebrated example, although many of the measures were highly subjective, needed great skill in interpretation and consumed huge amounts of time so that only small numbers of subjects could ever be studied using Murray's personological procedures. Nevertheless his work is an impressive beginning to the empirical study of personality which could prove a useful complement to the more rigorous, multivariate procedures advocated here. Actually these needs have been accepted by two test constructors Jackson (1967) and Edwards (1959). Despite this the scientific basis of Murray's work is not sufficient to use it as a foundation for the study of motivation nor is the questionnaire as used by Edwards and Jackson a truly suitable method for motivation assessment. The foundations of other theories as we have seen are manifestly unsatisfactory. Before we turn to an examination of the approach adopted by Cattell and his colleagues and to a study of their results, we should briefly discuss the views of experimental psychologists, whose attack on the problem of motivation is often wholly different.

MOTIVATION IN EXPERIMENTAL PSYCHOLOGY

To the operant conditioner the concept of motivation is virtually otiose. Thus for him the organism responds according to its past pattern of reinforcement.

The question therefore of why we do what we do involves the investigation of our schedules of reinforcement. If we manipulate these then we can manipulate behaviour. This is in essence the message (although only a part of it) of Skinner's work (e.g. Skinner, 1953). If in addition we take into account the work of the more Hullian learning theorists such as Dollard and Miller (1950), influenced by Pavlovian classical conditioning models, where we see that responses, i.e. behaviour, may become linked to stimuli far removed from those originally evoking them and that this classical conditioning process accounts for the dynamics of some behaviours, then it might be argued that we are wasting our time in studying motivation at all. Such an argument would maintain that the very term itself comes from an inappropriate analysis of the situation.

However, on closer examination it is evident that the Skinnerian reflexologist hides what we call motivation in an "incentive" commonly described environmentally, where we would look for needs in the animal itself. "Reinforcement" (the word "reward" would normally be better) implies instinctual drive, and one of the greatest of the learning theorists, Hull, clearly inserted drive and drive reduction in his model.

There are many problems in trying to integrate the vast number of experiments on rats in this reflexological framework, with human learning and motivation, as brought out by Cattell in *Personality and Learning Theory* (1976). The far more complex cognitive and emotional development of man is one of them, and another is the vague general use of "drive" by reflexologists compared to the progress made in discovering and measuring definite "ergs" in man, as will be described below. Furthermore, in the case of man as distinct from lower organisms it is by no means clear what events act as reinforcers partly because of the fact, so hated by reflexological psychologists, that men think and have feelings and are influenced by these.

Thus the study of motivation advantageously begins at this early stage of the scientific process with a study of the attitudes, feelings, thoughts etc that influence our behaviour, that act, in learning theory terms, as reinforcers. An example will clarify this issue. If a man has an image of himself as a fine scholar it is extremely reinforcing for his production of papers, if critics write that one of his latest creations is a notable contribution to a complex field. If, however, a colleague at work admires his hat it will be of no significance to his scholarly work nor in any other way unless he also has a self image as a well-dressed man. If this last is the case we can predict that he is likely to visit that hatter again, in other words we are able to account for, to say why, our scholar has gone to his hatter. Thus the study of motivation as a study of the important attitude structures influencing our behaviour in no way contradicts the learning theory analysis of motivation which renders the term redundant.

The ethologists (e.g. Tinbergen, 1953 and Lorenz, 1966) have attempted to argue that much animal behaviour can be understood in terms of responses released by sign stimuli—stimuli of especial significance to the particular organism. In addition they have invoked the concept of imprinting whereby at a critical period of development early in life (usually) certain behaviours are quickly learned and once learned are particularly difficult to eradicate. The most famous example is the duckling following its mother down to the water where the imprinting involves following the first moving object the duckling sees at a critical period after emerging from the egg. That comical sight of a row of ducklings waddling after a wellington-booted, pail-in-hand figure is now too well known to require further comment as an illustration of this phenomenon. However, phenomena such as these have not been demonstrated convincingly in man and in any case with the greater plasticity of behaviour in man due to his larger cortex it could well be the case that such imprinting could be wiped out by later conditioning, (See Slukin, 1974).

Physiological psychologists have also attempted to deal with motivation and Morgan (1943), for example, has developed a central (as distinct from a peripheral) theory of emotional activation and various activating, and inhibitory centres for discrete drives such as hunger, thirst and sleep have been allegedly found. For further details of the physiology readers must be referred elsewhere (e.g. Grossman, 1967) for in many ways the physiology of motivation is irrelevant to its psychology. It is clear that all our behaviours have physiological correlates but they are only correlates and are not identical with them. Thus to understand the psychology of memory involves our knowing the conditions, and factors influencing the acquisition and recall of different types of material. To know the physiology underlying this is simply irrelevant—indeed physiology and psychology are different universes of discourse.

From this brief general introductory discussion of motivation it is clear that, as was the case with the temperamental side of personality, the scientific study demands the use of multivariate methods of which at the present stage of the field factor analysis is by far the most useful, because it makes possible a discerning of *patterns*, and drives are, by their very nature, patterns. As we pointed out in our earliest discussion of factor analysis, a critical feature, especially of its exploratory use, is adequate sampling of the variables. In the case of temperamental traits, this was ensured, as far as possible, by the development of the semantic personality sphere. Thus our first point of examination must be of how well Cattell has sampled motivational variables.

THE MOTIVATIONAL SPHERE

The problem of trying to define the field of human motivation is that of knowing where to start. As we have seen, there is little agreement even among the most distinguished clinical theorists. Nevertheless most psychologists might be able to agree with McDougal in recognizing that there seem to be three aspects to motivated behaviour. The first is the tendency to attend spontaneously to some things rather than others. Thus for a young male audience even the best lecture on psychology would go unheard should Brigitte Bardot chance to enter the lecture theatre. Secondly, there tends to be a characteristic emotion specific to the drive and its action, as exemplified by fear, anger or sexual arousal. Finally the impulse is to a course of action which has a particular goal as its end, for example comforting a crying baby or pursuing a fleeing animal and eating it. If this is acceptable then a clear necessity for the scientific study of motivation is to establish how many drives there are. Only when this is done can we look at their specific goals and emotions.

Attitudes and their Measurement

Cattell (1957) has centred the exploration of motivation structures on the measurement of attitudes as the elemental "bricks". Thus the strength of an attitude is regarded as "the strength of a course of action, or tendency to a course of action, in response to a stimulus" (Cattell and Child, 1975). It is to be noted that this use of the word "attitude" differs considerably from its common use in sociology where attitudes are rather simply conceived as static opinions *for or against* objects, ideas or institutions; marriage to Negros, war and religion, being obvious examples. Furthermore, as we shall see, the measurement of attitudes involves the use of objective tests which we discussed in the last chapter and which therefore depend on far more than the mere verbalized opinions which form the basis of most attitude scales of the Likert and Thurstone type. The disadvantage of such verbal scales is not just that subjects may be lying but that there is no necessary correlations between words and action. Thus an employer can sincerely believe that he is not anti-semitic yet, somehow, it turns out that he never employs Jews. Since attitudes can colour our perception, should a Jew apply for a post he may be perceived as inferior to rivals—hence never appointed. Here then words and behaviour fail to correlate. On the other hand we may dislike Jews yet recognizing this as prejudice let it affect our behaviour as little as we can. Indeed from everyday observation it appears in the case of racial prejudice that some people overcompensate and favour the disadvantaged group more than they would if they did not perceive its members to be the possible victims of racial prejudice. These everyday examples illustrate the need in the measurement of attitude to use as many different types of observation as possible. Certainly verbal statements on their own are insufficient.

Given, then, the need to sample as wide a variety of behaviours as we can in attitude measurement, how should we set about the task? Cattell (1957) takes the view that attitudes can best be understood in the following way, a view endorsed in the more recent work of Cattell and Child (1975):

> In these circumstances (stimulus) I (organism) want (interest need) so much (of a certain intensity) to do this (specific goal, response) with that (relevant object).

I want to see a world ruled by reason, I want to be a great scientist, are two examples of attitudes fitting our analysis very accurately. Notice how this analysis embraces the nature of the course of action, the intensity of the interest in it and the object involved in it and is an amplification of the S-O-R model of some learning theorists because there are qualifying terms which take into account the magnitude and direction of the action.

Strength of Interest

With this model in mind we shall now look at the first problem of motivational measurement through the medium of interests and attitudes—strength of interest. Obviously two people can be interested in, say, cricket but to a markedly different degree. For example, the fanatic may watch every match his team plays, know the batting and bowling average of all players in the side and the number of times each has played for his country. Such a man probably has a fine cricket library, knows the records of Wisden by heart, and plays a little in the evening himself. He may perhaps perform some rather tedious but vital secretarial function without payment for the local club. On the other hand another man may describe himself as interested in cricket who watches the recorded highlights on the television sports news and skims the scores in his morning newspaper over breakfast. These illustrations show how strength of interest and motivation may be measured and how poverty stricken as a form of measurement is the typical Likert type attitude questionnaire where likes and dislikes are rated on a number of 5 point scales or even on a dichotomized yes/no basis. Thus our first subject will have a large store of information about cricket, there are likely to be definite physiological reactions to pictures of great cricketers which will leave the ignorant unaffected. It is highly likely that cricket stimuli will be misperceived or more easily learned by the lover than the non-interested subject, e.g. LDW may be misperceived as LBW and so on. The significance of maiden may be different.

By searching the literature for evidence of any relation between a psychological measurement and some criterion of motivation strength, a group at the University of Illinois (Horn, De Young, Miller, Radcliffe, Sweney, Cross and others) came up with some 68 expressions, from clinical, learning, perception and other areas of psychology—worthy of further investigation as objective measures of human motivations. These principles are set out in Table 9.1 taken from Cattell and Child (1975).

Examination of this table reveals that our cricket or base-ball enthusiast would be readily discriminated from his less interested subject. Thus preferences (1) would be suitable, a measure resembling the standard interest questionnaire, utilities choice (9) would also discriminate in that our subject spends unpaid time working for the club. Other variables in the list that would obviously be effective in this instance would be: 12–17, 28–30, 36, 42–47, 52–54 and 60.

TABLE 9.1

Some Principles of Motivation Measurement Applied to Constructing
Test Devices

With increase in interest in a course of action expect increase in:

1. **Preferences.** Readiness to admit preference for course of action.
2. **Autism:** misperception, distorted perception of objects, noises, etc., in accordance with interest (e.g. Bruner coin perception study).
3. **Autism:** misbelief. Distorted belief that facts favor course of action.
4. **Reasoning distortion:** means–ends. Readiness to argue that doubtfully effective means to goal are really effective.
5. **Reasoning distortion:** ends–means. Readiness to argue that ends will be easily reached by inapt means.
6. **Reasoning distortion:** inductive.
7. **Reasoning distortion:** deductive.
8. **Reasoning distortion:** eduction of relations in perception (e.g. analogies).
9. **Utilities choice.** Readiness to use land, labour, and capital for interest.
10. **Machiavelliism.** Willingness to use reprehensible means to achieve ends favoring interest.
11. **Fantasy choice.** Readiness to choose interest-related topic to read about, write about, or explain.
12. **Fantasy ruminations.** Time spent ruminating on interest-related material.
13. **Fantasy identification.** Prefer to be like individuals who favour course of action.
14. **Defensive reticence.** Low fluency in listing bad consequences of course of action.
15. **Defensive fluency.** Fluency in listing good consequences of course of action.
16. **Defensive fluency.** Fluency listing justifications for actions.
17. **Rationalization.** Readiness to interpret information in a way to make interest appear more respectable, etc., than it is.
18. **Naive projection.** Misperception of others as having one's own interests.
19. **True projection.** Misperception of others as exhibiting one's own reprehensible behaviour in connection with pursuit of interest.
20. **Id projection.** Misperception of others as having one's own primitive desire relating to interest.
21. **Superego projection.** Misperception of others as having one's own righteous beliefs relating to interest.
22. **Guilt sensitivity.** Expression of guilt feelings for non-participation in interest-related activities.
23. **Conflict involvement.** Time spent making decision under approach–approach conflict (both alternatives favour interest).
24. **Conflict involvement.** Time spent making decision under avoidance–avoidance conflict (both alternatives oppose interest).
25. **Threat reactivity:** psychogalvanic resistance drop when interest threatened.
26. **Threat reactivity:** increase cardiovascular output when interest threatened.
27. **Physiological involvement:** increase cardiovascular output when interest aroused (threatened or not).
28. **Physiological involvement:** finger temperature rise when interest aroused.
29. **Physiological involvement:** increase muscle tension when interest aroused.

(Continued)

Table 9.1—*cont.*

30. **Perceptual integration.** Organize unstructured material in accordance with interest.
31. **Perceptual closure.** Ability to see incomplete drawings as complete when material is related to interest.
32. **Selective perception.** Ease of finding interest-related material embedded in complex field.
33. **Sensory acuity.** Tendency to sense lights as brighter, sounds as louder, etc., when interest is aroused.
34. **Attentivity.** Resistance to distractive (lights, sounds, etc.) when attending to interest-related material.
35. **Spontaneous attention.** Involuntary movements with respect to interest-related stimuli (e.g. eye movements).
36. **Involvement.** Apparent speed with which time passes when occupied with interest.
37. **Persistence.** Continuation in work for interest in face of difficulty.
38. **Perseveration.** Maladaptive continuation with behaviour related to interest.
39. **Distractibility.** Inability to maintain attention when interest-related stimuli interfere.
40. **Retroactive inhibition** when interest-related task intervenes.
41. **Proactive inhibition** by interest-related task.
42. **Eagerness:** effort. Anticipation of expending much effort for course of action.
43. **Activity:** time. Time spent on course of action.
44. **Eagerness:** money. Anticipation of spending much money for course of action.
45. **Activity:** money. Money spent on course of action.
46. **Eagerness:** exploration. Readiness to undertake exploration to achieve interest-related ends.
47. **Impulsiveness:** decisions. Speed of decisions in favour of interest (low conflict).
48. **Impulsiveness:** agreements. Speed of agreeing with opinions favourable to interest.
49. **Decision strength.** Extremeness of certainty for position favouring course of action.
50. **Warm-up speed:** learning, Speed warming-up to learning task related to interest.
51. **Learning.** Speed learning interest-related material.
52. **Motor skills.** Apt performance to affect interest.
53. **Information.** Knowledge affecting and related to course of action.
54. **Resistance to extinction** of responses related to interest.
55. **Control.** Ability to co-ordinate activities in pursuit of interest.
56. **Availability:** fluency. Fluency in writing on cues related to course of action.
57. **Availability:** free association. Readiness to associate to interest-related material when not oriented by cue.
58. **Availability:** speed of free association. Number of associations when interest aroused.
59. **Availability:** oriented association. Readiness to associate interest-related material with given cue.

(Continued)

Table 9.1—*cont.*

---

60. **Availability:** memory. Free recall of interest-related material.
61. **Memory for rewards.** Immediate recall of reward associated with interest.
62. **Reminiscence.** Ward–Hovland effect. Increased recall over short interval of interest-related material.
63. **Reminiscence.** Ballard–Williams effect. Increased recall over long intervals of interest-related material.
64. **Zeigarnik recall.** Tendency to recall incompleted tasks associated with interest.
65. **Zeigarnik perseveration.** Readiness to return to incompleted task associated with interest.
66. **Defensive forgetfulness.** Inability to recall interest-related material if goal not achievable.
67. **Reflex facilitation.** Ease with which certain reflexes are evoked when interest aroused.
68. **Reflex inhibition.** Difficulty in evoking certain reflexes when interest aroused.

It has to be admitted that the evidence for the validity of these principles derived in the main from clinical psychology is not overwhelming, although there is some support from the results of factor analyzing the correlations between the measures—a procedure designed to investigate the problem of motivational strength. In the investigations which we are about to discuss, however, certain criterion variables which almost all would agree were indicative of high interest were included in the factor analysis to help identification of the factors, for example, life criterion scores of amount of time and money voluntarily spent on the interest. Before we discuss these results, the motivational factors emerging from the analysis, it will be helpful to examine a little more carefully the meaning of interest because in this way we shall be able to see that some of these measurement principles are indubitably valid. We must also mention briefly the importance of ipsative scoring so as to overcome some immediate objections to this approach to the measurement of motivation.

THE MEANING OF INTEREST

When we say that someone is interested in something this has to be inferred from his words and behaviour. Thus one piece of evidence, as the sociologists point out, are his claims of being interested. However we also infer it from behaviour as we saw in the case of the cricketer. Thus the child who spends his money voluntarily on Greek plays and his time in translating them into blank verse is said to be interested in Greek drama. Interest is simply a shorthand term for saying that he spends time, money and energy on the pursuit. To say a person is interested in or has an interest in anything has no other meaning than this. Consequently such variables as time and money spent and the like may be regarded as by definition valid. We do not have to demonstrate their validity as interest measures because they are, as it were, the interest itself. Thus if we can find factors loading high on these criterion variables then we can feel confident that they are interest or motivational factors. Before leaving this topic one further point remains. If these criterion measures are satisfactory why do we need to develop further motivational tests. First it is not easy to quantify accurately criterion measures of this kind. Furthermore there are in individual cases sources of error—some people may have little free time. In addition certainly for practical purposes such as vocational guidance where we may want to predict interest in the absence of criterion measures, criterion-saturated tests which allow quantification are highly desirable. One of the difficulties of using the amount of time spent voluntarily on an interest in estimating its strength, as is also the case with money and effort, turns on the meaning of voluntary. A family whose income is exactly sufficient to meet its essential needs (in contrast to Micawber's) can, by definition, spend nothing on interests of any sort. Rare though these cases may be in Western society this is by no means uncommon in India or Asia so that if we are interested in a full understanding of human motivation such national differences are important unwanted scources of variance in measurement. Even if we ignore cross-cultural studies, for the moment, as introducing too many problems of measurement in a field already difficult enough there are clearly similar large differences in any one culture. Thus if a millionaire spends £10,000 on his car, is he more interested in motoring than the engineering student who picks one up for £10 from a scrap heap? The solution to measurement problems of this kind lies in ipsative scoring which is used in most of Cattell's motivation tests.

To ipsatize the scores for any individual on a battery of tests requires us to treat each score as a deviation from *that subject's* mean. Thus at a stroke we eliminate many of the difficulties which we have discussed above. An example will make this clear. Suppose that we are using information as a measure of interest. Now it could well be that a highly intelligent and well informed person could score more highly on every information test than a person of moderate ability. Thus his cricket information score could be higher absolutely than his less intelligent rival but being uninterested in cricket expressed as a deviation from his mean this score would be low (for he would have scored higher on every other test). However, if our second subject's scores were ipsatized, his cricket score, since he was interested in cricket, would become a high score, thus accurately reflecting the difference in interest between himself and his more intelligent rival. In this way individual differences which would obscure motivation scores derived by these methods are eliminated. Incidentally, as we can see from this particular example, ipsatization would automatically eliminate the g factor of general ability (or more strictly, (Cattell, 1971) the g factors of fluid and crystallized ability) and differences of total motivation strength. It is, of course, equally effective with our examples of time and money since ipsatization automatically compensates for the total pool of money or time available and it could, therefore eventuate that our hypothetical student scores more highly than the millionaire, using money as the criterion.

RESULTS OF INVESTIGATIONS

Cattell (1957) reports a typical investigation into motivational strength which we shall scrutinize below. A sample of 374 adult males was administered a battery of objective T tests to tap major professional job attitudes, a respectable hobby or interest, a somewhat disreputable interest, an attitude with relatively strong unconscious roots and an attitude with a marked moral component. Not only did the objective tests contain those measures which we have previously suggested would be likely to be related to motivation—high level of information, perceptual skill, better memory for and attention to preferred material—but also physiological indices were used such as GSR, muscle tension, and blood pressure.

The ipsative scores were correlated and the correlation matrix was subjected to a rotated factor analysis. From this investigation 5 factors emerged which were tentatively identified and given Greek alphabetical names. Later investigations, as can be seen in the work of Cattell and Child (1975), have isolated a further two factors of motivational strength and all seven factors have been reliably identified in at least two investigations. The seven factors of motivational strength, primary motivational components, together with their descriptions are set out below.

I. *Alpha:* This factor is characterized by autism believing that one's desires are true and practicable (infantile omnipotence was the Freudian description). It loads on stated preferences, rapid decisions, fluency on cues, means and ends to desired goals and rationalization. It appears to be a component signifying determination to satisfy personal desires at the conscious level even when this is somewhat irrational. Cattell (1957) claims that "Clearly it represents a component of interest most nearly corresponding to the psychoanalytic concept of the id though we must be definite that we are redefining this as the conscious id". Indeed this factor is probably best regarded as an "I desire" component which is partly conscious and which has not been tested against reality. Although we shall be discussing the theoretical implications of these findings later, we should note here that Eysenck (1973) has objected to this factor being called an id factor on the grounds that the essential feature of the id was that it was unconscious and that since this is a partly conscious factor it is misleading to thus name it. Nevertheless, despite this, it does remain a fact that the general feel of the factor is indeed of the id when we remember that it was defined by Freud (1940) as "a cauldron of seething excitement. It is the core of our being within which the instincts operate and their sole endeavour is to seek satisfaction regardless of consequences, situation or logic."

II. *Beta:* this factor has been identified as a component of realized, integrated interest. The objective tests loading on this factor include high informational content relevant to the interest, perceptual skills and the capacity to learn in the apposite interest areas together with a regard for remote but realistic rewards. Cattell (1957) hypothesizes that the beta factor is one of interests acquired through habits and duty, fully conscious and integrated into the routine of daily life. Thus he argues that it corresponds closely to the Freudian concept of the ego—a view adhered to in the later work of Cattell and Child (1975). Even if we disregard for the moment the Freudian label we can see that factor beta is the strength of interest consciously and deliberately developed. This is the motivational strength factor that will influence our questionnaire replies to direct items about liking or disliking various tasks or occupations, as in the Strong or Kuder interest tests. The fact that there is more than one factor in strength of interests indicates the weaknesses of the older approach to interest measurement.

III. *Gamma:* this factor is harder to relate to psychoanalytic theory or any psychological theory than the other two factors we have so far considered. It loads on autism, fantasy, conscious preference for an activity, perseveration for a reward, and lack of information about the preferred activity. Cattell and Child (1975) argue that this factor has an "I ought to be interested" quality about it, which leads to a highly tentative identification of gamma with the superego. Actually this gamma factor was clear in some vocational interviewing that we undertook with a large sample of sixth-formers. Many of these claimed interests which they felt as intending university applicants they ought to have—intellectual and artistic interests for example. However any probing of these interests in terms of even elementary knowledge uncovered profound ignorance. Many a lover of Bach was convinced that he had written symphonies. Furthermore many of them claimed to be interested in jobs about which they knew nothing or had ideas so fantastic as to be literally wrong, most of these jobs being of high status although not necessarily lucrative, e.g. microbiologist or biochemist.

IV. *Delta:* this factor is almost entirely physiological in nature loading on blood pressure, PGR, and speed of decision making. This suggests that the autonomic response to stimuli of interest is measured by this factor. An example here would be the thrill running down the backbone or the goose pimples experienced by many people to certain musical passages or pictures. Cattell (1957) suggested that this factor could be the unconscious id.

V. *Epsilon:* this is a factor which seems to be related to conflict in that it loads on PGR, poorness of memory for given material and poorness of reminiscence. Clinical studies of word association have, since the time of Jung, indicated that poor memory of responses to such tests and large PGR indicates that the word is of emotional significance to the subjects, (indicative of complexes in the psychoanalytic jargon—sources of conflict below the level of awareness). It appears therefore that this epsilon factor could be an unconscious conflict factor.

The last two factors, *zeta* and *eta*, have appeared only in two studies so far and are less well defined and do not receive even tentative identification in Cattell and Child (1975). All that can be said about them is that zeta loads on decision strength and impulsiveness (in making decisions) while eta loads on fluency and persistence in a perceptual task.

These, then, are the seven factors of interest strength. The fact that there are seven means that our level of motivation or interest depends on our position on all these seven factors, particularly the first five which are the largest. Thus when we are estimating or predicting motivational strength we must have information about all these seven aspects just as, in the case of temperamental traits, it was necessary to measure all the primary factors. This finding is a great challenge to psychologists and an embarrassment to sociologists who have been measuring attitudes by a single score—a score comprehending predictively different kinds of motivation in a hodge-podge total. The challenge to psychologists is to develop theory to fit the undoubted fact of several components. Some initial light is thrown on them by the fact that they fall into two groups, as shown by second-order factoring. It will be remembered that in the ability and temperament fields correlated primary factors can be factor-analyzed to yield broader (but shallower) *second stratum factors*, e.g. anxiety across ego weakness, guilt proneness, ergic tension and other primaries. Similar methods have quickly revealed that three second-order factors emerge from the motivation primaries of which the first two are by far the most important. These are known as the *integrated* and *unintegrated* components. The integrated factor loads on the beta and gamma component (ego and superego), the unintegrated loads on alpha, delta and epsilon (conscious id, unconscious id and the conflict factor). These two factors tend, although precise rotation is difficult with so few points, to be negatively correlated. The meaning of these second order factors has not been fully worked out and there is a pressing need for more research into them. Nevertheless, as Cattell and Child (1975) point out, it is unlikely that they are ability factors because they have low correlations with ability tests. In addition the fact that the motivational tests are ipsatively scored makes the appearance of an ability factor of any kind highly unlikely. However we can tentatively think of these two second-order factors of interest strength as on the one hand, a component spontaneous and below the level of our awareness and on the other a component reflecting reality-oriented, information-based experience. Perhaps it is not too fanciful to see this factor analytic picture of motivation as resembling the psychoanalytic conflict of conscious *v.* unconscious.

Illustration of factors from real life

An illustration will clarify these factor analytic results. We shall restrict our discussion to the first three primary motivation factors—alpha, beta and gamma, id, ego and superego. Suppose that we have three surgeons, all of whom feel themselves highly interested in surgery, work long hours at the job and keep themselves up to date in the latest techniques (objective criteria of interest). For simple descriptive purposes they may be described as being equally interested in the profession. However the structure of their motivational strength could be entirely different. Thus in one the ego component may predominate: surgery enables him to live well, provide for his family, take his place in the community as a respected citizen and it gives him intellectual challenge. In addition he knows that it is a useful even vital job in society. In our second surgeon the superego component may predominate: his interest in surgery springs from the conviction that the most important thing in life is to alleviate human suffering, to apply modern scientific knowledge for the good of people. For such a man surgery is an obvious outlet. In our third example the id component may predominate: here the interest in surgery arises from a sadistic, aggressive pleasure in cutting up bodies, in the ghoulish side of surgery. Note that this id pleasure is not entirely unconscious and this surgeon would thoroughly enjoy his job. It is a fine illustration of the Freudian defence mechanism of sublimation. How much better for society it is that such drives are sublimated into surgery or, at a lower intellectual and social level, butchery, than that they are expressed in murder, as by Jack the Ripper. Of course such alpha and epsilon factor strength of interests can give us a fascination that seems inexplicable in our hobbies and interests. From these examples of an interest in surgery we can see that strength of interest is not the simple unifactorial phenomenon that simple measures hold it to be. However, it can be objected that, even were this analysis of interest strength correct, no practical or empirical consequences would follow different from those if interest strength were considered to be unifactorial.

Actually there are differences which our surgery example can well illustrate. Thus the ego surgeon (to shorten the phraseology) may well concentrate on those branches of surgery which are the most prestigious and lucrative (is not the birth passage said to be paved with gold?) and which enable him to live in the best part of the country. The superego on the other hand is likely to concentrate his work where he feels he is doing the most good. In Great Britain for example he is likely to be the kind of man who goes out into the developing countries and works for little material gain against hopeless odds. The id surgeon on the other hand is very different. In view of the Hippocratic oath these were the surgeons who performed surgical experiments without anaesthetics in German concentration camps. Some of the huge army of specialists in abortion could well be of this kind. In other words, if we know the structure of interest strength it may well be possible to predict what form the interest will take.

A difficulty with the work which we have discussed above lies in the problem of the validity and the practicability of the tests involved: many of the objective test devices need a laboratory to administer them. Since the understanding of the factors from experimental work both in personality and motivation derives from their practical application in clinical, educational and occupational psychology, this necessity for laboratory facilities has to some extent delayed research. Certainly it is a fair summary to say that far less is known about these factors of motivation than is the case with the temperamental traits.

However Cattell and his colleagues have developed three tests, the Motivational Analysis Test (MAT), a school version for use with adolescents (SMAT) and a version for younger children (CSMAT), which, using objective test devices of a pencil and paper type can be administered as easily and simply as a questionnaire. These tests yield measures of integrated and unintegrated interest tapping alpha, beta, gamma and epsilon components but excluding the physiological delta because it is difficult to measure. At this point in our discussion of motivation, however, we shall not discuss these tests further because they also measure *ergs* and *sentiments* and fit better into our later discussion of these concepts. However, it should be pointed out that recent research on changing motivation strength by experimental stimulation and deprivation shows that these objective motivation measures show change as would be expected under such changing circumstances.

Before we leave strength of interests to turn to a discussion of dynamic structure one point that we have mentioned parenthetically deserves attention. The analysis of interest strength into seven components means inevitably that unifactorial measures of interest cannot be satisfactory. However almost all the well known interest tests such as the Strong test and the Kuder are based on stated preferences, i.e. they measure mainly the alpha factor. Opinion surveys are also of this kind which no doubt accounts for their inaccuracy. Thus it was noticeable during the most recent British election that the opinion polls were more right than wrong (far better than chance) but were not able to gauge the actual swing in percentage terms. This fits well our claim that they were measuring but one factor affecting decisions. Nevertheless to be fair to the best interest tests, while they are theoretically weak, their construction by using criterion keying has ensured that in the practical situation they are effective. Thus by selecting items that discriminated successful from unsuccessful chemists for example a useful occupational scale was produced.

Summary
So far we have discussed Cattell's work in the area of motivational strength. Here we found that, contrary to the usual unifactorial sociological approach, motivational strength could only be fully understood as a multidimensional (7 dimensions, in fact) concept. These seven factors were extracted from the factor analysis of a battery of objective test devices. However, a more simple questionnaire form of objective test has been constructed (the MAT and its variants) suitable for practical as distinct from laboratory testing. Two second-order factors have also been extracted, integrated and unintegrated components of motivation.

DYNAMIC STRUCTURE MEASUREMENT

However apart from measuring interest strength, it is obvious that an important question in the study of motivation concerns the goals of human behaviour and the paths that lead to them—the dynamic structure. Indeed, the whole aim of putting the measurement of attitudes, the elements in our dynamic structure, upon a sound objective footing was to make possible for the first time a systematic, experimental investigation of the roots and ramifications of human dynamics. As we saw at the beginning of this chapter there has been a plethora of views based upon armchair speculation and clinical evidence among which there is little agreement. Consequently as was the case with the temperamental personality traits we cannot accept any of these theories unquestioningly as a basis of a scientific investigation of dynamic structure. Instead we have to sample as wide a variety of motivational variables as possible and hope to map out the field with the help of correlational methods.

The Dynamic Lattice

For example, if we suspect in a clinical patient that behaviour x and symptom y are operating as alternative expressions for the same drive, then the strength of their expressions should correlate negatively over time. And in correlations across people, assuming behaviour a, b, c and d are, say, manifestations of the sex drive, we should expect all to tend to be higher in the person with the stronger drive. Thus correlational, manipulative and factor analytic methods should be as capable of exposing underlying structures as they are in other domains e.g. abilities.

As a concept for describing the dynamic structure to be depicted, Cattell has proposed the *dynamic lattice*. This is the complex network of paths by which we attain our goals. To use this we have to establish what the goals and sub-goals are. A few examples will make this clear. A student may study law in order to become a lawyer, in order to earn money, in order to raise a family, in order to play a part in the community, etc, etc. Note that there comes a point in a sequence of this type when we can go no further, when there seems no reason over and above the one we have proposed. These ultimate or final goals are called by Cattell *ergs*, which, as we shall see, are roughly equivalent to the drives and instincts of former theories but, unlike those older and more vague concepts, ergs can be operationally defined by their replicable factor loadings and thus become useful scientific concepts. The dynamic lattice is therefore a flow chart of nearer and more remote dynamic goals. It must be noted also that these are not simply long chains of sub-goals and goals. Each sub-goal can serve more than one ergic goal. Thus we might go to a film to satisfy a large number of different goals and sub-goals. For example we go to relax in order to work better the next day, in order to earn money, and we enter the chain that we mentioned before. However we also go in order perhaps to please our spouse, in order to satisfy our need for sex or our need for security. We may also go in order to learn about the content of the film and so on. In other words the dynamic lattice seeks to untangle the complexity of motives that underlie all our attitudes and behaviour.

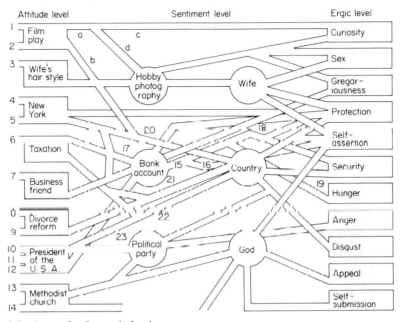

Fig. 9.1   Part of a dynamic lattice.

In the past the unravelling of the dynamic lattice relied on acute observation and clinical interview. For example a sudden increase in church going by a young girl is often regarded as motivated more by feeling for the vicar or one of the choir boys than religious awe, a hypothesis that may be easily checked by suggesting that she attend another church. In the more professional methods of the consulting room the clinical interview where we ask probing questions about interests may be used or the free association technique of psychoanalysis or even hypnosis. Psychoanalysis indeed is essentially concerned with the unravelling of the dynamic lattice. Its theories suggest that much of our motivation is unknown to us (unconscious) and they have attempted to specify the nature of this motivation. However, as this description makes clear, the fact that some of our motives are unconscious makes the value of clinical methodology uncertain. Thus what the analyst is forced to do is to infer what the dynamic lattice is in any particular person and there can be no way of substantiating these inferences. In addition there is the related problem of knowing how far back we should go in the search for goals. Thus if we finally trace back the chain of reasons to the need for food, we can go no further since there is a biological imperative to eat—strictly speaking, the alleviation of hunger is an ergic goal—existing in the constitution of the organism. However if a subject replies that he works as a chemist because he enjoys it he may refuse to go further. Subjectively this may be a sufficient reason. If he is asked why he enjoys it this may seem to him a meaningless question because he just does. Here the interview technique is exhausted. The psychoanalytic free-association could doubtless provide an inferred deeper goal accounting for this enjoyment. Certainly, intuitively, to posit a basic pleasure in chemistry erg is not convincing and we can argue that there must be some further underlying goal. Nevertheless, as we shall see some ultimate goals (sentiments rather than goals) are culturally derived yet still function as basic drives—career sentiment is an example of this. All this discussion illustrates the need for a method of investigating the dynamic lattice that goes further than interviews but is less inferential than free association.

It follows therefore that what we do in the study of motivation is to factor analyze a wide array of human interests. Thus we may measure a sample of forty attitudes among a representative sample of 200–300 subjects. If the correlations among these attitudes are subjected to factor analysis the resulting factors should represent the distant goals, i.e. ergs which account for these attitudes. For example if sexual drive or the sex erg is facilitated by going to the cinema, wearing attractive clothes and liking dancing then those in whom the sex erg is high should enjoy all these pursuits. Thus there will be correlations between these interests which will be accounted for by a sex erg factor. There is another interesting hypothesis which has not been fully researched as yet and which does not seem supported by the evidence but which needs careful consideration. It could be the case that each of these three activities on its own would satisfy the erg so that there would not be a positive correlation between these variables but a negative one. This would complicate the factor analytic solution, requiring the superimposing of an environmental circumstantial (alternative substitutes) factor upon the primary ergic tension factor, but, as we have said this does not seem to be the case. Thus the resulting factors should indicate what are the goals underlying interests and attitudes.

Before we examine the resulting motivational factors one important distinction has to be drawn. Factor analyzing the interests of a large sample of people (R technique) reveals the dynamic lattice *most common in our culture*. Although this is valuable to know it is necessarily different from the dynamic lattice within any one individual. If we wish to understand fully the motivation and behaviour of one person as we frequently do in the practical application of psychology in the clinic or in occupational guidance then we must unravel his particular dynamic lattice by repeated measurements of his attitudes and interests followed by the appropriate P factor analysis (see p. 21). Fortunately it has been shown by Cattell and Cross (1952) that the ergic factors obtained by P technique are the same as those obtained by the R technique involved in the study of subjects. Had this not been the case the logical problems involved in trying to reconcile two different sets of factors, inter- and intra-individual, would have set back for some time the study of the dynamic structure of motivation by factor analysis.

DYNAMIC STRUCTURE FACTORS: ERGS AND SENTIMENTS

Cattell (1957) and Cattell and Child (1975) both argue that the results of these factor analyses which we set out below are in broad agreement with the findings of ethologists with higher mammals, e.g. Lorenz (1966) and Tinbergen (1951) and with the early speculations of McDougall (1908), a result which would be of no surprise to Darwin at least. Our description of the ergs and sentiments shows those attitudes that load on the factor. Each attitude is expressed by a phrase which, however, is only a shorthand expression of it. This phrase is *not* an item from a questionnaire purportedly tapping the attitude. As we have made clear, all these factors are derived from objective (T data) tests, although some of these as in the MAT and SMAT are of the pencil and paper variety. The ergs and sentiments together with their descriptions are set out below and to aid interpretation we also set out Cattell's formal definition of ergs and sentiments. An erg is defined (Cattell, 1957) as "an innate reactive tendency, the behaviours of which are directed towards and cease at a particular consummatory goal activity." This definition makes it clear that it would be likely that the ergs would resemble the basic drives of mammals as described in zoology. Over and above this objective evidence for the proper number and nature of human drives the multivariate experimental approach has turned up a number of factor patterns which obviously belong to a different class. Whereas the attitudes clustering in ergs are different social approaches to the same consummatory "instinctual" goal, those in the new pattern may have different emotional "instinctual" qualities but all converge on one social goal, e.g. on home and family, religious organization, sports, careers. These have been called sentiments defined by Cattell and Child (1975) as "dynamic structures visible as common reaction patterns to persons, objects or social institutions and upon which all people seem to have some degree of endowment." They tend to show up in the dynamic lattice as intermediate sub-goals, between initial attitudes and final goals.

Before we go on to consider the relationship between these ergs and sentiments there are some important points that need to be made, as a background to our discussion. First, the fact that there is a limited number of ergs and sentiments points to obvious weaknesses in the chief earlier theoretical formulations of motives which we briefly discussed above. Thus if we followed McDougall or Murray there should be many more factors than have in fact appeared. Freudians, on the other hand, would have expected decidedly fewer than occur in our list and there should have been a primacy of the

TABLE 9.2

Ergs and Sentiments: Descriptions

Ergs	Attitude
Fear	I want my country to get more protection against the terror of the atom bomb
Sex	I want to fall in love with a beautiful woman
Gregariousness	I like to take an active part in sport and athletics
Parental Protectiveness	I want to help the distressed wherever they are
Exploration	I like to read books, newspapers and magazines
Self-assertion	I want to be smartly dressed with a personal appearance that commands attention
Narcism	I want to do a lot of smoking
Pugnacity	I want to destroy my country's enemies

Sentiments	Attitude
Religious	I want to feel that I am in touch with God or some principle in the universe that gives meaning and help in my struggles
Profession (Air Force)	I want to make my career (in the Air Force)
Sports	I like to watch and talk about athletic events
Self	I want to control impulses and mental processes
Superego	To satisfy sense of duty to church
Sweetheart	To bring gifts to sweetheart
Mechanical Interest	I enjoy a good car or motor-cycle for its own sake

sexual factor. Thus as regards numbers of drives it appears that no theorist was correct. However, some of the factor descriptions are more in line with theory. Thus the sexual erg is defined in the accepted manner, "I want to satisfy my sexual needs", being a high loading description. However the loadings of smoking drinking and music on this erg are impressive support for the Freudian concept of pregenital psychosexuality (in this case oral erotism (Freud, 1905)) and sublimation since aesthetic interests are held in psychoanalysis to be sublimated sexuality. However it must be pointed out that these data can be more simply explained than by psychoanalytic theory since it is the case that much sexual activity, especially among the young (the subjects of many of these motivation studies), takes place in an atmosphere of drinking and smoking and visits to the theatre and opera house are an integral part of dating for many students. Table 9.3 illustrates the relation of this factor analytic approach to motivation to the more theoretical traditional approach by setting out a full list of ergs and sentiments.

TABLE 9.3

Hypothesized List of Human Ergs

Goal title	Emotion	Status of evidence
Food-seeking	Hunger	
Mating	Sex	
Gregariousness	Loneliness	
Parental	Pity	
Exploration	Curiosity	Replicated factor; measurement
Escape to security	Fear	battery exists
Self-assertion	Pride	
Narcistic sex	Sensuousness	
Pugnacity	Anger	
Acquisitiveness	Greed	
Appeal	Despair	
Rest-seeking	Sleepiness	Factor, but of uncertain
Constructiveness	Creativity	independence
Self-abasement	Humility	
Disgust	Disgust	Factor absent for lack of
Laughter	Amusement	markers

Hypothesized List of Human Sentiments

S_1 *Profession*
S_2 *Parental family, home*
S_3 *Wife, sweetheart*
S_4 *The self-sentiment.* Physical and psychological self
S_5 *Superego*
S_6 *Religion.* This has emphasis on doctrine and practice, on high social and low esthetic values
S_7 *Sports and fitness.* Games, physical activity, hunting, military activity
S_8 *Mechanical interests*
S_9 *Scientific interests.* High theoretical, low political; math.
S_{10} *Business–economic.* Money administrative
S_{11} *Clerical interests*
S_{12} *Esthetic expressions*
S_{13} *Esthetic–literary appreciation.* Drama
S_{14} *Outdoor–manual.* Rural, nature-loving, gardening, averse to business and "cerebration"

S_{15} *Theoretical–logical.* Thinking, precision
S_{16} *Philosophical–historical.* Language, civics, social–cultural, esthetic rather than economic
S_{17} Patriotic–political
S_{18} *Sedentary–social games.* Diversion, play club and pub sociability; cards
S_{19} *Travel–geography.* Possibly Guilford's autism here
S_{20} *Education–school attachment*
S_{21} *Physical–home-decoration–furnishing*
S_{22} *Household–cooking*
S_{23} *News–communication.* Newspaper, radio, TV
S_{24} Clothes, self-adornment
S_{25} Animal pets
S_{26} Alcohol
S_{27} Hobbies not already specified

A glance at this full list reveals further interesting problems with respect to pugnacity which did not appear in the earliest factor analyses. This could be because aggression is a response to frustration rather than a source of energy in itself, as suggested by Dollard *et al.* (1939). Further studies, however, revealed that pugnacity, when the variables were increased, tended to fall on the same factor as fear and self assertion. This again could be explained by assuming that the repression once applied in Victorian Europe to sex now restrained aggression. However yet further studies (e.g. Horn, 1966) have produced a separate pugnacity factor. Thus it can be seen that pugnacity demands much further research although Cattell and Child (1975) hazard that it is a factor of small power which is parasitic on other drives for its energy.

These authors also point out that so far no factor resembling the territorial imperative (territory is important in understanding bird behaviour (e.g. Lack, 1943)) has so far emerged. It may be that one will be found as further studies are undertaken since it must be remembered that Cattell has not been able to sample the motivational sphere with the same thoroughness that he achieved with the personality sphere so that we cannot call the present list of ergs and sentiments definitive. Again it could be, and this seems a highly likely possibility, the case that in human beings the rather simple territorial imperative has become transformed into the infinitely more subtle and complex factor of self-assertion. In our fuller list in Table 9.3 the presence of a secondary sex factor Narcism, a factor of auto-erotic self directed sexuality or sensuality, is in full accord with Freudian theory which postulates just such an infantile narcissism from which most people largely but not entirely emerge. Such an erg we should postulate would be high among actors and entertainers perhaps indeed politicians. There is too a high negative correlation between this factor and superego which confirms Freudian theory since it would be the case that the more infantile aspects of sexuality would be sources of shame and guilt.

This list of ergs and sentiments while, as we have seen, not fitting with any precision the theoretical claims of any one worker certainly gives some kind of general support. Thus, as McDougall supposed, there are human dynamic structures which resemble those observed in lower organisms although there are rather fewer than would be expected from McDougall's writings. On the other hand Freud underestimated the number of human drives although his observations of the sex drive appear to have been shrewd. Nevertheless just because there is a similarity between these operationally defined factors and the speculative lists, we must not ignore the question as to whether we are talking about the same things. We have noted before (see p. 164) that an instinct was held to have three parts: the innate tendency to perceive certain objects as more significant than others, the innate tendency to experience emotion in relation to these perceptions and the conative impulse to perform certain acts rather than others in relation to these objects. It has to be admitted that up to the present none of these three steps has been demonstrated in connection with these ergs.

RELATION OF ERGS AND SENTIMENTS

As we have seen in the factor analyses of ergs and sentiments, career, family and home, wife or sweetheart, self-sentiment superego and religion are the most important sentiments and these appear in the MAT. Nevertheless Cattell and Child (1975) hypothesize that there are many more and they list from a study of the literature no less than 27. Many of these are simply equivalent to the interest categories of many interest tests e.g. the Brook Reaction Test (Heim *et al.*, 1969). Thus we find sport, mechanical interest, business clerical interest, outdoor manual interests, etc, all categories in the Strong and the Kuder tests. The relation between the basic biological goals, the ergs, and the culturally given sub-goals, the sentiments seems, from the factor loadings on the various attitudes to be one that is relatively unsystematic. Thus in our culture at least several sentiments are subsidiated to one erg and several ergs to one sentiment. Thus assertiveness may be expressed through self-sentiment, superego, career and parental home sentiments whereas career can express assertiveness, narcism, sex and security.

An important point which has not been extensively researched and on which well-checked data cannot be presented in either the manual to the MAT test (Cattell *et al.*, 1970) or Cattell and Child (1975) are the correlations between the ergs and sentiments and the higher-order factor structure. Cattell (1957) contains some information but gives little detail. Nevertheless it is worth noting that among sentiments all correlations with self, career and religion are positive and substantial a finding which presumably reflects the integration of citizenship, career and religion in the American culture. Among ergs, sex correlates negatively with narcism and fear. The inverse relation between sex and narcism supports the psychoanalytic claims about object libido investment and narcistic regression. As we have mentioned there are slight relationships between ergs and sentiments reflecting the fact that sentiments allow ergic expression. However even more interesting than these correlations are, of course the factors that account for them and these we shall now briefly discuss. These are second-order factors.

The only source for this (Cattell, 1957) consists of second-order analysis of the correlations between the primary motivation factors, the correlations being the mean values from three investigations. Although a clear simple structure was reached we have to be careful in interpreting the factors until they have been replicated and until their identification has been put to the test by other than factor-analytic methods. Factor 1, the largest of the six secondary motivation factors, contrasts fear, narcism, self and religious sentiment with sex and self assertion. It looks like a factor of ergic inhibition *v.* ergic expression. Whether this is of a cultural origin or whether it resembles the psychoanalytic regression from object love to narcissistic love (through fear) remains to be decided by further work. Factor 2 is of less interest contrasting sports and mechanical interests, which presumably simply reflects the empirical fact that in our culture people tend to like one or the other. Factor 3 defies explanation in that it combines narcism and the protectiveness erg, factor 4 seems related to career and the ergs expressed via this sentiment, while factor 5 contrasts gregariousness and rest seeking with curiosity and self assertion. Finally factor 6 relates fear with self sentiment. Cattell (1957) has argued that factors 2, 4 and 6 (perhaps even 1) would admit of explanation in terms of dynamics while 3, 5 and 1 suggest a temperament factor determining motivational expression. However much further research into the higher-order structure of ergs and sentiments combined with investigation of the factors in experimental studies needs to be done before we can raise the discussion beyond the bounds of speculation.

In the next chapter we shall turn to the examination of the meaning of the largest dynamic factors in the MAT and look at the situations which affect scores on these factors. Findings will also be related to other work in this area.

SUMMARY

1. The distinction between dynamics and temperament was discussed.
2. Pre-scientific theories of motivation which were largely clinical were examined and the attempts by experimental psychology to deal with motivation were scrutinized.
3. It was pointed out how attitudes held the key to motivational strength and these were used as the basis for motivation measurement by objective tests.
4. The meaning of "interest" in behavioural terms was explicated and the principles of objective motivation testing were set out.
5. The motivational strength factors were described.
6. The dynamic structure was then examined and the dynamic lattice was described.
7. Ergs and sentiments were defined and a list of those discovered was given.
8. Finally the relation of ergs and sentiments was set out.

Chapter 10

The Nature and Criterion Relations of Dynamic Structure Factors

PRACTICAL TESTS OF ERGS AND SENTIMENTS

In this chapter we propose to look more closely at practical aspects of motivation strength measurement, both because this will enrich the description of theoretical development as such in the last chapter, and because that development has led to steps important to the practical psychologist. The step most useful to practical psychology and to research has been the actual construction of motivation strength measuring devices in standard form for the principal ergs and sentiments of practical importance. Although ergic tension levels and sentiment strengths are measurable, admittedly as yet relatively crudely, by these devices, they need continuous improvement. Incidentally, one problem is that, by comparison with ability and temperament tests, there is much dependence in interest tests on the local and current cultural matrix. Thus, for example, in translation of measures for a given erg or sentiment more adaptation and more trial and error of item construction and validation are necessary than in older tests. The concept of, say, a sex erg or sentiment to career is as international as any other scientific conception, but the means by which it is recognized in the given culture may be local.

 The testing of dynamic structure strengths by objective methods (rather than verbal self-appraisal as in the Kuder, the Strong and many sociological attitude scales) has so far developed only three instruments: the Motivational

Analysis Test (MAT), Cattell *et al.* (1970) and a high school version, the School Motivation Analysis Test, (SMAT) as well as a test suitable for yet younger children, the CSMAT. In standard form they are group tests which employ four types of validated objective test device: autism, projection, word association and information. Three more tests are available if individual administration is possible; reaction time, galvanic skin response and systolic blood pressure. The MAT measures the strength of the ten largest dynamic factors (5 ergs and 5 sentiments): sex, assertiveness, fear, narcism and pugnacity (all ergs) and self-concept, career, sweetheart-spouse and home-parental sentiments. In addition total strength of interest may be measured using both the integrated and unintegrated components score. It should be noted that an attempt is being made by Sweney to measure, in a new test, the vocational interests measure, those sentiments which in our previous chapter we argued resembled the standard interests of the typical vocational guidance test. However little work has as yet been carried out with this VIM and we shall not discuss it further. To illustrate the ingenuity of the MAT we set out examples of the sub-tests below.

TABLE 10.1

Example of Items from MAT (Motivational Analysis Test)

	Autism
Self-assertion:	What percentage of people feel that a person's status is properly shown by his appearance and that "clothes make the man or woman"?

80%	50%	20%	0
3	2	1	0

Fear:	The money spent by cities to protect their citizens from atomic attack has gone up in ten years by:

20%	50%	100%	200%
0	1	2	3

Utilities

More research money should be spent on:

Self-assertion:	(a) Dressing the nation in smarter styles and new fabrics.
	(b) Finding cures for radiation sickness.

More newspaper articles should stress:

Super-ego:	(a) Self-control in facing sexual distractions.
Self-sentiment:	(b) Gaining happiness by being socially useful.

Information

A stoic is:

(a) a person who seeks pleasures of a physical nature.
(b) a basic coin of Ethiopia.
(c) *a person not affected by passions.*
(d) a small haystack in a field.   SELF-ASSERTION*

(Continued)

Table 10.1—*cont*

Which of the following has the highest reputation as a man of honesty and principle?

(a) Talleyrand
(b) Charlie Chaplin
(c) Theodore Roosevelt
(d) *Woodrow Wilson*   SUPER-EGO

Paired Words

Hot ⟨cross (*Super-ego*) / lips (*Sex*)   Country ⟨club (*Self-assertion*) / cottage (*Home*)

Autism

Self-sentiment: How many people feel it is more important to be honest than popular?

100%	80%	60%	40%	20%
4	3	2	1	0

Self-assertion: How many people would like to be head of the government?

90%	70%	50%	30%	10%
4	3	2	1	0

Information

What people think of you is called your:

(a) *reputation*
(b) experience
(c) disposition
(d) ambition   SELF-SENTIMENT

Which official is responsible for the accuracy of the financial report?

(a) President
(b) Vice-President
(c) Secretary
(d) *Treasurer*   SELF-ASSERTION

Paired Words

STUDENT ⟨body (*Self-assertion*) / learn (*Curiosity*)   BOOK ⟨Bank (*Acquisition*) / Bible (*Religious sentiment*)

Memory

Subject looks at this list for several seconds:		Then subject turns page and tries to pick previous words from this list:	
Bank	(*Acquisition*)	Defend	Most
Rest	(*Sensuality*)	Gloomy	Invitation
Invitation	(*Self-sentiment*)	Rest	Outline
Unselfish	(*Super-ego*)	Conceit	Century
Defend	(*Patriotism*)	Date	Unselfish
		Bank	Church

---

* (The categories presented in capitals are, of course, not printed on the test itself.)

Examination of Table 10.1 shows that, as is the case with objective tests, there is little *face* validity to these objective measures. Indeed face validity is avoided because it facilitates faking. It therefore becomes important to scrutinize the evidence for the validity of these factors. Thus operationally this question becomes one concerning the identification of the factors. Various kinds of validity coefficient can be obtained. A concurrent validity study would utilize correlations between the factors and some other measure of interest. However since we can have little confidence in other motivation measures this would not be convincing. A concrete validity study would, for example, attempt to predict some present or future criterion behaviour on the basis of MAT scores. However, it is obvious to readers that the establishment of such a criterion is no easy task. Cattell *et al.* (1970) in the test handbook rely on concept validity where the MAT factor scores are correlated with the factor scores obtained from the original construction study of the particular erg or sentiment. This, of course, means that we have to scrutinize the validity of these original studies. Now, as was pointed out in the last chapter, from the meaning of the word "interest" these factors are assured of some validity because criterion measures were used such as time or money spent on the particular interest.

Nevertheless when we scrutinize the best summaries of these original investigations (Cattell *et al.*, 1962 and Cattell and Horn, 1963) it becomes clear that the validity of these factors turns first on the highly replicable factor structure in the various studies of these ergs and sentiments defined by the descriptive loadings that we have discussed in the last chapter. What was at first lacking was any external source of validation. For example if we found deviant sex erg scores among sexual criminals or high sweetheart spouse sentiment among the newly married this could be regarded as external evidence for validity. This is a desirable feature for any dynamic test in that if we factored a battery of intelligence tests we would get replicable factor structures and patterns although they would not be motivational factors. Although the MAT, SMAT and CSMAT have been mostly available for less than a decade, there are already strategically chosen experiments showing that these ergic tensions and sentiment measures behave as would be expected in relation to concrete criteria. For example, Adelson (1952) showed that in subjects kept without water for two days the various perceptual and word association measures change as would be expected. Similarly, Cattell, Pawlik and De Young (1972) found that women students fasting for two days showed significant changes on a battery similar to the MAT designed to measure ergic tension on hunger. The theory that U and I components might change differently in response to stimulation and deprivation was tried (Cattell, Kawash and De Young 1972) on the sex erg, measured by the MAT. Significant change in young married males occurred after exposure to pornographic films, and in relation to the diary recording sexual relations. Although these experiments on the objective device measures in the MAT are new, there is evidence that as far as ergic tension levels are concerned they relate to concrete life criteria as theory would require.

Some of the studies of the MAT among different occupational groups also have a bearing on the validity of the ergs, and particularly the sentiments measured in that test. Thus Noty (in some unpublished research quoted by Cattell and Child, 1975) has examined the MAT score of high executives. It is interesting to note that contrary to expectation their career sentiment is only average although for those lower down the ladder it is higher. Doctors are higher on narcism than the general population and on self-sentiment, almost certainly the need achievement studied by McClelland and his colleagues (McClelland, 1961), two findings well in accord with the popular picture of the doctor. Similarly the low assertiveness and self senti-ment of the unemployed compared with the employed suits the nature of the variables. All these results are fully discussed in chapter 15 on industrial psychology. Here they are mentioned because they are modest support for the validity of the MAT.

Our discussion of the validity of ergs and sentiments has centered so far upon group scores yet, as was made clear in the previous chapter, the ergic pattern and dynamic structure of individuals is perhaps of greater significance for the validity of these variables. Thus with one individual we can study the impact of situations and events upon erg and sentiment scores in a way that is impossible with groups. For example, for one individual narcism may be sated by fine clothes, for another food may fulfil this function. Fortunately, two such individual case studies of ergs and sentiments exist and these will be discussed below.

ENVIRONMENTAL FACTORS INFLUENCING ERG AND SENTIMENT SCORES

The first of these investigations was that of Cattell and Cross (1952) who used objective test devices of the laboratory type to measure every day over an eighty day period 21 attitudes in one young male subject. In addition a diary and a clinical record were kept. It was therefore possible to plot the rise and fall of ergs and sentiments over this period and relate them to diary events. This eighty days was a particularly interesting time because the subject was rehearsing an important part in a play and was under pressure from the university to attend courses and from home to attend to science rather than drama. In view of this we should pay tribute to the nobility of the subject in enduring a battery of daily testing although we must stress that the tests were objective and hence not such as daily repetition would blunt. The results of this study can be easily summarized: there is a most impressive and clear relation between the rise and fall of ergs and sentiments over this period and the feelings of the subject as well as the actual life events. A few examples will make this clear.

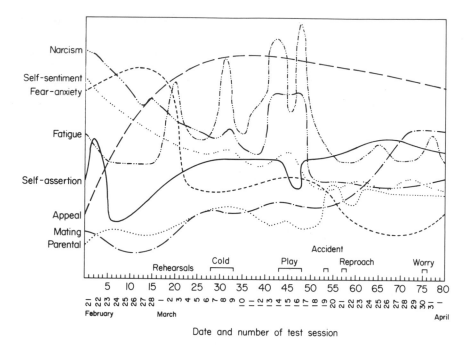

Fig. 10.1 Fluctuations in ergic tension over time.

A serious accident to his father caused the protective erg to rise sharply. A rise in the sex erg is connected with an increase in dating after the play was finished. The critical nights of the performance of the play show clear disturbances—a great rise in narcism, a slight rise in self-sentiment and a sharp relapse and recovery of the self-assertive erg. Evidence such as this is powerful support for the validity of the ergs and sentiments as measured by these laboratory objective test devices. Although factorial validity is important before we can feel confident that the factors do correspond to our non-factorial concepts (other than by name alone) such external validatory evidence is essential. However we must be clear that one case study on its own cannot prove the validity of these scales. Thus there is a very high correlation in intelligence between pairs of identical twins reared together—beyond 0.9,— which in view of the reliabilities of the tests is about as high as it could well be. However Hudson (1966) quotes an example of a pair of identical twins who differed in I.Q. by more than the standard deviation of the test, as if this individual case threw doubt on the genetic hypothesis of the origins of intelligence based upon the numerous twin studies of which Burt's is a fine example (Burt, 1966) and the more sophisticated MAVA studies of Cattell and his colleagues (Cattell, 1971). Of course there is one important difference between the example from Cattell and Cross (1952) and that of Hudson (1966) in that Hudson's example is contrary to all the other evidence whereas there is little other evidence concerning ergs and sentiments and none of it is contrary. Nevertheless we must be aware that case studies can be misleading. What is needed therefore is a plethora of such case studies. If all pointed the same way they would then constitute proof of validity. Unfortunately, however, the practical difficulties of repeated testing have ensured that the number of such investigations is not large. This is not only due to the psychologist's difficulties of repeated testing but in addition it is a severe strain on subjects.

The second investigation bearing on the validity of ergs and sentiments which utilized the individual case is that of Kline and Grindley (1974). This study differed from that of Cattell and Cross (1952) in that it was of shorter duration, being spread over the month of February. More importantly it used the MAT test which was completed every day by our young female subject just before going to bed: a detailed diary of thoughts and feelings that was confidential to the authors was also completed. One of the valuable aspects of this investigation lies in the fact that it examines the validity of the MAT which is the instrument used in the practical setting. Thus it is one thing to demonstrate that the complex objective test devices are valid and quite another to do so with the relatively simple and brief MAT. One obvious problem concerns the fact that the subject had to complete the same questionnaire on 28 occasions. Surely it could be argued that this would destroy the validity of the test. Would not, for example, the subject simply remember what she had put the night before? Certainly it was an aversive task and about half-way through the session we find several diary entries recording extreme boredom with the whole research especially the tests.

Yet another difficulty with this research design is to be found in possible contamination between the diary and the test results. To avoid this none of the tests was scored until the whole monthly session of testing was completed. Since the MAT is objective it is not easy without having scored the test to estimate one's score on the variables and the subject knew nothing about the test at the time. Thus although this investigation is not such as can yield clear proof of the validity of the test it nevertheless has an important bearing on it. Certainly it is possible that the results could be so clear that there could be no reasonable doubt of the relation of the scores to the diary events.

The first point worthy of note about the results was that with all variables other than career, which was almost constant during the month, there was a considerable fluctuation of scores—as evidenced by the large S.D.'s. Even granted that our subject was unusually volatile, it is clear that any one measure of the ergs and sentiments of this subject would have been highly unreliable. This finding, if replicated in other cases, implies that in applying the MAT we should always obtain more than one set of scores. It was also noteworthy that even the sentiments showed considerable fluctuation even if not so great, as in the case of the ergs.

On account of this fluctuation we attempted to relate the peaks and troughs of each one to the diary record. Clearly we cannot go into the details of each erg and the accompanying diary events. Nevertheless a few examples will show that there was unequivocal support in the case of this subject for the validity of the MAT. Thus during one weekend the fear erg was both extremely high and at the lowest point during the month. The diary revealed that at this time our subject was "really distressed" about driving an unsafe car to Bath. The fear erg dropped on her safe return to Exeter. The subject reports that driving does indeed frighten her, partly because she had been involved in a serious accident some time before the study began. Since the goal of the fear erg is defined by Cattell (1957) as "avoidance of illness, accident . . . and death" we can see that the fear erg had strong support for its validity.

The mating erg was high for this subject throughout the month and we do indeed find sexual desire expressed in the diary. Thus on day 10 the subject was longing for a wild affair and on day 12 felt her libido to be high, and was planning a seduction. On the day that the mating erg was highest the subject was taken to a party by a man on whom her sexual desire was focussed. One further fascinating point remains to be made about the sex erg. On the 24th as the sex erg was rising to its peak, the subject went into a delicatessen and bought a present of smoked eels for her father.

As an example of a sentiment career sentiment deserves comment. Career sentiment was uniformly low other than on day 6 when it rose. On this day our subject went for an interview for admission to a teacher-training course for the next year. There are no other career relevant items in the diary. This is a clear instance of fluctuation of scores being related to environmental events.

Kline and Grindley (1974) were able to link up most of the fluctuations in all the variables to clear environmental events or feelings expressed in the diary so that it seemed a reasonable conclusion to claim that the MAT was a valid test although we must bear in mind the caveats of this kind of case study.

This small personal investigation is a carefully documented illustration of our common sense experience both of our own behaviour and that of others that such variables as ergs and sentiments are not constant over time in the way that abilities and temperaments are. Thus, for example, sense of security is a feeling which may be provoked in an individual by a wide variety of different events: newspaper reports (e.g. of plane crashes or outbreaks of dysentery), his bank account or fear of illness in himself or others, all these can affect his level on a basic erg. Thus not only, in this case, will scores on the fear erg fluctuate (as we saw in our investigation with the unsafe car) from situation to situation and from time to time, but even the strengths of sentiments will alter steadily with learning or decay with time and circumstance. A sad and banal example of this concerns sentiments to spouse as the myriad divorces of the civilized world bear eloquent witness.

As ergic and sentiment levels change within the indiviual for the kind of reasons we have discussed, so his reactions to any particular concrete stimulation of interest will change. For example it can be shown that a person will show more of a startle response to some small stimulus when he is already in a state of fear tension about some important matter than in other circumstances. Macbeth started in his guilt at every sound while his wife but heard "the owls scream and the crickets cry." From all these examples it is clear that our everyday experience and our most acute literary observers have taught us that our drive levels vary with the stimulation from the environment and with their satisfaction. This last we have not bothered to mention because in most cases it is simply obvious. Our hunger is sated by a good meal and our sleep erg by sleep. The interesting part of the goal satisfaction aspect of drives lies in what constitutes satisfaction. Thus it is banal to argue that hunger is satisfied by food, but if psychoanalytic theory is correct and sex, for example, is satisfied, or sublimated, by artistic creation, then we are in a new and profoundly important area of research for a proper understanding and formulation of the dynamic lattice. Unfortunately at this point of trying to understand the situations and satisfactions affecting scores on dynamic traits the empirical quantified data stemming from research runs out and we are thrown back into the twisted and contradictory jungle of clinical theory. Investigations such as those by Cattell and Cross (1952) and Kline and Grindley (1974) are necessary to unravel this problem although very large numbers of subjects will have to be tested before any firm conclusions can be drawn.

One set of factors that influences drives is physiological in origin. However before discussing these at the end of this chapter we want to continue with our discussion of the psychological nature of dynamic traits and we shall now look at the relationship between dynamic motivation factors and the temperamental traits of personality.

RELATION OF DYNAMICS AND TEMPERAMENT

This relationship between disposition, motivation, and personality has long been of interest to psychologists. Individuals are regarded as being of amorous disposition such as Casanova or Don Juan, or assertive such as Petruchio or, in the language of the motivational variables of our discussion, people vary in the natural strength of their ergs. If we consider the subject in the Kline and Grindley (1974) study, volatile though she was, a mean value for each of the ergs was a useful descriptive set of scores. From it we could say that our subject was not interested in career but was highly sexed although, as we showed, there were considerable variations round these means depending upon the frustrations and satisfactions afforded by the environment. It is noteworthy in this respect that the subject in the Cattell and Cross (1952) investigation showed a far greater stability of scores. Indeed there is reason to think that at the time of the research the subject in Kline and Grindley's study was unusually disturbed and there can be little doubt that were the study to be repeated fluctuations in score would be less. Evidence for the basic stability of ergic tension level within individuals can be found in the Handbook to the MAT (Cattell *et al*. 1970) where the test-retest reliability coefficients with a five week interval are in the region of 0.5 to 0.6 for most of the variables. Cattell and Child (1975) even argue that these figures are underestimates because the measures are unreliable, but since these figures are themselves the reliability coefficients it seems somewhat circular to correct them for attenuation. For children the coefficients over a six month period are much smaller and this probably represents a realistic picture of genuine changes or function fluctuations among these subjects.

Thus there is some evidence from the investigations with objective motivation tests to support the notion that the fluctuation of ergic tension within individuals occurs round a mean which is relatively stable. Whether this is necessarily the case or whether it reflects the fact that most people live in a rather constant and consistent environment is not known. However, it is a meaningful question since it would be possible to test the hypothesis by comparing the MAT scores of groups whose environments had changed with controls: immigrants would be useful samples of this kind. If then our motivations are stable the relationship between them and temperament becomes of considerable interest.

In our early chapter on the value of factor analysis in the scientific study of behaviour it was pointed out that the personality sphere was assumed to be different and distinct from the ability and the dynamic spheres. Cattell indeed (e.g. Cattell and Child, 1975) has actually incorporated this view into a behavioural specification equation where any given behaviour is predictable in terms of scores on abilities, temperamental traits and dynamic traits. However in the case of dynamic traits we are scoring responses to interest in some specific behaviour. This can be narrow, as for example, interest in early Mauritius stamps or broad, as for example an interest in sex. In factor analytic terms the former would be a specific factor (at best a bloated specific) the latter would be a general factor with wide ramifications, as indeed we saw from the description of the sex erg in the last chapter which included smoking, drinking and theatre-going in addition to the expected sexual variables. With temperamental traits we are taking a measure broader than that of interest. Thus the surgent individual is quick and impulsive, resistant to fatigue. Such a trait might manifest itself in a wide variety of interests and therefore we should expect dynamic traits to have small correlations with a variety of temperamental traits rather than substantial correlations with one or two specific factors. However from this argument it is possible to conceive of a dynamic factor so broad that it produced styles of behaviour in a wide variety of different situations and contexts so that it becomes to all intents and purposes a temperamental trait.

A glance at Table 10.2 which shows the correlations between the personality factors and dynamic factors reveals that both predictions are true. Generally motivational and personality factors are independent but there are

Relation of Dynamic Modality Factors to General Personality Factors

Dynamic traits	A Affectia	B Intelligence	C Ego weakness	E Dominance	F Surgency	G Superego strength	H Parmia	I Premsia	L Protension	M Autia	N Shrewdness	O Guilt-proneness	Q₁ Radicalism	Q₂ Self-sufficiency	Q₃ Self-sentiment	Q₄ Ergic tension
Sex	.02	.15	.02	-.02	.11	-.30*	-.11	-.06	.20*	.31*	.11	.27*	.27*	.19*	-.31*	.31*
Gregariousness	.33*	.05	.15	-.01	.22*	-.18*	.17	-.06	-.18	.01	.01	.01	-.11	-.33*	-.12	.03
Parental protectiveness	.06	-.15	.09	-.25*	-.05	.12	-.08	.04	-.27	.01	-.15	.06	-.09	-.16	.03	.05
Exploration (curiosity)	-.14	.09	.01	.02	-.10	.07	-.06	.21*	.11	.13	-.09	.04	.29*	.13	.09	-.00
Fear; escape	-.07	-.12	-.09	-.01	-.16	.19*	.15	.01	-.05	-.17	-.02	-.20*	.09	-.13	.27*	-.23*
Self-assertion	.24*	.11	.06	.15	-.00	-.01	.32*	-.06	-.20*	.03	.03	-.06	.21*	-.12	.07	-.10
Narcistic v. superego	.02	.08	.05	.07	.13	-.37*	-.12	-.15	.21*	.35*	.12	.22*	.27*	.22*	-.39*	.26*
Air Force	.01	.01	.11	.23*	.13	.14	.38*	-.09	-.24*	-.13	.13	-.38*	-.05	-.07	.21*	-.41*
Sports	-.00	-.11	.02	-.02	-.08	-.06	-.02	-.16	-.12	-.03	-.01	-.09	-.20*	-.04	-.08	-.00
Religious sentiment	.01	-.18*	.03	-.19*	-.05	.26*	.01	.20*	-.14	-.22*	.16	-.12	-.34*	-.33*	.25*	-.10
Mechanical, materialistic interest	-.03	.10	.01	.10	.01	.11	.10	-.13	-.05	-.01	.04	-.12	.16	.15	.06	-.18*
Self-sentiment	.11	.10	.04	.20*	-.05	.13	.34*	.05	-.13*	-.15	-.02	-.22*	.06	-.18*	.34*	-.25*
Rest-seeking	-.10	.03	-.03	-.09	-.20*	.10	-.04	-.04	-.02	.04	.06	.14	.10	.05	.06	.09

* Significant at 1% level.

in a few cases substantial overlaps. The provenance of this table is important because it is a reliable set of results being a mixture of the original studies reported in Cattell (1957) and of some more recent researches. 74% of the correlations are non-significant and most of the significant ones are small. Indeed some of these may be little more than chance deviations from zero (inevitable in a large number of correlations). Indeed the only correlations of any size are that between temperamental superego, G, as measured by questionnaire and the superego (—narcism) dynamic structures in the MAT, and that between the self-sentiment, Q3 in the questionnaire and the dynamic self-sentiment. This is an interesting example of this "indifference of indicator" principle, i.e. the same personality structure will show itself through different media of observation. In this case, as Cattell and Child (1975) point out, if one allows for the effect of the two different instrument factors (questionnaire in one and objective motivation test in the other) the correlations could be well nigh perfect, showing that the same factors, superego and self-sentiment, are being measured in two different media. The main interest of this finding is in showing that if dynamic structure factors are broad enough (if in fact they are connected with general control and direction rather than specific kinds of interest) they can appear among general, broad, personality–temperamental factors. From this we can conclude that in *most* instances motivational factors are distinct from personality dimensions but that in two cases, superego and self-sentiment, the dynamic traits are so influential as to become in effect general personality traits affecting total style of interest expression.

PHYSIOLOGY OF MOTIVATION

Naturally in the motivation field one looks also for physiological associations, since, particularly in animal psychology the assumption is made that appetitive states reflect to some extent physiological states. Certainly the ethologists working with animals (see Tinbergen, 1951) have been forced by the evidence to take into account the physiological state of organisms in understanding motivation. Thus for the stickleback the red underside of another male provokes a territorial fighting display only when male hormones are active, in the breeding season. Similarly activating and inhibitory centres for various behaviours such as eating, drinking and sleeping have been found at the mid-brain level in mammals and these clearly must influence goal directed, i.e. motivated, behaviour. Since the physiology of the brain is highly complex both anatomically and biochemically we shall not attempt a detailed treatment of the field in this discussion. For the details of the physiology of motivation readers are referred to suitable texts such as Grossman (1967) or Thompson (1967).

Most physiological studies are, for obvious reasons, carried out on animals, although accident victims can provide vital human evidence, as can wars. Many of the findings rest either on electrical stimulation of the given site or on ablation where certain structures are cut or surgically removed and the resulting deficits are noted. Now these ablation techniques have certain obvious logical difficulties and we should be cautious in accepting the findings. If we were to take a radio set and sever a connection to the speaker we would fail to tune in to any programme. It is a totally false conclusion, however, to deduce that this connection subsumes tuning. Nevertheless, despite these problems, it seems that some concensus of view exists. Thus Isaacson *et al.* (1971) in their succinct review of the physiology of motivation make fairly positive claims about the primary motivational variables such as hunger or thirst which we shall briefly discuss.

Hunger

Even such an apparently obvious variable as hunger can be difficult to define and this complicates considerably the study of its physiology. Thus it might be defined in terms of the time since the subject's last meal, or how much was last eaten although these interact with past dietary experience, physical activity and age. Nevertheless, in considering the physiology of hunger (however measured), it is clear that there are two distinct sets of factors. Peripheral factors related to the state of the digestive system, blood composition, the amount of food in the stomach, and oral, taste and cutaneous receptors, for example, all play a part in the onset, maintenance and termination of eating. However, central factors, especially in the centres in the hypothalamic and limbic region of the mid-brain which are sensitive to food intake, are also important. We shall consider first the peripheral factors.

Cannon (1929) claimed that the stimulus for hunger was peripheral— contractions of the stomach, (for thirst it was dryness of the mouth), a theory that had, as Isaacson *et al.* (1971) point out, its origins in the 18th century. The fact that stomach contractions are correlated with hunger by no means demonstrates that these cause hunger. It could be of course that both the hunger and the contractions are caused by some central process. This is an example of the elementary error of confusing correlation with causation. Indeed, cutting the nerves to eliminate afferent impulses from the intestinal system does not appreciably affect the amount of food ingested. In addition surgical cases where portions of the stomach and intestine are removed, thus again eliminating contractions and gastric secretions which could supply feedback information to the brain on the state of the stomach show no disturbances of hunger (after surgical recovery). Indeed, it is often said that, those who have undergone extreme food deprivation report that stomach contractions cease after a few days whereas hunger persists.

Schachter (1967) has provided evidence, from an extremely ingenious set of experiments, that in the obese, eating is instigated not by internal cues such as hunger contractions but by environmental stimuli. Thus in experiments where a clock was artificially slowed or altered it was found that obese subjects ate if the clock indicated food time. Actually there were some nice contra-intuitive results in this study. For example the normal-weight person in this investigation would *not* eat if the clock showed food time in case it spoiled his meal. Furthermore since the obese person is cued to eat by environmental stimuli if the food is not appetizing he will not eat it whereas the normal subject will. This work is relevant to the study of motivation in two ways. In the first place, as Isaacson *et al.* (1971) argue, it shows the importance of peripheral cues in eating at least for the normals. Actually this is not strictly correct since by our previous argument it may be the case that the subject feels hungry (and eats) through some central mechanism of which he is unaware but attributes this to the hunger pangs of which he is all too conscious. Even more important from the point of view of the psychologist, however, although this is ignored by these authors, this work of Schachter indicates how psychological stimuli overide peripheral internal stimuli in eating. Thus not only do the obese ignore such internal signals and are cued to eat by environmental events (as ice cream sellers with their jangling chimes well know) but even normal subjects do this in that they used the clock as an excuse not to eat. It seems to us that the conclusion to be drawn from the work of Schachter is that psychological rather than peripheral events are important in eating.

Even if, therefore, stomach contractions cannot be said to cause eating there are other important peripheral factors, such as hormones. As food is digested so chemical changes in the blood occur: glucose level increases and digestive enzymes are released and any one of these could be an adequate stimulus for eating and for the control of eating.

It was demonstrated experimentally by the use of a denervated gastro-intestinal pouch that stomach contractions are dependent on chemical changes in the circulatory system, an argument supported by the finding that the blood of a starving dog when transfused into dogs that were replete produced stomach contractions. Similarly intravenous injections of glucose decrease gastric motility and Mayer (1955) has proposed a glucostatic theory of hunger in which the regulation of food intake was dependent on gluco-receptors in the hypothalamus. However if this theory were correct injections of glucose should sate the animal which is not the case. On the other hand destruction of the glucoreceptors in the hypothalamus by the injection of gold thyoglucose which is toxic produces uncontrolled eating. However with gross ablation (in effect) studies of this kind, as we have pointed out, we cannot strictly conclude that the damaged area subsumes the resulting deficient behaviour. From this we must conclude that peripheral factors, both hormonal and kinaesthetic, play some part in the regulation of food intake, as do psychological factors, but they are not sufficient in themselves.

The postulation of glucoreceptors in the hypothalamus introduces us however to our second set of physiological mechanisms, i.e. the central mechanisms. Isaacson *et al.* (1971) claim that over the last thirty years it has become evident that there are two centres responsible for the regulation of food intake, a feeding and a satiation centre. However Teitlebaum and Stellar (1954) found that after lesions in the feeding centre animals could be persuaded to feed again although they first had to be kept alive by artificial feeding and palatable food had to be available. This demonstrates that new centres can take over the lost function and it suggests that other centres of the brain are implicated in feeding. Indeed Isaacson *et al.* (1971) cite more recent evidence that indicates there is limbic control over satiation in the amygdala which controls in turn the hypothalamic centre.

We have devoted some space to the discussion of some of the physiological factors involved in hunger, without going into detail, to demonstrate the enormous complexity of the physiology and perhaps more importantly show that it adds little to our understanding of the psychology of hunger (and even less in the case of a more complex drive) because although in lower organisms the initiation and cessation of eating may be determined by the state of its relevant physiology the work of Schachter (1967) indicates that in human beings such physiological signals are ignored. Indeed the very existence of large numbers of over-weight people strongly suggests alone that physiological explanations of eating are doomed to failure. However this is not to say that physiology is useless in the study of motivation, rather that it should not be regarded as an explanation by itself. The clearest example of both the value and the shortcomings of physiology in psychology can be found in the recent work of Blakemore on the development of perception in cats. Here, particular feature analyzers have been found which, if not stimulated during the early infancy of the cat, cease to function and the cat thus has a visual deficit throughout its life. This early infant stimulation is normally present, of course, within the cat's environment. However from the viewpoint of psychology this physiological knowledge adds nothing to our understanding because we restate the findings of work by saying that there is a critical period for visual development where visual stimulation is essential and without this there will be visual deficiencies in the cat. In this case the physiology is a pleasant but unnecessary addition to psychological knowledge.

Research with human beings shows that some ergic tension levels are affected by physiological deprivation. Thus an individual who has not eaten for a long time can become highly sensitive to the sight and smell of food. Furthermore their thoughts and fantasies become increasingly concerned with food. Thus Cherry Garrard in his celebrated account of his journey to the Pole with Scott reports constantly on the succulence of his fantasies. If we were measuring the hunger erg we should expect objective T tests such as the fluency test or the misperception test to be influenced in part by physiological factors, and as we have seen above, it is experimentally demonstrable with the MAT that hunger and thirst (with MAT-like measures) and sex measures respond significantly to physiological and related conditions.

OTHER FACTORS AFFECTING ERGIC TENSION LEVEL

In addition the tension level in a particular erg is in part determined by its history. Levy (1934) showed that puppies that were allowed different amounts of sucking in infancy during feeding indulged in different amounts of non-nutritive sucking, a finding that has sometimes been taken to confirm the Freudian concept of oral erotism (see Kline, 1972, for a full discussion of this topic). Freud was one of the first personality theorists to state explicitly the importance of early infantile experience on adult drives. Psychoanalytic theory can be conceived as an attempt to specify in great detail just what are the critical experiences in our early life. Ethologists too have emphasized the importance of early experience with the notion of imprinting, which we have discussed (p. 164).

Physiological deprivation and the past history of the subject (referred to by learning theorists as past patterns of reinforcement) affect ergic tension level. In addition internal stimuli can affect it. The sexual drive is a case in point which can be high in the absence of external stimuli. On the other hand it can be roused by external stimuli, as we discussed at the beginning of our examination of factors influencing drive strength. Indeed as Beech (1956) has shown, and all know from their own experience, external stimuli in the form of people or pictures and internal stimuli in the form of fantasies are powerful influences on the sex erg. This means that when the stimulus value for, say, sex drops to zero, ergic strength or tension does not necessarily die away completely. From this analysis of factors influencing ergic tension level we are now in a position to generate an equation that will account for ergic strength. Thus we might write: E, ergic tension, is a function of the stimulus situation $(S + k)$ where k is a constant introduced to embrace the fact that when the stimulus is zero (no girl in sight) ergic strength does not necessarily disappear, multiplied by the need strength $(C + H)$ where H is the past history of the ergic satisfaction and C reflects the inborn, constitutional difference in needs. However, as we saw in our previous discussion, ergic level is also affected by the current state of gratification. This must enter any equation and will be represented by G while absence of gratification will be $-G$. Since gratification can operate in respect of both the physiological component (P) and the consummatory behaviour satisfactions it is necessary to symbolize it with two different constants, a and b, for the two domains of action. (This finding that both the physiological condition, e.g. food in the stomach, and consummatory *behaviour*, e.g. grasping and chewing food, are distinct parts of the satisfaction is most clearly shown in animal experiment, notably for example in the survey by Kimble (1961).) The equation reads in full: $E = (S + k)[C + H + (P - aG) - bG]$.

This formula is useful in that it is a brief expression of three important concepts: (a) drive strength (b) need strength and (c) ergic tension level. Drive strength is an individual's natural strength of drive at his time of life discounting current stimulation and gratification conditions. From the equation we can see that this includes C, H and P. Need strength is the strength of need at the time, it is inherent in the person and taking into account his current gratification but excluding stimulation. Finally there is the ergic tension level itself which is the final outcome as measured by the MAT and the SMAT resulting from the combination of need strength and stimulation level. Cattell and Child (1975) have made minor modifications to this formula* in their latest work on motivation but not such as to affect our understanding of its basic concepts, which is the main value of this equation at present for it enables the researcher to concentrate on the important variables—need strength and drive strength. Indeed efforts have been made by Cattell and colleagues, using this model as a basis, to elaborate it and of course to check it. Some of this work will be described below.

CHECKS ON ERGIC TENSION EQUATION

As the above formulation is put to experimental checks it becomes necessary to vary stimulus and gratification independently. Let us look a little more closely at the evidence already briefly cited above. That these measures of ergic tension were found e.g. by Adelson (1952) and others (as we saw earlier in this chapter) to respond in humans as expected to non-gratification of thirst has already been mentioned. (See also Bruner and Goodman's evidence of other perceptual measures changing with desire, 1947). The experiments on the hunger and sex ergs also fit the model, and Dickman's work on fear, though not conclusive, agrees with that of Tsushima (1960) on anxiety, in showing significant shift on the objective test scores in *some* variables. On the usual total score, however, both Dickman and Bolz got ambiguous results. Sweney may have the answer to this in saying that fear is peculiar in that the autism test, for example, works in the opposite direction, i.e. instead of leading to illusions of escape it leads to over-estimation of danger. In Dickman's study the experimental task was the delivery of a spontaneous lecture to a group (fearful for freshmen); in the second study, subjects were given the impression that they were about to receive a severe electric shock. A final investigation required subjects to read horrendous material on the increased incidence and symptomatology of venereal diseases, a procedure which it was felt should affect both fear and sexual ergs. In the first two experiments the hypothesized increase in fear erg in the experimental groups did not occur. Thus it could be that the measures of the fear erg were simply invalid or, a more likely hypothesis, it could be that the experimental manipulations were simply not fear arousing. After all the expected electric shock in a reputable university laboratory is not analogous to that expected by a prisoner who has been condemned to death or by a Nazi victim. This failure points up clearly the problem of lifelike experimental manipulation that is within an ethical

* (See p. 212.)

code compared with the real-life studies of the type reported previously. The fear erg was reduced from occasion one to two in the experimental group. Perhaps, the whole laboratory situation was highly frightening in itself so that familiarity by the second occasion was sufficient to reduce the scores— certainly enough to outweigh the experimental manipulation. From these two studies the only fair conclusion is that the experimental manipulation of fear is not easy.

In the third experiment, however, where the VD material was presented, there was a significant increase in the fear erg whereas with the control group there was no significant change (all measures being the MAT unintegrated fear score). This is good support for the validity of the MAT fear erg which it will be noted was also strongly supported in the real-life study by Kline and Grindley (1974). This demonstrates neatly that the kind of equation that was developed above is at least an approximate description of the factors influencing ergic tension. It also confirms the well known clinical claim that fear of VD especially when for some reason it reaches pathological proportions is a powerful inhibitor of adequate sexual performance and adjustment. It is reassuring to get this common sense result because psychologists would (in a clinical sense) predict that subjects would have been temporarily put off sex by this medical material. Whether it would, however, in this normal sample have affected sexual activity given the opportunity with pleasant partners is perhaps a different matter.

Cattell, Kawash and De Young (1972) have also carried out studies of the sex and hunger ergs using experimental manipulation of the drives and special versions of the MAT. To arouse the sex drive the experimental group was shown erotic slides. As hypothesized the sex erg score rose. Cattell and Child (1975) argue that this supports the equation we have discussed previously. On the other hand if we presented the results as showing that males were sexually aroused by erotic pictures it would cause little sensation in Soho, for example. Rather this kind of manipulative experiment is good support for the validity of the sex erg scale in this version of the MAT. A further investigation had the experimental subjects abstain from eating for around 29 hours. In these the hunger erg was increased—a finding which supports our equation and the validity of the hunger erg in the special version of the test.

Since a possible limitation of these studies is that there is no link with criterion behaviour (though using the usual analysis of variance design in relation to stimulation and non-stimulation) an attempt was made to overcome this by dividing the experimental group in the study of the sex erg into two groups based upon whether they had rated the slides as highly arousing or not, from which a measure of need strength was produced. It was found that the subjects most aroused by the slides were those with the highest sex erg scores and analysis of behavioural data on sexual behaviour and relations after the study confirmed this claim. There is little doubt from the follow-up results that sex erg scores are related to sexual behaviour. Finally it should be noted in this study of the sex erg that it was the unintegrated score that was related to the sexual arousal. Thus it may be that it is the U score that reflects *state* (depending upon gratification and stimulation) whereas the I score reflects the more enduring trait score.

All these experiments and the life studies discussed before show that ergs and to some extent sentiments are affected by life experiences as we should intuitively expect. The validity of the MAT scores and the motivational factors is therefore strongly supported.

These findings confirm, in general, the viability of the equation for ergic strength that we have further postulated. Cattell and Child (1975) have attempted to develop this somewhat but, as they admit, such work is largely speculative being in advance of the evidence.

Finally, now that we have looked at some of the factors affecting the strength of motivation as revealed in experiment and in life studies (and found good support for much clinical intuition), we must look at some of the other work on motivation which, if it lacks the multivariate sophistication of ergs and sentiments, is at least based upon quantified data and which has been found useful in the practical situation.

OTHER WORKS ON MOTIVATION: THE STRONG TEST

Despite the theoretical advances in the MAT, and its replicated factor structure, probably the most widely used interest test in America is of a more traditional verbal kind—the Strong Vocational Interest Blank (see Strong *et al.*, 1971 for the latest edition). This was first produced in 1927, and does not apply to motivation as the clinician knows it but to interest in jobs only. Buros (1972) is able to cite almost 1,100 references to this test. The test has been extensively revised by Campbell (1971) to the extent of new items, new item weights and new scoring keys and although in the manual it is argued that the new and old forms are strictly comparable and that the vast amount of research knowledge concerning the old scales applies still to the new, Williams *et al.* (1968) found differences between the two forms sufficient in some cases to induce different interpretations of the results. Despite this, for the purposes of our brief discussion, we shall assume that both forms are parallel. The question we want to answer concerns the reasons why we have not devoted as much or more space to the Strong variables as motivational factors as we have to the MAT variables when, as is clear, the Strong is the more widely used test. An examination of the empirical basis of the SVIB will quickly provide our answer.

In its original form the SVIB contained 400 items, occupations, school subjects, activities and personal peculiarities to which subjects had to respond like or dislike, plus forced choice items of a similar kind. As we have pointed out previously, the SVIB is a criterion-keyed test, i.e. items were selected if they discriminated one occupational group from another and from the general population. To improve discrimination items were weighted for particular occupations positively and negatively. Separate keys were available for each occupation and for the male form of the test there were more than 50 such keys covering a diverse range of jobs. The new test, as we indicated above, has replaced many of the items which were no longer appropriate, removed the weighting system which is inevitably too tied down to the sample on which it is based, increased and updated the occupational keys and provided, in addition, a set of more general interest scales such as adventure, agriculture and military interests. Some of these basic interest scales have common items, however, so that they are inevitably not independent.

The weakness of this Strong test from the viewpoint of the investigation of motivational factors resides in the fact that it was criterion-keyed. This means that the variables are not necessarily psychologically meaningful as we have discussed (see pp. 54–55). The fact that an individual scores high on a scale which discriminates chemical engineers, for example, from other occupational groups, may mean that he will be a satisfied chemical engineer (a purely empirical question, to be decided on the evidence) but it does not mean that he has a chemical interest, because chemical engineers may differ in a wide variety of ways from other occupational groups. This does not mean that the scale would not be highly effective in vocational guidance or selection, and further research might identify accurately in factorial terms the variable measured by it so that it could be given psychological meaning. However, this has not been done in the case of the SVIB. Even if such criterion-keyed scales are effective practically there is still good reason in the practical vocational guidance setting to prefer factor-analytically derived psychologically meaningful scales. Readers must be referred to chapter 15 for a discussion of these points. It should be clear from this discussion that the Strong test cannot be valuable in the study of motivation.

THE BROOK REACTION TEST

Most of the other commonly used interest tests such as the Kuder Occupational Interest Survey (Kuder 1970), the Edwards PPI and the Jackson test (both still leaning on Murray's list of needs) have been constructed by the same methods as the Strong so that all our arguments apply equally to these. A different approach to the measurement of interest and the establishment of motivational variables is that adopted by Heim *et al.* (1969) in the Brook Reaction Test. This test consists of eighty stimulus words orally delivered, one every 12 seconds, to which subjects have to give their first association, the one that follows that and so on until the next stimulus word is presented. The test consists of a pre-recorded tape and subjects have to write down their responses. The stimulus words are ambiguous in that they either have more than one meaning e.g. "swift" or else they are homophonous e.g. "ark" ("arc").

The data for each subject in the Brook Test consist of the associations to the stimulus words which are then classified into 22 interest categories plus a category for unclassifiable words. For each stimulus word 4 points of interest are available to be distributed through the interest categories of the response. There are 22 interest categories available, which include all the intuitively important groups, e.g. aesthetic, business, food, outdoor and sport. A few examples (not from the actual test) will make the scoring clear. To the stimulus word "swift" three subjects might thus reply: (1) swallow, woodpecker, kingfisher, heron; (2) swallow, roast beef, apple pie and (3) Red Rum, Arkle, Pat Taafe. The first response is entirely made up of birds and is therefore classified as biological interests, 4 points. The second response contains a bird and food responses and the bird is itself by name related to eating. This would be scored as food interest 3 points biological interest 1 point. The third response refers to famous race horses and a jockey. This would be (if Alice Heim had not unfortunately omitted horse racing from her scoring keys) sport 3 points and people 1 point, (since it is a convention of the scoring system that mention of a living person is thus scored.).

These examples illustrate clearly the strengths and weakness of the Brook Test. On the credit side, it is in Cattell's terms an objective test since it is impossible to fake or to guess the purport of the test. Attempts to distort results by leaving responses out or thinking of something else are easily detected by the inevitable omissions (except for the verbally brilliant). Furthermore the test avoids the silliness associated with many conventional interest tests which force subjects to choose between alternatives which they equally hate—a procedure which intelligent British subjects find entirely objectionable and which destroys test rapport if indeed they even complete the test. On the debit side, however, there is clearly great subjectivity of scoring, and the interest categories are quite arbitrary. It must be noted that the rationale of the test is similar to that of some of Cattell's interest test in that we should expect (see Horn's (1968) principles, p. 167) more relevant associations in our fields of interest than in other subjects.

Because of the promise of this test which avoids the pitfalls of the conventional interest test which in any case loads only on one of Cattell's motivational strength factors, Kline (1969b, 1970b) and Kline and Thomas (1971, 1972) have investigated its reliability and validity, researches which we shall summarize briefly. For each stimulus word Alice Heim has provided a manual with all the common responses scored. In this way with experience it is possible to classify with reasonable confidence and speed (although scoring takes over an hour) most responses into interest categories. Nevertheless is it a reliable procedure? If it is not the test cannot be valid. Kline (1969b) examined the reliability of scoring and the internal consistency of the test by comparing scores on the first 40 stimuli with scores derived from the last 40. High reliability would indicate both that the test was consistent and that it could be reliably scored, otherwise there would be poor agreement between halves. In fact the reliability of the scales was around 0.8, which, in view of the scoring procedure, is surprisingly high. This does not mean that the scores are valid merely that the scales can be consistently scored.

Heim *et al.* (1969), in the manual to the test, present almost no evidence concerning its validity other than the fact that members of certain student societies did have scores high on the relevant Brook scales. Kline (1970) in an attempt to examine the independence of the scales, which, as we have said, were virtually arbitrary categories of interest, and to investigate the correlates of the scales, administered the Brook test and the 16PF test. This was chosen because there is some *a priori* reason stemming from the work of Jung with word associations to think that word associations would be related more to personality than interest. However, correlations between the scales and a rotated factor analysis showed that Brook scores were reasonably independent and only modestly related to the Cattell factors. This was only a pilot study with small numbers so that a detailed account of the results is inappropriate. What we can conclude is that the Brook test could be valid and is certainly reliable. This is a test which demands further focussed research preferably with the MAT or better with some of the other motivational objective test variables.

WORK OF HOLLAND

The work of Holland in the sphere of motivation also deserves mention. Holland (1965) has developed the Vocational Preference Inventory which is classified as a personality test in Buros (1972) and by Cronbach (1970). Because this test is intimately bound up with Holland's theories of vocational interest, it seems better to think of it as a measure of motivation and there is little doubt that it is concerned with the dynamics rather than the temperamental side of personality. The V.P.I. consists of 11 scales: realistic, intellectual, social, conventional, enterprising, artistic, self control, masculinity, status, infrequency of response and acquiescence. The items from which these scales are derived are 160 occupational titles to which subjects have to indicate like or dislike.

This test is the empirical basis of Holland's theory of vocational choice which is, of course, a dynamic theory and which is described in Holland (1966) and elaborated in two research reports (Holland and Whitney, 1968, Holland *et al.*, 1969). There are four cardinal points to Holland's theory of vocational choice. The first states that in Western culture most people can be categorized into one of six types: Realistic, Intellectual, Social, Conventional, Enterprising and Artistic. The second claims that there are six kinds of environment, corresponding to the groups. Thirdly, it is claimed that people search for environments and vocations that enable them to exercise their skills and abilities, express their attitudes and to avoid unpleasant roles. The final point is that a person's behaviour can be explained by the interaction of his personality pattern and his environment.

First we shall look at Holland's notion of types. This typology is, as might be expected, intuitive, although it has empirical tinges. All literature relevant to occupational choice and success was searched and if any description regardless of technical quality was found to be statistically significant at least twice it was utilized in the categorization. From this search Holland found that he was able to classify all descriptions into the six types. The problem here, with this arbitrary classification of descriptions, is that we have no means of knowing whether this is the only way of classifying the material or even the most elegant way. Furthermore there is no check on whether other investigators would categorize the material in this way. Such intuitive groupings are very different from the statistical categorizations provided by a factor analysis rotated to simple structure or, perhaps more appropriate in this instance, by the Taxonome programme.

We shall look below at the description of one of the types, as derived from the literature, and before this we must note that in the theory each type is described in terms of a theoretical model orientation. This is a cluster of adapted behaviours, needs, self-concepts, goals, preferred roles and abilities. The resemblance of a person to each of the six model orientations is his personality pattern and the model which the person most resembles is his personality type. A description of the realistic type, as an example, will help to clarify Holland's work.

The realistic type is masculine, stable and materialist, a person who favours the goal of objective manipulation rather than subjective intellectual and social goals. This is a summary of the empirical data derived from the literature of which a selection is set out. He prefers occupations such as plumber, photographer, power-shovel operator, in fact technical and engineering jobs. He is a conventional man, with a simple outlook, of parents who tend to be foreign-born, poorly educated, of lower socio-economic status and with few books in the house.

This is a sample from the description by Holland (1966) of the realistic type. We can here only give a sample to catch the flavour of these digests of research although we have a fuller and more detailed analysis of these types in Kline (1975). Granted then that Holland has found six types in the literature, the theory depends much on its quantification. As it stands, based upon research literature, there is insufficient support for it. Holland has proposed several methods of categorizing subjects into types. One approach is frankly qualitative. Thus if a subject's interests or occupation are characteristic of a type he is classified accordingly. The other method is quantitative and relies on the V.P.I. which we have already briefly described.

From eighty-four job titles (fourteen jobs for each of the six types) subjects choose those that appeal to them. The higher they score on any scale, the more they resemble that type. Thus the highest score represents a subject's dominant personality type. The profile of his scores reflects his personality pattern. Despite this quantification it should be obvious that this procedure validates the theory little better, if at all, than the previous qualitative method. Thus the theory states that certain types prefer certain occupations. However to find out, as occurs with the V.P.I., that certain people prefer certain occupations and thus classify them into types is no less arbitrary than the original classification. The only advantage it has is that it at least establishes that groups of occupations tend to be liked.

That this is all the V.P.I. scales do is confirmed by the fact that certain scales of the Strong and Kuder interest tests are also claimed to pick out types. What is needed, to provide empirical support for Holland's theory, is further different and independent evidence that people who prefer certain groups of occupations are similar in other ways also. Unless this is done all the V.P.I. scores can demonstrate is the fact that subjects who like one occupation tend to like others similar to it—a not very remarkable finding.

This leads us to conclude in the absence of further evidence that, as yet, Holland's typological theorizing about motivation, even in the relatively limited field of occupational motivation, is, despite the existence of a test yielding quantified scores, nothing more than a speculative hypothesis which demands quantitative support. On the other hand, some of the practical findings with the V.P.I. especially in the field of vocational guidance and the prediction of occupational success strongly suggest that the V.P.I. is a useful measure. As has been pointed out by Kline (1975) it is one thing to predict occupational success another to predict change and this latter the V.P.I. can do—if the personality pattern is inconsistent. However even if of practical use, Holland's theory does not provide a new motivational theory.

WORK OF HERZBERG

Finally mention should be made of Herzberg who has developed an elaborate theory of work motivation which is also a more general theory of motivation. Several publications have appeared where this theory has been set out (e.g. Herzberg *et al.*, 1959) culminating in "Work and the Nature of Man" (1966). We shall briefly summarize this theory and look at its experimental basis because it has found useful application in occupational psychology.

Underlying Herzberg's work is an untested psychological assumption of the duality of man's nature. He postulates that there are two underlying needs for man: the need to avoid pain and physical deprivation and the need to grow psychologically. This latter need obviously requires definition and Herzberg argues that such growth constitutes "knowing more, seeing more relationships in what we know, being creative, being effective in ambiguous situations, maintaining individuality in the face of pressures of the group and attaining real psychological growth". Thus we can see that Herzberg has postulated a two factor theory of human motivation where the factors are clearly complex higher-order entities. However any resemblance to Cattell's factorial studies of motivation which we have discussed earlier in the chapter (see p. 183) ends here. For although the second-order factor structure of ergs and sentiments has not been worked out, the first of Herzberg's factors groups together the fear erg with hunger and thirst ergs (which do not appear particularly important in a generally over-fed Western world). However there is nothing in the correlation matrix of the ergs and sentiments which even slightly suggests this bipolar opposition of these three ergs to the others. Furthermore the definition of psychological growth postulates ergs which Cattell has not found evidence for, as is clear from the ergic list on p. 181.

Although it is true that Cattell cannot claim to have sampled the whole motivational sphere with the same confidence as in the case of the semantic personality sphere, nevertheless it is unlikely that major ergs and sentiments would have been missed, unless of course, there is something wrong fundamentally with the approach to motivation typified in the MAT—which indeed Herzberg's theory would suggest. This is why we are examining this work for it is clear that in the second set of factors there are ergs and sentiments entirely different from those claimed by Cattell to be the most important in human motivation. Thus in Cattell's system there is no equivalent of knowing more, seeing more relationships or being creative. Part of this second-order factor is subsumed under the ergs of self assertion and narcism. It should also be pointed out here that the last part of Herzberg's definition is uselessly tautologous since it defines psychological growth in terms of psychological growth. Since this theory is different from that of Cattell we must now examine its evidential basis.

The original study on which the theory rests concerned 200 accountants and engineers who were a cross section, it was claimed, of Pittsburgh industry. Subjects were interviewed and had to recall a time when they had strong positive feelings towards their jobs. These feelings were then probed for their effects on their behaviour and their job performance. This gave rise to job satisfaction factors. A similar interview was also held but this time concerning negative feelings about jobs giving rise to, by the same process, job dissatisfaction factors. Five factors were identified as important as satisfaction— achievement, recognition for achievement, work itself, responsibility and advancement while the factors affecting job dissatisfaction were compnay policy and administration, supervision, salary, interpersonal relations and working conditions. Although it cannot be too strongly emphasized that the use of the word "factors" here is only in its vernacular sense, the point of interest is that Herzberg's satisfiers and dissatisfiers are equivalent to orthogonal factors. Thus if responsibility makes a man feel satisfied with his job, lack of responsibility does not make him dissatisfied. Similarly, removing sources of dissatisfaction does not, if these results are correct, produce satisfaction. This theory is not banal in that this distinction between satisfiers and dissatisfiers could not have been intuitively made. Thus far the theory is concerned solely with work satisfaction. However, it is elevated into a motivational theory by an extension of the argument.

The dissatisfier factors are held to describe the environment and are conceived of as hygiene factors whereas the satisfiers are thought of as motivators. At this point the basic assumptions of the theory are brought into play. Hygiene factors lead to job dissatisfaction because of the need to avoid unpleasantness while the motivators lead to satisfaction because they lead the individual to feel that he is growing psychologically. In effect this means that the satisfiers are drives. Certainly if we look at the satisfaction factors we can see resemblance to some of the ergs and sentiments discovered by factor analysis although it would appear that the factors identified by Herzberg are far from factor pure (hardly surprising in that they were the end product of a subjective classification of interview data). Nevertheless it is possible that among the satisfiers, the motivators, are to be found self-assertion and self-sentiment and narcism. This theorizing by Herzberg is intimately related to his assumptions of two basic needs, which are purely hypothetical and rest on the intuitive analysis of interview data. It is mentioned here because it is highly interesting in its possibilities for occupational psychology and because Herzberg has attempted to provide some validating data.

The basic objections to these researches by Herzberg and his colleagues stem from the subjective nature of the factors and the problems inherent in interview data. We intend to add little here to the considerable body of evidence that interviews are notoriously unreliable and invalid (as many years ago was pointed out by Vernon and Parry (1949) in their study of war office selection procedures). In addition, when interviews are used as sources of evidence for a theory then they are strongly subject to the kinds of distortion that have been discussed by Rosenthal (1964) in the notion of experimenter bias. Also, as was the case with the work of Holland which we discussed above, the subjective grouping of interview responses into these factors is a totally different (and quite unscientific) procedure from a statistical categorization by multivariate analysis. Herzberg (1966) cites a number of studies all using interviews which largely support the initial Pittsburgh findings. These are open to all the objections that we have raised, though the fact that all the findings are confirmatory gives one a little more confidence in the claims. What is needed, however, are findings dependent on quite different data.

Schwartz (1959) categorized responses into similar but different factors from those of Herzberg in a sample of air force officers, a finding which reinforces the necessity for an objective, statistical sorting procedure. Halpern (1965) constructed rating scales to measure these factors in a sample of students. Although the results were not identical to those of the Pittsburgh studies at least this research demonstrates that the interview can be improved upon as a measure of the factors.

Relevant to the accurate study of these motivator factors are factor analytic investigations of work attitudes and satisfactions. As we have tried to indicate it seems from the description of Herzberg's factors that they should emerge from factor analyses if they are indeed meaningful constructs with which to conceptualize the data. Smith *et al.* (1969) provide a summary of previous studies which are difficult to reconcile and claim that four factors seem to have been isolated—a general satisfaction factor, a pay factor, a work factor, a supervision factor and a co-worker factor. These factors do not support Herzberg's claims and are of little interest to us as students of motivation in that they all seem to be factors associated with occupations rather than people. It is to be noted that all these factors are commonplace in that an *a priori* classification of job satisfactions would not probably be much different. Too much weight should not be attached to these results since in the main they were obtained from investigations which used simple attitude scales which as we have seen from our discussion of motivational factors discovered by Cattell are loaded only on the alpha component of attitudinal strength. Actually it is ironic that Smith *et al.* (1969) in their own investigation failed to confirm these factors or those of Herzberg. More recently Gulliksen and Gulliksen (1972) in a large scale investigation of worker satisfactions using factor analysis again failed to confirm Herzberg's work: indeed they found that lack of recognition lead to job dissatisfaction which is the opposite of the predictions from Herzberg's theory. However the validity of the scales used in these researches has not been convincingly demonstrated, most investigators relying on face validity, so that we should not like to use these results to disprove the work of Herzberg. In conclusion we would argue that Herzberg's work demands proper quantification and we should like to see the relation between his factors and those of the MAT, where relevant, drawn out.

This rapid survey of some of the more influential motivational theories in the practical world of occupational psychology demonstrates that despite the reasonable level of predictive success obtained by the blindly empirical methods of Strong and Kuder and despite the rather elaborate theorizing of Holland and Herzberg, nothing like a clear theory of (a) validation of motivation strength measurement *per se* or (b) the dynamic structure in the typical human being, has been established by these workers. Holland's factors need to be better technically related to the temperamental and the motivational factors of Cattell while more objective ways of measuring Herzberg's factors must be developed before they can emerge from the realm of interesting hypotheses. As it stands the area of motivation which is certainly a more difficult field to quantify with any precision than the personality sphere has still been illuminated, as we might expect from our early chapters on the rationale of multivariate methods and the scientific method, only by the proper use of factor analysis and associated manipulative experiment. In the case of motivation Cattell and his several colleagues have established with some confidence (a) five factors of motivational strength and (b) some ten dynamic structures: five ergs and five sentiments.

SUMMARY

1. The tests developed to measure the dynamic structure factors described in the previous chapter were described together with some of the evidence pertaining to their validity.
2. Some studies illuminating the environmental influences on ergs and sentiments were discussed, including manipulative laboratory studies and real-life field studies both with groups and individuals.
3. The relation of dynamic and temperamental factors in personality was examined.
4. Modern work on the physiology of motivation was discussed but it was claimed from the work of Schachter that psychological factors, at least in human beings, were more important than physiological in the understanding of motivation.
5. Other factors affecting ergic tension level such as the past history of the animal and recent experiences were also introduced so that the *ergic tension level equation* could be set up.
6. Manipulative studies checking on this equation were then described and it was shown to be largely confirmed.
7. Finally some other work on motivation was critically examined: the Strong Test, the Brook Reaction Test, the researches of Holland and the investigations by Herzberg.

FOOTNOTE TO P. 200

In modified form the formula is (Cattell and Child, 1975):

$$E_k = (S)[L] = \overbrace{(S_k + Z) \underbrace{[c(C + H + I) + \underbrace{\{(P_k - aG_k) + (N_k - b\bar{G}_k)\}\}}_{\text{APPETITIVE STATE STRENGTH}}]}_{\text{NEED STRENGTH}}}^{\text{ERGIC TENSION}}$$

The difference from the original formula is that L (the individual's liability to the particular ergic tension) is introduced, as is Z, a term representing the self-stimulation which occurs in the complete absence of external stimulation. The other new terms are I, the investment quality of the erg, N, a neural need for discharge and c, a constant to account for the possibility that provocation can act differently on appetitive and non-appetitive need strength components.

Chapter 11

Traits, Moods and States

DISTINCTION BETWEEN TRAITS, MOODS AND STATES AND METHODS OF MEASUREMENT

So far in our discussion of personality we have concentrated largely on traits. Thus we isolated in the personality sphere 23 temperamental traits together with 7 others in the abnormal sphere. An obvious objection to an analysis of personality which stops at traits is that there are such conditions as states and moods. Just before an important examination or a visit to the dentist we are likely to be highly anxious. When it is all over, if things have not gone too badly and when we have had time to relax we are likely to feel a definite relief, less anxious than usual. The central tendency as regards anxiety, which is particular to each individual, is what we have previously discussed as trait anxiety, appearing as a second-order Q factor and a T factor. However the anxiety that we felt in the examples above is state anxiety reflecting changes in our external environment. Internal changes can have the same effect. Thus if we wake up in the night with a severe stomach pain and sweating profusely we should probably feel highly anxious trying to recall the symptoms of stomach cancer or wondering whether we have food poisoning or whether we have been in contact with some unpleasant disease. Anxiety is therefore both a temperamental trait and a state which fluctuates over time depending upon internal or external stimuli.

Indeed in the understanding and prediction of human behaviour it might be the case that it is better to be able to measure states and moods than traits. Many wives know how to handle their husbands if they have had a bad day at work, i.e. are enraged or angry at the way things have worked out. The list of such moods and states in everyday life and literature is huge—descriptive terms like fearful, enraged, sullen, sulky, moody and so on abound. In fact this distinction between the relatively enduring trait the central tendency for any variable for an individual and a mood or state which fluctuates over time is exceedingly useful in answering an objection which some subjects make to personality questionnaires—namely that sometimes they are dominant sometimes not. They are here referring to the state, whereas the questionnaire (factor E) refers to the trait. This being said it is obviously important to be able to distinguish traits from moods and states, and when we want to measure a person on a trait we should ideally measure him on several occasions and take an average.

Two techniques have been used by Cattell and his colleagues in the differentiation of moods and states from traits, *P factor analysis* and *dR analysis*, although these always have to be combined with the standard R technique. P technique, first used in the study of moods by Cattell and Rhymer (1947), involves the study of one individual where he is tested on a battery of variables repeatedly over a period of time. Thus he may take, for example, forty T tests which seem likely to reflect states and moods, being scored on them every day for a period of three months. By factor analysis of the correlations between these variables over time, moods and states which are genuinely unitary entities should clearly be revealed. We can then as a further source of information examine some of the associated physiological conditions and environmental provocations thus providing psychology with further insights into the real nature of these mood states. In fact this technique has been used, as we have seen, in the study of ergs and sentiments where motivational tests were related to diary events.

Differential R technique (dR) involves measuring subjects on two occasions with the same battery of tests. The differences between the scores on the two occasions are then subjected to factor analysis. The rationale of this method is that such an analysis will reveal the dimension underlying differences in scores—in fact moods and states. This method is somewhat more practical for research purposes than P technique since it requires a dedication to psychological testing unusual even among psychologists to complete so many testing sessions as are inevitably involved in P technique. Differential R analysis involves only two sessions.

Questions of practicality apart, we must now look at the problem of the comparability of results with the two techniques. With P technique, obviously, we see the pattern of responses over a period of time of one subject. We can never, however, be certain that the patterns that do emerge are not idiosyncratic to our subject. With dR technique the limitation lies in the fact that we only sample two occasions and some traumatic event could grossly affect results. Thus in the latter case our sampling of occasions rather than subject is weak. One possibility suggested by Cattell (1973) is to combine the two methods of testing say 10 subjects on 20 occasions (not so rigorous as pure P technique) on a battery of variables. The subjects are then put into a series such that 200 occasions can be used. This is a *chain P technique* and yields state and mood patterns commonly defined across people and occasions. This therefore is obviously the best method in that it overcomes the limitations of P and dR technique on their own. However so arduous is the data collection that it has been little applied yet in practice although Cattell and Bolz (1973) have one such study.

It appears that state response patterns as source traits change relatively little with different people and stimuli. This seems at first contra-intuitive, indeed simply wrong, in that we all know people whose expressions of rage and anger are quite different; sullen silence *v* savage punching of the nearest object. Furthermore our anxiety and annoyance at missing a train are usually differently expressed from our similar feelings at, say, failing an exam. The explanation is that different people use different combinations of the basic factors—producing surface states just as obvious as the clusters we have called surface traits. This uniqueness of combination is probably due to early learning experiences.

There are a number of difficulties with these methods which must be briefly discussed so that we can allay some apparently reasonable doubts and criticisms. First we must examine the psychological and psychometric effect of continually taking the same tests. Certainly in the study by Kline and Grindley (1974) the subject complained of the boredom of doing the MAT. However the considerable scatter of scores over the month was empirical evidence that the subject did not remember the previous responses and simply put what fitted the moment. Cattell (1973) argues that boredom and learning trends exist but that they can probably be factored out. Another difficulty is that there is no *a priori* reason why the pattern of a waxing mood or state should be the same as the pattern of a state waning in response to some declining stimulus. If the patterns are different it could account for the difficulty of matching Q and T source states. Again there is the further problem of deciding whether two states such as depression and elation are the opposite poles of a continuum state or distinct states. Of course if they are distinct they are also highly correlated (oblique) and certainly the research that we shall discuss below indicates that source states are more highly correlated than the corresponding source traits. There is no contradiction in thinking of distinct but correlated source states (anxiety and depression would be obvious examples), or of typical sequences of states.

This question of distinct states or negatively correlated or bipolar dimensions has concerned chiefly the factors arousal and fatigue and elation and depression. Very precise factor analysis (where every effort is made to reach adequate simple structure) seems to show that elation and depression are not just opposites nor are arousal and fatigue but this is not to deny that the question is a difficult one. There is a final problem that we shall not discuss here at any length: there is the possibility that state response patterns are not additive and linear (as implied in the factor analytic model) but are curvilinear and interactive. However, until empirical work demonstrates that the simple model is insufficient it is wise to continue with it.

The objections above are related to the model of state and trait differences implicit in the approach advocated by Cattell. One other statistical point that can lead to problems is the fact that difference scores have double the standard error of a single score (the sum of the individual standard errors). This problem has led Cronbach (1970) to advocate avoiding such difference scores. However just as strict behaviourism loses out by its refusal to consider states of mind because these are not public events so does this suggestion. Since the essence of science is change and causal sequence this is indeed throwing away the baby with the bath water. Cattell (1973) more sensibly advocates methods which minimize the error variance. One other problem remains that is perhaps more serious. Some states or moods are exceedingly volatile and change rapidly. Such changes could be missed by sampling once a day and studies are needed although so far they have not been carried out that test at intervals far smaller than this.

THE PERSONALITY STATE SPHERE

In the factor analytic study of moods and states it is necessary to define the personality sphere. This is done not only by assembling all the words for moods and states but also with reference to quite extensive work that has been carried on by psychologists since the 1920s in the field of emotion and its physiology. On this basis the early studies of states by Cattell and his colleagues (e.g., Cattell, Cattell and Rhymer, 1947) were begun. These explorative studies which gradually blocked in the field will not be discussed here. Instead we shall set out the main state factors that have emerged from the research programme. However before we do this two points must be made.

First it will be noticed that we have separated from this discussion the work on motivation and interests—the ergs and sentiments which we discussed in the previous two chapters. Since we showed that these clearly fluctuate in response to environmental and internal stimuli they might perhaps be conceptualized as moods or states. However, it still seems that there are real differences between *general states* such as depression or fatigue and *specific motivational states* such as hunger or sex. Ultimately, as Cattell and Child (1975) point out, research will have to elucidate the relation between them.

The second point concerns the development of mood scales by other investigators. Most of these have used, essentially, adjective check lists and subjected them to R factor analysis, the work of Nowlis (Nowlis and Green, 1957) and Clyde (1963) typify this approach. Thus in the Clyde mood scale, for example, (which is described by Lykken, 1972, as sophisticated) subjects indicate how well 48 adjectives describe them. In the original construction of the tests these ratings were subjected to an orthogonal Varimax factor analysis and 6 mood factors were obtained—friendly, aggressive, clear thinking, unhappy and dizzy (the scale is intended for use in drug studies with abnormals). However the inescapable fact of logic is that however appealing these factors are as measures of moods they were reached only by R technique, based upon scores from one occasion. There is no guarantee, therefore, that they discriminate states from traits. The factors could as easily be traits. This is why we do not here concern ourselves with mood scales and results obtained from them where only R factor analysis was used.

Cattell and Scheier (1961) have carried out extensive work on anxiety in an attempt to elucidate the vital distinction between state and trait anxiety (work which we shall be examining later in this chapter). However in the course of this work they carried out a dR study of the 16PF test where the retest period was nine months. This study, which has been replicated many times since that date, typifies one approach to the study of moods—namely a search for states in manifestations which are also expressive of personality, rather than data made up to cover common conceptions of states. We shall now first discuss the results from this type of research.

dR FACTORS FROM Q DATA

As Table 11.1 shows four second-order factors were found in the Cattell and Scheier (1961) study with the 16PF test which closely replicated those in the realm of second-order traits. Two others were not an obvious fit, although, because the error variance (as we have discussed above) is considerable, the simple structure obtained was not as good as that with R technique among traits. Indeed these results have been replicated around thirty times so that we are forced to conclude that all trait patterns have their corresponding state patterns. How is this finding to be interpreted?

While it is intuitively sensible that anxiety should both be a state and a trait, this is by no means the case with the other second-order factors, especially exvia. There is no suggestion in the literature from the time of Jung downwards that extraversion is a state. One possible solution, logically, since R technique cannot discriminate states and traits is that all the R factors (hitherto held to be traits) are really states. However the findings in the analogous field of abilities where the isolation of g factors has been so conclusive militates against this possibility. It is nonsense in the light of all the evidence and common sense to conceive of intellectual abilities as states. One *ad hoc* solution would be to invent a new concept of *trait change factors* which

TABLE 11.1

State Patterns at Second Order

First-Order Factor	Second-Order Factor I: Extraversion-Introversion or Exvia-Invia		First-Order Factor	Second-Order Factor II: Anxiety	
	State	Trait		State	Trait
A	38	42	Q_4	44	67
F	22	40	O	20	60
H	12	35	Q_3	-51	-53
Q_2	-39	-32	C	-53	-49
M	-36	-26	L	08	45
Q_1	-20	-19	H	-06	-32
L	-12	-14	M	18	30

First-Order Factor	Second-Order Factor III: Cortertia		First-Order Factor	Second-Order Factor IV: Independence	
	State	Trait		State	Trait
I	-50	-44	N	21	32
N	50	37	E	52	28
A	-18	-28	Q_1	12	27
Q_3	04	21	F	17	14
C	08	17	Q_3	-07	-01
O	(13)	-17	C	(02)	-15

Note: These loadings (decimals omitted) give the form of differential R-technique (dR) factors on the basis of 16 PF primaries (Adult). N = 95 normal male and female students retested after nine months.

TABLE 11.2

Second-Order Change Structures on a Broader Basis of Normal and Pathological Primaries

	I	II	III	IV	VIII	Depression	Psychoticism	(9)
A	54		-32					
C		-55		32				
E	57			36	(08)	28		-59
F	95			06	(-09)			
G	24				69			
H	49	(-02)	-47	29	-23			-28
I		-72						
L		(-03)		62	-33			
M			-44	(-15)				
O	34	38	-33					
Q_1				86	-27			
Q_2	-40		-37	41				-38
Q_3	-44	-54			62			
Q_4		96						
D_1	21					55		
D_2				29		55		28
D_3				-37	-28	35		-25
D_4				-49		54		59
D_5		23				51		
D_6	32	30				54		
D_7						83		
Pa			36				66	
Pp	-20			-24			(10)	-59
Sc			27				61	
Ag				-35			45	
Ps							74	

Note: Decimal points omitted as in all factor-loading tables. Intelligence B and shrewdness N have been omitted as variables since they define no factor. Second-order factors V, VI, and VII are not recorded; two are not present and VI has no loading on the pathological factor except 0.32 on Pp psychopathic. The label "untamedness" given to VI is fully supported by this new association. The anxiety factor has only a trivial association with depression items (the factors, however, correlate 0.3); superego loads anxious depression; except for D_3 brooding discontent the depression primaries all load roughly to an equal degree on the general depression factor. The existence of the general psychosis state—loading highest on the general psychosis primary Ps and omitting the psychopathic primary—is a new discovery.

supposes that personality traits, at least, are not entirely fixed and that their relatively small variance can be observed through dR technique. However, the development of new concepts, unless inescapable, offends the scientific law of parsimony and is thus to be avoided. Another possibility is that the results are some kind of statistical artifact. Extensive study of the statistical processes involved summarized in Cattell (1966) demonstrates that the results cannot be accounted for in this way. In addition, as we shall see, support for these factors (whether of mood or trait change) comes from P technique studies. Just as it can be shown that these change factors are not statistical artifacts so it can be demonstrated that the hypothesis that traits are really states is untenable by checks on the variance and on the stability coefficients of states and traits. This has been done and R technique factors are not states.

Thus we are forced to accept the finding with the 16PF that change factors exist, especially at the second-order corresponding to trait factors. Although no study exists of the 23 factors (the 16PF supplement) research into the combined 16PF and pathological primaries has been carried out by Wecko-witz (quoted in Cattell, 1973). Table 11.2 sets out the result.

This table makes it clear that in this research on nearly 200 subjects normal and abnormal who were retested after three months, four trait states were confirmed: anxiety, cortertia, exvia, pathemia and independence. General depression and psychoticism appear as change factors. Cattell (1973) argues that it is likely that, although the evidence is less clear, the other second-order traits have their corresponding change factors: discreetness, subjectivity, intelligence and good-upbringing.

These are the states or change factors that have been discovered through the application of dR technique to Q data. Shortly we shall examine the findings that have emerged from the study of objective tests which are much more suitable than Q data for P technique but this preliminary outline of the change factors and the observation that these form a parallel set with trait factors is useful in trying to establish the nature of these mood and state factors, the trait change factors and traits.

DIFFERENCES BETWEEN STATES AND TRAITS

So far, for the sake of simplicity, we have assumed that there is a distinction between traits and states, in that states are transitory, traits permanent. However these terms have no absolute meaning. Is a state that lasts years not a trait? How long can a state last before it becomes a trait? Some states, e.g. awe perhaps at a wonderful natural phenomenon such as the aurora borealis or disappointment at a calamitous event, are short. Others such as grief may be prolonged even indeed till death. Furthermore it is to be noted that all the factors which have been isolated by dR technique used with questionnaires must necessarily refer to states of some duration in that testing is in the order of 45 minutes. Even T tests take about 5 minutes to administer and we always need for adequate reliability a battery of such measures. Brief, fleeting states are inevitably missed.

This fact of their being no absolute distinction between traits and states affects our interpretation of the dR factors above which mimic trait patterns. So far we have not tried to distinguish state factors from possible trait-change factors mainly because P or dR factors can be either and there is no way of discriminating between the two. Criterion evidence about each of these factors might enable us to make the distinction empirically and this is the ideal solution. This research has not yet been carried out. In its absence an arbitrary definition is needed and one neat one, which still remains the best has been suggested by Cattell (1973). Since traits do fluctuate over time due to growth, decline and more local reasons, if we measure people on several occasions the between people variance is greater than the between occasions variance. In the case of states the variance is greater between occasions than persons.

Given this distinction between states and traits the nature of trait change factors can be clarified. If personality growth is uniform rather than phasic (like a tree rather than an amphibian) it follows that trait change patterns (representing growth and decline) will closely resemble trait patterns whereas the state pattern need resemble traits only by chance. There is a further complication to this argument: since R analysis produces factors that may be states or traits, states can be distinguished from traits if they appear in both R analysis and dR and P analysis. Traits only appear in R analysis. However, as we have seen, trait change factors can be distinguished from state factors if they mimic trait factors. Thus states appear in R, dR and P analyses, traits only in R analysis and change factors in dR and P technique. Change factor patterns resemble trait patterns and states need not resemble traits (although in the case of anxiety it does).

From this is clear that it is a complex problem to make clear distinctions between traits, states and trait-change factors although the arguments we have presented mean that in some specific cases we can be reasonably confident of our factor definition.

STATE FACTORS FROM P TECHNIQUE

So far we have discussed the state and trait-change factors that have emerged from the study of Q data and the state sphere defined by the personality sphere. We must now turn to the factors that have emerged from the study of the mood sphere defined in terms of variables set up to cover the state sphere specifically. The original study utilized P technique applied to specially written questionnaire items, observer ratings and a large variety of objective T tests including physiological measures. All these tests were given to the sample on each of 55 days. The results of this first study (Cattell, Cattell and Rhymer, 1947) confirmed what we have already shown with dR technique namely that factors apparently identical to Q primaries A, C, F, G and H appeared together with two second-order factors exvia and anxiety. In addition there was a general second-order factor of general fatigue.

For the student interested in fresh advances in experimental methods as such it should be pointed out that factor analysis can be combined with the manipulative procedures of classical experiment. In P techniques stimuli can be manipulated and their magnitudes correlated in with state response magnitudes. Thus Cattell and Scheier (1961) report a P technique study on eight depressive neurotics in which on half the occasions a stress was introduced. From the 34 physiological and questionnaire variables eight factors appeared, of which five were identified. These were anxiety, pathemia effort stress, adrenergic system responses, and a state of raised pulse rate and serum cholesterol level. Important here was the finding that effort stress and anxiety are distinct and that anxiety does not raise cholesterol level. Again it was noteworthy that anxiety was not produced by the stress interview but rather effort stress.

Van Egeren (1963) studied T data, physiological data and Q data from the 16PF test and the 7 depression factors discussed in our chapter on the abnormal personality sphere. Here it was found that depression was implicated not only in anxiety but also in regression. Since, compared with traits, the study of moods and states is young and there are severe problems in trying to distinguish between states, trait change and trait factors it is not possible to discuss it in detail here. Readers must be referred to Cattell (1973) although even this discussion needs amplification from the original papers. All we can do here is to summarize this work by setting out the state factors that have been most reliably replicated in the various studies. These findings are based largely on the definitive work of Curran (1968) and Nesselroade (Cattell and Nesselroade, 1973).

State Factors

All this work with physiological tests, T data and Q data has yielded 8 source states which are simply measured in the *Eight State Questionnaire* (Curran and Cattell, 1974). The source states are: exvia, anxiety, depression, arousal, fatigue, guilt, depression and stress-regression. Some idea of the nature of these factors can be gained by looking at the variables loading on the factors. Thus state anxiety loads on susceptibility to annoyance, lack of confidence in new skills, highly emotional comments, pulse increase to cold pressor test and raised blood cholinesterase. In some respects these loadings are similar to those of trait anxiety—in the case of the annoyances and the comments tests. This means that when a person is made anxious by some event he resembles the person who is neurotically anxious all the time. The elation factor loads inter alia on high verbal fluency and brief reaction time. This means that when we are elated we act quickly, talk a lot and respond spontaneously. The truth of this picture is surely supported if we watch, for example, people who have just met after a long separation.

Some attempt has been made to examine the second-order structure among states although results are not clear, partly because of the imperfect match between Q and T factors and also because T factors at the first order appear to parallel second-order Q factors. At the third order three replicable factors emerge (alpha, beta and gamma) which may underlly not psychological structures but environmental factors. Thus alpha loading on exvia and anxiety might be the kind of situation that increases anxious introversion—having to enter a crowded room is an obvious example. Beta loading on depression and guilt (negatively) and positively on fatigue could represent high work demands. As Flugel (1945) points out many men after a spell of hard work feel that they have earned a break and can enjoy some relaxation such as sailing or golf. However if work has been left undone the pleasure is spoiled. Factor Beta may reflect this kind of situation which Flugel interprets psychoanalytically as demonstrating a primitive kind of reparation. Gamma loading on stress and regression may well represent overwork. Obviously these speculations should not be pressed too far without further evidence but these third-order factors can certainly be interpreted.

Summary of Findings
As a result of studying mood states based upon factor traits in the normal and abnormal personality sphere 10 states have been found of which the most important are: anxiety, exvia, cortertia, independence, general depression and psychoticism. From the study of moods and states based upon objective tests and physiological measures considerable overlap with the previous findings occurred but stress, fatigue, arousal, regression and some lesser depression factors have been identified. Considerable problems were noted in the conceptual discrimination of states, trait-change and trait factors.

Thus far in this chapter we have discussed the methodology involved in the study of moods and states. We have also given brief descriptions of the source states so far discovered. One of these, however, anxiety, is so important in clinical and indeed in educational psychology that we shall examine it in more detail.

THE NATURE OF ANXIETY

Anxiety is seen by Cattell (1972b) as a suspension of behavioural expression paradoxically combined with a heightening of dynamic readiness. Its implied inability to cope is the probable reason why associated with it are variables such as lack of confidence, irritability, the tendency to agree, reduction of self-sentiment and guilt. *State anxiety* is characterized by loadings on such physiological variables as high systolic pulse pressure, faster heart rate, faster respiration rate, and lower pH saliva. These physiological changes clearly discriminate state anxiety from the response patterns associated with anger, effort and fear.

This state pattern contrasts clearly with anxiety as a trait. In Q data state anxiety emphasizes the sense of the inability to cope (C— and Q3—) but shows less protension (L), guilt (O) and the temperamental tendency to react to threat (H—). In addition the physiological indices, some of which we have mentioned above, are more prevalent in the state loadings.

We have been keen to stress the distinction between state and trait anxiety because they are both such important variables in the analysis of personality both temperament and mood. Anxiety is one of the largest second-order temperamental Q factors clearly implicated in neurosis and in a wide variety of behaviour—for example academic performance (Cattell and Butcher, 1968). Accurate measurement means that we must be able to distinguish fully state and trait anxiety—especially when we are interested in the trait. If we were concerned with the relation of anxiety to examination scores and on the day we administered the anxiety measure one of the school buses had narrowly avoided a serious road accident, the failure to discriminate the two types of anxiety would be fatal. This state/trait distinction has been demonstrated by Cattell *et al.* (1974) among adolescents although, as yet, there is no fully developed test for the state anxiety.

Cattell and his associates are not the only workers in the area of anxiety to attempt to measure state and trait anxiety separately. Spielberger and his associates (Spielberger *et al.*, 1970) have produced a state and trait anxiety inventory (STAI). The rationale for item selection is item variability: items of low reliability over time are regarded as state anxiety items. Stable items are trait items, all being face valid for anxiety a distinction supported by Gaudy *et al.* (1975). However there are obvious problems with this rationale (all of which we have discussed earlier in this book): first items cannot be properly selected simply by content. More importantly, items can be unreliable for psychometric reasons such as ambiguity of statement (i.e. simply poor reliability). Item fluctuation is a necessary but not sufficient condition for state items. Spielberger's state scale could be an unreliable trait scale. Indeed Nesselroade (1973) in a factor analytic study of the STAI together with markers from the Cattell Anxiety State factor and Curran's depression state factor found that there were indeed two factors in the STAI but that they appeared as two states (neither of them anxiety). Instead these scales loaded clearly on the depression and stress scores. Since there are three or four clear factors in this area it could be argued that these fine distinctions between anxiety, stress and depression are largely semantic. However as Cattell (1973) points out, the two Cattell anxiety factors on which the Spielberger factors failed to load are linked to anxiety almost however it is measured—high correlations with Eysenck's N and with the Manifest Anxiety Scale.

A further research by Nesselroade and Cable (1973 and 1974) using R technique found two clear anxiety factors which were interpreted as trait and state anxiety and which are available as tests in Barton's (1973b) Central State and Trait Kit. All this evidence is a clear indication that anxiety as a state can be discriminated from trait anxiety and as we shall see in later chapters on educational and clinical applications of these findings this distinction is highly useful.

STATE THEORIES

In a behavioural specification equation we have seen how we would insert values for ability, personality and motivational variables. However as we have frequently shown throughout this chapter momentary moods and states are important and can profoundly affect behavioural response. This is why we have been forced despite the complexity of the problem to enter the field of state measurement. How therefore are we to use the state variables that we have discussed in this chapter? To insert them into the equation means that we must have some underlying theory or model of how they operate within the field of personality. In real terms the picture seems simple if we could have accurate measurements of all the moods relevant to the behaviour in question. Since work with mood scales is still in its infancy we do not intend to develop any models here in detail. They are still in the realms of speculation. However there seems little doubt, as Cattell (1973) points out, that a modulation model does fit the data as known now. In this it is assumed that there is a *state liability trait* corresponding to each particular state, and that there are individual differences on each of these state liability traits. The liability value is transformed by a modulator which expresses the average stimulation for most people to a particular stimulus for a particular state. An obvious problem here lies in the measurement of such stimuli which can be either internal or external—virtually a separate area of research in itself although there is no reason why it should not be done as the measurement of states becomes more precise. The sort of questions we are referring to are the effects on fear of a charging bull or a drunken labourer with an iron bar. While these effects may be relatively homogeneous the study of stimuli for sex for example would appear far more complex. What would an average score mean? How could we compare two film stars, say Brigitte Bardot and Britt Ekland? For the man for whom Bardot represents sexual perfection an average stimulus value is meaningless as it is for the man who finds her unattractive. However, these are practical problems which research methods may well be able to overcome as they are developed. Perhaps the most notable feature of this model is the fact that a fourth concept (beyond traits state and trait-change factors) has been introduced—the state liability trait.

SITUATIONALISM

At this point mention must be made of the work of Mischel (1968, 1971, 1973) who has criticized trait theories of personality, and hence the approach adopted in this book on a variety of grounds.

Mischel (1973) points out that the trait approach assumes that there are factors of dispositions underlying behaviour, a problem quite distinct from their empirical status. He argues in the behaviourist tradition that such assumptions are naive and unwarranted. We see, for example, a child, not doing his homework and call him lazy. We then categorize the child as being high on "laziness" a trait and then use this as some causal explanation. While this argument is sound, if we can convincingly demonstrate that such trait factors do make sense of a wide variety of behaviours, as we can through factor analysis as a method, then this empirical demonstration makes the logical point irrelevant.

Mischel (1968) has argued that in the field of personality there is insufficient consistency across situations to support the hypotheses of underlying dispositional traits. "Response patterns", he writes (p. 177) "even in highly similar situations often fail to be strongly related." In the sphere of ability Mischel allows a certain consistency but not otherwise. The factors which we have discussed throughout this book would be regarded as artifacts of the *situations* i.e. inventories, ratings and objective tests. Thus to understand behaviour we have to observe the stimuli eliciting it. Bowers (1973) regards this viewpoint as situationalism.

One obvious argument against this position is that in fact people are perceived as being relatively consistent. As we have observed before we would be surprised to find a circus ringmaster consulting the archives of the Bodleian library. This argument however is brushed aside not only by Mischel (1968) but by earlier writers, e.g. Vernon, 1964. The constancy is only apparent. It reflects the observer's stereotypes, e.g. clever but cunning Jews, aggressive West Indians, noisy bookmakers, etc., the tendency for a halo effect in any judgemental procedure and the tendency to ignore contrary evidence.

Even worse the very traits themselves are held to reflect only the categories used by raters in assessing personality, rather than any real aspect of personality. Thus Mischel (1971) describes studies where ratings of subjects revealed 5 factors. However when the raters were required to rate subjects whom they had seen for a brief period only, so that any ratings would be purely imaginary the factorial structure remains the same. Hence the argument is put forward that ratings reflect raters rather than subjects.

These appear to be severe objections. How are they to be answered? There are two clear answers to these problems.

Cattell's rating procedures, as we have discussed, were developed with extreme care. They are perhaps the most detailed ratings that have been produced (see Cattell, 1957, for the full description). This means that many of the objections to ratings made by Mischel fall away. They were essentially behavioural observations. They were not likely to be simply the categories of the raters.

The Cattell factors are not simply categories of terms defining personality, independent of behaviour itself. If they were, we would not find the huge range of psychologically meaningful data, in terms of differences between occupational and clinical groups, developmental trends and correlations with various criteria that form the substance of this book. There would be no external, construct validity. In other words, empirical findings contradict the argument.

This is not to deny that situational determinants influence behaviour. Of course this is the case. We behave differently in different situations. Only a psychotic, not an extravert, eats celery or dry toast in the British Museum Library. However these situational determinants are taken account of (theoretically) in the specification equation (see p. 268). What is argued is that the differences in behaviour across situations reflect themselves our position on the temperamental, mood and dynamic traits. There is no real antithesis between the situational and the trait view in a proper understanding of factorial psychology.

SUMMARY

1. A distinction was drawn between traits and moods and states. The special methods to study states were described—dR and P techniques in factor-analysis.
2. The personality state sphere was defined and the dR factors which have emerged from Q data were discussed.
3. A more detailed discussion of differences between states and traits in the light of dR factors was made. Traits can appear only in R analysis. States can appear in R, dR and P analysis while state-change factors can appear only in dR and P techniques.
4. The state factors emerging from P technique were described and special attention was paid to the vital distinction between state and trait anxiety.
5. A state theory was described so that state factors could be fitted into the specification equation.
6. The work of Mischel (situationalism) was discussed in the light of the specification equation.

Chapter 12

Personality and Structured Learning Theory

THE HISTORICAL INDEPENDENCE OF REFLEXOLOGICAL LEARNING THEORY AND PERSONALITY STRUCTURE THEORY

For the first half of this century personality theory and learning theory proceeded on parallel courses   possibly meeting at infinity, but certainly not in that era. Rather desperate attempts—as in the Kentucky Symposium (1955)—were then made to bring them together, since the ambitions of a unified science demanded an end to this malformation in the middle of psychology. This artificial attempt at connection repeatedly broke down, and a genuine possibility of knitting the two areas began only a decade ago with the advent of what has come to be called *structured learning theory*.

The reasons for the chasm between these two major theory areas are relatively clear. Reflexological learning theory, which is sometimes inaccurately equated with behaviourism, in the work of Pavlov, Watson and others, began with reflexes. At first they were physiological reflexes in the stomach and salivary glands, and then twitches of a dog's leg, and, later, autonomic reactions of fright or some other emotion. Both in this branch of classical learning experiment and in the learning of nonsense syllables, some highly specific piece of behaviour is eventually plotted in a graph against some time sequence of repetitions and rewards. This carefully cultivated, but narrow line of reflexological learning theory, has brought appreciable, but by no means

229

completely intelligible, order into such learning, as instanced in the work of Skinner (1953), Kimble (1961), Deese (1952) and many others.

While this was progressing the personality theorists, starting with ideas of structure, and the conflict of structures which emerged from clinical psychology, notably that of Freud, proceeded to develop personality measurement as a necessary basis for more experimental work. That work, with data from observations, questionnaires and objective tests, culminated in the sixties, as we have seen, with tolerably precise conceptions of personality structure in ability, temperament, and motivational fields. It went further and discovered the typical age development curves for abilities and personality traits, objectified the measurement and action of the transient emotional states, and brought operational methods to bear on dynamic conflict and related processes.

The impasse between personality theory and learning theory was evident in a mutually empty-handed attempt at bargaining. The personality theorist said to the learning theorist, "Here I have a substantial and practically effective knowledge of personality structure. That structure must have arisen either by genetic maturation, by learning, especially social learning (or by an interaction of both). How does learning theory account for these structures?" But learning theory was silent, for it had concerned itself only with specific bits of behaviour and with learning curves derived in any case largely from the rat. It is true that learning theorists like Hull (1943), Mowrer (1950) and Tolman (1952) had posited some structures, such as drives—or, rather, "drive", since they offered no evidence like that in chapters 9 and 10, on the number and nature of actual drives. Behaviour therapy began to apply reflexological principles to broader behaviour than simple reflexes, though there was no adequate proof that this extension would apply. In any case, it has never concerned itself with the broad structures of the personality theorist and it has remained for very recent work by Barton, De Young, Bartsch, Dielman and a few others who are personality researchers enriching learning theory to show that measures on these structures will change significantly under various life treatments (as discussed in chapters 9 and 10).

THE TRI-VECTOR ANALYSIS OF LEARNING IN THE TOTAL PERSONALITY

It is obvious that the appearance of personality structures, and perhaps also their development and change (except for maturational patterns, as in ergs or fluid intelligence) must be accounted for by some schedule of repetition and reward which occurs *with simultaneous strength for all elements of the pattern.* If such an influence impinged more on some people than others, e.g. in the inhibition factor, UI.17, if children in some families were subjected to more restraint over a whole series of behaviours than those in other families, then a factor pattern of the kind we discover in many areas of measured behaviour would emerge.

The shift from measuring learning on a stray bit of behaviour to measuring it on some meaningful unitary pattern of behaviour is a part, but by no means the whole, of structured learning theory. The existence of what has been called *integration learning* as contrasted with *means-end learning* (operant conditioning) can also be precisely conceptualized and formulated for experiment. Such integration learning, incidentally, should be seen in the whole perspective of recognizable processes in personality change over time, and Table 12.1 can perhaps convey this perspective most quickly.

Integrative learning is stated above in a dynamic context, but it applies also to skills and other traits which can be brought into combination. In what manner, however, can it be quantitatively expressed? Let us consider the full behaviour specification equation, covering not only the action of traits but also of states, as studied in the preceding chapter. Ambient situations, i.e. the situation around the focal stimulus to which one is reacting, *modulate* a characteristic proneness or liability, L, of the individual to a particular individual, i, to the particular emotional state, x, by a modulating index peculiar to the situation t, written s_t. The resultant state level for the given individual i, on state x, at time t, is thus:

$$S_{x.i.t} = s_{xt} L_{xi} \qquad (12.1)$$

However, there is evidence that many supposed traits also modulate. For example, a person who in trait terms is an ambitious person, may have this ambition stimulated by an ambient situation of success. It is safest, therefore, to write the behaviour equation with modulators for all terms, thus:

$$a_{ijk} = b_{j1} s_{k1} T_{1i} + \cdots + b_{jn} s_{kn} T_{ni} \qquad (12.2)$$

where there are n traits involved in the behaviour a_j. Here the b's are *behavioural indices* (factor loadings) showing how much each trait contributes to, i.e. bears upon, the response a_j. As seen earlier, all b's here will have a j subscript because they are peculiar to the behaviour j. A list of values, such as extends here from b_{j1} to b_{jn}, is called, in calculation, a *vector*. So the discovered set of b_j values from 1 to n may be called the *bearing vector*, i.e. a statement of the bearing of one's endowment on those traits upon the behaviour a_j.

But the behaviour j (responding to a focal stimulus h, not included here) is carried out by a state-trait liability affected by the ambient situation, k, so the modulators all have k as a subscript, like s_{k1} and s_{kn} above. The series of s_k's constitute what may be called a *situation or involvement vector*. It tells how much the person has become emotionally involved in that situation, partly perhaps through innate responses to cues and partly from past experiences in that situation. For example, a behaviour therapist practising behaviour modification may have a patient with altogether too high an anxiety elevation

TABLE 12.1

Sources of Behaviour Change: Acquisition and Volution

1. Acquisition: *(Modification by Experience)*	1(a) *Learning (and Forgetting)*	1(a)(i) *CE.* Coexcitation Learning (Classical Conditioning, CRI) (Principle: coexistent excitation)
		1(a)(ii) *ME.* Means-end Learning (Operant or instrumental Conditioning, CRII) (Principle: connected reward)
		1(a)(iii) *IE.* Integrative Learning (Integration among immediate ends) (Principle: goal hierarchy formation)
		1(a)(iv) *GM.* Ergic Goal Modification (Sublimation, some imprinting) (Principle: second best modified goal acceptance) [Energy-economics changes]
	1(b) *Transformation* (Capacity Change from Direct Physiological Modification by Environment)	Central Nervous System and brain injury Hormonal over development and exhaustion Vitamin deficiency, altitude, oxygen shortage, etc. Drug exposure
2. Volution: *(Endogenous Modification by Intrinsic Time-controlled Constitutional, Life Processes)*		2(a) Maturation or Evolution (Genetic capacities) 2(b) Aging or Involution (Genetic capacities) 2(c) Time-determined Cyclical Changes and Appetitive Effects

Learning defined as change in the response usually given to a particular stimulus and which can be shown to be related to events specifically connected with the response.

Transformation defined as change simply through undergoing exposure to conditions. The term is thus proposed for specialization here as environmentally determined change which is *not* learning and not acquired in a goal directed learning experience, but through passive experience.

Volution: Covering evolution and involution: Change not dependent on experience, either passive or in active learning, but only on time and normal physiological process.

to the situation, k, of "leaving home". His therapeutic success would be evaluated by the extent to which he reduces s_{kx}, where x is the anxiety trait. (The psychometrist will note this s_k is now in individual factor analysis: P-technique.)

Now the full *description* of behaviour at a given moment, as in 12.2 above, is essential for a full description of a *change* in behaviour, and an adequately refined description of the change in behaviour is an indispensable preliminary to research aimed to *explain* the change by learning. Typically, as we have seen, learning theory has set out only to explain a "scalar" increment in the quantity a_{ijk}, but structured learning theory asks learning experiment to concern itself with the change in three vectors: the *trait vector* (since the profile of trait scores also constitutes a vector); the *bearing vector* and the *involvement vector*. That is to say, it implies first, in the *trait vector* that we never learn just one isolated bit of behaviour but that learning is a *multi-dimensional change in relation to a multidimensional situation*. Even a rat taught to press a lever in a Skinner box is not learning that only. He is learning some accommodation to being picked up by the experimenter, a reduction of fear on being put into the box, and so on.

The involvement vector is, of course, extremely important in personality learning, for it defines what changes take place in our fixations and phobias for situations, and the way in which our interests and attitudes have become developed around objects. Changes in the bearing vector are also important, for they describe changes in integration—in the way in which we bring our various traits and ergic expressions into more harmonious and effective action under the influence of experience and rewards.

As to the way in which the above changes in vectors are calculated, the reader must be referred to rather complex factor analytic procedures (Cattell, 1976). Here we need only note that we have a two stage process: (i) presenting the personality theorists' more sophisticated models of what changes constitute learning, and (ii) employing learning theory principles in *explaining* the changes.

DYNAMIC STRUCTURE AND THE DYNAMIC CALCULUS IN THE EXPLANATION OF LEARNING

Personality theory has a contribution to make in the latter which is almost as novel and substantial as in the former. Setting aside for the moment the classical conditioning process, given as the lesser division in table 12.1 and concentrating on what has been called operant conditioning, instrumental conditioning, and (perhaps with less pomp of pedantry and more relevance and brevity, means-end learning), let us look at *reinforcement*. Reinforcement is an ambiguous term. It probably embraces different causal actions in classical and operant conditioning, and it is used both for the fact of an increment in response and the fact of reward. For clarity we will use the term *reward* as that which affects operant (means-end) learning. What structured learning theory brings from the structuring of the motivation and dynamic realm is a capability in defining the *nature* of any given reward more precisely and meaningfully than was previously possible. Hull spoke of "drive in the abstract", but actually we have no evidence that the ergic tension of the different ergs—fear, sex, hunger, etc.—behaves in the same way in learning and remembering. Indeed, there are indications that a conditioned response learnt under fear, for example, extinguishes far less readily than one learnt under, say, hunger.

The whole area concerned with the nature and role of motivation in human learning has remained a blank page in reflexological learning theory, but in structured learning theory it can be handled with elegance. The motives behind any course of action are given in the specification equation in the trait-state vector of values. If we accept the tension reduction statement of rewards, then the reward for either an habitual action or a new response can be defined as the change in the values for the various ergic tensions in the vector of ergic tension. Most human reward is complex, and needs a vector of values to represent the pattern of its quality. The same is in principle true of animal learning, though an experimenter is perhaps entitled to assume that he is, say, rewarding food seeking when he provides food in the goal box. However, even there, as the results of Haverland and others described by Cattell and Child (1975) show, hours of food deprivation is not a very good measure, by psychometric test standards, of the intensity of hunger. More direct measures on the ergic tension level of the animal are needed, paralleling those we described in Chapter 10 for the motivation components in humans.

The whole of what has been described in Chapter 10 under the *dynamic calculus* is relevant to the present theory of structured learning; for motivation remains the central determiner in learning. Temperament factors aside (as largely genetic in origin) the largest factors in personality structure are the sentiments and those abilities which, unlike intelligence, are largely acquired. The acquisition of the sentiment patterns so far discovered—those to home, school, sport, career, and the self-sentiment—is a trial and error process, much like the rat in the maze, in which certain preferred, habitual paths of behaviour are set up in what has been defined (p. 176) as the *dynamic lattice*.

The "maze" which is set up for us as beings born into historical cultures, is that of our particular culture and our immediate socio-physical surroundings. Within this framework our various ergic tensions work themselves out by trial and error into paths in the lattice which maximize satisfaction. There are schedules of reinforcement (reward) provided forces, as Skinner convincingly points out, so that our sentiment structures come to be models of the moulds from which they are cast. However, different people have different degrees of interest in say, sport or career, and it is these differences which permit us by factor analysis to recognize the pattern of the sentiment factor.

Each sentiment pattern, as Chapter 9 shows, gives satisfaction to several ergs, to a degree demonstrable by the ergic factor pattern, and each erg gains satisfaction through several sentiments.

THE MORE REFINED ANALYSIS OF REINFORCEMENT IN HUMAN LEARNING

This covers what might be called the topography of the personality structure, and the general nature of the reward process, specified more exactly in structured learning theory by the "reduction vector" of ergic tensions than has previously been possible. However, the nature of the general process by which reward increases the likelihood of reinstatement of a particular response has not been described. The theory here has two concepts: that of *cognitive excitation*—a cerebral excitation of a cognitive perception and its associated connections, as when a rat sees a new pathway in a maze or a person contemplates the cognitive complexities of a problem in his life. This is assumed to be stimulated at the point in time t_x in Fig. 12.1. The second concept is that of ergic tension already defined in Chapter 9 along with the devices for measuring, in humans, its level in terms of motivation components U and I. In diagram (b) in Fig. 12.1, we see the organism entering the situation at a high level of ergic tension. Let us suppose that at time t_y a response is made to the cognitive stimulus h, which has produced the cognitive excitation, and that this particular response at t_y leads to ergic satisfaction. Other responses $(j_1, j_2,$ etc.) may have been made without such success, but j_n solves the problem and leads to the great reduction in ergic tension shown in (b) at t_y.

By mechanisms still only speculative even in general learning theory, this reduction of tension "stamps in" the connection between h, the cognitive stimulus, and j, the response by a new course of action. (This "stamping in" we call engraming.) What the dynamic calculus in structured learning theory contributes to the existing all-too-general and vague law, is a model, which can be formulated in an equation, for the increase in the future likelihood of making the response j to the stimulus h. For the more detailed handling of the meaning and form of the equation the student must be referred to more advanced treatments (Cattell, 1976). But it is supposed that this learning is a summation or product function of: (i) the amount of the diminishing cognitive reverberation existing at the moment of action, t_y, and (ii) the magnitude of the reduction of ergic tension $(E_{tx} - E_{ty})$, arising at that moment. That is to say, it is a function of the two curves at (a) and (b) in Fig. 12.1, together.

It will be noted that what we represent as $(E_{tx} - E_{ty})$ is actually a whole series of such expressions, one for each of n ergs. (This would be written, as a total ergic reduction, $\sum^{k=n} b_p(E_{ptx} - E_{pty})$, where p is any erg and b is some weight which allows for the possibility that different ergic tensions have different potencies in reinforcement, as speculated above.)

Actual research is only on the threshold of investigating these relations but we do have the means to measure separate ergic tensions in man and there is preliminary evidence (Cattell and Dielman, 1974) that animal psychologists could make these more analytical measurements. Thus Cattell and Dielman ran 128 rats through several mazes, subjecting the rats to various degrees of hunger, thirst and insecurity (fear of shock). They took most measures which animal psychologists regard as indicators of strength of motivation, and, in fact, covered 36 measured expressions. Seven definable factors were found which resembled, as far as one can infer across so wide a zoological gap, the seven primary motivation manifestation factors found in man. Granted the possibility of this more refined vector measurement of the reward in various courses of action a more thorough investigation of the acquisition of personality structure changes in man becomes possible.

"INVESTMENT" ACTION AND OTHER SHAPERS OF STRUCTURE IN THE LEARNING EQUATION

As a completion of this picture of the rise of structure we must not forget to take into account the effects of the other terms in the learning equation. There are ability and personality terms, as well as motivation and reward terms. Indeed, the psychologist of classroom results has for the last fifty years predicted from the ability traits and left the motivation out. Typically, as will be seen in the chapter on education below, about one quarter of the variance in school examinations is contributed by abilities, a quarter by personality traits, a quarter by motivation, and a quarter by luck and circumstance. We are not concerned here with the school application, but only with noting that the *structural form* of newly learnt traits will be accounted for by the form of existing traits as well as by the patterns of reward so far discussed. A classical example of this is the ability trait we call crystallized general intelligence, which derives by hypothesis from a learning equation in which the individual's endowment in fluid general intelligence plays a prominent part. The argument here is that crystallized intelligence appears as a general factor largely because (a) fluid intelligence and (b) the uniform exposure of children to the standard school curriculum, are also both general factors which produce the crystallized intelligence factor (first as a cluster) by their overlap, as shown in Fig. 12.2.

Together they operate in the learning equation to produce a new general factor, crystallized intelligence, in some degree mimicking them both. Such a phenomenon and its explanation have been called the "investment theory" of new pattern development, because existing patterns "invest themselves" in the new, and, granted any degree of uniformity in the reward schedule, produce new factor patterns related to the old.

The full picture of personality structure acquisition requires reference also

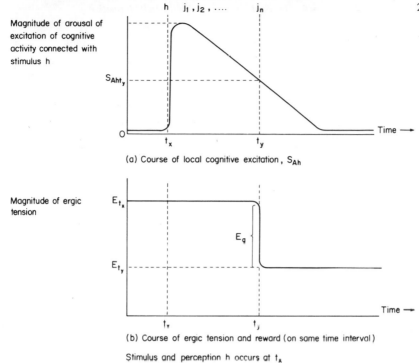

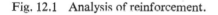

(a) Course of local cognitive excitation, S_{Ah}

(b) Course of ergic tension and reward (on same time interval)

Stimulus and perception h occurs at t_x

Responses j_1, j_2 etc. follow until j_n at t_y gives immediate satisfaction $(E_{t_x} - E_{t_y})$

Fig. 12.1   Analysis of reinforcement.

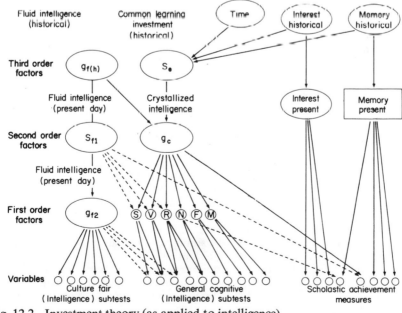

Fig. 12.2   Investment theory (as applied to intelligence).

to the formation of subsidiary sentiments from pre-existing ones, much as a large business corporation may find it advantageous to set up subsidiaries to minister to particular needs. A person with a sentiment about mathematics, for example, may find that he needs to read Russian articles, and sets out to learn the Russian language. This is a large enough undertaking to be said to constitute a sentiment in itself. The new sentiment is instrumental to the old, and the motivation it draws upon comes from the ergic investment resources already made in the mathematics' sentiment. Animal psychologists have studied this under the name of "secondary reinforcement".

A problem in studying human personality change through learning is that rewards are often quite subtle and symbolic rather than as simple as the rat being given bran mash. Nevertheless, at least in principle, the dynamic calculus enables us to track down the ergic nature of the satisfactions from rewards, concrete or abstract, and to understand the learning change accordingly.

SUMMARY

1. "Classical" learning theory, which is centrally reflexological in nature, has for half a century had relatively little useful interaction with personality theory, or with personality modification practices in school or clinic.
2. In the last twenty years several attempts at bridging the gap between the two fields of theory have been made, but only in the last decade have these been successful, largely through personality theory contributing the concepts of *structured learning theory*—a multivariate approach in contrast to the bivariate approach of reflexology.
3. The personality theorist feels the need of a learning theory to explain the undoubted existence of structures in ability and motivation traits. He sees also the need to recognize a category of *integrative learning* in addition to classical conditioning and simple means-end learning. This is done by substituting for a plotted change on a single variable the change on three vectors in the behaviour specification equation.
4. The tri-vector description of learning change recognizes that learning is a multidimensional change in response to a multidimensional stimulus situation, and can be recorded in a vector of change scores for (a) a *trait vector*, (b) a *bearing vector* of behavioural indices showing the changing bearing of factors on a performance and (c) an *involvement vector* showing the changing emotional-motivational involvement in the situation.
5. Structured learning theory contributes also to the explanation of these changes by introducing the possibility of measuring reinforcement by a vector of reductions on the main ergic tension factors. Furthermore it expresses the learning process itself as a function of residual level in a cognitive excitation process from the stimulus, in interaction with the ergic tension reduction from the ensuing action.
6. The growth of structure occurs partly by insightful and partly by trial and error procedures, in relation to reward schedules set up by social structures in the culture. The sentiment structures, found as factors, result from in-

dividual differences in exposure to these social institutions, and their form in the individual replicates these social moulds.

7. The above are not the only sources of acquired unitary patterns. The picture of personality learning includes also the role of existing personality and ability factors in the learning equations for the rise of new factors. Thus by investment action new factors are formed representing especially strong overlaps of two or more existing factors. Secondly, new sentiments come into existence as necessary instruments subsidiated to the requirements of existing sentiments.

Chapter 13

The Application of the Factor Analytic Studies of Personality to Clinical Psychology

IMPORTANCE OF PERSONALITY MEASUREMENT IN CLINICAL PSYCHOLOGY

From the work that we have discussed in the first 12 chapters of this book we have seen that through factor analysis a large number of temperamental traits, moods and states, together with some important motivational factors have been identified. In varying degrees these factors have been subjected to a considerable amount of study. In this chapter we want to examine the value of this research for clinical psychology, defined here as that branch of psychology associated with mental illness, excluding educational psychology which we discuss in the next chapter. We shall not only consider the practical application of these findings in the diagnosis and treatment of mental illness but we shall also discuss what light they can throw on more theoretical considerations in clinical psychology such as the aetiology of mental illness. One reason for doing this is that the value of the research into personality for clinical psychology is one criterion by which the value of the whole enterprise can be judged. Thus the factor analytic work of Spearman and Thurstone before the war in the analysis of abilities has proved widely applicable in selection procedures. There can be no doubt that tests developed to measure the major ability factors are far more effective instruments for selection than any other means. Such findings are one practical vindication for the factor analytic picture of abilities.

In the same way we can now examine the impact of factorial studies of personality on clinical psychology. We have chosen clinical psychology first before educational and industrial psychology which we also discuss in later chapters because it is to this field that the findings are most germane. Mental illness is one of the most severe forms of illness in terms of the need for medical care and attention, if only because of the average length of hospitalization. Psychoses are the most serious group of mental illnesses, including schizophrenia and manic-depression, because it is these conditions that are least amenable to treatment and give rise to the majority of long term mental patients. Neuroses on the other hand are less severe and are often treated by short-term hospitalization or even in out-patient sessions. Typical common neuroses are phobias, such as agoraphobia, the fear of going out, compulsive rituals and anxious depression. The incidence of neurosis is uncertain because many sufferers seek relief through non-specialized agencies such as ministers of religion or general practitioners but it could well be that about one in five adults at some time suffer from neurotic symptoms.

With so large an incidence of neurosis in modern industrial society (and incidentally as the studies of Field (1960) clearly indicate mental disturbance in rural Ghana, an area by no standards industrialized, is just about as widespread as in America or Great Britain) the cost of adequate treatment for all sufferers is obviously immense. Indeed modern psychotherapy, of whatever school, is not highly effective so that treatment is usually prolonged and often unsuccessful. It can be argued that it would be prudent to increase expenditure on fundamental research into mental illness rather than pour vast amounts into therapy programmes of uncertain outcome and dubious rationale. Prudent not just in terms of saving money but of ultimately improving treatment. Certainly in the case of cancer the most promising leads have often come not from applied research directly into the problem but from fundamental research into biochemistry, virology and genetics. Without a sound knowledge of the basic underlying science, applied science is a hit or miss procedure and there can be no doubt that at present, as in the case of cancer again, in psychotherapy and clinical psychology we are short of the basic knowledge.

This phrase "basic knowledge" is comfortingly vague. It hides us from defining precisely what knowledge we need properly to understand the problems of clinical psychology. Really there would appear to be two basic sets of questions to which we need answers. First there are the questions concerning the different types of mental illness: how should mental illnesses be classified? What are the causes (in the sense of antecedents) of different mental disorders? Are some quantitatively different from normal states or are they qualitatively different? Is depression merely an extension of the depression that almost all of us from time to time suffer? These are typical of the problems concerning mental disturbances. The second set of questions relates to therapy itself: what type of therapy is best for what disorder? It could be the case that psychoanalytic therapy was effective for, say, depression, behaviour therapy for phobias and non-directive (Rogerian) therapy for anxiety. There may be an important interaction between the personality of the patient and the personality of the therapist which entirely outweighs the type of therapy the therapist happens to use. Almost all schools of psychotherapy have emphasized the importance of this interaction. Indeed Freud once said of Jung that all was well with him because he understood transference. It could be that extraverted patients do well with extraverted therapists and vice versa. Another important area of study in therapy is to try to isolate the critical interchanges that occur during therapy: what, in other words, does a successful therapist say or do that less successful practitioners do not?

It is these questions which are not yet fully answered that bedevil the practice and theory of clinical psychology and in this chapter we shall examine the factor analytic findings in personality and motivation in relation to them.

It would be wrong and unjust to the enormous efforts of clinical psychologists and researchers to imagine that before the development of factor analytic personality tests no attempts had been made to develop tests and measures to attack some of these problems. Two of the most widely used psychological tests in the world—the Rorschach and the Minnesota Multiphasic Personality Inventory (MMPI)—were developed for precisely this purpose. Neither of these tests (fully discussed on pp. 139 and 54 respectively), however useful they may be in practice, can yield theoretical insights in the way that factored tests are able.

Another problem, of clinical psychology which was perhaps the reason that special tests were developed without reference to normal personality and one which certainly coloured all the thinking about the problems of mental illness was what has been referred to as "the medical model". This assumes that mental illness is like physical illness, that there is some cause (analogous to a virus or parasite) which has to be removed if the illness is to be cured. With this model of mental disease it made sense to study the mentally ill without reference to the normal since their psychological processes were likely to be completely different just as, in the case of tape worm, for example, the digestive process is radically changed in that most of the nutriment is going into the worm rather than the body. In mental illness however, as Freud stressed (although this aspect of his views is still not completely accepted in psychiatry), there seems to be far less difference between health and illness: in fact they may be regarded as on a continuum. Many forms of mental disturbance are like exaggerations of the normal traits found in most people, just as certain classes of physical disorder, such as diabetes or an allergic form of rheumatism, are dysfunctions and imbalances in normal processes. If this view is accepted then it is nonsensical to develop special tests for the mentally sick that have no reference to norms. This argument is not to deny that some psychotic disorders may be the result of brain damage as in the paranoid delusions of tertiary syphilis where the disease is much more like the physical disease model. However it is to be noted that even these grossly disturbed behaviours (despite the physical cause) are extreme exaggerations of normal perceptual and cognitive processes. Thus one important problem, the relation of the normal to the abnormal, can be attacked by the use of tests with psychological meaning.

With this preamble we must now turn to some more specific questions. The first we shall examine is the meaning and nature of neuroticism.

Neuroticism

The definition of neuroticism given by any psychologist or psychiatrist is likely to reflect the school of thought to which he belongs. To the psychoanalyst neuroticism is a symptom of imbalance between the ego, superego and id. "Where id was there shall ego be" is the succinct aim of pyschoanalytic therapy, in the words of Freud (1933). Thus for him neuroticism is largely a motivational problem and in terms of the factors discussed in this book is concerned with the dynamic rather than the temperamental traits. Many other eclectic workers however seem to equate neuroticism with anxiety. Indeed in our discussion of the second-order temperamental factors we noted that Eysenck labelled his anxiety factor as N, neuroticism. However there can be little doubt from its high correlation with other anxiety factors that it is anxiety, the work of Hundal *et al.* (1972) in India where N was factored with a large number of other anxiety measures being fairly conclusive. An even more powerful argument against identifying neuroticism with anxiety was the finding discussed in detail by Cattell (1973) that neurotics differed from normals on E, F, N and especially I and other factors. Thus all justification for Eysenck's idiosyncratic label is removed and we recognize that the neurotic has some systematic character differences over and above his anxiety.

Perhaps the most important definition of neuroticism is that advocated by the European phenomenological school of psychiatry, best exemplified in the work of Schneider (1958) on psychopathic personalities. He argues that the only objective meaningful definition of neuroticism is the pattern of behaviour shown by neurotics. Neurotics are defined operationally in that they are those people who seek treatment for mental disturbance or are sent by their relations and friends because their feelings and behaviour are a burden to themselves or others. This definition of neurosis is really a socially bound definition in that behaviour that would be so classified in one society might not be in another. This definition strictly includes the psychotics, but these can then be afterwards differentiated by further criteria such as thought disorder or lack of contact with reality. With this concept of neuroticism it is clear that the factorial dimensions of personality and motivation are exceedingly useful because they enable us to see in what way neurotics (thus defined) differ psychologically from normals.

DIFFERENTIATION OF NORMALS FROM ABNORMALS AND OF ABNORMAL GROUPS

We have fully discussed the MMPI in Chapter 5 so that it is unnecessary to examine it here in any detail. Suffice it to say that it will discriminate hypochondriacs, depressives, hysterics, psychopathic deviates, homosexuals, paranoids, psychasthenics, schizophrenics and hypomanics, if these groups have been classified by similar criteria to those in the standardization sample. As we also pointed out in Chapter 5, psychiatric diagnosis is not highly reliable and results are rarely as clear cut as the scales nominally suggest. There can be no doubt that the scales do differentiate normal from psychiatric groups, although on what psychological basis is not clear since the scales were constructed entirely empirically. The MMPI undoubtedly represents a successful pre-factorial attempt to discriminate normals from abnormals and to differentiate among abnormal groups. We shall return to this test later in this section when we scrutinize the factorial differentiation of normals and neurotics since, as readers will remember, the abnormal personality sphere was partly defined by MMPI items.

Projective tests have also been widely used in the study of neurotics. However, as Eysenck (1959) has pointed out, the reliability and validity of projective tests used in the traditional way is poor. The subjective interpretations usually hinge around a specific personality theory which may be of dubious validity itself or refer to matters specific to the patient involved which make the findings of little interest to the scientific study of personality. Thus, for example standard interpretations of the TAT are based upon Murray's 1938 personality theory which proposed a large number of human needs and environmental presses corresponding to them. Alternatively it is possible to make *ad hoc* interpretations of TAT protocols in the light of other knowledge about the subject. Used in this way the TAT has revealed considerable differences between neurotics and normals but as with the MMPI the psychological meaning of these discriminating variables is often by no means obvious. Yet another method, perhaps the earliest, deserves mention—the word association test. Jung (1918) early on in his psychiatric practice observed that the word associations of normals differed from those of abnormals both as regards content and latency of response (as we have discussed in Chapter 8 on objective tests). Jung naturally interpreted these findings in terms of his own dynamic theories and abnormal responses or latencies were held to be symptomatic of repressed materials or complexes. Much research is required to tie down the meaning of such results.

These pre-factorial findings (of which there are many thousands) indicate clearly that neurotics differ from normals although they do not indicate in any clear way how they differ. For this, what is needed is to compare neurotics and normals on those personality factors that have been found to underly normal personality. Since, as we have seen from earlier chapters, much is known about the psychological nature of these factors, such comparisons are likely to give us meaningful insights into the nature of neurosis and when comparisons are made between different neurotic and psychotic groups similar useful information should be obtained. First we shall examine differences with Q data.

Q DATA RESULTS

So much research has been carried out over the years that a detailed description of the findings is impossible in this chapter. Nevertheless we shall attempt to summarize the main results. Before we set these out it is necessary to recall that most of the work has been carried out with the standard 16PF factors which, as we shall see, were well able to make useful discriminations among various neurotic, alcoholic, drug addict, etc. groups. However it has become increasingly clear that though the normal personality factors do an excellent job in distinguishing and understanding such neurotic and maladjusted types, they miss some dimensions in the psychotic. Thus the 16PF gives distinctive profiles as shown below for the former, but on the psychotic one gets only the pre-psychotic personality or traits which describe why the psychosis expresses itself in the given manner. For example, schizophrenics are shown as introverted and manics as extraverted.

Consequently, in the late sixties a thorough factor analytic search was carried out among abnormal behaviour items, as in the MMPI, various psychotic depression scales and other clinically developed items. The result was 12 pathological dimensions beyond the 16 normal dimensions in the 16PF as described in chapter 4. The 16 normal (but in clinical types of item) and the 12 pathological (in thoroughly clinical expressive) scales were then put together and standardized as parts 1 and 2 of the Clinical Analysis Questionnaire (CAQ). The CAQ so constructed is likely, as it gets more wide use, to give valuable information on the psychotic reaction. However, some clinicians may still feel that the factors common to both normal and abnormal samples are the more important and these are the factors in the 16PF test. Again we must stress that the Cattell factors are basic source traits and not simply surface trait *syndromes* that can be observed by a psychiatrist. Although the lack of the abnormal personality factors has not proved serious for the study of neurosis, homosexuality, delinquency and drug addiction, it has had more influence on the result with psychotics who are less like normals than neurotics in being differentiated on these abnormal factors, as Eysenck and Eysenck (1968) have found in their studies of the psychoticism factor.

One further point deserves to be made. In Mahrer (1970) Cattell introduces the concept of depth psychometry as a useful diagnostic and prognostic tool. Vidal (1972) has used a similar procedure which involves working out the relative influence on second-order factors of the various primaries in temperamental trait measurement. This can greatly improve understanding and prediction in the individual case. Depth psychometry itself referred to the insight from combined use of source traits and surface traits. This, of course, is precisely what is possible from the two halves of the CAQ where the normal factors and the abnormal factors derived from the MMPI are measured, and from the standard application of the MMPI. Thus the same position on a surface trait syndrome in the MMPI can be reached by a variety of composite scores on the personality source trait factors. Knowing what can be called the individual factorial composition of a trait syndrome score can increase the efficiency of prognosis and, according to Freedman and Kaplan (1967), can even suggest different treatments and goals of treatments. Depth psychometry is a highly specialized and complex subject which we can discuss no further here. Suffice it to say, however, that it is one promising approach in clinical psychology which, if it turns out to be successful, will alone justify the use of factored concepts in clinical work.

As we can see from Table 13.1, an impressive amount of evidence has accumulated, about different neurotic groups in terms of the 16PF factors. However, since there is too much information to take in at a glance, Table 13.2 presents the means scores of a general neurotic sample which enables us first of all to see how neurotics differ from normals. This information will then enable us to grasp better the import of Table 13.1.

Normal Neurotic Distinction

From Table 13.2 it is clear that the neurotic is, compared with normals, low on ego strength (C−), tends to be weak and submissive (E−), is desurgent and inhibited (F−), but has low superego strength (G−). In addition to this he is timid (H−) in the sense of physiologically overacting to threat and is highly anxious and guilty (O and Q4). This description is interesting in the light of the many claims that have been made about neurosis based upon clinical intuition. Freud conceived of neurosis as an imbalance between ego superego and id. This view is partly supported by the finding that neurotics *are* low on

TABLE 13.1

Profiles for Specific Neurotic Types

Source Trait			A	B	C	E	F	G	H	I	L	M	N	O	Q₁	Q₂	Q₃	Q₄	QI	QII	QIII	QIV
	N																					
Anxiety Reaction	80	M ——	5.9	6.9	2.8	3.7	3.5	4.3	4.3	7.1	7.5	6.4	5.2	8.5	5.4	6.1	4.5	7.8	3.8	8.3	3.4	5.0
		σ	2.1	2.0	2.3	2.1	2.1	2.1	2.4	1.9	2.3	2.3	2.1	2.6	1.5	1.9	2.3	2.5				
Conversion Reaction	31	M – – –	4.9	6.5	4.2	5.7	4.1	5.2	4.2	5.2	6.1	5.2	5.7	6.9	4.7	6.2	5.0	7.7	4.4	7.2	5.5	5.1
		σ	1.9	2.4	2.0	2.6	1.8	2.1	1.5	2.6	2.8	2.4	2.3	2.6	1.9	2.0	2.3	2.2				
Depressive Reaction	70	M ······	5.4	5.4	2.7	3.9	3.5	4.5	4.9	7.1	7.4	7.0	5.5	7.5	5.2	6.2	4.5	8.1	4.0	8.0	4.1	5.3
		σ	2.1	1.8	2.2	2.1	1.9	1.5	2.6	1.8	2.2	1.8	1.9	2.1	1.5	1.3	1.5	2.0				
Obsessive Compulsive	29	M –––·–	5.9	6.1	4.8	3.7	3.8	4.9	3.7	6.7	5.3	6.0	4.8	7.7	4.4	5.4	4.4	7.7	4.1	7.5	3.5	4.0
		σ	2.3	1.8	1.9	2.0	2.4	2.0	2.2	2.3	2.5	1.7	2.3	2.3	1.3	1.6	2.1	2.2				

		A	B	C	E	F	G	H	I	L	M	N	O	Q_1	Q_2	Q_3	Q_4	QI	QII	QIII	QIV
Inadequate Personality 54	M	5.9	5.1	3.8	5.1	5.4	4.3	4.1	6.3	7.0	7.3	5.5	7.7	5.9	6.7	5.2	7.4	4.6	7.5	4.6	6.0
	σ	1.9	2.0	3.1	3.0	2.7	2.5	2.2	2.1	1.8	2.0	2.8	1.9	1.8	2.7	2.5	2.6				
Psychosomatic 76	M	5.2	6.9	4.9	5.3	4.8	5.0	5.0	5.1	5.5	4.7	5.6	6.4	4.2	6.2	5.1	6.8	4.9	6.5	5.6	4.8
	σ	1.9	2.6	2.0	2.1	1.7	2.2	2.8	1.2	2.3	2.4	2.3	3.4	2.1	2.1	2.2	2.0				

Notes: All profiles in this figure are based on combined male and female data.

Data for these profiles have been taken from Court (1965), Karson (1960), and from unpublished data provided by Dr. K. Delhees (SUNY, Binghampton); Dr. R. M. Dreger (Louisiana State University); Dr. R. P. Fischer (Fenton Company, Williamstown, West Virginia); Dr. I. McDonald (Porirua Mental Hospital, New Zealand); Dr. H. N. McLeod (Toronto Psychiatric Hospital, Canada); Dr. L. A. Pennington (Danville VA Hospital, Illinois); and Professor S. B. Sells (Texas Christian University).

TABLE 13.2

General Neurotic Profile

Source Trait	A	B	C	E	F	G	H	I	L	M	N	O	Q_1	Q_2	Q_3	Q_4	QI	QII	QIII	QIV
M	5.8	6.5	3.0	4.0	3.6	4.6	4.3	7.0	7.2	6.5	5.4	8.1	5.4	6.1	4.4	8.0	4.0	8.2	3.6	5.0
σ	2.1	2.0	2.3	2.1	2.1	2.0	2.4	2.0	2.3	2.1	2.0	2.5	1.5	1.7	2.1	2.3				

Notes: This profile is based on data from 272 males and females.

ego strength—where id was there shall ego be. On the other hand Freud argued that neurotics tended to be ruled by their superego. This is not supported by the low G but against this neurotics are high on Q4 and O, a pattern that is not unlike Freud's description of the superego. The superego (G) scores are noteworthy in the light of psychoanalytic theory and the work of Mowrer (1950). Freud argued (e.g. 1933) that an important problem for neurotics was the excessive severity (strength) of their superego which gave rise to feelings of guilt and did not permit sufficient id expression. Mowrer, however, argued that the neurotic felt guilty because *he was* guilty: his superego was not highly developed: it was not strong but weak and the neurotic defied conscience. The tables do not really support either view although they incline more to orthodox psychoanalytic theory. Factor G is not as high as would have been predicted from the theory. On the other hand it cannot be called low by any standard. Factor O, as both have argued, the guilt-proneness factor, is high. At the second order we can see that the neurotic is an anxious inviant or introvert. Although this is a grossly simplified description (similar to that obtained from Eysenck's EPI), unless we apply the depth psychometric techniques to the data advocated by Vidal (1972), we can see that most clinicians are right in thinking of the neurotic as plagued by anxiety. According to Freud, indeed, this anxiety sprung from the feeling that id material was about to burst through the defences (note the low ego strength) and flood the ego. From Table 13.2 we can see clearly that, to conclude our description, the neurotics are more anxious and less determined and decisive than normals a picture which gives some support for the Freudian view of the neurotic in general, although it must be observed that this approach cannot impinge on one issue that is central to Freudian theory—the Oedipus complex.

Examination of this neurotic profile can be useful in providing us with some understanding of how the mental disturbance arises in the individual. Thus we can see that they are above the mean on M, autia or absent-minded, bohemianism. This dimension is related to subjectivity and disregard of the external world and the high M scorer, wrapped up in his own thoughts, is unlikely to pay much attention to simple practicalities and tends to fit facts to theories rather than theories to facts. Indeed it can be argued that almost all the grand theorizers, such as Marx and Freud, indeed even Eysenck, have had high M in their make up. It is these tendencies which would edge people into absurd emotional positions which then could be hotbeds for neurotic breakdowns. Again neurotics are high on I. Now we have pointed out earlier in our detailed descriptions of the factors that the high I individual is sensitive emotionally, capricious and generally the kind of person who is described as a great big spoiled baby. It is also known that high I is fostered by over-indulgent, early upbringing (postulated by Freud early on in his psychoanalytic work as likely to induce, through fixation, permanent marks on the adult character) which could easily bring this attitude where frustrated needs cannot be handled. Thus the more realistic low I individual will be able to reconcile himself to certain deprivations which are inherent in civilized society, whereas the high scorer will be unable to give up the impulse or accept the consequences—producing the typical neurotic hesitation.

We have already discussed how low C fits the Freudian theory of the development of neurosis and the disparity of the G score and O and Q4 to that theory. However the low E, lack of dominance, is noteworthy. Since, as we shall see later, this is not found in all varieties of neurosis and pathological disorder it is likely that the low score is the consequence (rather than the cause) of the disorder; for low E has been found to be the consequence of many illnesses and misfortunes. The low F, lack of energy, is also marked in neurotics. Actually low E and F are responses to major frustrations which would account for their importance in mental disorder. However Freud, who had also observed the neurotic fatigue and depression of spirit (asthenia), postulated that it was due to the battle between ego and id. The ego spending all its time involved in neurotic defences had used up all its energy.

Since it is possible to calculate from the 16PF factor scores various surface trait scores, an index of the severity of neurosis can be worked out from the 16PF test. This can be derived directly from the factor scores by an appropriate weighting of factors that is given in the Handbook to the test. Alternatively a special 40 item test the NSQ has been developed for this purpose. The use of this special instrument is only recommended where a screening test for neurosis is needed and there is not time to administer the 16PF.

The NSQ enables us to evaluate with reasonable accuracy the *extent* of a patient's disturbance and an obvious use for example could be for a general practitioner to decide on its scores whether an individual should be referred for psychiatric treatment. However as we have indicated, it is far more important from the viewpoint of understanding mental illness and evolving rational therapeutic procedures to know the total personality *structure* of a patient. For this, of course, the NSQ is not satisfactory and the 16PF and hopefully its pathological additions needs to be used.

DIFFERENCES BETWEEN NEUROTIC GROUPS

What we must now examine, therefore, is the personality structure of the different neurotic groups. In a text of this kind, not exclusively devoted to the study of clinical psychology, we cannot go carefully through each of the profiles in Table 13.1. However, we can look at the scores of the different groups on what are clearly the most important factors to see what light they throw on the aetiology and prognosis of the various mental disturbances.

The first thing to notice is factor C—ego strength. Immediately we can see at a glance that almost all the groups in the table are low on this factor. The only exceptions are some of the physically handicapped, e.g. the blind and those with locomotor difficulties, which are not really neurotic groups. The finding that heart disease patients are low on C is support for the implication of psychological factors in this illness. Indeed we can safely say that low C, as Freud claimed, is a feature almost universal among neurotics and psychotics.

The interesting groups are the rare exceptions. These are the psychopaths and the paranoids. The case of the psychopaths is particularly relevant. These are characterized by their complete amorality. To further their own ends they will stop at nothing and seem particularly immune to feelings of guilt. Thus their high ego strength is not inaccurate. Their difficulties do not arise from inability to control their feelings and emotions, almost the contrary. If this interpretation is correct then we would expect a very low G, guilt proneness, or superego. This is indeed what we find on the 16PF scores for G is their lowest score, and no group scores below them. Our interpretations must be cautious because this was a small sample of only 15 psychopaths. These were carefully selected from a larger criminal group as being by common diagnostic agreement "pure" psychopaths, so these results are impressive support for the value of the 16PF test in clinical research. We find here a credible picture of the personality of the psychopath wherein his main weakness—the failure to develop a conscience—is highlighted. While it is difficult to suggest a treatment for this since conscience appears to be laid down in our earliest years, it does suggest that we concentrate on future prevention by trying to stress the importance of the family in child rearing. These findings also relate to the work of Bowlby (1944) with delinquent youths who found that interrupted mothering and the resulting failure to form strong attachments was implicated in psychopathy although this work was of course clinical rather than statistical.

The paranoids were the other group (admittedly psychotic rather than neurotic) whose C score was not abnormally low. What kind of psychological sense does this make? The paranoid is usually defined by the fact of his delusions of persecution which are often developed into a complex system of enormous ingenuity. Ideas of self reference are usually present. For a fuller description readers are referred to Mayer-Gross, Slater and Roth (1967). In Freudian theory based upon the interpretation of the diaries of Judge Schreber by Freud it is postulated that the persecutory feelings are the result of vigorous ego defences: homosexual impulses become hostile feelings due to reaction formation and these become transformed into feelings of persecution by the defence of projection. Thus paranoids are a group characterized by strong ego. This interpretation would imply that id tension should be high (Q4) but this is not really the case. Nevertheless the fact that paranoids as a group do not show a low C score certainly is in accord with one theoretical formulation.

Factor O, guilt proneness, is not useful in discriminating different neurotic and maladjusted groups because all have raised scores on this dimension, thus supporting the psychoanalytic claim that guilt feelings (conceptualized as emanating from the superego) are important in the development of neurosis (Freud, 1933). The psychopathic group is merely at the general population mean for guilt which as we have pointed out fits the description although we should have expected a particularly low score. Q4 is also an important component in mental disturbance reflecting ergic tension and frustration. An examination of Q4 group means in Table 13.1 is instructive. It shows generally that, as we should expect, the physical disorders are around the population mean in id tension, as are the psychoses. It is the neuroses which show the elevated score. Among the highest scorers are those groups which intuitive clinical theory would hypothesize: alcoholics, exhibitionists and homosexuals—all symptoms of inner conflict.

From this brief look at some of the more important primary factors in neurosis it is clear that the 16PF test can go a long way in explicating the neuroses in terms of personality structure. In other words we are beginning to understand why it is that some individuals when subjected to environmental stress remain relatively unaffected (high C for example), why some take refuge in drink (high guilt and ergic tension), and while others yet again become psychopaths, never having developed a superego.

Of course, if psychologists or others want to deal only with a simplified picture (despite considerable loss of information) they can examine the differences in terms of *second-order* factors only. Thus, if we compare neurotics with normals on the second order factor derived by scoring weights from the 16PF primaries we find that the neurotic group is high on anxiety, introversion, and subduedness (opposite to independence, Q4) while it is about average for pathemia.

Consideration of Cattell's second-order findings brings us by an obvious progression to the possibility of comparisons with the work of Eysenck with the EPI. As is to be expected from the close relationships between the EPI factors and the *second-orders* of the Cattell 16PF HSPQ, CPQ and other primary scales which we have fully examined earlier in this book, results with psychiatric groups are very similar. Indeed the results reported in the Handbook to the EPI (Eysenck and Eysenck, 1964), support our discussion of the previous paragraph in most important respects. We find that compared with normals neurotic groups are strongly introverted, as also are psychotic groups. As is to be expected from Eysenckian personality theory (Eysenck, 1967) the hysterical group are the most extravert. However, to be precise, both his results and those on the 16PF show that anxiety hysterics are *less* extraverted than normals. His sample of female prisoners are however (again as fits the Eysenckian theory of crime (Eysenck, 1964)) more extravert than normals, and Cattell's findings with psychopaths and criminals support this. Nevertheless as Cochrane (1973) has pointed out, not all empirical studies support this finding that prisoners are more extravert. Actually in the light of the concept of delinquent sub-cultures it would be improbable if all prisoners were more extraverted than normal since the extraversion is held to underlie the failure to learn the mores of society (extraversion being negatively correlated with conditionability). However the delinquent sub-culture concept implies that criminals have not failed to learn the mores of society but have learned the wrong (delinquent) mores. The disparity of findings which we have mentioned implies that there are distinct populations of criminals: some may well have failed to learn any mores and thus fit the Eysenckian model, others may have learned the wrong things; as Euripides said "evil communication makes evil men". The typing of different types of crime on 16PF profiles by Scheier and by Horn substantiates this existence of quite distinct groups.

The results with the N factor, which as we have shown, is better regarded as *anxiety* (QI1 among the second orders) again confirm the findings from the Cattell scales. Most abnormal groups are more than one standard deviation on anxiety beyond the mean for normals—with the exception of schizophrenics whose anxiety level is about normal. Thus with the exception of hysterics and schizophrenics in Eysenck's system the abnormal individual is the introverted neurotic. There can be little doubt that even if we eschew the complexities of depth psychometry as advocated by Vidal (1972) there is considerably less recorded information and richness of implication for the clinical psychologist from the EPI than from the 16PF.

Enough has now been said about findings on the normal factors derived from Q data to see that they can give us useful insights into the dysfunction of personality structure which occurs in various psychiatric groups. It is time now to leave the normal factors and turn to the information that can be obtained from the 12 new abnormal source trait measures.

FINDINGS WITH ABNORMAL Q FACTORS

The NSQ was designed to measure the degree of neurosis but using items differentiating neurotics from normals on the standard personality factors. As far as proved statistically possible it accounted for the MMPI surface trait syndromes in terms of the normal personality sphere. It was obvious from factorial studies with the MMPI and with special scales developed for psychiatric use that there were extra factors accounting for some abnormal forms of behaviour, particularly those regarded as psychotic rather than neurotic. As described above, these factors, 12 in number, were eventually isolated and a full description of them may be found in Chapter 4. We now want to examine their value in clinical psychology. Most of our discussion will be based upon the work carried out with the CAQ (Delhees and Cattell, 1971) which, measuring 28 factors (16 normal and 12 pathological), attempts to index psychotic behaviour syndromes in terms of pathological factors and is thus for psychosis what the NSQ is for neurosis.

Examination of Table 13.1 shows clearly that the 16PF factors distinguish well between normal and neurotics and delinquents and other anti-social acting-out disturbances. It is equally clear that there appears to be little difference between psychotics and normals except on a few factors and in a few instances. This finding agrees with the general clinical evidence (as found, for example in Mayer-Gross, Slater and Roth, 1967), that in the psychoses behaviours are seen that cut across normal personality expression. Thus the Bayesian study of psychiatric symptoms by Smith (1966) showed clearly that the psychoses involve little disturbance of personality structure whereas with the neuroses, as we have seen, there is a characteristically exaggerated personality structure. It was for this reason that the twelve abnormal pathological factors were searched for and found.

Immediately we can see from table 13.3 that all the six nosological groups are separated from normals on all factors except psychasthenia (As). Furthermore there is effective discrimination between the abnormal groups. It is noteworthy that neurotics are also discriminated from normals on the pathological primaries as well as psychotics although these two categories will be distinguished on the normal factors in the CAQ. Table 13.3 also shows that the first order depression factors are useful in discriminating among the abnormal groups even though these are not generally thought of as particularly involving depression. This is interesting because, as we discussed earlier (see p. 119) these depression factors are highly correlated and their full meaning is not well understood: indeed it might be preferable to use the three second-order depression factors.

May (1971), the original source of the data in table 13.3, worked out discriminant functions based upon these factor scores to maximize separation of the groups. Three dimensions were found necessary to do this. One separated all pathological groups from normals, a second separates at one pole the two schizophrenic groups from neurotics at the other. The third separates the brain damaged and the personality disorder groups from the others. Assignment to groups of individuals based upon weighted scores showed a high degree of agreement with psychiatric diagnosis. As we have discussed in our chapter on multivariate techniques, the discriminant function is ideal for discriminating groups but is not so suitable for theoretical analysis because, unless repeatedly replicated, it makes too much of chance differences between the particular samples involved in the study. Furthermore it presupposes that there is real segregation, without much overlap, in the psychiatrically chosen groups which the tests are asked to discriminate. (The traditional psychiatric categories may not be like those which Taxonome sorts into empirically derived groups.)

Nevertheless this work with the abnormal factors suggests clearly the aspects of personality that are affected in the psychoses. Such work also has a theoretical bearing on how we conceive of psychosis. It is clearly quite wrong to think of psychosis as on some kind of continuum of mental health with the healthy, i.e. supposing the healthy to be at one pole followed by neurotics and ending with psychotics at the other extreme. Psychosis would appear to be a

TABLE 13.3

On the 12 Pathological Primaries (CAQ)[a]

Two Groups[b] Examined for Differences	D_1	D_2	D_3	D_4	D_5	D_6	D_7	Pa	Pp	As	Ps	Sc
1–5		*−										
1–6		**−					**−				**−	
1–7	**+	**+	**+	**+	**+	**+	**+	**+	**+		**+	**+
2–5				*−		**−	*−		**−			
2–6		**−				**−	*−		*−		*−	
2–7	**+	**+	**+	**+	**+	**+	**+	**+	**+		**+	**+
3–5									**−			

3–6	** +	** +	** +	** +	** +	** +	** –	** +	** +	*
3–7	+	+	+	+	+	+	+	+	+	** +
4–5	* –	–	–	* –	* –		* –	* –	** –	* –
4–6	** –	** –	** –	** –	** –	** –	** –	** –	** –	
4–7	** +	** +	** +	** +	** +	** +	** +	** +	** +	** +
5–7	** +	** +	** +	** +	** +	** +	** +	** +	** +	** +
6–7	** +	** +	** +	** +	** +	** +	** +	** +	** +	** +

a Each row examines differences of each pathological syndrome group in turn from the normal group—7 (see paired numbers on left). A plus shows the group on the left is higher and a minus lower. The degree of significance of the difference is shown by an asterisk (P<.05) or two asterisks (P<.01) (by Tukey's HSD test). Data from May (1971).

b (1) paranoid schizophrenics, (2) chronic schizophrenics, (3) organic brain damage, (4) personality disorders, (5) neurotics, (6) affective disorders, (7) normal controls.

separate dimension from neurosis. Neurosis, in the light of the 16PF results, could be seen as the result of a disturbance of normal personality structure. Psychosis, as the text books have long argued, is something very different and is perhaps the result of biochemical disturbance, although this has not been convincingly demonstrated. It would be wrong to neglect the impact of psychological factors on psychotic behaviour simply because it is qualitatively different from neurosis. The work of Laing (1960) for example showed convincingly that in some cases at least the apparently bizarre symptomatology of psychotics represents their attempt to communicate what is essentially a bizarre life experience in a "schizogenic" family.

Parallel to Cattell's work showing a second-order general psychoticism factor in the abnormal personality sphere has been the work by Eysenck and his Maudsley colleagues on the psychoticism scale P. This which, as we have shown, is best regarded as a second-order factor which has emerged at the first order through under-factoring lines up with Cattell's second-order psychoticism factor and is well able to distinguish psychotic from normal and neurotic groups.

Most of the findings which we have so far discussed are relevant to the aetiology of the various disturbances and to theoretical insights rather than to treatment. Nevertheless some of the results with Q data do have bearings on therapy. One important issue is the extent of change as the result of psychotherapy. Now the issue of how to measure the outcome of psychotherapy is exceedingly complex and one which we do not intend to discuss in any detail here. Nevertheless it does not appear unreasonable in the light of the discriminations between neurotics, psychotics and normals which we have discussed above, to postulate that whatever therapy is applied should produce therapeutic improvement shown by personality changes in scale scores moving towards the normal. It is to be noted that this is particularly the case with the source traits measured by the CAQ. This is because they are the fundamental underlying dimensions of personality in contradistinction to scores on specific criterion symptom-keyed test devices which simply discriminate normals from psychiatric groups on surface traits. Changes on the source traits reflect actual personality change. Changes in specific test scores may reflect only symptom change which, except to the behaviour modifiers' school, is not the sole aim of psychotherapy. Given this argument, it follows that the monitoring of therapeutic change over the course of therapy in terms of personality factors enables the therapist to see what happens as he goes along and thus guides his own procedures.

For example Hunt *et al.* (1959) and Rickels *et al.* (1965) have shown with students and private clinical patients, respectively, that psychotherapy increases ego strength, dominance and surgency and lowers anxiety. Reference to Table 13.1 indicates that this is personality change towards normality and is not merely change. For change as such, and even the extinction of some narrow symptoms, could after all be for the worse, i.e. exacerbating the, neurotic factors. Furthermore these changes make psychological sense in that low ego strength is seen as actually bringing about neurotic reactions and reduction of anxiety is obviously helpful.

At the moment it is only fair to add that the study of therapy in terms of structural personality change is not sufficiently advanced for the practical guidance of treatment. However it is the task of research to relate different procedures and strategies to such change so that psychotherapy may have a rational as well as an intuitive basis.

One other important field of treatment on which the factorial study of personality bears is that of delinquency and criminality. We have seen previously how Eysenck's theory has claimed that criminals should comprise mainly neurotic extraverts. More clinically based theory sees delinquency as some sort of acting out of neurotic problems with the result that, with children especially, there has been considerable emphasis on the treatment rather than the punishment of delinquents. It is fair to point out that just what this treatment should be is rarely specified and there is certainly no evidence supporting the value of any particular treatment. Recently the work of Pierson *et al.* (1966) on delinquents transferred to residential schools with constant and consistent discipline, has shown, on the HSPQ, a steady and significant rise in the ego strength factor, C, and the self sentiment factor, Q3. By extending tests through several equivalent forms a sensitivity of measurement can evidently be achieved sufficient to compare therapies.

Psychoanalytic theorizing would suggest that the neurotic and the criminal were alike in that they were not ego controlled (as the mature well balanced man should be) but were different in that the criminal had a defective superego (G in the factor series) and self sentiment (Q3 in the series) whereas the neurotic's was overactive.

Work with delinquent and criminal groups with the 16PF and HSPQ tests can illuminate this problem. First reference to Table 13.1 shows that as this theory would predict criminals of all types with the exception of psychopaths are low on ego strength, as was the case with the neurotic groups. This is not a new discovery since it was anticipated in the brilliant investigation of London gangs by Burt (1948b) in the *Young Delinquent*. Here he noted the high emotionality of these delinquent children, a factor which he considered innate. Studies with factor C, as we have shown in Chapter 7, indicate that there is a constitutional component but that it is also susceptible to environmental influence. Factor G, superego, is also low (although not excessively low, except in homosexuals and psychopaths) which again supports the clinical notions. Another important finding is that there is a tendency for the criminals to be more extravert than normal although E, dominance, is more involved than is usual among normal groups. As was the case with neurotics, a knowledge of the personality structure of the criminal should enable therapy to be put onto a rational basis, although, as yet treatment methods are not advanced.

We have to be careful however in assuming that delinquents are necessarily the same as adult criminals—so that the comparison with Burt's findings may not be altogether apposite. Thus Pierson and Kelly (1963) who gave the HSPQ to every delinquent institutionalized youth in Washington State found that they were high on A, C, E, I, and J but were low on Q3 and D. Cattell in the Handbook to the HSPQ (Cattell and Beloff, 1960) finds that delinquent samples are low on B and G. A large scale study of delinquents in Scotland (McQuaid, 1970) found that they were low on intelligence and superego strength (G) but high on ergic tension (Q4). At the second-order level they were anxious introverts although it must be pointed out that compared with the American controls all Scots tend to be both anxious and introverted. From these investigations it would appear that for delinquents the low ego strength that was noted with adult criminals does not appear. Rather we find high ergic tension and low superego. Thus the delinquent behaviour would appear to reflect not the low ego strength, the inability to tolerate frustration, but rather the strength of the drives. This high ergic tension combined with low intelligence and superego is enough to create delinquent anti-social behaviour, for example the senseless destructiveness of some adolescents. The low intelligence may, of course contribute to their being caught.

These results suggest that it may be the case that young criminals' offences occur because of the overwhelming strength of their drives which may moderate later in life whereas the adult offenders break the law because their defences are particularly weak. Clearly follow up studies of delinquents to trace their pattern of personality development need to be carried out. However the findings with criminals as a whole do support the Freudian dynamic interpretation of crime.

So much for the impact of Q personality factors on clinical psychology: as we have seen they provide useful insights into the nature of neuroses and psychoses and could be with further research valuable in guiding the course of psychotherapy.

OBJECTIVE T FACTORS IN CLINICAL PSYCHOLOGY

In our chapter on objective tests and objective personality factors we were able to show that they measured factors that were clearly different from those in L and Q data. One possibility was that T factors were effectively broader than primary Q and L factors and were therefore equivalent to second-order factors in these domains. While we were able to show substantial overlap between some T factors and some second-orders, the ineluctable fact remained that there were far more T factors than second-orders. While there was reason to think that the most important L and Q factors had been extracted, this was not the case with objective factors. There can be little doubt that some of these at least are measuring aspects of personality that are untouched by the other methods. For this reason, if no other, it is necessary to ask how important they are in clinical psychology.

One other point needs to be considered. Many of the differences between normals, neurotics, psychotics and delinquents, which we have discussed above, despite their obvious psychological sense have to be treated with some discretion because the effects of the neurosis or psychosis may have affected the responses to questionnaires rather than radically changed the personality structure. This is a logical rather than a likely possibility but one that cannot be entirely dismissed as a source of the differences noted, especially when we realize that thought disorder is a characteristic affliction and symptom of psychosis and forms the basis of a highly efficient diagnostic test for schizophrenia—the Rep. Test (Bannister and Fransella, 1966). Objective test data, especially where the tests do not involve questionnaire-like items, will go a long way to obviate these objections.

There are now a considerable number of research findings in clinical psychology with objective tests. Much of this work has been fully discussed and surveyed in the excellent monograph on clinical diagnosis using objective test batteries by Cattell, Schmidt and Bjerstedt (1972) which forms the basis of our discussion in this chapter and to which readers must be referred for further details.

Cattell *et al.* (1972) carried out a detailed study of 114 subjects including involutional psychotics, manic depressivenes, depressive reactives, anxiety reactives, schizophrenics and manics plus controls who were tested twice on a battery of objective tests designed to measure the objective source traits set out in Chapter 8 and on the depression scales of the CAQ. R analysis to investigate traits and dR analysis to investigate states was carried out.

Results

The most important finding in this study we shall describe only briefly, in that it is more relevant to our chapter on objective factors rather than to this one on the application of the findings to clinical psychology. This finding was that the number and nature of factors in this mixed sample of subjects proved essentially the same as that which had emerged from the study of separate groups of psychotics, normals and mixed groups of hospital patients. In this research the clearest factors were (by universal index number): 16, 17, 20, 21, 23, 24, 28, 30, 32 and 33. Two new factors were also found.

The second-order structure among these primaries, however, turned out to be different from that with normals although it was similar to other studies of mental patients. The largest of the second-order factor was clear and well replicated and proves to be one generally associated with clinical cases. This is psychasthenia or general mental slowness. There is a technical problem with the rotation of second-order factors—the relatively few points for the establishment of simple structure, the absence of hyperplane stuff, which demands a confactor rotation (see Chapter 2, p. 19). Consequently the identification and interpretation of second orders in T data must wait on further research. In this same large sample studied by Schmidt the state and state change factors by dR technique revealed mostly factors previously found, but with some new ones which were not identified.

This brief résumé of the foundations of the Schmidt study is important when we come in the next section to examine the clinical discriminations among these T factors. It was at once evident that the discriminations were in good agreement with previous results which means that we can regard them with some confidence. A variety of analyses was used on the data to investigate group differences including analyses of variance, multiple regression and discriminant functions. The discriminant function analysis and the multiple regression have to be treated with care because, as we discussed in our chapter on multivariate techniques, these methods are highly influenced by the characteristics of the particular samples in the research. Nevertheless the findings can be summarized as set out below:

(a) In the clinical area the most important factors for discriminations are, in descending order: U.I.19, independence, U.I.21, exuberance, U.I.23, mobilization of energy, U.I.25 realism and U.I.28, asthenia. These results are based upon the discriminant function analysis. From the multiple regression the characteristics of each syndrome group were determined. These are set out in (b) below:

(b) *Involutional depressives* 21— (suppressibility), 19— (subduedness), 20 (herd conformity) and 28 (asthenia).

Other psychotic depressives 19— (subduedness), 21— (suppressibility), 23— (regression) and 25— (tensinflexia).

Depressive neurotics 19— (subduedness), 23— (regression), 21— (suppressibility) and 25— (tensinflexia).

Schizophrenics 23— (regression), 19— (subduedness), 25— (tensinflexia), 33 (dismay) and factor 11 (unlabelled).

Manics are high on 23—, 19— and 25—. Compared with other clinical groups manics are high on 30— (disofrustance), 24— (low anxiety), 17— (trustingness) and 28— (self-assuredness).

By using the scores on these traits it was found possible to classify correctly into their psychiatric groups 75 percent of the subjects. When the state and trait change factors were added in the figure rose to 93% —well beyond the usual with psychiatric diagnoses. Since the original classifications were psychiatric diagnoses it is pertinent to ask how such a high figure could come about, particularly in view of the sampling problems associated with discriminant functions. The important variable here is probably the special care that was taken to select patients. Patients were only chosen when, wherever possible, there was independent agreement between psychiatrists. Every care was taken to avoid the effects of medication.

For more precise details of the weights for the various factors readers must be referred to the original publication by Cattell *et al.* (1972). Enough has been described to enable us to draw a number of conclusions concerning the use of objective personality tests in clinical psychology.

First, there can be little doubt of their discriminatory diagnostic power. These results demonstrate that they are at least as good as any other instruments. Indeed, the combined placement when state factors were included is excellent. The Rorschach studies of depressives and schizophrenics by Holley (1973) which we have discussed on p. 32 are even better, but this only indicates that the proper use of this projective test, as is the case with these objective tests factors, has been neglected. So our first conclusion must be that for clinicians there is much to be gained in precision and continuity of diagnosis by use of the Q data scales (CAQ, 16PF, EPI, HSPQ) and T data (the OA or Objective Analytic) batteries.

However, as we have stressed throughout this chapter, there is the added advantage for clinical psychology—beyond immediate diagnosis—in utilizing tests of source traits, namely that source traits have psychological meaning in terms of personality structure. As we argued in the case of Q factors, to know that psychotic groups differ on factors 23, 19 and 25 gives us insight into the nature of the psychosis and may well be able to guide our therapeutic procedures. The insight it gives is a function of our knowledge of the particular source traits. Thus to be told that a patient is low on g_f (fluid ability), to select the psychological factor about which perhaps most is known, tells the knowledgeable psychologist (as distinct from the ignorant group who question the notion of intelligence and regard all intellectual differences as reflections of poor upbringing) an enormous amount. He will be able to make a large number of predictions on the strength of this single score. Unfortunately it cannot be claimed, as our discussion of objective test factors in Chapter 8 indicates, that we know enough about these T factors for our insights to be as penetrating as we have every reason to expect they eventually will be. This is partly because clinicians have not yet taken them up and applied them as widely as they have older methods. When enough data has been collected in the natural course of clinical psychology it may well be possible to know with considerable certainty what kinds of therapies will help different types of patients. One approach may, for instance, be helpful for those with low scores on U.I.25, quite another for those low on U.I.19. Again it may be possible to predict different outcomes for patients with different personality structures: some may have to be careful to avoid exacerbating circumstances as far as possible, perhaps stressful jobs, others we may confidently regard as unlikely to relapse.

Now, of course, this is equally true of the Q factor results but it is well to remind ourselves here of the advantages of objective tests to the clinician compared with other forms of measurement so that the pressing need for this further research can become clear. These are the impossibility of distortion, the elimination of response sets and the fact that objective tests can be of many kinds, thus eliminating instrument or method variance. There is another advantage in the clinic for objective tests. Items often require subjects to state what they usually do, so that for patients who may have been for many years incapacitated by their problems we tend to get a somewhat artificial result reflecting their ill rather than their new behaviour (if psychotherapy has in fact wrought any changes). Now this is an important point if we are to check and guide the progress of psychotherapy through structured personality testing. There is one further advantage that objective tests have: from their nature they are more suitable for re-testing patients on several occasions than are questionnaires. The disadvantage of the OA batteries relative to the questionnaires is that they take appreciably more time and skill for their administration. It is this which undoubtedly continues to account for the lag in their necessary wider use in the clinical field. Another reason, trivial yet real, is that until 1975 psychologists had to pick up the tests themselves from numerous scattered research articles. But as of 1975 the publication of a "streamlined" 10 factor battery by Schmidt and Hacker in Germany, and by Schuerger in a British-American edition by IPAT, along with handbooks and standardizations, should greatly facilitate use by clinicians and other professions in applied psychology. Furthermore, we may surely expect that training in these personality test administrative skills will take its place in professional courses alongside training in intelligence testing, etc., in the near future.

Although our discussion of the value of objective tests has been based to a large extent on a book by Cattell and Scheier (1961) and the monograph by Cattell *et al.* (1972) this is because they are the most extensive and careful of the researches reported in the literature of objective tests in the clinical settings. Furthermore it must be stressed it confirms the previous smaller studies. For further details of these readers must be referred to the original publications: Sankar (1969); Cattell and Killian (1967); Cattell and Schuerger (1970); Cattell and Tatro (1966) and Cattell *et al.* (1971) to name only some of the papers.

Initially, there were two main centres of research on personality structure, by Q and T data, using the new multivariate factor analytic experimental techniques, that of Cattell and his many associates at the Laboratory of Personality Analysis set up in 1945 at the University of Illinois and that of Eysenck and his associates at the Maudsley Hospital in London. Sparks from these fires have since brought illuminating work from several other centres notably in Britain, the U.S.A., Germany, India, Australia, Canada and Japan, but certain original differences of emphasis continue. Our concern is primarily with the mutually confirmed concepts, but in one area—that of nomenclature —a difference of labels has caused confusion needing to be resolved here.

In the objective (T data) researches the clinical interests of the Maudsley group produced concentration on those factors which they called U.I.23

neuroticism, U.I.25, psychoticism, and U.I.32 extraversion among the 20 factors (U.I.16 through U.I.35) reached by the broad "personality sphere" approach of the Illinois group. As to the factor patterns of these three factors, identified by their index numbers 23, 25 and 32, there is no longer any disagreement. But Cattell, Scheier, Barton and others have repeatedly shown that a factor U.I.24 is anxiety and that this correlates fully with the questionnaire second-order anxiety Q2. They point out that what Eysenck has called neuroticism in Q-data, namely Q2, and what he calls neuroticism in T-data, namely U.I.23, are two different source traits. Furthermore, Cattell and Scheier (1961) found *six* T-data factors distinguishing neurotics from normals as powerfully as U.I.23 does, and their interpretative term for U.I.23 was *Regression* (based on psychoanalytic similarities). We are left, therefore, with three factors in Q data—Q1, Q2 and Q5—called by Cattell *exvia, anxiety* and *psychoticism*, which align with three T-data factors— U.I.32, U.I.24, and U.I.25—given by him the same, consistent labels. On the other hand the alignment of terms does not hold in the Eysenck series since U.I.23 (which he calls neuroticism and Cattell regression) is distinct from U.I.24, anxiety, which actually aligns with the second-order Q factor which he calls neuroticism. This verbal confusion has of course caused considerable conceptual confusion in all except those thoroughly familiar with the factor loadings. Obviously it would be best if a third party investigated the factual basis of this confusion, namely whether the anxiety ("neuroticism") questionnaire Q2 lines up with U.I.23 (regression, neuroticism) or U.I.24 anxiety.

Incidentally, the conceptual distinction of types and traits is also involved in the confusion of nomenclature. Cattell and Scheir's findings (1961) show (either in Q or T data) that a neurotic is a "type" distinguished from normals not by a single factor but by half a dozen (as an orange is distinguished from an apple on several dimensions of description). With this elucidation we can better follow the considerable clinical research of the Maudsley group.

Eysenck's P scale (psychoticism) second-order factor which discriminates psychotics (hence psychoticism) is by far of the greatest relevance to this chapter especially since there was no questionnaire measure of P before 1968 (Eysenck and Eysenck, 1968) so that elucidation had to rely on T test measurement. Even now there is no published version of the P scale and the items are still considered best used only for research.* Eysenck (1967) has argued that his P factor, as determined by objective tests, is similar to that found in the study by Cattell and Tatro (1966). Since this latter study is in full accord with the later investigation which we have examined in detail above it will suffice to describe the tests that load most highly on the objective test P (U.I.25 in Cattell's series). Gestalt Completion, alternating perspective, size of writing and copying, computational skill, where the emphasis is

---

* The E.P.Q. has just been published (Eysenck and Eysenck, 1975) which contains a P scale.

on the capacity to reason well with numbers rather than on Thurstone's numerical ability factor, and mirror drawing are objective tests which load both on Eysenck's P factor and on Cattell's U.I.25. In most cases in the Gestalt Completion test subjects are given incomplete drawings and they are required to say what they would be like if completed. Psychotics make faster but more inaccurate responses. In the alternating perspective test psychotics show a greater alternation than controls. Finally psychotics tend to write larger when copying and to copy figures in a manner that is too large for the paper although some may produce minute drawings.

We have previously discussed our reasons for doubting the title of psychoticism for this factor (whether measured by questionnaire or objective test)—since psychotics were differentiated by other factors also. Rather it would appear to match U.I.25, which is fully described in our chapter on objective factors to which the descriptive term "*tense inflexibility*" has been applied. In conclusion we can say that Eysenck's work on psychoticism at the Maudsley Hospital is yet further evidence that objective tests of temperament have a valuable part to play in the elucidation of clinical psychological problems. We must hope that a new generation of practising clinicians will multiply their use.

DYNAMIC FACTORS IN CLINICAL PSYCHOLOGY

So far in this chapter we have examined the utility of measures of temperament in clinical psychology. We have found that both neurotics and psychotics differ in personality patterns from normals and among themselves in ways that give us useful insight into the aetiology and guidelines into the treatment of mental disturbance. The findings of research in this area provide conclusive proof of the advantages of factored dimensions over scales (as in the MMPI) which merely give statistical differentiation between groups.

However, most of the great clinical theorists, especially those of a psychoanalytic orientation, conceive of mental illness in terms of dynamics—dynamic conflict. Terms such as mental disturbance, emotional imbalance and the very notion of conflict show how deep rooted this concept of mental illness has become. In our two chapters on motivation we showed how factor analysis had begun to translate some of these clinical entities into quantified variables although the work in this area was considerably less advanced than was the case with temperament. It will be remembered that there emerged 10 sentiments and ergs which acted as rather basic drives or motivators of behaviour. In addition three motivational components, alpha beta and gamma were found to underly motivational strength. We must now discuss the value of these findings in the understanding of mental illness, what has been called quantified psychoanalysis.

Differences Between Normals and Psychiatric Groups on Ergs and Sentiments

From our chapter on the objective measurement of motivation and the elucidation of dynamic structures by factor analysis [with ergs (drives) and sentiments (acquired interest structures)] the reader will perceive that measures in this domain are most capable of any of carrying on and extending the approach to clinical understanding through dynamics which has characterized the classical approaches of Freud, Jung, Adler and many others.

The two instruments which have developed from this basic research as convenient and standardized tests are the MAT (Motivational Analysis Test) and the SMAT (the equivalent School Motivational Analysis Test for younger ages). Psychometrists accustomed only to ability tests have unfortunately misconstrued the low homogeneities of these factored tests as a defect when in fact they are deliberately planned on newer psychometric principles (see Cattell, 1973, Chapter 9) which show that in broad personality and dynamic factor measures a low homogeneity of items is desirable. Even from an untutored common sense standpoint it is clear that if we wish to measure, say, a person's dominance we should take not some narrow area of expression, say his behaviour in the office but also his behaviour in sport, in the home, and so on. Broader sampling means, in psychometric terms, lower homogeneity coefficients, but in terms of a multiple correlation with this general factor, it means higher validities. The broader sampling in MAT and SMAT leads to quite low homogeneities, with high concept validities, and we shall shall show in the evidence which follows that these objective tests have more substantial concrete validities against real life clinical criteria than is usual in motivation and interest measures of a subjective "check list" kind. The study by Kline and Grindley (1974) indicates there are considerable fluctuations over time on these scores (which are by no means to be regarded as errors) so that we may not expect such large differences between normals and neurotics to obtain with motivational traits as was the case with temperament.

Cattell and Child (1975) survey what few researches have so far been reported. Caffelt and Sweeney (1965) administered the MAT to a sample of 19 criminals convicted for crimes of violence. If we consider that the difference between the unintegrated and the integrated MAT scores (see p. 186) is a measure of conflict, then we can see from the results that the criminals are highly conflicted on career, sex, self-sentiment and the need for security. In other words it is in these areas of life that there appears to be frustration. However over aggression (pugnacity and assertiveness) there is no conflict, presumably because criminals directly expressed it, thus contravening the laws of the society. There is an interesting comparison with thieves in this investigation. Here we find again conflict over self-sentiment (a convicted thief can hardly have a good self image) fear and security, presumably fear of prison, but the highest concerns narcism. Cattell and Child (1975) argue that this suggests that the motive for stealing is to live a rich luxurious life. This does not seem altogether convincing because if this were the case we should expect a greater incidence of robbery among the poverty stricken and a smaller incidence among those with sufficient than appears to be the case. However all discussion must be tentative on account of the sample sizes.

A useful contrast group for the criminals was supplied by Davis (1966) who tested a group of students training for the ministry. These showed almost no conflict other than for sweetheart-sentiment—a finding which would be expected with students (especially of theology) where sexual outlets are, even today, limited. However, the psychoanalytic view of religious fervour is by no means benign (Freud, 1927) since it is held to reflect Oedipal conflicts. It is noteworthy therefore, that the home-parental conflict score is the next highest.

May and Sweney (1965) worked with 30 schizophrenics. It is well known that the home background is implicated in schizophrenia (although not, of course, the only factor) as can be seen in the work of Laing (e.g. 1960) on schizophrenic families and in the double-bind hypothesis of Bateson *et al.* (1956). Hence it was interesting to note considerable conflict on the home-parental sentiment. The overall career-sentiment score was high which perhaps reflects the well known tendency of schizophrenics, as the disease begins, to have increasing work problems and finally lose their jobs. The sex erg was highly conflicted which suggests that sexual problems are important in schizophrenia—a finding which confirms clinical impressions. Thus this study of schizophrenics in no way seems contrary to psychological sense although it does not strikingly confirm any particular theoretical viewpoint.

All these studies, as Cattell and Child (1975) point out, indicate that the MAT could be highly valuable in disentangling the dynamics of neurosis and psychosis and could be far more reliable than the clinical impressions of most clinicians.

P Technique
P factor analysis demands that we factor the correlations between variables measured repeatedly on one person. In our discussion of moods and states we saw how such methods were used in this field. In the study of motivation P technique reveals the dynamics of behaviour when the fluctuations of ergic tensions are related to particular specific behaviours. Kline and Grindley (1974) used the MAT in just such a study although the actual P factor analysis was not carried out. The full value of P analysis for clinical psychology can be seen most clearly when we come to examine the specification equation.

THE SPECIFICATION EQUATION

The equation $a_{iJ} = b_{j1}E_{1i} + b_{j2}E_{2i}$ (Cattell and Child, 1975) shows how an attitude, or cause of action, a_{iJ}, has its strength best estimated for an individual, i, by the strength of his two ergic tensions $E_1 E_2$ (if only 2 ergs are involved) and the weight of the indices $b_{J_i}b_{J_2}$ (found by factor analysis). In effect, if a P analysis can be given so that the weights may be found this equation gives us for each individual in each of his behaviours a quantified psychoanalysis. Thus, for example, P analysis of a subject could tell us the dynamics of his painting a picture. Does it really reduce sexual and Oedipal drives, as Freud claims? A P analysis of an artist could unlock some of these creative secrets.

This specification equation can be used in clinical psychology. If we test all ergs and sentiments, preferably by objective test rather than MAT (see p. 191 for reasons) for a patient undergoing treatment everyday, we can see how his symptoms and behaviour are related to ergic patterns. This indeed, for each patient, is a quantified psychoanalysis. In addition, if we put therapeutic variables into the analysis, we can see the effects (if any!) of psychotherapy. Thus P technique plus the specification equation could be the most powerful tool in understanding the dynamics and hence treatment of mental illness. Such studies, however, remain to be done partly because the pressures of time on practising clinicians preclude the use of so many tests.

In our discussion of ergs and sentiments we pointed out that there was a similarity between the Freudian unconscious and the unintegrated component of motivation. Similarly the conscious is not unlike the integrated part. In our chapter on the intensity of motivational strength it was hypothesized, albeit tentatively, that the epsilon factor, loading on physiological indices, might be associated with the unconscious aspect of motivation. Now if P technique applied to objective tests really is a quantitative psychoanalysis then somehow it must relate motivational changes and changes in behaviour to unconscious mental activity.

Although this is a complex topic which we cannot deal with in full here (Cattell and Child, 1975, treat it in some detail) we can at least indicate how these motivational measures can go some way to uncovering the maze of motivation that psychoanalysis has found to underly human behaviour. Of course the results will not be precisely as Freud described them, but this is the strength of the method that it allows the profound insights of depth psychologists to be modified in the light of the clinical evidence.

THE ADJUSTMENT PROCESS CHART

This chart is useful in conceptualizing motivation in terms of ergs and sentiments and yet still accounting for the known variability of behaviour. When an erg is stimulated there occurs the first dynamic crossroad or chiasm, A, where there are three possible outcomes. Ai provides immediate satisfaction, and the drive decreases. If there is no satisfaction there is either obstruction (having to join a long queue for food with the possibility of having to leave before we get anything) or complete deprivation. Attempts to overcome the

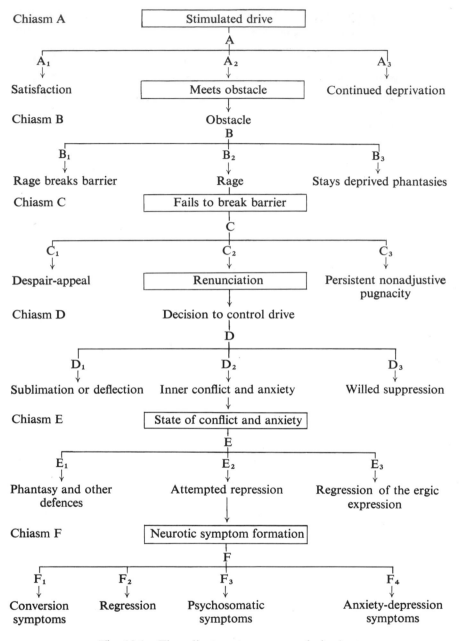

Fig. 13.1   The adjustment process analysis chart

barrier lead to chiasm B. Extreme rage could enable our subject to break the barrier—perhaps just rudely push to the front or falsely claim that he is a diabetic and must have food. However if he fails he continues enraged or has phantasies about food. The remainder of the APA chart indicates what can happen when the erg remains unsatisfied no matter how we turn until at last it is repressed at E3, thus leading to pathological symptoms. Now it must be realized that this chart is an attempt within the Cattell system, which deals with quantified variables and discreet events, to encapsulate the subtle complexities of psychoanalytic theorizing. At present it is speculative and we could not apply the APA chart to any given neurotic or psychotic syndrome.

We hope that it is clear that with P technique and the objective measurement of motivation, the APA chart could be applied to individuals. Clearly from the chart the critical points for clinical psychology are the chiasms towards the end of the system where after long frustration pathological symptoms are beginning to occur. Cattell and Sweney (1964), in what remains the only such study, investigated conflicts in children at these later chiasms by factoring all the clinical symptoms of conflict (slips of the tongue, muscle tension, vacillation, etc.) at three loci: reading comics or going to Sunday school, looking after younger siblings or pets, and pleasing peer or parents. Six factors occurred which loaded consistently across the three loci of conflict. These factors were identified as cognitive disturbance relating to suppression, perceptual vigilance, phantasy, muscle tension, to name the clearest. This work is a sound way of filling in empirically the responses in the APA chart, especially when it is realized that anxiety as was shown by the work of Cattell and Scheier (1961) is a further conflict factor. If sufficient work were done with large samples of patients utilizing the model of the APA chart, P analysis would not only provide a quantified psychoanalysis for individuals but for whole syndromes and nosological categories.

In our chapters on traits of temperament and states we have had full definitions of anxiety which was regarded in psychoanalysis as of critical importance in the development of neurosis. We have been careful to distinguish anxiety as a trait and anxiety as a state. As we know from the physiological loadings on the anxiety factors, there is the important physiological aspect of anxiety. In learning theory terms the experience of anxiety is the experience of physiological events which we have learned to call anxiety. The importance of anxiety in motivation is this: much of our behaviour is motivated by ergs and sentiments. However in our culture, as the APA chart shows, the expression of these ergs is prohibited and by the level of Chiasm 4 or 5 it is transformed into anxiety and directed into pathological forms of expression. Anxiety is not the only transformation although it may be the most important since the factor analysis by Cattell and Sweney (1964) showed at least six other conflict factors. Krug (1971) factored together these conflict measures and the ergs and sentiments and found that they loaded on the same factors, thus suggesting that these too, as in the case of anxiety, take their energy from the basic ergs and sentiments. Although far more empirical research is needed in this field, it is safe to say that anxiety level is a function of intensity of ergic arousal, amount of thwarting and control of expression and temperamental traits, C, low ego strength, H, high threat susceptibility, O, guilt proneness and Q3, low self sentiment. In conclusion, we can say that P technique combined with the APA chart can give us an insight into major sources of conflict of which in traditional clinical psychology anxiety is the best known. We should note how at this level temperament and motivational factors interact in the development of anxiety.

SUMMARY

1. The importance of personality measurement in the diagnosis and treatment of the mentally ill was discussed. Stress was laid on the value of measuring the majour source traits of personality.
2. The differentiation of normals from abnormals and among different abnormal groups in terms of Q data was examined. Factors which distinguished neurotics from normals and psychotics from both groups were found to agree with clinical theories and to make sound psychological sense.
3. The results with T factors were also discussed and these were found highly impressive: the need for further practical use was demonstrated.
4. The value of dynamic factors for clinical psychology was also demonstrated. The specification equation, P factor analysis and the adjustment process chart were shown to be capable of providing a quantified psychoanalysis.
5. It was concluded that factored personality tests could put both diagnosis and treatment on to a more efficient and rational basis.

Chapter 14

The Application of Structural Findings in Personality and Motivation to Educational Psychology

INTRODUCTION

There is no absolute distinction between clinical and educational psychology. Thus a child with severe behaviour problems in school is likely to come under the aegis of an educational psychologist rather than a clinician. Consequently, it is rather an arbitrary distinction that we shall make in this chapter. We follow the academic convenience of defining educational psychology as concerned with psychological problems affecting education.

Until recently in Great Britain, since 1920 there has been a selective secondary school education, the basis of selection being the intelligence test. Now a great surge of public opprobrium has been directed against 11 plus selection on the grounds that intelligence tests only measure skill at intelligence tests and that all differences are the changeable result of environmental differences. The fact that both these popular views are, in the light of research, substantially wrong, appears to affect political, administrative decisions not at all. It is a strange irony that the first use of intelligence tests in Britain for selection on a wide scale was in Northumberland under the guidance of the factor analyst Godfrey Thomson who knew that in his own village previous selection methods by attainment tests had grossly favoured those from professional homes and that the balance could be righted to a great extent by the use of intelligence tests. Intelligence tests realized the aim of "Opening Careers to Talent"! Now the argument for equal opportunity is strangely used against them, contrary to the evidence. Lest anyone think that such bias does not exist today, in a survey of Liverpool schools carried out by Tempest (1971) teachers were asked to nominate highly intelligent pupils. Although in some cases they were correct, a large number of pupils were selected whose distinguishing features were a large pair of glasses and a nice white collar. Similarly, some unprepossessing but highly intelligent children were missed. The intelligence test is still the best at unearthing the village Hampden.

As psychological measurement progressed from abilities to personality, research evidence grew supporting the shrewd observations of experienced teachers that personality and character differences could be as important as intelligence in deciding fitness for higher education. Unfortunately these scientific advances were caught in the backwash of uninformed prejudice against intelligence testing. At the moment some sceptical educators will say that any hope of increasing the efficiency of selection procedures for school or university by the addition of more tests, say, of personality and motivation, is remote. Furthermore in educational psychology itself there is, in some circles, a general retreat from quantification and experimental methods. Indeed a group of anti-experimental psychologists has split off as a new sect of "Humanistic" psychologists. It is not only with this retreat from scientific rigor that experimental and psychometric, mathematical psychology finds its advance encumbered at the present moment. Misunderstandings of the findings on the extent of heredity in abilities have in some countries become entangled in politics and ethnic rivalries. In America, for example, some minorities do better than the national average, but others, e.g. the blacks and Mexicans, score below average, as Jensen and Eysenck have independently shown. The interpretation of these results is, of course, quite a different matter, and raciologists (as opposed to racists who claim superiority, or ignoracists who claim ability differences are *a priori* impossible) have cautiously called for much more research. The finding that some ethnic groups do less well, on average, in intelligence and scholastic tests has undoubtedly caused emotional rejection of testing. The minorities may be small but the vehemence of their public protests against tests has, in some countries, interfered with the legitimate and effective use of tests in the majority to select according to merit. It is in the context of this mood—temporary but substantial—that we must make our statements on the application of psychology to the classroom and the educational system.

THE RELATION OF ACADEMIC SUCCESS TO PERSONALITY

Although some recent studies have used T data, much work on this question for practical reasons has involved questionnaires. Our discussion will, therefore, concentrate on these results.

There has been, in both Great Britain and America, a flood of research in this field which has become so well known that we shall be content here to summarize the most important findings. Since there are disagreements in the results obtained in America and Great Britain we shall deal separately with each country where necessary. Entwistle (1972) and Warburton (1968b) contain excellent surveys of the research in Great Britain and we shall lean heavily on these papers in this section. Before we scrutinize the results we must point out that for practical purposes results with the Eysenck and Cattell second-order factors are in perfect agreement and we shall not distinguish between these factors. At the primary factor level, obviously we can refer only to work with the 16PF, H.S.P.Q and C.P.Q. scales.

Two tables are useful reference points for our discussion. Table 14.1 shows the results of a careful American investigation where the relative weights of ability and personality variables can be seen. Table 14.2 summarizes 25 studies in Great Britain.

Primary School Results

In both America and Great Britain, as the tables show, there is good agreement. In second-order terms the stable extravert is the most successful. Eysenck and Cookson (1969) with a sample of 4,000 children in their last year in the primary school is a reliable confirmation of this result. Furthermore they found no trace of a curvilinear relationship that some earlier workers (e.g., Savage, 1966) had done. As Sarason *et al.* (1960) found in America, at all levels of anxiety, there are deleterious effects on academic performance. At the age of 13 there are some indications of sex differences in the results. Thus Entwistle and Cunningham (1968) found that extraverted stable boys were superior in school work. However the successful girls were stable introverts.

When considering these results we have to be careful not to confuse psychological with statistical significance. In many of these studies the correlations are small (around 0.2) so that only 4% of the variance is explained.

In American schools, Butcher and Cattell (1968) and Barton, Dielman and Cattell (1971) have reported in a book and several articles (one of which is the source of our Table 14.1) detailed studies of the relationship of school performance to personality and ability factors. From Table 14.1 it is clear that intelligence (gf) is a more important determinant of academic performance than any one personality factor with children of this age. G, conscientiousness, is the best predictor among the personality factors which accords with common sense. These correlations are small although a multiple correlation between the criterion and all the factors would probably be substantial. The differences in correlations between different school subjects are generally small and we shall not discuss them. These American findings when the second-order factors are calculated from the primaries confirm the British results with second-order factors.

Secondary and Higher Education

Table 14.2 summarizes the results at various age groups in Great Britain. From this it is clear that in Great Britain the introverted-neurotic is superior in school work. There is a startling change-over at the age of 15 (previously

TABLE 14.1

Personality, Motivation, and Intelligence Variables Related to School Grades and Achievement Scores

Correlation of Personality and Intelligence Variables with Grades

						Personality Factors									
	A	B	C	D	E	F	G	H	I	J	O	Q_2	Q_3	Q_4	CFIQ
Grade 6 (N = 169)															
Subject areas															
Spelling	22[a]	32[a]	13	−08	−11	−21[a]	30[a]	24[a]	00	−07	−17	−07	20[b]	−12	36[a]
English	23[a]	43[a]	10	−09	−13	−18	34[a]	20[b]	08	−08	−16[b]	−06	25[a]	−08	45[a]
Social studies	21[a]	47[a]	10	−04	−15	−15	35[a]	15	10	−04	−18[b]	−05	22[a]	−08	47[a]
Mathematics	19[b]	40[a]	03	−04	−12	−15	28[a]	13	−05	−10	−11	−02	19[b]	−06	45[a]
Science	24[a]	41[a]	10	−01	−10	−19[b]	31[a]	16[b]	09	−05	−20[b]	−04	25[a]	−03	41[a]
Grade 7 (N = 142)															
Spelling	13	28[a]	11	−11	01	05	22[a]	14	−21[a]	−22[a]	−09	−13	−02	−07	38[a]
English	10	45[a]	12	08	00	09	31[a]	20[b]	−13	−32[a]	−17[b]	−18[b]	23[a]	07	53[a]
Social studies	07	54[a]	12	12	−03	13	37[a]	13	−10	−30[a]	−17[b]	−17	22[a]	08	56[a]
Mathematics	11	40[a]	14	−08	01	03	31[a]	18[b]	−24[a]	−14	−24[a]	−10	23[a]	02	54[a]
Science	03	30[a]	09	04	−06	04	16[b]	04	−01	−20[b]	−09	−06	11	08	43[a]

[a] P < 0.01.
[b] P < 0.05.

Note: From Barton, Dielman, and Cattell (1971). Decimal points are omitted. CFIQ means Culture Fair Intelligence Test.

the *stable* extrovert was better). In higher education the studies are about split: some show stable introverts perform better, others show neurotic introverts to be superior.

In America, on the other hand, at these levels the stable introvert is always superior. Early on in education the A + (affectia) individual does better in the social classroom situation. The other two important primaries in the extrovert complex behave as opposites, the divergent (F) and self sufficient (Q2) pupil does better. (This illustrates the complex nature of this second order exvia factor and raises doubts about using it in predictions. The primaries give a decidedly higher prediction.) In anxiety (C−, H−, L, O, Q3− and Q4) on the other hand, the primaries act alike. However, the results are coupled with the Eysenck neuroticism scale in that *non*-anxious introverts are found to do better at all age levels.

Regardless of differences due to whatever differentiates the Cattell anxiety and the Eysenck N scale, the important global result for education prediction and selection is that the addition of personality measures to ability measures can already substantially increase predictions and understanding of school learning, as shown by Cattell and Butcher (1968) who obtained a multiple correlation between grades and the HSPQ of 0.462 which rose on correction to 0.597.

This now leaves a difficult question. Why are the American results at the secondary level different from the British in respect of anxiety, which correlates negatively with success in America (as one might expect) but positively in Great Britain? To this, at present, there would appear to be no adequate answer: clearly interaction studies of classroom behaviour in the two countries would be needed for a proper empirical answer.

In higher education in Great Britain, introverts are superior in performance. Correlations range in size from −0.26 downwards and in no case was extraversion significantly correlated with academic success. As regards anxiety, there is a split, stable students sometimes doing better, while in other studies neurotic students are the more successful. Entwistle (1972) argues that a rough fit to these results is obtained by seeing them as reflections of subject differences. The stable introvert is best at natural sciences or history: the neurotic introvert excels at engineering and at languages, as Furneaux (1957) found. The social sciences would appear to be intermediate between these poles since Kline and Gale (1971) found no correlation between performance in psychology and either E or N.

In America there are again consistent results although here the non-anxious introvert is the successful student. However Cattell (1957) has shown that the anxiety may be a consequence rather than a cause of the poor performance.

Before leaving these correlational studies with personality traits and attempting to explain them one further set of findings may be of interest. It appears that the same relationships between academic performance and

TABLE 14.2

Summary of Results from Studies Using Cattell's Inventories: Direction of Correlation Coefficients with Scholastic Attainment (Adapted from Warburton, 1968b, Table 3)

Second-order Factor	Primary Source Trait	Age Group							
		Under 12		12–14		15–17		Over 17	
		+	−	+	−	+	−	+	−
Anxiety/Neuroticism	Instability (C−)	0	3	0	1	3	0	3	2
	Tenseness (Q$_4$+)	0	1	0	1	1	0	5	1
	Insecurity (O+)	0	0	0	2	1	0	1	1
	Bad-temperedness (D+)	0	1	0	2	2	0	0	0
	Unreliability (Q$_3$−)	0	1	0	5	0	2	0	2
	Suspiciousness (L+)	0	0	0	0	0	0	2	2
	Total	0	6	0	11	7	2	11	8
Introversion (1)	Aloofness (A−)	0	0	0	6	3	0	0	1
	Desurgency (F−)	0	3	0	0	8	0	3	1
	Shyness (H−)	0	2	0	2	3	0	1	0
	Total	0	5	0	8	14	0	4	2

Introversion (2)									
Submissiveness (E−)	0	1	0	7	0	4	0	1	2
Independence (Q$_2$−)	1	0	0	3	0	3	0	1	0
Total	1	1	0	10	0	7	0	2	2
Tendermindedness									
Tendermindedness (I+)	0	0	0	1	0	2	0	3	0
Unaffectedness (N−)	0	0	0	0	0	0	0	1	0
Total	0	0	0	1	0	2	0	4	0
Radicalism									
Bohemianism (M+)	0	0	0	0	0	0	0	4	0
Radicalism (Q$_1$+)	0	0	0	0	0	0	0	1	0
Total	0	0	0	0	0	0	0	5	0
Morality									
Conscientiousness (G+)	2	0	1	6	0	4	0	2	3

The signs following the letters in parentheses indicate the direction of scoring on the trait. For example, shyness is inferred from low scores (negative sign) on trait "H".

personality as in Great Britain obtain in cultures very different. Thus Kline (1966) and Honess and Kline (1974a) working with Ghanaian university students and Ugandan (Buganda tribe) high school pupils found essentially that the neurotic introvert was best in attainment. These studies utilized the EPI and the JEPI. Fears that the tests were not valid in these cultures, thus rendering the findings of little value, were dispelled by careful item analyses and in one case factor analysis, (Kline, 1967b and Honess and Kline, 1974b). Actually in Ghana results with the second-order 16PF factors yielded even higher correlations than with the EPI so that there can be little chance of some kind of freak results.

The interpretation of these results relating introversion–extraversion to academic performance is straightforward if we accept the general finding that extraverts are the best primary school performers whereas the best university students are the introverts. At the level of higher education the introvert is probably favoured because he is bookish and quiet and academic education is of this kind. After all the constant party attender (one of the items in the EPI) cannot be both working and socializing. Furthermore if we can accept the definition of the extravert as stimulus hungry, ever seeking what may arouse him (Eysenck, 1967) then it must be admitted that many of the lectures which form an integral part certainly of British higher education are not likely to appeal to the extravert. At the primary school, on the other hand, the more modern teaching methods practised where the emphasis is on project work and where pupils are encouraged to work at their own speed at what they like, as far as is possible, are likely to favour the extravert in the sense that under such conditions he produces his best performance.

In the case of Neuroticism at the level of higher education we have two difficult questions. The first, as at the secondary level, concerns the difference between Great Britain, the African samples and America. There seems to be no adequate explanation of the cultural difference. Certainly the American results where the non-anxious student is superior in educational performance fits the clinical findings of educational psychologists. Schonell (1944) has argued this, claiming that the majority of educational difficulties were rooted in emotional problems.

The British results could be explained if we were to argue that the mildly neurotic student, when warned by low marks or his teacher's threats that he is not doing well, makes a greater effort whereas the non-anxious student does just enough to avoid being thrown out. This then would allow for the fact of the *highly* anxious student going to pieces in the examination. However this interpretation does not accurately reflect the British findings, since it implies a curvilinear relationship which is not often found: nor does it account for subject differences. If it were correct it makes the American findings inexplicable. As Entwistle (1972) argues, there is no satisfactory account of the British findings. Perhaps a confounding variable in these studies is the inadequate separation of state and trait anxiety.

At our present state of knowledge we are not in a position to elaborate on the different relationships with personality variables that are found among the different disciplines. These may reflect differences of teaching method or the fact that different kinds of people (in terms of personality pattern) are attracted into the different disciplines (see our chapter on the use of factorial findings in occupational psychology for a discussion of this point). Thus it would not be surprising if different personalities excelled at the complexities of English literary criticism and the rigors of pure mathematics. However apart from such extreme cases interpretation is difficult and inclined to be *post hoc*.

It was in an effort to get at some of the underlying variables of this problem that we undertook the cross-cultural studies, to which we have previously referred in Uganda and Ghana. Here we argued that in the very different social milieu and culture of these tropical countries it would not be surprising if educational performance were affected by personality variables different from those in the West. However such was not the case. This suggests, but does not prove, that the explanation of the relationship between personality and academic performance lies in the actual teaching process, as it is carried out in western style education. There can be little doubt that in this respect Ghanian and Ugandan education still shows the influence of British colonialism. Support for this argument comes from the fact that in India, where education has a similar British model, the same relationships have been found (Madan, 1967).

If this interpretation is correct then it follows that the next exploratory steps in this area of research must be detailed classroom interaction studies where one can observe precisely what transpires in the course of lessons between teachers and taught having previously measured both pupils' and teachers' personality patterns. If this were done we might be able radically to improve the effectiveness of teaching. Thus we might find that extraverts taught extraverts better than introverts, and vice versa, or that certain teaching methods impaired the performance of pupils with certain personality configurations. Such studies could illuminate the nature of effective teaching and thus make teacher education and selection more rational. Thus it seems to us that personality and academic performance studies should now leave the psychometric laboratory and advance into the classroom.

Before we leave the research relating personality to academic performance there are some other results that we must discuss briefly. We have previously pointed out that although there can be little doubt that the Cattell Q factors are the most important factors in the personality sphere there are nevertheless other factorists who have isolated different dimensions in their research. The majority of these have been shown in this book to overlap substantially with those of Cattell but the work of Grygier (1961) did seem to have revealed factors that were not found in the Cattell system although the definitive factorial work to locate the factors in the personality sphere has not been carried out. However these Grygier scales have been related to academic performance at the university by Hamilton (1970).

In this investigation of students it was found that there were positive correlations between some of the scales and success in the arts and sciences examinations, to such an extent that Hamilton (1970) argued that selection could be improved if these scores were to be included in a multiple regression equation. It would not be useful to describe the detailed correlational findings because, as we have fully discussed, the validity of the DPI is open to doubt (see Kline, 1968). What is important is the fact that there are correlations at all with this personality test and that they were at least as good as those with AH5 (Heim *et al.*, 1970) which is an excellent high level intelligence test loading largely on g_f. Of course this is not to argue that intelligence is not an important determinant of academic success, only that this sample is already selected for intelligence so that the correlation is attenuated through homogeneity. Thus this work by Hamilton (1970) is yet further evidence of the importance of personality variables in the determination of academic performance.

THE RELATIONSHIP BETWEEN PERSONALITY AND ACADEMIC PERFORMANCE

In this section we have shown clearly that at different ages different personality variables are important in academic success. At the second-order level extraversion and stability favour academic performance at the primary school. As the children get older there seems to be a change to introversion so that at the student age the introvert is almost always superior to the extravert. The role of neuroticism is not so clear, but the neurotic introvert is favoured in some disciplines. However, in the majority of achievement situations, in early school, mid school, university, military training, air pilot training etc., the correlation of success is with low anxiety as defined precisely by the second order anxiety factor. These results are not simple to explain although in part they may be accounted for by the teaching methods usual in western education. Further studies have yielded similar findings in other cultures than western ones and in addition very different personality dimensions have been found to be correlated with academic performance.

THE RELATION OF MOTIVATIONAL FACTORS TO ACADEMIC PERFORMANCE

Unfortunately in this area of study it is not possible to be as systematic as was the case with personality. Research is in its infancy and outside the work of Barton, Butcher, Child, Dielman, Lawlis, and Sweney there is not much of a consistent nature. There are some investigations with various age groups which have been extensively described in Cattell and Child (1975), which we shall summarize here. Almost all the studies have been carried out with the MAT and its school version the SMAT, which were fully discussed in Chapter 10.

Cattell and Butcher in a study mentioned in the previous section administered the SMAT as well as the HSPQ to their sample of 13 and 14-year-old high school pupils. Here it was found that the SMAT had a multiple correlation with school achievement of 0.164 which rose on correction for attenuation to 0.482. This is only a modest degree of predictive power. However added in to the HSPQ the figure rose to 0.449 (0.717 corrected). If intelligence was also added in the final multiple correlation was 0.650 (corrected 0.813). If we ignore the corrected figures this final multiple correlation is still impressively high. Furthermore it illustrates that even if, in this study by Cattell and Butcher (1968), the MAT on its own did not contribute much to the prediction, its variance was quite separate from that of either personality or ability. The SMAT, in brief, usefully improves the prediction of academic performance.

Cattell, Barton and Dielman (1972) produced similar results although the predictions were somewhat superior. In mathematics and reading, the figures were from 38–64 percent. When the integrated and the unintegrated components were analyzed separately, as might be expected from our definition of the integrated component as the conscious, systematic, reality based interest, this did turn out the better predictor of the two. These results support the work quoted by Cattell and Child (1975) of Cattell, Sealey and Sweney where it was estimated that around 25 percent of the variance in academic performance was accounted for by motivational variables.

Cattell and Child (1975) attempt to integrate the findings relating school achievement to individual ergs and sentiments from some of the very fine grained analyses carried out in various publications by Cattell, Barton and Dielman (1972), Dielman, Barton and Cattell (1971 and 1973). The results can be summarized by the following claim. The academic achiever is high on the total (I plus U) curiosity score, self-sentiment (I) and superego (I) but low on pugnacity (T), gregariousness (I) and narcism (T). Since education, in the west at least, stresses educational attainment it is hardly surprising that self sentiment, the drive to be acceptable is positively correlated with academic success. Similarly it is hardly surprising that superego the drive to do things properly "if a job's worth doing its worth doing well" is correlated with academic achievement. It is noteworthy too that these ergs both appear as temperamental traits and are positively correlated with academic performance. One other point that we discussed in our chapters on motivation is interesting: n ach, the achievement motive, was related to self sentiment and superego. Thus what was considered by McClelland *et al.* (1953) to be a basic human drive, discovered by criterion keyed studies with the TAT and confirmed by other tests and in the thematic analysis of literature, was shown to be compounded of at least two factorially derived functional unities. Certainly if these two ergs are related to the achievement motive it makes sense that they should affect academic performance. We might, by similar *a priori* arguments, have expected that self-assertion would be correlated with academic success. However, no studies show any significant relationship. Self-assertion is concerned with competitiveness and mastery of nature and it is possible that the self assertive person expresses his drive in fields where he can express it (i.e. successfully) so that self assertion is expressed in successful academic performance but nowhere else. Since superego and self sentiment are both factors nurtured within families these correlations may go some way to explaining the social class differences noted in educational performance.

That curiosity should be associated with school performance would be expected (other than by cynics of typical school syllabuses). Gregariousness is negatively related to achievement. Partly this is practical: if we spend much of our time socializing, there is simply less time for academic work. Furthermore those who enjoy social events are not likely to take pleasure in the essentially lonely activity of learning and scholarship. A similar result was found in our studies of the temperamental traits when we remember that extraversion contains an important social component.

There would appear to be no obvious reason to account for the fact that pugnacity is associated with low academic achievement as a *cause*. However, as a *consequence* it becomes clear. Reference to the APA chart (p. 269) shows that failures can lead to pugnacity so that it may be the case that the pugnacity is the result of failure rather than the cause. Findings of this kind could be used as rational support for comprehensive schools for the sense of failure created by the selection exam could perhaps account in part for the severe discipline problems associated with the old selective schools.

Narcism, it will be remembered, was described as a factor of self-indulgence, a liking for luxury and a fear of work. On common sense grounds therefore we would expect the negative correlation with academic achievement that was in fact observed. However there is a difficulty in this *post hoc* explanation. If a child, for example, has grown up in a family where academic performance is prized before all then it is conceivable that part of his narcism will be involved in such prowess. However, it is possible that what psychoanalysis called narcism is actually represented factor analytically by two distinct source trait concepts: the *erg* (need) narcism and the *sentiment* we call the self sentiment. There is evidence on every hand that a more strongly invested self sentiment is positively correlated with scholastic and other achievement. It is thus not surprising that the sensual egocentrism of narcism is negatively related, and the strength of the self sentiment positively related to real world achievement. For example in many Jewish homes, academic success is prized not just for its rewards but as a worthwhile objective in itself so that in this group narcism would be expected to correlate positively rather than negatively as in the studies so far reported.

The sex erg is an important variable especially because so great an importance has been attached to it as a drive by psychoanalysts, even if their definition is somewhat more broad than that of the factorially defined erg. Cattell and Butcher (1968) found that there was a negative correlation between unintegrated sex (U component) and academic performance. Cattell, Barton and Dielman found the same, but in integrated sex (I component) the opposite held. In psychoanalytic theory activity (almost of any kind) especially that involving great effort is regarded as a sublimation of the sex drive. This should mean that those who direct their sexual energy into work will have less remaining for direct ergic expression. There should therefore be a negative correlation between unintegrated sex and academic achievement. Since sexual activity itself is a highly absorbing and time consuming activity, those with high drive will be likely to be less successful than others at academic pursuits. On the other hand satisfaction of the sex drive tends to stop preoccupation with it so that academic work can be pursued without distraction. All these considerations would lead us to expect a negative correlation between sex drive and academic performance.

Studies of the kind reported in Cattell and Cross (1952) and by Kline and Grindley (1974), where fluctuations of ergic tensions are related to real-life events, are necessary to answer the kind of questions posed in the last paragraphs (see pp. 189 and 191 for descriptions of these investigations). The essence of the problem lies in the nature of the drive itself. If expression lowers the drive, and these studies suggest that it does, then there can be little doubt that a negative correlation is to be expected between academic performance and sex. A high sex score means no expression either sublimated or direct so that the academic work could not be regarded as a substitute. Thus there would be no reason to postulate a positive correlation.

So far in this discussion of the impact of the multivariate study of personality and motivation upon educational performance we have concentrated upon accounting for the results as they have occurred in the research reports. However, Cattell and his colleagues have attempted to embrace these findings and others which we have discussed throughout the book within a coherent theory of learning and development—structured learning theory. Since this is particularly apposite to education we must now discuss briefly how structured learning theory deals with all these findings.

EDUCATION AND STRUCTURED LEARNING THEORY

We have looked in Chapter 12 at a new development of learning theory which is so radical a development out of and beyond reflexological learning theory that it may take some years for traditional learning theory courses to assimilate and use it. It will be remembered that it differs (a) in observing and recording learning changes not only in specific behaviours but also in describable and measurable ability, temperament, and motivation structures, which are of interest and use to personality theory and should be to learning theory. The most far-sighted educators, from Plato through to modern, educational theorists today have maintained that education of personality and character is in the last resort more important than that of mere academic skills. Unfortunately, until quite recently, skills and academic knowledge have been relatively accurately measurable in examinations and personality and motivational developments have not. The result has been that, in spite of pious lip service to educational ideals of personality and character development, the practical attention has been to what is tangible in "classroom results".

Structured learning theory differs also in (b) not assuming that these complex changes over the whole spectrum of an individual's growth can be reported in changes in trait elements as such. Instead they must be encompassed conceptually as changes in the combinations of resources brought to bear in response to situation, and therefore in the manner of integration of the personality. Let us remind the reader that this is handled technically in Chapter 12 by a statistical treatment that uses a mathematical representation in three *vectors*, as follows:

(i) *The trait vector*. This reflects the changes in abilities, personality traits and motivational factors. Thus, for example, when a child learns how to behave himself when he is taken out, this learning will be represented in part by changes on the trait vector (specifically, perhaps, on factor A, sociability).

(ii) *The bearing vector*. This reflects the change in the bearing of traits upon the action. As we learn different things so the way in which we combine our capacities to bring them to bear (hence the name) on any performance will be changed. Thus as an example we can think of the person who as a boy takes up egg collecting because he enjoys the thrill of climbing trees. As he learns more about eggs there may develop a different biological interest and thus the same behaviour is maintained but by a different combination of traits.

(iii) *The situation or involvement vector*. This reflects the changes in the emotive meaning of a situation. Thus a beautiful girl coming into the ambit of a young man has a different effect if he is alone, out with his wife or with his mother.

From this it is clear that structured learning theory offers a tri-vector formulation of learning. All learning can be described in terms of changes in these three vectors.

In as much as this is a theory involving vectors it is possible to develop formulae through the use of matrix algebra to predict some learning performance which can then be put to the test experimentally and with the hunger and sex drive this has been done at least as regards the first two vectors, the trait and the bearing vector. For details of these procedures readers are referred to Cattell (1975).

Apart from the formal advantages of this theory in that it allows of precise mathematical prediction, it has several points which deserve note. First it explicitly recognizes that learning is a three dimensional process.

Second it posits that all the individual's traits and states are involved in learning and that learning affects all states and traits. Finally structured learning theory by means of the mathematics mentioned above is able to define the changes taking place through given types of experience. The APA chart provides the basis for coding these experiences (see p. 269).

More important than any of these points, however, is the claim made by Cattell and Child (1975) that structured learning theory is able to formulate the reinforcement which in the terms of operant conditioning maintains behaviour. This is so significant for theories of personality that it deserves further comment. Thus Kline (1972) has argued that psychoanalytic theory and neo-behaviourism (operant conditioning as a basis for personality) are not opposed as many adherents of these schools seem to think e.g. Eysenck (1953). For example in the case of agoraphobia the behaviourist claims that the avoidance behaviour has been reinforced and that it represents the learning of a maladaptive response. The psychoanalytic view however is that agoraphobia denotes a reaction formation against sexuality, the patient (usually a woman) wanting to be raped everytime she goes out and reacting against it by never wanting to leave the house (Fenichel, 1945). We are not here claiming that this rather fantastic psychoanalytic notion is correct. However what it represents is an attempt based upon clinical data to state in a common neurotic complaint what the reinforcement is that maintains the behaviour. Crudely, the analyst says the reinforcement is the avoidance of sexual temptation. Now we have argued that psychoanalytic theory is in this respect superior to learning theory because it attempts, even if incorrectly, to describe the reinforcement. Now merely to state that the behaviour *is* reinforced is a truism of little value for it inevitably follows from the notion of conditioning. Unfortunately in the case of psychoanalysis we cannot be sure how much of the theory is correct because it is notoriously hard to test although as we have shown (Kline, 1972) some of the basic tenets do have some objective support. Structured learning theory does, however, claim to define reinforcement, but in a strictly testable and quantifiable way. Reinforcement is conceptualized in terms of structured learning theory as the difference in ergic tension before and after learning. Since, as we have seen, there are a large number of ergs and sentiments then reinforcement for learning comes from tension reduction on a large number of drives, not just one.

That is why to come back to our educational topic we normally feel that we learn things better when we are interested in them because as we saw in our study of interests we are usually interested in things (by definition) when we are ergically involved with them. Thus, for example, for adolescents vocationally oriented learning may be far more successful because it influences ergs and sentiments such as career, mating and spouse which are likely to be affected by having a good job in contradistinction to the more abstract study of Greek grammar. On this argument we might say that it would be unlikely that anybody would learn Greek grammar but for able children it may enable the expression of self-assertion, self sentiment and career, classics fitting one for emoluments both in this world and the next.

If we look back at the relationship of ergs to academic success we can perhaps see in terms of structured learning theory why it is that curiosity, self sentiment and superego have positive correlations. If, as happens in middle-class professional families particularly, there is an identification of success and achievement with academic performance, then it is obvious that self sentiment will be related to it. Good performance will reduce tension here. As Freud postulated with the notion of the Oedipus complex, perhaps all we are saying in achievement is "look I am a good boy". Since, except for the unusually gifted, academic success demands hard work, the superego is necessarily related positively to success as is, for obvious reasons, curiosity.

It seems arguable that structured learning theory suggesting the nature of the reinforcement for academic success, given that we know what ergs are involved with it, is supported albeit in an imprecise manner by these findings with the motivational variables. Of course structured learning theory has been developed by Cattell to explain the rather more diffuse and fundamental learning underlying the development of personality as we saw in Chapter 12 rather than with the specific educational objective in mind. There is little doubt that it is able to account for the correlations observed between ergs and academic performance and is, of course, more systematic than any *ad hoc* specific explanations could be.

IMPLICATIONS FOR THE PRACTICE OF EDUCATIONAL PSYCHOLOGY

Finally in this chapter we should like to consider the implication of these findings for the professional practice rather than the theory of educational psychology. Since there are various functions and aims in this profession we shall have to consider them separately.

One important aspect of educational psychology is helping the child with educational problems who is not getting on well at school. This of course involves diagnostic and therapeutic questions. The diagnostic problem involves attempting to discover the source of the difficulties. For this it is obvious that the psychologist must use tests of ability. In this book the sphere of abilities has been considered outside the scope of personality and motivation although it is always convenient to have some ideas of a client's intelligence— hence the insertion of factor B in the 16PF test. We may be blessed with an ideal temperament and motivation for academic pursuits, but if we lack the intellectual ability then all is in vain. In other words, the reasons for educational failure may lie in the sphere of abilities, temperament, motivation or the particular personal problems of the client and his family. This is not a matter of either/or: some unfortunate clients will have difficulties in all these areas, others in just one. Furthermore, as is obvious, there is an interaction between some of these variables. For example a highly anxious child may be made even worse by the fact that his mother is frequently away in hospital. Here is an environmental source of difficulty exacerbated by the temperament of the child. In another case it may well be that the effects are almost unnoticed, as is suggested by the later work of Bowlby (e.g. Bowlby, 1969).

This is not the place to pontificate on methods of practical educational psychology. Good diagnosis necessitates that the intellectual status of the client is firmly established with reliable tests of the main cognitive factors. This involves tests of fluid and crystallized ability, verbal, numerical and spatial ability. Possibly with older subjects aptitudes might be assessed although as Kline (1975) has argued the use of measures of aptitude is vitiated by the ineluctable fact of the two g factors which means that the scale scores are usually highly correlated so that any *differential* value is strictly limited. Once however we know the intellectual abilities of our clients we are in a position to judge the nature of the educational problem. If the scores are poor then we can advise the teachers that the courses are too difficult. Calculus for the student of poor general ability and numerical skill is a waste of time. The obverse of this problem is frequently noted—the highly gifted child with g_f in the top 0.2 percent of the population languishing in an undistinguished position in class, a child who without special stimulus is largely wasting his time at school at least as far as intellectual development is concerned. Thus the use of ability tests indicates those students whose problems are dullness. This does not mean that they have no other difficulties but there can be little doubt that for young children the constant frustration of being asked to perform academic work that is too difficult is likely to lead to behaviour problems (see the APA chart on p. 269). Much more important than this function of ability tests is the other group which they reveal those whose intellectual abilities are such as could not account for their educational problems, average and able children who are doing badly. For these children the application of personality and motivation tests appears especially useful.

It should be evident by now that we advocate the use of factored personality tests where the variables have been shown to be those that are the most fundamental in the description of temperament and dynamics. Thus if we find that one of the subjects is highly anxious and extraverted this in part explains the difficulties over academic work. High anxiety is known to disrupt behaviour and as we have seen at the secondary level extraverts do not do well.

One objection to the use of tests in this way in educational psychology is that even if we find out that a child is, say, extraverted and use that as a partial explanation of failure, this is not a useful procedure. It can be considered equivalent to saying that X has failed because he is a failure. The educational psychologist is expected to do something about the problems, not simply reiterate that they are problems. Here, however, if we merely label a child extraverted, there is some force in this objection. Nevertheless a sensible possibility, especially if the classroom interaction studies bear out the hypotheses suggested earlier in this chapter, that the basis of the negative correlation between extraversion and performance lies in the teaching methods, is to attempt to select teachers in a school and allocate pupils to them on the basis of personality. This way we could thus tailor teaching procedures to the personality of pupils.

None of this is to deny the importance of the experiences that each pupil has in his family and home. Testing of this type is not a replacement for the kind of interview aimed at discovering the personal problems and difficulties (if any) of the children referred to the educational psychologist. There is an interaction with experience and personality in the widest sense. Indeed this is precisely what the tri-vector theory of structured learning theory is about. If, over the years, educational psychologists were to keep records of all their subjects in terms of scores on the basic factors of ability personality and motivation longitudinal studies would enable us, as was the case with clinical psychology discussed in the previous chapter, to find out how subjects with various personality patterns reacted to various environmental traumata. In this way we would be able to discover the vulnerable children. The educational psychologist and the social worker working together with the psychiatrist would be able to give special help and support perhaps before trouble ever appeared where it seemed necessary. A scheme of this sort envisages that when, as is usual in Great Britain from time to time in school, medical records are taken of a child's weight and height, so routine factor measures of personality motivation and ability would also be taken. In fact this is an unlikely procedure since public opinion is strongly against the notion of psychological tests. Young has successfully satirized in "The Rise of the Meritocracy" the concept of a state where intellectual merit was the key to success. It is evident that in Great Britain the notion of blood still runs strong, a striking testimony perhaps to the influence of the horse on the English ruling classes. Nevertheless longitudinal studies of children, where the impact of the environment entered the analysis, could do much for the alleviation of children's problems if, having recognized them, we knew how to treat them.

This brings us on to the other crucial side of educational psychology ultimately more important than the recognition and diagnosis of children at risk and in difficulties. This is treatment. At present, although behaviour therapy is having some success in certain problem areas, especially with subnormal children there are no guaranteed treatments for educational difficulties in the way that, for example, vaccination inevitably defeats smallpox. Indeed since some educational problems are rooted in the family, treatment also requires that we treat this, a task in which it is probably unreasonable to expect educational psychology to succeed. Follow-up studies of children who have been tested at regular intervals, as we suggested above should, as we argued in our previous chapter on clinical psychology, enable us to work out what kinds of treatments and therapeutic procedure are most likely to be useful with what kinds of children. In this way we could maximize the effectiveness of therapy and the results would give us insight into the nature of educational disability.

SUMMARY

1. Personality variables have been shown to be correlated with academic success. At the primary school the stable extravert does best, later the neurotic or anxious introvert, although there are variations with subjects studied. Since these are findings which have been replicated in other cultures it was tentatively argued that teaching methods might be responsible for them. Interaction classroom research was advocated to solve the problem.
2. Motivational variables have been also shown to be correlated with academic performance. Here it was found that superego and self sentiment, together with curiosity, were positively correlated with academic performance while narcism, sex and gregariousness were negatively correlated. These results made good psychological sense and, it was argued, could account for the social class differences noted in educational performance at least in part (differences in intelligence also being important).
3. The relevance of structured learning theory for education was discussed. In this all learning is conceptualized in terms of three vectors, the trait vector, the bearing vector and the situation vector. The importance of this theory, apart from its ability to make precise predictions about learning, is that it attempts to pin down the nature of reinforcement. This is seen as the tension reduction in ergs. Structured learning theory can thus give a systematic account of the motivational results discussed in 2.
4. The impact of these findings upon the practice of educational psychology was discussed. Although contrary to prevailing public opinion, the advantages to both treatment and diagnosis of regular measurement of the major factorially defined variables of ability, personality and motivation were pointed out.

Chapter 15

Personality and Motivation Factors in Occupational and Social Psychology

INTRODUCTION

Occupational psychology is usually taken to embrace the fields of vocational guidance, selection and training, the management of systems and organization for the maximum economic efficiency and human satisfaction (the former being impossible without the latter) and the design of machinery for error free use (ergonomics). Thus a complete coverage of occupational psychology would include an extremely wide range of knowledge, as can be seen on examination of any comprehensive text in this area, e.g. Gilmer (1966).

In this chapter, we shall be concerned in the main with two aspects of industrial psychology: vocational guidance and selection. Since this involves inevitably some job description this will have to be briefly discussed.

Difference Between Vocational Guidance and Selection

It is a curious fact that although most adults spend much of their waking life at work what work they actually do is often decided by accident. Until recently, with the advent of counselling services in schools with some element of vocational guidance, most adults had no rational basis for choosing a job, an equal limitation we may say of vocational selection. The reason for this is simple. There is probably a range of jobs that each of us could do, with reference to our abilities, personality and interests. Only recently have we been able to measure interest and personality with anything like the precision of good ability tests. Accurate assessment has not therefore, been possible.

However, a major reason for adjustment to occupation not reaching a good scientific foundation is that job demands, in terms of psychological characteristics, are not known. From this logical analysis it is clear that vocational guidance and selection must be concerned with two things: job specification and person specification. In this respect vocational guidance and selection are similar. Nevertheless there are differences between these procedures which must be discussed before the full impact of the factored tests described in this book can be grasped. In vocational guidance clients want to be helped. Guidance is usually a voluntary process. This means that deliberate distortions such as lying and refusal to broach certain subjects which can affect Q data have minimal influence on test scores. This is particularly true if the testing side of vocational guidance is carried out within a counselling situation where good rapport has been established between counsellor and client. In vocational guidance the interests of tester and testee are one.

In vocational selection, however, the case is different. Here the subject usually wants the job even if he would not be particularly good at it. The selectors, however, want the best person. Here therefore the interests of the parties are not the same. It behoves the applicant to appear in the best light so that there is every possibility of distortion. Many personality inventories are manifestly transparent. What applicant for a salesman would admit to finding difficulty in getting on with people, being shy and diffident and being poor at persuading others? For selection purposes the use of Q data must be cautious. Here indeed T data come into their own.

Before we come to examine the quite considerable array of facts that have been collected concerning the personality and motivational characteristics of different occupational groups, we must mention how we intend to deal with job demands, the characteristics of different jobs since, as we shall see, these permeate our discussion of both vocational guidance and selection. One approach and one favoured by Cattell and also by Strong (1943) and Kuder

(1970) in the development of their interest tests is to define a job in terms of the *psychological characteristics of those actually doing it*. This approach has been dealt with in our discussion of interest tests (see Chapter 10), so that there is no need for lengthy discussion. Suffice it to say that there is a logical difficulty with this method in that there is no guarantee that the most suitable people are in the right position, particularly when selection procedures are so haphazard. Furthermore most jobs have not been organized in an ideal way so that critical necessities of any particular post may be, in fact, inessentials of the job, as when for example, outmoded machinery makes special operational demands. Employers may seek out unnecessary skills and abilities. The British civil service used to favour a qualification in classics although there was no clear evidence that classical scholars were better than those of other disciplines. A study of the attributes of higher civil servants could have been most misleading. Perhaps even more important than this is the fact that the demands of jobs change rapidly. The advent of computers at all levels of information processing has meant, to take the civil service as an example again, that competent administrators must know what can and cannot be expected from computers, knowledge and insight that a classical education is unlikely to provide. Job change means that the method of describing an occupation in terms of the attributes of those in it may be inevitably wrong.

All these problems by no means entirely vitiate this approach to job classification. Some occupational psychologists, however, have turned to job description. Job description is not, of course, a novel procedure. Oakley *et al.* (1937) at the National Institute of Industrial Psychology had quite elaborate descriptions of many jobs, but these were little more than intuitive although based on observation and common sense. In similar vein and highly useful in practice is the seven-point plan of Rodger (1952). However more modern exponents of job description and task analysis (of whom Gagné (1965) would be a good example), which are regarded as part of systems analysis, berate these early attempts at job description. They consider them to be unsystematic with no agreed terminology. Instead task description and analysis carried out within the framework of system development have enabled a far more objective approach to job description to be used. In order to evaluate properly the contribution to vocational guidance and selection made by the factor analytic findings of Cattell and his colleagues we must briefly describe task analysis and description within systems development.

Task Analysis and Description

Although this is a highly elaborate procedure for our purposes the basic principles are all that is important to grasp. Our summary will be based upon two excellent descriptive papers by Miller (1965, 1966) to whom readers are referred for further details, although a more extended discussion of this topic can be found in Kline (1975). A system is conceived of in these terms as designed for some human purpose. Thus a radio would not be designed in isolation but as a system of which the human operator and listener is a part. Similarly, a car would be considered to be part of a transport system for driver and passengers. In this way we would radically alter many design features; for example many very large cars have little room for passengers. This same method of thinking, when applied to tasks, forces exceedingly precise job descriptions to be developed.

The first requirement is task analysis, i.e. a highly detailed set of instructions for carrying out a job. Without this, it is argued by Miller, work on human factors within occupational psychology is guesswork. This is the objection to the intuitive, sensible but unsystematic approach of the seven-point plan. Undoubtedly the plan in the hands of a sensitive and insightful psychologist will work well. However, there are not many such people and the aim of a scientific system of vocational guidance and selection is to be able to rely on its methodology rather than the skills of the people implementing it.

Task analysis which enables us to see what has to be done shows up the errors of job description. Our discussion of these will clarify the concept. First, a general job description can lead to irrelevant requirements. For example clinical psychologists are required to know statistics. However *as the job is presently conceived* they rarely make use of these skills—all they actually use are the skills needed for understanding scientific papers. If the requirement were dropped there would be virtually no loss of job efficiency. Now this example has been chosen because it highlights the strengths of task analysis and the weakness of matching scores to occupational profiles. Up to now clinical psychologists have tended to ignore the work of the factor analysts partly because the statistical notions are overwhelming. Thus if we were to find a typical profile of psychological characteristics of clinical psychologists it would fall short of our ideal because at present, as a group, they have insufficient statistical knowledge. A matching procedure therefore would inevitably be unsatisfactory. One other advantage of the task analysis is also brought home to us in this example. It has highlighted the fact that, at present, clinical psychology demands no statistical knowledge. It reveals that records are not kept, for example, in a form easily amenable to computer analysis—an aspect of clinical psychology which we have argued is highly important. Task analysis demonstrates what aspects of the job are not being adequately carried out, as well as highlighting unnecessary (but not in our clinical example) demands for qualification and training.

A second fault of intuitive job description is that it can underestimate the demands of a job. If the sequence of steps in a job can vary, more is entailed than simple knowledge of the steps themselves. A third error is the failure to identify emergency procedures that may have to be known. For example, a lorry driver ought to be able to carry out his own simple repairs such as replacing fan belts or headlights and diagnosing starter motor problems. Without this facility much time will be wasted waiting for repairs. A fourth fault of general description is the converse of the third—the overemphasis on the unlikely emergency. A simple and obvious example can be taken from music. String players are not taught to play on less strings than normal as a training for the occasion when one breaks. These errors which task analysis avoids compel us to think with great clarity about what various jobs involve and lead up to the related task description.

Miller (1965, 1966) regards task description as a statement of the requirements of a job in minutely detailed form and proposes an algorithm which ensures reasonable success. First the function of the task must be stated. Then the environmental conditions affecting the task should be set out. Those relevant to the example of lorry driving are; in mud, at night, on motorways, in crowded city centres, 90° turns to be reversed through only one foot wider than lorries. Finally, other contingencies have to be listed, such as the need to be able to carry out repairs, read maps, or load up lorries. These illustrations show that task description and analysis combine together to enable us to gain a detailed understanding of the requirements of a job. When this has been achieved we are in a position to estimate the psychological characteristics demanded by it. Such estimates do of course have to be validated against real life criteria and compared with results obtained from people working in the various occupations. Job analysis and description are very useful in helping to determine the psychological demands of jobs—a prerequisite of rational vocational guidance and selection.

We are not arguing that job evaluation of this detailed kind is impossible outside the concepts of systems development. This is clearly not the case. There is no doubt that the methods advocated here imply that we must make the detailed descriptions that are necessary for adequate psychological evaluation. Given this full description, the advantages of it stand out. First task analysis and description can apply to new and to changed jobs. This is most important in any complex technological society where occupational demands are frequently changing. Secondary school teaching is a good example of this. The new group methods of teaching now in favour involve a different approach to teaching and hence a very different type of teacher is necessary. Carpentry too examplifies this change. The emphasis has switched from great skill where time was of little consequence to great speed where the carpenter is fitting pre-cut pieces into position. The fact of job change means that occupational profiles based upon the scores of those in post are not as useful as might be expected. This method overcomes the problem of bad job design which can destroy empirical attempts to determine the psychological characteristics of those doing the job. If a particular job needs some special skill, because the machinery is poorly designed or located in the factory, this skill will be an important part (but not an intrinsic part) of job success. Selecting men on this basis is absurd since it is far better to modify the machine. That such factors can also apply to the fields of personality and motivation is demonstrated by the example of noise. It has been shown that there are personality differences in the effects of noise on performance (Broadbent,

1971). Thus in a noisy factory job we are likely to find personality differences are of some influence on efficiency. It is probably a better solution to silence the machinery (if that is possible) than to select men who can stand the environment.

In summary we should like to see job specification in terms of the psychological profiles of those carrying out the job and estimates of the psychological demands based upon task description and analysis. When this is done rational vocational guidance and selection can begin—turning on the assessment of both men and jobs.

However, if we reduce vocational guidance and selection to procedures (whatever they may be) of fitting men to jobs or, in the case of new jobs, to men, we are still ignoring a number of important problems.

Distribution of Talent in Society

A vital issue concerns the appropriate division of human resources throughout society. Thus almost all admit the value of education and that the quality of teachers must be as high as possible. However if all teachers were as highly trained and as suited to the profession by virtue of ability, temperament and motivation, as is desirable, because so many teachers are needed, other professional jobs demanding similarly high levels of training and talent would be denuded of ability. This is a common problem of developing countries who channel much of their educated manpower into education, to the detriment of efficiency in many other aspects of administration. Related to this is the level of salary that any society deems appropriate for jobs. Until recently, teachers and nurses in the United Kingdom would appear to have been underpaid. Governments would appear to have been relying on a sense of vocation to attract able people into these professions. However the fact that a job (such as estate agent) which demands relatively low levels of training and ability is so much more valued in terms of salary means that many able people are attracted to this with a consequent loss to the community.

In vocational guidance it may eventuate that a client seems to be equally suited to several different occupations. To some extent much depends on how many others are likely to be directed to these positions. For example if we are faced with a client who wants and seems able to be both mathematics teacher and actuary since the latter are more difficult to obtain it may be sensible from the point of view of society to train him as an actuary rather than a teacher. However whether such value judgements can or should be made by individuals concerned with vocational guidance is another matter. Even this brief discussion, however, indicates that vocational guidance and selection inevitably involve the problem of human resources in society.

There is a further and yet more severe difficulty in rational vocational guidance—the difficulty of getting even moderate reliability and validity into a criterion of job success against which validity studies of all procedures must ultimately be established.

The Problem of the Criterion in Job Success

Ghiselli (1966) has demonstrated in a survey of more than 10,000 investigations that overall there was a correlation between success in any job and intelligence of around 0.3. Such a survey, of course, involved an examination of the criteria of occupational success. This is critical to a proper evaluation of Ghiselli's work since many and varied were the criteria in so vast a number of studies. Ghiselli (1966) contains an excellent summary of this problem which is equally germane to the use of factor analytic personality and motivation tests in occupational psychology. For a full discussion readers must be referred to Ghiselli (1966) or to Kline (1975). Here we can but summarize the problems. First there is a large number of different criteria for job success that can be used. Those most frequently found in Ghiselli's survey were: ratings by supervisors (the most common), output, errors, wastage, volume of sales, and number of new accounts. Obviously not all these criteria apply to all jobs. Thus the last two variables are applicable to salesmen but useless for teachers. Ideally we ought to use as many criteria as possible for each job. In the case of a production line job, output, errors, wastage, damage to machinery might all be useful, depending on the extent to which they were correlated. If they were highly correlated there would be little point in using all of them although if there were zero correlations between them the value of combining them into one score is questionable.

A difficulty with the establishment of these criteria lies in the fact that many of them are not reliable, a fault which applies especially to supervisors' ratings. This unreliability naturally sets a limit on the size of any possible correlations. Another problem arises from the fact that the abilities for the acquisition of a skill are not necessarily the same as those required for its maintenance. This means that results obtained with some criteria are dependent upon the time at which the study was undertaken. Ghiselli (1966) found it useful to distinguish two broad categories of criteria of job success: capacity to absorb training and proficiency at the task itself. Many existing personality and ability specifications for jobs, e.g. those for school teachers and nurses, are based on success in the training period rather than in later practice. There are exceptions to this, as in the specification equation in the 16PF Handbook for success as a bakery rounds salesman and a car driver, the former being based on actual earnings over the year of more than a hundred salesmen and the latter on the inverse of the number of recorded accidents.

This discussion makes it clear that it is difficult to establish with any confidence a criterion of success in most occupations. The best we can hope for is to combine as many measures as possible although it is almost certain that any correlations will be heavily compounded with error, and thus likely to be lower than in ideal conditions. Readers must be aware of all these difficulties when we come to examine attempts to predict occupational success using factored tests of personality and motivation.

We have argued here that the essence of rational vocational guidance and selection lies in accurate job assessment and person assessment. The former would appear best carried out by a combination of task analysis and description and a definition of the psychological characteristics of a job in terms of those holding the post. A difficulty involved in studies of this kind lies in the establishment of an adequate set of criteria for job success. Assessment of men as we have stressed should be in terms of source traits.

In this book, concerned with temperamental and dynamic traits, we will not discuss ability factors of which the most important are the two g factors, fluid and crystallized ability (Cattell, 1971) and the primary ability factors, the fruits of Thurstone's (1938) pioneering work on rotation to simple structure. For a discussion of source traits in the sphere of abilities we must refer readers to Cattell (1971). For their value to vocational guidance and selection, Ghiselli's (1966) survey bears eloquent witness. Kline (1975) also discusses fully the use of ability tests in assessment.

Here we shall concentrate on the use of personality and motivation factors for guidance and selection, recalling the arguments of chapter 10 on interest tests and our arguments in the last two chapters on educational and clinical applications concerning the advantages of measuring recognized personality dimensions rather than entirely atheoretical hotch-potch collections of variables that happen to discriminate one occupational group from another as in the Strong Interest Blank (see chapter 10 for a full discussion). In this way we can gain insight and understanding into what makes for vocational success and satisfaction because the variables have psychological meaning.

PERSONALITY FACTORS IN OCCUPATIONAL PSYCHOLOGY: VOCATIONAL GUIDANCE AND SELECTION

Since this has turned out to be, over the years, an area of application which has been of great practical value there has accrued a vast amount of information—so much indeed, that in the Handbook to the 16PF test alone (Cattell *et al.*, 1970) more than 100 pages are devoted to it. We could not include all this information in this chapter. What we shall do is to outline the various methods by which the full power of these factors can be utilized and then give illustrations of some of the most striking results.

Actually the methods we are about to discuss find applications beyond occupational psychology, in the educational and clinical fields in the previous two chapters. However, since they are most useful, given our current knowledge, in occupational psychology we examine them here rather than previously. The two methods are the *Adjustment* or "type placement" method and the *effectiveness* or "performance" approach. Although these methods are sometimes considered to be alternatives there can be little doubt that they are better regarded as complementary.

The Adjustment or Type Placement Method. In essence this answers the question does individual A belong to Type X? In occupational psychology this means does our client or subject up for selection resemble those in a given job or jobs. This entails matching an individual's profile of scores (on, say, the 16PF) with a profile representing the occupants of a job. Obviously this method can be used in clinical psychology "does our patient fall into the depressive or schizophrenic groups?" In educational psychology "does our subject resemble high achievers academically?" would be a typical question.

This first method suffers the disadvantages (which are discussed on p. 295) in using the occupants of a given job as a criterion group. They may not be ideal for the job and we have no measure of their performance. Where reliable criterion evidence on performance is available, the psychologist will probably prefer the specification equation weighting abilities and personality, etc., factors in the best multiple regression. There remain two arguments for the present approach, one pragmatic, based on the term "adjustment" above and one statistical, based on the term type. The latter says that emphasis must be put on the total pattern or "gestalt" by the pattern similarity coefficient, r_p, between the person and the typical person in the job. The specification equation might weight power of engine and slimness of fuselage in predicting speed of a plane, though they cannot compensate for each other indefinitely—a slim body and a weak engine or a powerful engine with a broad fuselage will not work too well. It is the right combination that does the best job. Statistically, the use of types and pattern similarity coefficients is an advantage.

The pragmatic argument involves socio-economic considerations. Doubtless plumbing could be better done by a man with the intelligence and spatial sense that would make him a superb surgeon. But a man is in *economic* (not in religious or social terms) a commodity and will tend to reach his natural wage by laws of supply and demand. So he will not stay a plumber, even though he does the job extremely well, if he has capacities which—in the jargon of employment—"overqualify" him. Nor is it desirable for society, with its limited resources of genetic ability and educational funds, to have its resources of high skill go into plumbing rather than surgery. In a society open to talents—a meritocracy—there is a movement towards the best distribution for society as a whole and what society can "afford" for a given occupation is shown in the equilibrium reached. One says "movement towards" because until psychological knowledge of jobs and individuals is more advanced, the movement is relatively haphazard and inefficient, and justice is not done. But, to a degree, the fact that people have stayed in a job is some indication that they and society are "adjusted" in a compromise equilibrium. Incidentally, a statistical allowance is suggested by Tatsuoka and Cattell in the 16PF Handbook for connecting the required occupational profile on this assumption of inefficiencies in reaching that profile in the actual incumbents.

The Effectiveness or Fitness by Performance Method. This entails the estimation of the goodness of performance of the criterion by using some mathematical function of the factor scores. The linear regression, or specification, equation is the most widely used of these functions. As we have pointed out there is now a considerable body of research where the beta weights of the 16PF factors have been worked out in respect of a large number of occupations. All the user is required to do is to multiply the sten score on each factor for any individual by the beta weight for the particular job. The addition of these weighted scores then enables us to see how closely the subject fits the job (or the clinical category in clinical applications). Linear regression is virtually the only model used in studies of this kind although there is no logical reason why this should be the case.

Use of the Adjustment Approach in Vocational Guidance and Selection

There are two questions to be answered concerning the use of this method for practical guidance and selection. The first relates to how the matching of individual to group profile is actually to be done. The second concerns what we do when the match has been made.

Some experienced clinicians and counsellors, especially where there is no computer assistance, match by eye. This is a highly subjective procedure which involves usually private weighting of some of the factors. Since in some cases the statistical evidence is still not available there is obviously room for such clinical intuitions. However, as Meehl (1954) demonstrated, clinical intuition is inferior to statistically based decision making and there can be no doubt that the best solution is to match an individual's profile of score to the various group profiles using r_p, the pattern similarity coefficient (Cattell, 1949). The details of this computation need not concern us here although calculation is simple and various aids are supplied in the Handbook to the 16PF test.

When we have found the occupational groups that a subject most resembles in terms of r_p we should not advocate in either guidance or selection the mechanical use of these procedures. This is because the reliability and validity of the tests, although good, is not perfect, so that in the individual case there is room for error. There are difficulties in the use of criterion groups with this method so that we would always want to ensure that the results were appropriate by careful interviewing, and discussion in the case of guidance. This is not to elevate the interview above tests but simply to recognize that it can provide a useful amplification for test scores.

One of the least satisfactory features of vocational guidance is the tendency for subjects, especially youngsters who have little self-knowledge, to seize upon the results especially of interest tests and, by virtue of the results, claim that they are interested in the categories in which they scored high. Until the reliability and validity of personality and motivation tests is far higher than at present and until we know more about the normal life course and stability of interests through such structured dynamic measures as the MAT, mechanical use of the scores without tempering psychological advice is to be avoided.

We have already discussed the problem of the proper distribution of abilities and skills throughout society. This is relevant to practical vocational guidance. A subject who fits a rare group would be well advised to enter it—not only is there less competition but there is the need of society to have that job well done. The ethical problem of what contributes a useful or valuable job is ultimately a personal decision for the subject himself and, as such, is beyond the scope of this book.

Use of the Effectiveness (Fitness by Performance) Approach in Vocational Guidance and Selection

Problems of measurement apart, this would appear to be a superior method to the one discussed above because it deals with what we want to know—actual performance in the job, the criterion behaviour. Ideally the factor weights would be obtained by carrying out a factor analysis where the criterion scores (note the plural) are put into the analysis together with our predictor variables (in this example the 16PF factors). However a more practicable method and the one therefore much more commonly used is to administer the 16PF to a group for whom criterion scores have been obtained and to correlate the factor scores with the criteria. This has the disadvantage (compared with the first procedure) that the correlations are affected by the reliability and validity of the factor scales—so that values lower than in the first method are obtained.

The specification equation uses weights which modify the correlations of the factors with the criterion according to the correlations between the factors themselves, as is done in calculating any multiple regression equation on a criterion. The standard matrix algebra to do this is set out in the Handbook for the 16PF tests where readers must refer for full details. Given that we have worked out the specification equation we get a series of weights (the beta weights) for multiplying each factor scale score for a given individual. Since this is a linear additive model, the greater the weighted total for any subject, the better he is likely to do in that occupation. Since, as we have indicated, criterion measures are difficult to obtain, Tatsuoka and Cattell (1970) have worked out adjustment specification equations based upon group profiles. This may be regarded as the best of both worlds.

Again, as was the case with the first method, because of the problems of criterion measurement and imperfect tests we would not like to see either guidance or selection mechanically based upon these scores. Thus to select one candidate over another just because his fit was better, 7.84 rather than 6.91, would not seem sensible. How to use these scores in practice is discussed in some detail in the Handbook to the test (Cattell *et al.*, 1970). This is a specialized topic which we shall not pursue here.

The Two File System

For the practical convenience of test users Cattell (1957) has proposed the two file system which maximizes the value of both the methods which we have discussed above in vocational selection and guidance. The two file system entails that the test user has files of mean profiles and specification weights for the sixteen factors (and, indeed, any other factors if the data are available) on all the relevant categories (clinical syndromes for the clinical psychologist, for example). These data constitute the *constants file*. In the personnel score file are the factor scores of the subjects with whom the psychologist has to deal. Then when any personnel decisions have to be taken a computer analysis of the files can present all the results for the individuals concerned in terms of the specification equation and the adjustment method.

It would certainly seem valuable, if, before interviewing subjects, the psychologist had studied the data presented by the two file system. The practical application of this system depends upon the availability of computers with large storage facilities, but there is no reason why it could not be used by large organizations.

Specification equations and profile scores on the 16PF factors have been collected for a large variety of occupational groups. So far our discussion has turned upon how these are best used in the practical solution of vocational selection and guidance problems. One of the great advantages of the factored over the criterion keyed test consists in the psychological meaningfulness of the discriminations. So it is this theoretical issue that we are now going to examine. We do not intend here to quote the huge array of results for various occupations: that would be merely bewildering. Rather we shall highlight some of the more interesting and provocative profiles or equations. For the full lists readers must be referred to the Handbook to the 16PF Test (Cattell *et al.*, 1970).

Specification Equations and Occupational Profiles (16PF)

Accident proneness has been examined, an important variable in vocational selection especially where in certain jobs we need to eliminate accidents as far as possible, as in public-service driving for example. Here the specification equation reveals the power of factor-analytic variables. Thus the highest leading variables are G and M. This means that having a strong superego, restraining behaviour on the grounds of morality and foresight, leads to freedom from accidents. Autia (M) on the other hand favours accidents because it tends to cut the individual off from external checks and the reality of his dangerous behaviour. Certainly it could be objected that these findings are obvious but as we have seen in the history of psychology much clinical intuition which seemed so obvious turns out to be wrong. As the great Creighton (1899) invincibly argued, it was obvious that the principal cause of the Black Death was the evil miasma emanating from corpses.

An interesting case which illustrates our argument is that of retail salesmen. Here the stereotypic view of the successful salesman as a dominant extravert, while not entirely wrong, needs modification. Thus dominance is not an advantage for E is negatively weighted in the specification equation. Furthermore although the extravert primary traits of A, F, and H are important (doubtless the reason why salesmen seem so extravert) Q2 is negatively weighted. Here then research enables us to modify our intuitions and thus improve both guidance and selection. Again we must note the psychological meaning of these results, a far cry from the discriminations between occupational groups made by such instruments as the Strong Vocational Interest Blank.

Table 15.1 which simply gives a sample of the occupational findings with the 16PF test illustrates better than any discussion the value of the 16PF test for understanding the psychology of vocations. It is worth noting that on A sizia, (withdrawn, detached, aloof), physicists and artists are the lowest scoring of our groups. This neatly fits the picture of the thoughtful, reserved scientist working out his problems alone. It is also interesting that these two groups together with writers are the highest on intelligence. Conversely the highest scorers on factor A are business executives. Perhaps this is why so much business is apparently done over dinner and drinks. A business executive has to be high on A simply because other executives are and a mismatch on a factor of this kind automatically makes the individual a misfit. If we look at factor C, ego strength, the ability to make firm reality based decisions, we find that the two highest scores are those of the physicists again and of airline pilots. The importance of C for airline pilots is obvious. It is gratifying for nervous travellers that this is indeed the case. The fact that physicists should be high on C is not so obvious although there can be little doubt that the ability to maintain original and possibly unpopular lines of thought essential in any science would be greatly facilitated by high ego strength. A good example of this can be taken from recent psychology: to maintain that intelligence is largely genetically determined and to quote the evidence upon which the claim is based is today to be branded a fascist pig. Certainly these words and worse were used to the second author of this book and Lysenck was physically attacked for using this argument at the University of London.

A further point deserves notice: the more extreme scores a group has the more rare it is bound to be, since extreme scores are statistically abnormal. This probably accounts for why in any population there are relatively few writers and physicists, groups which possess extreme scores, as the table shows, on a variety of factors. Artists, too, fit this bill. Accountants on the other hand of whom there are a large number in any highly developed capitalist society have no such extreme scores. This finding again supports our claim that the use of factored personality tests gives us real insight into the psychology of careers and vocations.

We have now given sufficient illustrations of the value of the 16PF questionnaire in occupational psychology. Readers can scan for themselves the scores quoted in this chapter and draw their own conclusions about the nature of various professions and occupations. Many more sets of scores can be found in the Handbook (Cattell *et al.*, 1970) to the test.

So far we have indicated two possible methods for using 16PF scores in

TABLE 15.1

Personality Profiles for Varied Occupations

Occupation	N	Sex	A	B	C	E	F	G	H	I	L	M	N	O	Q_1	Q_2	Q_3	Q_4
Accountants (American)	94	m	7.1	7.9	4.9	5.5	4.9	6.4	5.6	4.5	6.3	6.1	6.6	5.7	6.3	6.2	5.8	5.1
Airline hostesses	139	f	6.6	6.1	7.5	5.9	6.8	7.1	7.7	5.0	3.8	4.3	6.8	3.6	6.4	4.1	7.7	2.8
Airline pilots	360	m	5.1	7.2	7.8	6.0	6.7	7.2	6.9	3.8	3.7	4.1	5.7	3.5	5.8	5.1	7.5	3.0
Artists	64	m, f	3.1	8.8	7.0	6.8	3.9	3.7	7.0	9.2	5.0	8.9	4.4	4.8	6.4	7.0	6.3	6.3
Business executives	178	m	7.8	7.5	5.7	5.8	5.3	5.5	6.6	5.6	5.4	5.7	6.2	5.5	6.4	5.5	5.8	5.3
Electricians	67	m	4.6	6.6	7.2	5.5	4.9	5.7	5.7	3.9	4.4	3.7	6.4	3.8	4.5	5.7	6.6	4.8
Industrial plant foremen	165	m	5.1	6.5	5.4	5.1	4.5	5.8	5.1	5.1	4.5	4.9	5.7	5.7	5.6	5.5	5.6	5.4
Military (army) cadets	1282	m	5.4	6.0	6.1	5.6	5.9	6.4	5.7	5.0	5.2	5.4	6.1	4.6	5.5	4.4	6.3	5.2
Miners (Australian)	137	m	5.2	5.8	6.1	5.6	5.9	5.5	4.8	4.6	5.0	4.4	5.9	5.6	5.7	5.3	5.9	5.3
Nursing students	176	f	5.3	6.1	6.2	4.8	5.8	5.5	4.8	4.7	6.1	6.0	6.1	5.7	5.4	4.5	5.8	5.8
Physicians	170	m	5.4	6.2	5.4	4.8	5.6	5.1	5.4	5.7	5.4	5.5	5.8	5.5	5.6	6.4	6.1	5.0
Physicists	91	m	2.8	9.6	7.3	6.2	3.1	3.9	6.1	6.8	3.8	4.9	5.6	3.7	5.6	6.3	7.2	5.1
Policemen	106	m	6.0	5.0	6.0	6.5	5.1	5.7	5.5	3.9	5.2	4.4	5.3	5.0	4.7	4.8	5.9	5.5
Teachers (elementary)	1280	f	5.6	6.5	5.0	5.5	5.5	5.7	5.6	5.9	5.0	5.4	5.8	5.1	5.5	5.7	6.0	5.3
Teachers (elementary)	88	m	5.7	6.6	5.7	5.1	5.9	5.6	5.5	5.9	5.4	5.8	5.0	5.6	5.3	4.7	5.5	5.5
Teachers (junior high)	94	f	4.3	6.9	5.4	6.7	6.0	4.1	5.8	5.2	5.3	6.7	6.1	4.8	6.7	5.2	6.0	4.8
Teachers (junior high)	132	m	3.7	6.1	5.0	5.4	5.4	5.4	5.0	5.8	5.3	6.4	5.3	5.9	5.8	5.4	5.3	5.5
Teachers (senior high)	92	f	4.5	6.8	5.5	6.2	5.8	4.4	6.3	5.5	5.4	6.6	6.2	4.7	6.6	5.4	5.8	4.3
Teachers (senior high)	177	m	4.4	6.2	5.2	5.3	5.4	5.1	5.3	5.8	5.6	6.0	5.4	5.8	5.9	5.6	5.2	5.2
Writers	89	m, f	4.1	9.7	6.6	8.1	4.6	3.2	7.0	7.9	5.3	7.3	5.1	5.4	6.9	7.2	5.7	6.9

Note: Norms used in converting these group profiles from raw scores to sten scores are those for general population, except where groups are indicated as students (in which case student norms were used). All values are in tens (population mean 5.5). Standard deviations within occupations are also given in table of 73 occupational groups from which these 15 are taken (Cattell, Eber, and Tatsuoka, 1970; p. 175).

vocational guidance and selection. We have also seen how the use of factored scores leads to theoretical insights into the nature of occupations. At one point these theoretical gains actually have direct practical application. Thus, for example, some source traits, such as A and H, are largely genetically determined whereas others are more heavily influenced by the environment. Factors I, G and F are examples of the latter. To know from the profiles of scores which type of factors give rise to the fit affects our judgement of it. Thus if the major discrepancies are on the largely genetically determined factors we know that the subject is unlikely to become more suited to the group. If, however, the discrepancies are on factors which decline with age (and our young subjects score on these was too high) then we know that in the future there is likely to be an even better fit.

The 16PF test is a valuable test in vocational guidance and selection although, since it covers only the general personality temperament domain, the MAT is needed to cover the dynamic area, just about doubling prediction. As Cattell and Butcher (1968) have shown, the use of the 16PF without the MAT is not enough. Moreover, the user must be highly skilled in understanding the 16PF source traits, and the question also arises whether it should be used with or without an interview. On the last the range of opinion is wide. Eysenck argues that an interview introduces nothing but error and prejudice: other psychologists feel they cannot do without it. It is probably safer, used with test results on hand, as a device to fill in some gaps in the test evidence.

OBJECTIVE T TESTS

The method of fitting obtained scores to occupational profiles and specification equations can be used with any test provided that the profiles and equations exist. Thus the methods could be used with T data. Unfortunately in the temperamental field sufficient occupational T data have not yet been collected. However we can still examine T factors in vocational guidance and selection for any theoretical insights that they may provide. One advantage with objective tests lies in the fact that their meaning is hidden from subjects so that for selection at least they would be more suitable than the questionnaires that we have examined above.

Since vocational guidance and selection is carried out largely for practical purposes, sometimes by those without a considerable training in psychology, objective tests have seldom been used. It is therefore not possible to comment on their value. Two tests which we have previously examined the Music Preference test of Personality and the Humour test of Personality were designed with industrial applications in mind. As yet there is insufficient evidence for their utility in industrial psychology although it would be interesting to try both tests out on different occupational groups.

Results with Other Factored Personality Tests

In chapter 6 we showed that most factorial results of any technical merit largely confirm the Cattell personality factors. However Grygier (1961) has developed the Dynamic Personality Inventory and work with this test indicates that although the validity of the scales is dubious there are significant differences between faculty members at university—arts, architecture and science (Hamilton, 1970, Stringer, 1967). Work by Kline and Knowles (in preparation) with artists also shows that these are discriminated from normals. There is little doubt that, given further research of an extensive kind, the DPI might become useful in vocational guidance. However until factorial work has located these particular scales in the general personality sphere, it is difficult to interpret any differences found between groups (occupational or otherwise) with this test.

Kline (1971) has developed a test of anal or obsessional character, Ai3Q, which, he has shown, measures a factor not covered by the 16PF test, although probably of relatively small variance. This test again distinguishes artists from controls and also student psychologists who score low, whereas mathematicians and scientists score high. Since this is a meaningful scale both factorially and in terms of psychoanalytic theory these are interesting results which could be valuable in vocational guidance and selection.

Eysenck's E and N, as measured by the EPI, deserve mention. While there is no doubt that these two factors are essentially the exvia and anxiety of the second-order factors of Cattell, we must note that they are less useful in guidance and selection than the primary factors of the 16PF because they contain less information. Furthermore we cannot apply the depth psychometric techniques (which we discussed in our chapter on clinical applications) and which could prove, with further research, highly valuable in vocational guidance. Two factors, albeit the largest, are not sufficient for sensitive personality measurement.

So much for temperamental traits in vocational guidance and selection. We must now turn to the use of dynamic and motivational strength factors, which have further predictive power.

THE MAT IN VOCATIONAL GUIDANCE AND SELECTION: DYNAMIC TRAITS IN OCCUPATIONAL PSYCHOLOGY

As we have discussed in the chapters on motivation and its factorial measurement, the main dynamic factors are conceived of as ergs, the basic goals of behaviour, and sentiments which are culturally moulded goals. The dynamic lattice has been developed to account for observed behaviours in ultimate ergic terms. As an example it could be argued that high career sentiment allowed the eventual expression of a number of ergs such as security, hunger, acquisitiveness and self-assertion and the attraction of a job could depend upon the number of different ergs for which it allowed expression. This analysis of job satisfaction would certainly account for the findings of Herzberg, (see Chapter 10) where money was not found to be a satisfier although lack of money was a dissatisfier. Ergic satisfaction could be the key to vocational satisfaction. All this, however, is speculative and we must now turn to the evidence which consists largely of the scores on the MAT of different occupational groups.

Before we discuss these, as we hope is clear from our section on the 16PF test, it must be realized that we can apply those methods to the MAT also—the adjustment technique and the fitness by performance approach. All that we have said about the relative efficiency of these methods with respect to their use with the 16PF applies equally to the MAT and we shall not repeat the arguments here.

Cattell and Child (1975) present some interesting profiles, although on small samples, of Presidents of Insurance Companies and successful business men. To take the Presidents first, the outstanding feature was their high score for narcism and self-sentiment and their low score for superego. This confirms the left wing stereotype of the highly successful executive as ruthless, without conscience, indulging himself in the pleasures of life, and striving to be the top man. It is interesting to note that his career sentiment is only average, perhaps because, as Cattell and Child (1975) point out, he has arrived—a viewpoint succinctly stated by an Indian professor who claimed that he had given up research because he had reached the top. One other score deserves mention: the home parental sentiment was low indicating possibly that this small but highly successful sample had achieved so well that they could confidently break away from all dependence on their parents.

This example of the high executive group highlights with great clarity a major weakness of the adjustment method. There is no mistaking the low superego score. However few could argue that this is necessarily desirable. It must be presumed that Nixon fits the pattern extremely well and low superego led to Watergate. This is not intended as a political statement: it merely shows that an adjustment method may perpetuate undesirable as well as desirable characteristics.

The typical successful businessman profile, quoted in Cattell and Child (1975), as might be expected, does not differ much from that of the top executives. Those differences there are support the psychological meaning of the ergs and sentiments and hence their utilization in a rational scheme of vocational guidance and selection. The main discriminating factors are: career sentiment (high), assertiveness (high) and sweetheart-spouse (low). As we ponder upon these differences we should first consider that these men, unlike the first sample, have not yet reached the top. For them the career drive has some meaning. At the top some new goal has to be set. The American President can, it must be supposed, aim still to be the best president there has ever been. Assertiveness is higher presumably because when we have reached the top, again it has become obvious, and there is no need for strident evidence.

The low sweetheart spouse sentiment may reflect the time spent at work, they have married their work rather than their wives—a common complaint of those married to high achieving men. When success comes, then perhaps more time can be spent with the family.

These are the main features of the two profiles which would appear to be of obvious interest to those concerned with vocational guidance and selection. There is a further point of more theoretical interest. Among the top executives there was a considerable difference between the integrated (average) and unintegrated (high) sex erg. This suggests the possibility that the sex drive was being channelled into work since this pattern is typical of unfulfilled sexual tension. This finding therefore supports the Freudian notion of sublimation.

Skelton (1968) administered the MAT to officer cadets and computed biserial correlations between each factor and passing or failing the selection procedure. As with our previous samples we must be cautious in interpreting the results because there were in all only 52 cadets. The results certainly fit common sense in that the successful group were less attached to their parents, less fearful, more self assertive and more career minded, a reasonable description of a keen army officer.

Cattell and Child (1975) have a table showing the MAT scores of various occupational groups which we reproduce below.

Although readers can peruse this table and speculate about it themselves

TABLE 15.2

MAT Sten Scores (Rounded) for Various Occupational Groups

Occupation	N	Career	Home	Fear	Narcism	Superego	Self-sent.	Mating	Pugnacity	Assertion	Sweetheart
Army Officers	44	6	4	5	8	4	5	6	7	5	6
Theological seminary males (clergymen)	279	5	4	4	6	6	6	5	5	4	6
Teachers	64	5	3	5	3	5	7	6	5	5	6
Physicians	112	6	3	6	8	6	7	5	6	5	4
Executives	20	6	3	5	10	1	10	8	4	5	6
Disabled workers	34	6	5	6	5	6	4	5	5	4	5
Construction workers	17	8	4	5	6	4	5	4	7	7	6
Engineer supervisors	27	7	5	5	5	5	5	5	5	5	5
Engineers	23	7	5	5	5	5	5	5	5	6	6
College students	100	5	4	5	3	4	4	3	4	4	4
Chronically unemployed	75	5	4	8	4	5	5	4	4	2	3
Violent criminals	19	5	4	7	3	5	5	2	5	5	3
Non-violent criminals	19	5	5	5	3	5	5	3	5	4	4
Schizophrenics	30	8	7	4	3	8	4	5	2	5	5

there are a few noteworthy features which we should like to mention. All that we say must be given the status of hypothesis rather than fact since at the moment there is a desperate need for this test and the SMAT to be taken up by field workers so that much more data can become available: in addition the numbers in some of the samples are smaller than desirable. First there seems to be no doubt that education makes people more independent of their home, as indeed ought to be the case if any kind of change is ever to come about. This is demonstrated by the fact that most of the educated groups are low on the home-parental sentiment, even clergymen who professionally, as it were, are advocates of the family life. Similarly highly trained groups have a higher self sentiment than the rest as if in America at least this very education which enable them to break away from the family also makes them feel confident. It could be, of course, that the high self-sentiment makes them confident enough to be able to break away from the family. It is interesting to remember, apropos of this point, that Freud (1940) argued that it was the task of the adolescent to do just this to grow away from the family—to resolve the Oedipus and castration complexes. It would be hopeful, if it turns out that education can contribute to this kind of maturity.

Another interesting score is the high fear erg score of the chronically unemployed. This confirms that they are in a state of insecurity. The only other group who score almost as high are the violent criminals. Whether the unemployed person's insecurity is due to the lack of a job or is part of a wider personality disorder that contributes to their unemployment is not clear. That the violent criminals are fearful supports a Freudian notion of violent men projecting their own violence on to others and then acting accordingly in apparent self defence. Clergymen, for instance, are low on fear.

Other interesting aspects of the table are the narcism scores. As we have had reason to point out before, high scores on this erg are found in the high status groups, low scores in the low status groups. Those who have experienced the finer material pleasures of life find that they enjoy them—a powerful confirmation of learning theories and no doubt the essential mechanism behind the easy corruptability of those in positions of power.

College students score below the average on most of the MAT variables. Presumably this is because being a student allows little outlet for many of these drives. What is needed here is the comparison between their U and I scores. Finally a curious score is that of the construction workers on career sentiment. Intuitively there seems no reason for this. Further comment is inappropriate since the sample was so small.

The above discussion of the scores of different groups confirms what our earlier more detailed examination of three groups showed—that the MAT does give useful insights into the motivations of workers without which rational vocational guidance and selection is not possible. So far the data are too flimsy for the construction of even a tentative theory of occupational satisfaction and success. That task has had to be left for those investigators who are not constricted by factual observation to the same extent as those working with multivariate techniques. Nevertheless the examples which we have discussed above do confirm the kind of approach subsumed by the dynamic lattice—that all our behaviour may be seen as an attempt to express our fundamental drives (ergs and sentiments) in a way appropriate to our temperament, abilities and experience.

Almost all our scrutiny of the research with the MAT in relation to occupations has been concerned with our first method, the adjustment method, which as we have seen is not without its disadvantages. Although the second method of obtaining specification equations against the criterion of job efficiency has not yet been highly developed for the MAT some equivalent procedures although far less precise have provided some useful information. Cattell and Child (1975) show that satisfactory job performance is associated with high career and self assertion and low fear. Such findings are hardly surprising although they confirm the importance of confidence and insecurity in achievement, a finding strikingly reminiscent of Harlow's wire-mother reared monkeys in the open field test, who could only adopt the foetal position. Lawlis (1971) as we have seen correlated the MAT scores with unemployability. He argued from the results that the unemployed person is basically afraid to express himself—negative correlation with assertiveness and career sentiment. As with the school phobic, work might expose inadequacy. Since having no job affects position in society and attractiveness as a prospective or actual spouse we not unexpectedly find negative correlations with self-sentiment and sweetheart-spouse sentiment. Now whether it is correct to think of this rather negative picture of the unemployed as causing, or as the result of, unemployment cannot of course be settled by correlational studies. What is clear, however, is that associated with unemployability is a whole constellation of negative effects in respect of motivation. If we were to hazard a guess, then there is probably a circularity such that a disposition tending towards unemployability is exacerbated by being unemployed.

All this makes clear that the MAT is a highly useful test for vocational guidance and selection. Since, as yet, the necessary specification equations have not been developed, the test cannot be used with the precision of the 16PF. When it is combined with other test scores and the interview to form the basis of vocational decisions it adds in much valuable information. Perhaps its most valuable function is as a basic research instrument for occupational psychology. Thus since the ergs and sentiments have psychological meaning to know how groups differ from each other and deviate from the norm and to know how the factors correlate with criteria for job success must inevitably give us understanding in this area. In addition it will enable us to see how the dynamic lattice is constructed in an area of behaviour which for most adults in the Western world occupies the majority of their waking time. In brief the occupational use of the MAT will lead to both practical and theoretical advances in the understanding of the dynamics of behaviour.

APPLICATIONS OF FACTORIAL FINDINGS IN SOCIAL PSYCHOLOGY

Since some of the findings are relevant to the problems which we have discussed in this chapter it is fitting to examine the social psychological work that has utilized factorial variables. This research falls naturally into separate fields and we shall begin with a discussion of leadership—a topic clearly relevant to occupational psychology.

Leadership

There can be no doubt of the importance of leadership in the world. Fromm (1974) has argued indeed that it is a critical task for democratic nations to uncover the major determinants of such leaders as Hitler or Stalin in order to ensure that such men never rise again. Hitler, to use Fromm's vivid phraseology, did not have horns and it is idle to think that should another begin to rise again he would be easily recognized and thus put down. The questions that obviously spring to mind concern the nature of great leaders: what qualities enable men to lead others often voluntarily to disaster, to abnegate their normal standards of morals or discretion "not for me to reason why ..."? Can leaders be made (as the Army hope) or are they born? If the former how are they to be trained? The old Public schools of Britain put their faith in cold baths and the classics for the leaders of that Empire upon which the sun was never to set. To some extent the answer to some of these questions can now be made, an answer resting upon evidence rather than opinion and it is to this evidence that we shall now turn.

Research of Cattell and Stice (1960)

In a series of researches 100 groups each of ten men were set into competition with each other on a variety of tasks including construction work, committee procedures, code cracking, tugs of war and tests of the groups' honesty in dealing with each other. There were rewards for the groups with the best performances. Different forms of groups were tried out for example a leaderless group, a group where the leader was elected and a group which had a leader from the start.

These researches indicated that in the conditions of this experiment where the groups had to achieve certain ends there was a definite preference for an elected leader. This was the best way to get things done. So much for Rousseau's speculation in the face of this "that man is born free but is everywhere in chains" and that therefore we should struggle to break them. However, equally important as the fact that groups prefer to be led if they can choose their leaders was the fact that three types of leader could be recognized—popular leaders (voted as likeable), effective leaders (those who are judged as the most efficient regardless of popularity) and technical leaders (those who produce the greatest number of solutions to the the group's

TABLE 15.3

Differences Between Leaders and Nonleaders Using the 16PF

Personality factor	Observers' leaders (effective)				Elected leaders (popular)			
	L	Non-L	d	C.R.	L	Non-L	Ld	C.R.
A	18.3	19.7	−1.4	—	18.6	17.4	1.2	—
B	12.5	11.7	0.8	—	10.9	10.3	0.6	—
C	36.1	34.2	1.9	2.2*	34.8	34.0	0.8	—
E	27.0	26.0	1.0	—	25.2	24.4	0.8	—
F	26.1	26.2	−0.1	—	26.4	22.5	3.9	4.6
G	22.4	21.3	1.1	—	22.4	20.8	1.6	3.6
H	39.8	35.8	4.0	3.4	36.6	33.2	3.4	3.2
I	9.8	10.6	−0.8	—	10.0	10.6	−0.6	—
L	16.8	17.8	−1.0	—	17.9	18.6	−0.7	—
M	18.6	19.8	−0.8	—	18.6	20.2	−1.6	2.5*
N	23.0	22.2	0.8	—	21.4	20.7	0.7	—
O	11.3	13.6	−2.3	2.4*	13.0	15.9	−2.9	2.7
Q_1	21.5	21.2	0.3	—	19.7	19.8	−0.1	—
Q_2	15.9	14.5	1.4	—	13.6	14.6	−1.0	—
Q_3	26.7	24.6	2.1	2.2*	26.0	23.6	2.4	2.1*
Q_4	12.0	15.0	−3.0	2.2*	14.7	16.0	−1.3	—
N	43	100			92	233		

Personality factor	Frequency leadership acts (technical)					
	High L'ship	Mid L'ship	Low L'ship	d_1 (H − L)	(H − M)	(C.R.)
A	17.8	17.9	17.5	0.3	−0.1	—
B	11.4	10.4	9.7	1.7	1 0	4.2
C	35.1	34.1	33.6	1.5	1.0	—
E	25.6	24.4	24.0	1.6	1.2	—
F	26.9	25.6	25.0	1.9	1.3	2.5*
G	22.1	21.0	20.6	1.5	1.1	3.1
H	36.7	33.3	32.9	3.8	3.4	3.1
I	9.8	10.7	10.7	−0.9	−0.9	—
L	18.1	18.6	18.4	−0.3	−0.5	—
M	19.0	20.1	20.1	−1.1	−1.1	—
N	21.9	20.4	20.6	1.3	1.5	—
O	13.3	15.4	16.2	−2.9	−2.1	2.2*
Q_1	19.9	20.3	18.8	1.1	−0.4	—
Q_2	14.1	14.1	14.1	0.0	0.0	—
Q_3	25.8	34.3	23.2	2.6	1.5	3.4
Q_4	14.7	16.3	16.4	−1.7	−1.6	—
N	90	140	90			

Source: Stice (1951).
* Significant at 5% level. All other critical ratio C.R. figures shown are significant beyond 1% level.

problems even though they might not actually be called leader). Cattell and Child (1975) on the basis of these three operational definitions have offered an objective definition of a leader (other than the person thus designated) namely "the group member whose removal brings about a greater change in syntality values than that of any other member". The syntality of a group is defined as that which determines what a group will do in any given situation (and is thus analogous to the personality of an individual).

Some points about these profiles are worthy of notice. First all three types of leader are high on H, Q3 and O- (to reverse the sign). Elected and effective leaders are also high on G. This means that the two dynamic factors which are so pervasive that they appear also as temperamental traits (self sentiment and superego) are also important in leadership. In other words attitudes connected with self-preservation, self-control will-power (Q3) high morals fair play and dependability (G) are essential in good leadership. This makes powerful psychological sense particularly when we add in the traits of H adventurousness and O-, freedom from worry. What is particularly interesting is that, as we shall see in our final chapter, these two traits Q3 and G are also important in the integration of personality—fuel indeed to the argument that training for leadership is training for life. In addition to this it is clear from Table 15.3 that intelligence is an important quality of leadership especially, as is to be expected from the definition, technical leaders. It is important that the intelligence gap between leaders and the group should not be too large, perhaps the reason, as Terman's work suggests, that scientists have not usually reached high positions in politics although there are (see p. 306) other personality differences between leaders and scientists notably in the second-order of exvia.

Superego appears to be important in leadership in that fair-mindedness and standing up for right were regarded as highly desirable in leaders. Certainly it is a commonplace of politics that offences against morality are often sufficient reason for resignation.

Studies such as these which are discussed in greater detail in Cattell and Child (1975) make clear the nature of leadership. Although far more research needs to be done before we can confidently assert what kinds of people make the best leaders there is no doubting the importance of H, B, G, Q3, O- and perhaps F. These findings imply that leadership can be trained but that a certain basic personality pattern is needed if we are to be successful in such training.

Differences in Culture Patterns

We have had occasion to mention in our chapters on the temperamental factors that there were national differences between the samples from different countries. Although some of these made good psychological sense interpretation always has to be cautious because of the technical problems in cross-cultural personality testing and in obtaining genuinely representative national samples, difficulties fully discussed in Kline (1976). In addition to measuring the personality of typical subjects representing a culture, it is possible to measure the culture patterns themselves (which can be seen as depending to some extent at least upon such personality variables) and subject these to factor analysis. The interest of this from the viewpoint of personality is that cultural features and institutions are thought by some anthropologists (e.g. Kardiner, 1945) to affect personality and such a view is implicit in psychoanalytic theory and indeed in all theoretical formulations which stress the importance of environmental factors in personality development. Factor analysis of culture patterns together with a study of national differences in personality could provide firm tests of these anthropological "culture and personality" hypotheses. Unfortunately sufficient research has not yet been carried out to enable this to be done, although the early preliminary studies of cultures deserve mention.

When the mean values for different nations on such variables as group aggression, internal tension, frequency of international treaties and power consumed are subjected to factor analysis the resulting factors are naturally the major dimensions of culture. The most important of these are cultural pressure, size, morale and economic-educational level (Cattell, 1957). Psychologically, cultural pressure is the most interesting because it seems to reflect the level in a culture of the circuiting of drive goal behaviour, i.e. the complexity of the dynamic lattice. It loads on such variables as creativity (art, music, etc.) proneness to war, urbanization and suicide, institutional behaviours postulated in psychoanalytic theory as sublimations and defensive procedures.

As was mentioned, if the scores on such dimensions as these could be reliably established and related to the corresponding national personality characteristics and other environmental variables important social anthropological advances could be made.

Differences Among Small Groups
In the research described above in relation to factorially based studies of leadership, summarized by Cattell and Stice (1960), factorial analysis of the groups also yielded factors expressing small group syntality analogous to the cultural factors which we discussed in the previous paragraph. Since the relevance of these factors is to social psychology rather than personality, the subject of this book, it will be sufficient to mention the larger of these factors.

Four factors described group morale and explicated the coherence of small groups suggesting that the commonsense term morale is in fact multifactorial. The four factors were: *leadership synergy*, loading confidence of leader and a sense of common purpose; *immediate or gregarious synergy*, loading on group organization, orderliness of procedure and good group performance; the last two factors were less well defined although they can be labelled as *reward morale* where the emphasis is on the smooth functioning of the group and *role morale* where the satisfaction for opportunities offered by the group is important.

The interest of these factors for the study of personality lies in their relation to the characteristics of members of the group. If these were understood it might be possible to form highly effective groups where this was required as in certain industrial and military applications. At present, as Cattell and Child (1975) point out, the first factor appears to be unrelated to the characteristics of the group members. However the second factor is related to absence of suspicion (L), guilt and tension (Q4 and O) and to high ego strength and group dependence (C and Q2-). To some extent however the characteristics of "the good group member" must depend upon the nature of the group. As we have pointed out elsewhere good academics tend to be introverted so that research groups would probably function better with introverts than extraverts. This would not necessarily apply in other cases.

From this it is clear that further research into the characteristics of successful groups both in terms of group variables and the characteristics of the members could prove useful in occupational psychology.

Political Values

A few other points where the factorial studies of personality impinge on social psychology deserve mention, albeit briefly. In the psychology of politics Eysenck has confirmed the importance of two factors—radicalism *v.* conservatism and tough *v.* tender mindedness in the determination of political beliefs, thereby empirically confirming earlier claims of William James. Thus fascists and communists resemble each other on one of these factors, both being tough minded but differ on the other, communists (it is claimed) being radical. This may have been true when the studies were undertaken in the early fifties. However there must come a time when communist doctrines become enshrined as orthodoxy and no longer appeal to the radical but to the conservative. Similar results to those of Eysenck have been obtained by Cattell and his colleagues where the importance of both these factors—I and Q1—in political beliefs was clear.

As we saw in our chapter on motivational structure attitudes depend to a large extent upon ergs and sentiments, the dynamic lattice going some way to explaining how attitudes subsume ultimately ergic expression. However I is a temperamental factor that can clearly influence a wide variety of beliefs: the sensitive I+ individual has a fundamental belief in the benignity of the world. For him man is naturally good, is corrupted by a corrupt society, needs no laws, a set of beliefs that has never been destroyed by the harsh realities of life. Hence the protected family background of the high I individual which is regularly found. The tough minded individual on the other hand is down to earth, tied in to reality. Cattell (1965) has even speculated that I is on the increase in modern civilized societies where disease and hunger and death itself have been made remote. However in India, contrary to this hypothesis, premsia is also high.

From this it is clear that temperamental traits especially I and Q1 can have a considerable influence on the political beliefs and fundamental values of people in western society. It is interesting to note here that the F scale of the authoritarian personality (Adorno *et al.*, 1951) and the Dogmatism scale of Rokeach (1960) are specific embodiments of these two factors.

Roles

A major stumbling block in the prediction of behaviour from personality traits alone is the fact that people have roles. Sometimes when the role is accompanied by particular uniforms and ceremonies we cannot mistake it, as is the case with military or academic dignitaries. However there are roles more subtle than this that some people play largely unconsciously as part of their everyday life. Berne (1968) in his concepts of transactional analysis has explored much of this aspect of human behaviour. The helpless creature is a role which some women play well and the household martyr is another example.

Formal roles, as typified in many jobs, obviously considerably modify behaviour. A policeman on night duty in a town walks the streets trying the handles of doors. If we know a man is a policeman we could predict this behaviour, but not otherwise: indeed a non-policeman doing this would be speedily arrested. Thus to be able to predict fully a man's behaviour we must know his formal role. The non-formal roles which people adopt are an integral part of their personality and consequently may not so powerfully disrupt prediction based upon the major temperamental and dynamic factors. It may be the case (although the necessary research has not been carried out) that we can predict the non-formal roles that people slip into. Certainly that is implied in some of the clinical theories of personality. Adler, for example, considered that our style of life, very much a role in the sense we are discussing, was determined in early childhood (Adler, 1927). Freud, too, with his notion of oral dependent character traits, came near to postulating a role such as the helpless one mentioned above.

An important question, then, is how are we to recognize roles. Q matrix analysis (not to be confused with Q technique which locate dimensions not types) where the similarity of people rather than variables is recorded using r_p, a pattern similarity coefficient (Cattell, 1949) or the G index (Holley, 1973) if the data are in dichotomous form, is a commonly used method. Common usage sometimes refers to such a type as a "role" but Cattell's (1973) model also considers a role as a factor—one of special skills and readinesses evolved by social expectations. Taxonome (Coulter and Cattell, 1966) is a computer device which takes up the r_p matrix and systematically picks out the clusters of people. Notice that if we insert ordinary personality or dynamic factor measures into Taxonome "species", "types" or categories emerge. If the basic data of the analysis are social role behaviours, then functional roles which reflect occupations are likely to emerge as "skill factors". Thus postmen would be easily defined by: walks regularly up and down streets, puts letters and parcels through some doors, opens mail boxes and collects the contents, wears a certain uniform, etc.

It follows that, if an individual can satisfactorily enact a role he must possess certain response tendencies which are cued off by the relevant stimuli, the responses being the role behaviour. A mechanic for example on seeing a car engine may automatically check plugs, oil and water, on duty. Even when not in his role, he may still respond like this to the relevant stimuli (especially if he's a keen mechanic). These response tendencies should load up therefore on a factor like a temperamental trait.

However these *role factors* can be distinguished from *personality-temperamental factors*. First they are evident in only a few situations. A postman can only be distinguished from non-postmen in respect to his responses to letters and mail boxes. Furthermore there is relatively little variance in role behaviour. Thus a miner either cuts coal or not. If he does not, he does not, in an ideal world, long remain a miner. Similarly a bus or train driver either covers his route or not.

Subjectively role is a mental set which modifies all ordinary responses. Thus as university teachers we might feel compelled to correct poor logic or incorrect facts when talking with our students. We are usually, indeed, on the lookout for such errors. However if mixing socially with them, we should probably not do so. The pedant who carries the classroom into everyday life, i.e. who plays his role beyond the confines of his job is a much mocked figure of literature, "and still the wonder grew that one small head should carry all he knew". This role factor affects our perception of the situation. Thus a policeman off duty might admire a powerful speeding car and applaud its driver. On duty he would stop and fine him. Clearly in the prediction of behaviour role factors, as we said, need to be taken into account.

In practical terms the influence of role factors in the measurement of personality is a source of error that we must strive to eliminate, just as we eliminate instrument factors such as response sets (see p. 37). This can be done by ensuring that the samples of behaviour we use in our measuring instruments are widely varied, covering a large number of commonly adopted roles. Surgency, F, illustrates this well, for this factor is highly loaded on talkativeness. However if all our samples of talkativeness were taken from work situations, role factors would intrude. Librarians, nuns, diplomats and court ushers say little, salesmen, lecturers, commentators and politicians all talk too much in the course of their occupations. Conversely if we are interested in how strongly an individual has adopted a role we should sample a wide variety of different traits.

From this discussion it is clear that role factors can intrude on the validity of personality factors as such unless steps are taken to ensure that this does not happen. But in any complete prediction of behaviour role factors are by definition specific and narrow in effect and only when the major motivation and temperamental factors are established would we like to see role factors extensively studied. Nevertheless it is true that they should be ultimately included in the complete description of personality.

SUMMARY

1. Some difficulties and problems were discussed; differences between vocational guidance and selection, task analysis and description, practicalities of vocational advice, the criterion of job success.
2. Personality factors in guidance and selection: the adjustment method and the efficiency in performance method were compared, and the practical advantages of the two file system were pointed out.
3. Some typical 16PF personality profiles for various occupational groups were examined and the psychological meanings and insights into occupational satisfaction were discussed.
4. The value of objective T tests and other factored tests in vocational problems was assessed.
5. The value of the MAT both to the theory of motivational expression in general and to vocational guidance in particular was explicated in the light of recent research.
6. Finally the bearing of our factorial findings on topics in social psychology was examined. It was shown that leaders could be trained given a certain basic personality structure. Culture patterns and the effectiveness of small groups, and political values were all discussed. The concept of role particularly as it affected the prediction equation was also scrutinized and it was concluded that its influence could be eliminated.

Chapter 16

Conclusions and Theoretical Implications

THE CONCEPTS DEVELOPED BY QUANTITATIVE RESEARCH

In the early chapters of the book we showed how factor-analysis rotated to simple structure can give a parsimonious and replicable account of data so that in effect a factor-analytic description is a quantified theoretical statement. Since we have examined such concepts in the field of temperament, mood and motivation (the main corpus of our book), in our final chapter two tasks now remain.

(i) We must discuss the bearing of these results on the best known personality theories which have been, in the main, clinically derived and lack quantification.

(ii) We must outline how the personality components revealed by factor analysis can be put together to form a coherent theory—one based upon replicable, quantified concepts.

To achieve these two aims it is necessary to summarize as succinctly as possible the main findings so that readers can have them clearly in mind in our theoretical discussions. To this end we have set out the results in a number of tables.

The Temperamental Factors

(i) In L and Q data discrepant findings were shown to be due largely to the technical inadequacies of much research especially in respect of the number of significant factors and in obtaining simple structure. Nevertheless, in Q and L data 23 normal and 12 pathological primary factors have been enumerated and described.

Table 16.1 sets out these factors

(ii) In T data. Objective tests of temperament yielded factors which were roughly equivalent to the second-order Q and L factors. The T factors of largest variance are set out in Table 16.2

Table 16.2 sets out the T factors

Moods and States

Multivariate analysis was also applied to moods and states. Despite the logical and statistical problems of R analysis in this area P and dR analysis revealed state and state change factors. The most important of these are set out in Table 16.3

Table 16.3 sets out state and state change factors

Dynamic Factors

Three factors accounted for much of the variance in motivational strength. However 10 factors seemed best to embrace the aims or goals of behaviour—ergs which resemble basic biological drives and sentiments which are culturally moulded drives. The dynamic lattice was proposed by which behaviours far removed apparently from biological drives can be understood in ergic terms.

Table 16.4 sets out the strength of motivation factors

Table 16.5 sets out the ergs and sentiments

In these tables we can see the main substantive findings of the multivariate analysis of personality. The remainder of the book was devoted to an account of this structure in terms of developmental laws which necessitated the establishment of structured learning theory. This will be introduced as it bears on the second task of this chapter—the formulation of a coherent personality theory. Finally we looked at the relevance of these findings to three important areas of applied psychology—clinical, educational and occupational—and some of the discussion in these sections will be of relevance to our theoretical discussion below.

To execute our first task, it will be simplest to consider the relevance of these findings to theories under separate heads: temperament, mood and dynamics. What we write here is a condensed summary, an explication of points that were necessarily made as various factors were discussed throughout the whole book. It may be inevitable that we seem to do injustice to some theories of personality through reasons of brevity. Some subtlety may be lost. However, these are summaries and they should not be regarded as the final word. Kline (1972) devoted more than 400 pages to a similar study of Freudian theory alone. One further point needs to be remembered: the factors in our five tables represent replicable experimental findings, to a precision not generally characteristic of the concepts and variables of clinical theories.

BEARING OF TEMPERAMENTAL Q AND L FACTORS ON PERSONALITY THEORY

Obviously we cannot examine the fit of these factors to all personality theories. We shall, therefore, restrict ourselves to those discussed in the best surveys of the subject, e.g. Cartwright (1974), Pervin (1972), Sarason (1972) and Hall and Lindzey (1952).

Clinically Derived Depth Psychologies
One clear conclusion can be drawn relevant to depth psychology (psychoanalytically derived theories). None of these theories suggested a large number of primary factors as shown in our Table 16.1. Freudian theory has implicit in part of it at least (psychosexual theory) a three factor theory of personality with oral, anal and phallic characters. There is virtually no sign of these in the factorial results, although, as we showed, there is some evidence for the anal and oral character, but as factors of only small variance (see chapter 5). The major factors of 16.1 cannot be held to support this aspect of Freudian theory.

Once this argument is accepted it automatically means that many of the other analytic theorists are refuted for they described similar traits differing only in their hypothesized aetiology. Fromm (1949) proposed a series of characters including the marketing character, the hoarding character and the necrophilous (as distinct from biophilous) character of whom Hitler was the supreme example, all more or less equivalent to the Freudian psychosexual syndromes. Reich (1945) had a similar set with yet different nomenclature and Blum (1953) has pointed out that even Karen Horney (1939) followed this pattern despite her rejection of psychosexual theory. All these claims are refuted by the results. Furthermore none of the second or third order factors, either, are anywhere near these hypotheses.

Among these psychoanalysts, Jung needs more careful consideration for he proposed, as a basic discriminating orientation, extraversion–introversion. In addition he hypothesized four modes of operation—thinking, intuiting, sensing and feeling so that in Jung's theory there are really eight types. One of the two most important second-order factors is of course introversion-extraversion although exvia seems a preferable label to avoid confusion with the Jungian concept which is certainly *not* identical. The two are similar in that both are concerned with the outward contrasted with the inward looking personality. However Jung proposed a typology: subjects were either extraverts or introverts whereas the factorial concept is a dimension on which people vary in position. In addition there is no hint of the four orientations unless by some stretch of the imagination they can be equated with emphasis on some of the primary traits in exvia—such as surgency F, affectia A, parmia H, etc. Thus it is sensible to rename the measurable factor exvia–invia to avoid confusion. Perhaps an even more important reason for renaming is that the factor is *not* a vague, verbally defined construct. Instead it is operationally and precisely defined by its factor loadings. We are again forced to conclude that Jung got closer than the other depth psychologists to one of the secondary factors but that his concept was essentially dissimilar, being typological.

There are many aspects to Freudian personality theory other than psychosexual fixation. There is the effectively tri-factorial theory of ego, id and superego and the bi-factor theory of eros and thanatos.

As regards the life and death instincts, it can be safely argued that none of the factors gives them any support (see Table 16.1). This is important because it not only confirms the views of Fenichel (1945) in the classic psychoanalytic tradition that these concepts are best left alone as metaphysical rather than psychological categories, but in addition it runs counter to the work of those influential modern analysts, Melanie Klein and Fromm who have made considerable use of them in their work. Fromm (1973), for example, regards thanatos as valuable in understanding Hitler.

The topological theory, however, does receive much better support. Thus Warburton's (1968) fourth-order factorization of questionnaire data (despite its technical shortcomings as a pilot study) produced two factors which were named as morality *v.* thrust. These resemble to some extent ego and superego factors and perhaps, therefore, could be regarded as some confirmation of the topological theory. However this study should not be taken as definitive because of the problems of correctly identifying the factors through rotational problems almost inevitable at the fourth-order where there are few variables to be located and no hyperplane stuff.

However as we discussed in chapters 7 and 13, topological Freudian theory is much better supported by the first-order primary factors C and G ego and superego. Thus C was low in neurotics, as predicted in the theory, although G was not quite as high as might be expected. However the descriptions of these factors, obtained from empirical studies, are good confirmation. In the test manual (Cattell *et al.*, 1970) the C- person is described as easily annoyed by things and people, dissatisfied with everything, family, the world, his life, and as showing typical neurotic symptomatology. C rises after lobotomy and successful psychotherapy and is found high in occupations where subjects have to face and meet problems and decisions. This is essentially the reality orientation of the Freudian ego.

Factor G equally resembles the Freudian superego. The descriptive terms of the high G scorer are revealing: persevering, determined, responsible, ordered, dominated by a sense of duty, concerned about moral standards and rules. A problem in the questionnaire measurement of G which has caused some to argue that it is no more than "middle class morality" is its susceptibility to distortion. Criminals seeking parole can score high, adolescents and bohemians in revolt low, while often clearly showing good reliable conscientious behaviour in other spheres. However the negative correlations with delinquency, sociopathic behaviour, and homosexuality and the positive correlations with achievement do support the psychoanalytic identification. For further discussion of the relevance of the scores of neurotics on G to psychoanalytic clinical theory and the work of Mowrer readers must turn to chapter 14.

From all this discussion it is clear that the Q and L temperamental factors, except for ego and superego by Freud, and extraversion by Jung, cannot be held to support the claims of the psychodynamic psychologists. This is particularly unfortunate because depth psychology claims the kinds of universals that in an accurate description of personality would be expected to emerge as factors.

Other Theoretical Positions Proposed in the Last Half-Century

Murray's (1938) Personology is mainly concerned with the dynamics of behaviour so that the temperamental factors are not relevant to his theory. Discussion of Murray, therefore, will be found below in our section on the theoretical bearing of Cattell's motivational factors. Allport (1937) too is not truly relevant to this discussion for he stressed the individuality of people and regarded common dimensions, even if they existed, as being of relatively little importance in the study of personality. Actually the test of Allport's theorizing lies not in the establishment of various factors but in whether, contrary to his views, specification equations and predictions can be made with them. The same is true of Mischel (1968) who, as a disciple of Allport, objects to common traits and argues essentially for a "chaotic personality" composed of nothing but a swarm of atomistic specifics, due to the particular Skinnerian conditioning by innumerable life events. The evidence against this is simply the large "communalities" found whenever their alleged specific behaviours are mutually correlated (but see p. 225 for a full discussion of these points).

If the factors can predict only with a low degree of accuracy various aspects of behaviour then this failure supports Allport's views that individual events, the particulars of one person's experiences and feelings are the essential data for the study of personality. However as we have seen throughout this book especially in the three chapters devoted to clinical, educational and occupational psychology, this is far from the case. Highly effective predictions can be made although, as we stressed, in the practical application of the factorial tests to vocational selection and guidance, some note of personal events should be taken. There can be no doubt that these predictions especially from the temperamental factors, but best in combination with motivational and ability factors, give the lie to Allport's scientifically gloomy claims. Clearly, common dimensions of personality are important and we must conclude, therefore that the practical power of the factorial study of personality actually runs counter to Allport's claims.

Theories from Physical and Biological Associations

Physique and personality theories have long been popular among armchair speculators and literary men as we showed in our introductory chapter to this book. Two of these theories that of Kretschmer (1925) and Sheldon (Sheldon and Stevens 1942) have achieved some kind of scientific repute and they are usually discussed in the standard text books on personality. Sheldon's work is noteworthy for its attempt at scientific measurement of physique and for a highly appealing style in discussing the personality patterns claimed to be related to the varieties of physique. Thus, for example, the personality of the person who is predominantly endomorphic was described, *inter alia*, as voraciously sucking at the rich breast of mother earth. Kretschmer's work is justly famous for it undoubtedly contains much acute and penetrating clinical observation.

This is not the place to criticize these theories on general grounds e.g. that in the case of Kretschmer the extreme physiques he described are rarely found and that consequently the mixed physique makes personality prediction difficult; or that the measurements of physique so laboriously worked out by Sheldon may well not be applicable beyond his rather special sample of Harvard undergraduates and that as the concentration camps showed, physique is affected by diet. Endomorphs become not as Sheldon and Stevens claimed "starved endomorphs" but ectomorphs. All we shall do here is to see to what extent the temperamental factors in table 16.1 are in accord with the broadly similar personality descriptions of both these writers.

The Sheldon descriptions of the typical ectomorphic and mesomorphic temperament were based upon the correlations between rating scales so that we might expect some relation to the original L data of Cattell and others who have factored "behaviour *in situ*".

However, from a statistical point of view Sheldon's "dimensions" are actually clusters not factor dimensions and since he applied no tests whatever for number of dimensions he was able to emerge with three (like Eysenck, though the two sets of three prove to have no alignment). Actually his distortion of this data to three seems to have been dictated by his prior settling upon three dimensions of physique, essentially the same as Kretschmer's though given different names. Nevertheless, if we allow for this loss of precision through reducing the "dimensions" some rough alignment with concepts from more completed factor analyses can be recognized, both in Sheldon's and in Kretschmer's descriptions.

Thus cerebrotonia, the ectomorphic temperament, resembles primary factor A, at the negative pole so that withdrawn, aloof, severe schizoid would be adequate descriptions of the cerebrotonic personality. Viscerotonia, the endomorphic personality, is like $A+$ and extraversion as well as anxiety with its mood swings and is in effect the opposite of cerebrotonia. Falstaff is a good example of this, bonhomous and cheerful (but not quite to the last). The mesomorphic temperament, somatotonia, is typified by push and drive and is thus close to $E+$.

It is claimed by Eysenck (1970) that the correlations between temperament and physique reported in Sheldon are inconsistent and contain computing error. In addition, Sheldon failed to include, as pointed out above, many factors which are equally important in the description of personality. We may conclude that this temperamental picture therefore was not wrong but inaccurate albeit employing dimensions that have been shown to be important.

In respect of physique this work by Sheldon has not been followed up although there are slight relationships as found by the Rees–Eysenck index. Since his description was not factor pure it is not surprising that no such high relationship between physique and the Cattell factors has been found. The largest is a correlation of F, surgency, with body breadth, but it is still only about 0.25. Some workers (e.g. Glueck and Glueck, 1960) have examined the relationships of physique to other variables, in their case criminal delinquency, and there does seem to be a significant link between mesomorphy and violent offences. This, however, is very different from the original claims of a close correlation between physique and personality.

Kretschmer's two main temperamental continua, the cycloid or circular personality varying from moody in the normal to manic depressive in the psychotic and the schizoid again varying in severity from normal to psychotic are similar to second order factors of exvia and anxiety. These descriptions are tribute to Kretschmer's clinical acumen, and they are supported and clarified by the factorial work. However his notion that the psychotic temperament is an extreme form of the neurotic which is in turn the extreme of the normal is not entirely supported. Thus the 16PF factors are largely found in neurotics but psychotics appear to differ in respect of other special abnormal factors of which Eysenck's P is a good example.

In summary, therefore, we can see that the physique and personality theorists are not confirmed by the factor analytic work: they exaggerated the relation between physique and temperament and these analyses of personality were too erratic—with the exception of Kretschmer's use of definite psychotic syndromes—to have yielded relationships even if some existed. Nevertheless in the temperamental field, the variables they used do at least appear in some form in factorial work in contrast to the psychoanalytic temperamental traits. However this comparison does some injustice to the Freudians who were more interested in the dynamics of behaviour. We examine these again in our section on the theoretical import of the motivational factors.

SOURCE TRAITS CONCERNED WITH ABNORMAL BEHAVIOUR

Up to this point in our study of the theoretical import of the temperamental factors we have ignored, except in commenting on the work of Kretschmer, the abnormal factors. It first became evident in the domain of Q data that factors could be found in clinical and mental hospital subjects, and with items describing abnormal behaviour, that are of too small variance to emerge clearly in the normal range as reference to the abnormal factors in Table 16.1 shows, (see chapter 13 for full discussion). 12 such primaries appear in the Clinical Analysis Questionnaire that are not in normals, though the 16 normal primaries exist (as part 1 of the CAQ) in clinic and hospital subjects. At the second order the CAQ yields a general psychotic factor, as found also in Eysenck's research, and a general depression factor (spanning the 7 primary depression factors in the CAQ).

The fact that the 16PF gave excellent separation of neurotics from normals and among the neurotic syndromes, but not of psychotics (until extended into the CAQ with the new pathological factors) is of considerable interest in relation to the debates extending over many decades in psychiatry as to whether psychoticism is just a more severe form of neuroticism or a totally different dimension. The independent studies of Cattell and Eysenck agree in decisively favouring the second view.

Although the clinically based depth psychological theories are notoriously difficult to tie down these findings are in general support of such theories, though not necessarily confirming their specific points. Thus in psychoanalytic theorizing neuroticism is seen as the result of inefficient defence mechanisms whereas psychoticism results from the breakdown of defences so that unconscious material actually enters consciousness. This, of course, accounts for the bizarre hallucinatory symptoms of almost all psychoses. Since we all, in order to remain mentally healthy within the terms of psychoanalytic theory, use defences, the neurotic is essentially similar to the normal. When the defences have broken, however, we could expect different feelings and behaviours—hence the special abnormal factors that have been observed. Since anxiety is central to the Freudian concept of neurosis where it signifies the breakdown of the defences, the importance of the anxiety factor, at the second order, must be regarded as essentially confirmatory.

T Factors

Table 16.2 sets out most important T factors. It is an interesting fact, awaiting more theoretical explanation, that the personality source traits emerging from T data (objective behavioural measures) have been more potent than those from questionnaires in giving diagnostic separation of various kinds of neurotics and psychotics. The results by Schmidt (1972) summarized in Table 16.6 (fully discussed in chapter 13) show high agreement with the directions of deviation expected from earlier research (notably that of Scheier) and a high significance of difference on at least five dimensions. With weighted combinations of scores on these both Schmidt and May (1971) were able to get a degree of diagnostic separation of various forms of psychoses and neuroses which, in psychometric terms, came very close indeed to the criterion presented by the consensus of a diagnostic panel of psychiatrists. Here again some of the more diagnostic factors are more clearly found in a mixed normal and pathological group than in a thoroughly normal one. This has bearing on a second much debated theoretic issue: are mental disorders diseases of a specific kind as are most physical diseases, or are they dysfunctions and abnormal extremes in essentially normal processes? The evidence on neuroses as a whole point to the latter, but in psychoses and in some dimensions of neuroses it seems from the score distributions that we are dealing with what looks like a normal disease process.

The matter can be illustrated by the T data trait U.I.23, which, in the pathological direction, is measured by a battery including high motor-perceptual rigidity, sway suggestibility, rapid increase of errors when forced to hurry, and inability to combine habits in a new way that are functioning well as single habits. This factor was called neuroticism by Eysenck, its co-discoverer, and regression by Cattell, because (a) neurotics separate equally on some other factors, and (b) it is high in both neurotics and psychotics (see Table 16.6). This factor becomes of small variance in groups of healthy children and in military flying cadets selected for stability and competence. It is as if extension in the "unhealthy" direction occurs only when some deteriorative process sets in. Whereas one sense of abnormality is to be far out in either direction from a mean, in this there is only one direction— deterioration from a normal level, and this surely is what is meant more specifically by disease.

In general, therefore, we must conclude that empirical factors resulting from multivariate analysis not so much fail to support the intuitive, clinically based personality theories of what we have called the pre-scientific era of personality, as add new dimensions of explanation. Nor is the latter surprising when we consider the nature of source traits. The best clinicians could only hope to pick out surface traits or syndromes unless gifted with phenomenal insight. Perhaps, indeed, as his theory supposes, Freud was, because at the fourth order, far removed from observation, there is some agreement between the factors and psychoanalytic theory. These results, however, must be considered as very strong support for our claim that multivariate methods are superior to observation unaided by statistical analysis. The fact is that most of the writers in the sphere of temperament could not pick out the critical variables.

MOODS, STATE AND STATE CHANGE FACTORS

With these factors set out in Table 16.3 as we have discussed in chapter 11, Cattell has virtually broken new ground. The concept of state and trait change factors is simply not found in earlier personality theory. It was surprising too to find change factors equivalent to most of the primary factors so that we are forced to a conclusion that all the temperamental trait factors must fluctuate around their mean for each individual. This again is not a feature of any personality theory.

Moods are well known to everybody through personal experience but they have not been blended into any theory perhaps because their apparent simplicity made it seem hardly worthwhile. Thus, for example, anger might be seen as a response to frustration, fear as a response to some particular situation, such as a charging bull or the crackle of snipers' bullets.

Only in the field of motivation and certain aspects of abnormal psychology have earlier theorists incorporated moods and states as serious parts of their work. In motivation which we shall discuss separately since there is a special set of factors relevant to it, most theorists see changes as resulting from satisfaction privation, excitation or inhibition of the drive whether through external or internal factors or a combination of both. However with traits this has rarely been the case. Indeed some psychometrists (e.g. Anastasi, 1961) have regarded such changes as a source of unreliability of measurement and have thus sacrificed validity before the altar of reliability although this argument must not be used to support the use of unreliable tests. She suggests that accurate measurement should involve the mean of several readings, so that trait change factors are effectively negated, and, of course, this is true if we are concerned only with traits.

In abnormal psychology on the other hand, clinical psychologists would have had to be obtuse indeed to fail to recognize such state factors as anxiety or depression. Many are the theories attempting to account for the difference between states and traits in the abnormal sphere but these are irrelevant to our purpose. Our conclusions must be that the factor analytic study of moods and states has revealed dimensions which, in psychometrics have never previously received any role or recognition, and which in clinical psychology have never been given precision of pattern or measurement. Major mood states such as anxiety, depression, stress, arousal have been confirmed. This work (except in the clinical instances) neither confirms or denies any particular theory. Rather it emphasizes the problems facing clinicians in trying to develop theories. A new theoretical formulation is urgently needed.

DYNAMIC FACTORS

It will be remembered from chapters 9 and 10 that there were two kinds of dynamic factor which had emerged from the studies of Cattell and his associates, those concerned with strength of motive summarized in Table 16.4 and those concerned with the goals of action set out in Table 16.5.

Strength of Motivation Factors

These were given Greek alphabetical names and only the first three of the six were given descriptive titles, conscious id, ego and superego. The fact that some of the factors cannot be named strongly suggests that they resemble nothing in the clinically based theories of motivation as was the case with the mood and state factors discussed above. Similarly the Freudian nomenclature of the first three factors implies a resemblance at least, if not an identity with the Freudian model. As we discussed earlier, alpha, the id factor, is a *conscious* factor and therefore is different from the psychoanalytic concept, although it has the same irrational quality of wish and desire. Furthermore there was another physiological factor which might conceivably refer to the true unconscious Id.

As these factors stand they do give confirmation of the classical psychoanalytic approach which sees all behaviour as a function of the balance between ego, id and superego. These factor analytic findings certainly do not support the Adlerian theory of motivation which is seen almost exclusively as a two factor phenomenon, achievement and social interest being the two factors. It might be possible to argue that beta and gamma represent these Adlerian concepts (albeit in the vaguest fashion) but the largest alpha factor finds no place. Jungian theory, like that of Freud is also tri-factorial. However Jung's factors would be those of ego, personal and racial or collective unconscious. The last factor which is truly the most important to Jung's system and the one essentially and distinctively Jungian, certainly does not appear among the Cattell factors. As for the other depth psychologists, it is difficult to conceptualize their claims in factorial terms although perhaps Fromm's theory implies the operation of a number of defensive strategies, which do not appear in the empirical findings.

What is clear is that these researches into motivational strength lend some support to Freudian theory which however in the light of the results (if reliably confirmed) needs some modification. Other depth psychological theories are not confirmed and we must conclude therefore that in this sphere of personality, Freud's clinical insights were not far wide of the mark. We have considered here only depth psychologists because these alone conceive of motivational strength separately from the goals of behaviour and action. Most theorists of motivation see it in terms of goals and motivational strength depends upon the balance of frustration satisfaction and excitation (internal and external) in respect of these goals. To some extent Freudian theory also conceptualizes motivational strength in these terms as well (as has become well known throughout the world—the dangers of sexual frustration). We must, therefore, now examine the theoretical import of the findings concerning goals—a teleological view of behaviour which is anathema to scientific method.

Motivational Factors, Ergs and Sentiments

The first point to notice about the list of the most important ergs and sentiments so far found in the factor analytic research and set out in Table 16.5 is that as a list it corresponds to no theoretical description of goals in the literature. This means that none of the theories is supported and some are refuted. As was the case with all the other types of factor the results demand their own theory: the factors are the observations for which a theory must account and since the observations had not generally been made before it is inevitable that a new theory must be developed. Nevertheless it is worth noting how closely various theorists have got to these results.

Tables 16.7 and 16.8 set out respectively the main needs of Murray (1938) and the propensities of McDougall (1932), although McDougall also suggested that a wide variety of sentiments was important in allowing expression of the native propensities.

First let us consider the relevance of Cattell's and his colleagues findings (especially Barton, Bartsch, Gross, Dielman, Miller and Sweney at Illinois) to the work of McDougall as discussed in "The Energies of Men" (1932). First of all the basic concept of the dynamic lattice and the dynamic calculus deliberately resembles the view of McDougall. Thus McDougall (1932) writes (p. 227)

"I ... confidently ... regard the native propensities ... as the mainsprings of all human and animal activity ... Nevertheless ... few of the activities of the adult man spring directly from his native propensities: the great majority derive their energy only indirectly from those sources by way of the sentiments within which the propensities are organised."

Table 16.8 shows, if we compare it with Table 16.6, that McDougall came far closer with his list of propensities to the factorially based ergs than did Murray (1938), see Table 16.7, Freud, for whom the sexual drive was paramount, Adler or Jung. One point we should note here: Freud is supported in splitting the erotic need into a heterosexual object attachment and a narcissistic component. The relevance of these results to psychoanalysis will be discussed in a later section.

From this it is clear that McDougall's analysis of motivation in terms of propensities and sentiments was not far wide of the mark. The factor-analytic studies have enabled us to add precision to his description and given us objective measuring instruments.

Cofer and Appley (1964) have characterized ethologists as being rooted in zoology rather than psychology so that they are interested in the evolution of behaviour often concentrating their work on sub-human organisms. Furthermore they "like their animals" so that they tend to eschew the laboratory experiment preferring accurate field observation and a naturalist's approach which may not be fully objective. On these criteria we can see that McDougall might well be regarded as an early ethologist. At this point then we can see to what extent Cattell's dynamic findings bear on modern human ethology.

Ethology

As Eibl-Eibesfeldt (1975) points out, ethologists in their study of motivation tend to concentrate on the releasing stimuli—for example, the red underside of a stickleback provokes territorial aggression in its rival—rather than on listing instincts or goals of behaviour. Thus many of Tinbergen's (1951) examples concern such basic biological drives as the reproduction instinct, a major instinct which is seen to underly a higher level of behaviour, e.g. fighting, nest-building, mating or care of offspring, which in turn underlies the consummatory behaviours, e.g. biting, clawing, boring, fertilizing the eggs, etc. In addition ethology concentrates also on very precise descriptions of behaviour.

Tinbergen's model resembles closely that of McDougall (1932) and Cattell, as discussed in the dynamic lattice. The major instinct is equivalent to the erg, the consummatory behaviours are equivalent to the behaviour involved in expressing any particular attitude. The secondary levels e.g. nest-building are equivalent in terms of the model to sentiments. The emphasis on precise observation, in situ, is also echoed in the work of Cattell and his colleagues, although the practical methodology is quite different. From this it is clear that Cattell's work on motivation *could* be thought of as human ethology. It is clear from Eibl-Eibesfeldt (1975) that it is not thus categorized by the few researchers in this field.

If the model of motivation implicit in the work of Cattell resembles that of the ethologists, in explicit detail there are great differences. Thus Cattell's work, as we have seen, is concentrated upon listing the goals—ergs and sentiments, whereas Tinbergen (1951) writing of motivation argues that little is known about the instincts of man although they are crucial in his motivation. Cofer and Appley (1964) however show that Tinbergen claims (on the rather poor evidence of analogies with animal behaviour and his own experience) the following instinctual patterns: locomotion, sex-behaviour, food-seeking, sleep and care of the body surface.

Two points stand out concerning this list of instincts. First it does not bear close resemblance to the patterns found by factor analysis. Indeed it clearly shows the biological influences on ethology. In the second place there is no mention of aggression as an instinct.

However, Lorenz (1966) is absolutely clear that it is a human instinct. The spontaneity of aggression is what makes it so dangerous. Acute readers will notice that in the Tinbergen model which we discussed above aggression is a second-level behaviour in the service of a major instinct. There is, even among ethologists, no agreement on the major drives of human behaviour. Eibl-Eidesfeldt (1975) in his survey of the ethological position makes no attempt to list what are considered to be the most important human drives.

Apart from its obvious social importance, the view of aggression as instinctive or not is clearly of considerable theoretical significance in the understanding of human behaviour. Lorenz in the typical ethological tradition has argued that the aggressive instinct was of evolutionary importance to man, enabling him to survive as a species. Now, of course, ironically, such selective breeding threatens disaster. Such a view of man has quite different implications from say that of learning theorists such as Dollard *et al.* (1939) where aggression is seen as a response to frustration. Some biologists, notably Dart (1957), have argued that man is instinctively aggressive and hence can never be truly tamed because he is descended from a carnivorous ape-man, although there is no agreement on this point of man's descent. Finally, aggression has some place in our list of ergs, since pugnacity has been clearly identified.

In summary, the ethological, biological view of motivation is not broadly different from that of Cattell and his colleagues. Behaviour is seen as hierarchically organized in the service of instincts. There is too a good emphasis on precise observation. Where they differ however is in results. The ethologists have studied lower organisms rather than man and their behavioural observations have not yielded, as they themselves admit, a full account of human drives.

The Work of Murray

As we can see from Table 16.8 Murray (1938) postulated a large number of needs. In addition there were corresponding environmental presses—i.e. the environmental pressures relevant to each need, in our culture considerable for sex, for example. The first point to notice is that there is only slight agreement between the list of Murray's needs and the source traits isolated by factor analysis. There is little work on the excitatory stimuli relevant to ergs and sentiments (in effect research on the presses). Now that ergs and sentiments can be reliably measured with some ease by such tests as the MAT and SMAT (see chapter 10), the opportunity now exists for such exploratory work. The studies by Kline and Grindley (1974), Cross and Cattell (1952), Dielman, Cattell and Kawash (1971) are small beginnings although more extensive work is in progress in Illinois. However at present there is no firm evidence on the presses and we can only discuss the needs in Table 16.8.

Murray, as we have stated, postulated far more needs than have been found by factor-analysis. This is almost certainly because, with his clinical methods and psychodynamic orientation, Murray was dealing essentially with surface traits. Although Murray's work on personology has been neglected, partly because of the vast labour of data collection, one aspect of it, need achievement, has been taken up by a number of researchers, especially McClelland (1961) in various publications. Before we turn to this work we should summarize our view of Murray. Murray's needs are probably surface traits being based on brilliant clinical interpretation of subjective data. It would be interesting and perhaps profitable to reanalyze data of this type with objective scoring procedures and modern multivariate statistical analysis.

Need Achievement

McClelland and his colleagues claim that the major drive especially in high achieving societies is N.Ach. the drive to succeed for achievement. The influence of this drive was originally inferred from TAT protocols although similar inferences have been made from the art and literature of societies as well as from simple questionnaires. Nevertheless since the importance of this drive has been demonstrated in a number of studies comparing entrepreneurs and executives (Hundal 1970, just for example) it is reasonable to see how it fits into Cattell's system of ergs and sentiments. As soon as we consider the dynamic lattice we can see that there is little difficulty in accounting for N.Ach. Thus it is a multi-factorial concept comprised of a mixture of self-assertion, career, self-sentiment etc. favoured, as its exponents point out, by particular family and social environments. In other words in western society both now and in the past (e.g. Renaissance Venice) certain modes of behaviour, e.g. developing a complex banking or import system, have fulfilled a number of drives and sentiments. Such behaviour can be conveniently described as need achievement (virtually a surface motivational trait) but is better understood in terms of its underlying ergs and sentiments. The weakness in the McClelland and Atkinson "need for achievement" research is that it is treated as a single need, much as Murray hypothesized, whereas objective motivation measurement and analysis shows it to consist of an erg of self assertion, a sentiment to career, and especially the self sentiment. In cultural comparisons such as McClelland and Atkinson made we are left in ignorance of the roles of these separate forces, because they did not recognize the relevance of the dynamic calculus.

Mention of the achievement motive leads us back in time to its indubitable precursor, the inferiority complex of Adler and to dynamic psychology. Adler emphasized above all this "upward drive" the real need to overcome inferiority. Thus if he were correct we should expect to find one drive of vastly greater importance than all others. In fact this is not the case and it appears likely that Adler was misled by his poor sampling techniques, i.e. his reliance on small clinical samples of patients. It is possible that his patients were suffering from problems relating to this drive rather than any others (or perhaps this was Adler's own difficulty). As was the case with the achievement motive, the inferiority complex would appear to be a surface trait of some factorial complexity. Nevertheless the factor-analytic results cannot uphold the importance of the inferiority complex in understanding human motivation.

As regards the other main psychoanalytic theorists, the factor analytic results again show that their clinical intuitions were wide of the mark. Freud would certainly have expected the sexual drive to be the most important and pugnacity (aggression) would also have been emphasized. The results indicate that Freud, as his critics have always claimed, did put too much stress on the sex erg, which is however, extremely important. One feature of the factor analytic findings is worth noting in respect of Freudian theory—the dynamic lattice. This fits a psychoanalytic model quite well (although closely tied to quantified observation), just as it fits McDougall's. Freud claimed many apparent asexual activities ultimately expressed the sexual drive, and in the dynamic lattice we see how many activities express sentiments and ergs which are apparently remote. In this respect, the expression of drives through behaviours that are not obviously connected, factor analysis concurs with psychoanalytic theory. On the other hand, just as McDougall overestimated the number of drives, so Freud clearly underestimated them.

Freud later postulated a two factor theory of motivation—eros and thanatos, concepts that have proved unamenable to measurement and have been ignored in psychoanalytic circles except by Melanie Klein and, more recently, by Fromm (1974) who has used thanatos as an explanatory concept in the psychological analysis of Hitler. There is no support whatever in the factorial results for this aspect of psychoanalytic theory. Jung too, receives no confirmation from this research.

Since, the factorial results that form the main corpus of this book support only a small minority of the theories developed without the aid of multivariate research, we must now examine the attempts that have been made to integrate these quantitatively derived concepts themselves into some sort of coherent theory. Factor analysis has been excellent, as the name suggests in the analysis of personality. Of itself, however, it leaves unanswered the question of personality synthesis or integration. After factor-analysis, personality, like Humpty Dumpty, needs to be put together again.

ATTEMPTS TO ACCOUNT FOR FACTORIAL FINDINGS

Only two of the factorists discussed are actively concerned with this second problem—the development of a personality theory that is tied to the observed factors. First we shall deal with the work of Eysenck. We shall discuss his theorizing rather briefly because, as we have pointed out earlier, there are severe problems both in the theory itself and perhaps more importantly in the observation that it is supposed to subsume, mainly due to the fact that Eysenck has chosen to work with second-order factors so that the observational base of the theory is relatively coarse grained.

Eysenck's Personality Theory

Eysenck has claimed that his two most important factors, neuroticism and extraversion, are related to the lability of the autonomic nervous system and the excitability of the central nervous system respectively. This latter is of great significance because it means that conditionability is related to extra-version–introversion, extraverts being harder to condition than introverts, a fact that accounts for a huge variety of behavioural differences. Thus in the psychology of criminals it follows that some at least (those who have failed to learn the mores of society) must be more extraverted than normal because, manifestly, the conditioning procedures offered by society have failed to work.

Eysenck is well known in Great Britain as a leading exponent of behaviour therapy, a treatment based upon theories of learning, especially classical conditioning and therefore tied closely into Eysenck's factorial findings. Here the significance of the high N score can be seen for the highly labile autonomic nervous system of the high N scorer allows physiological responses (which are subjectively conceived of as anxiety) to be conditioned to inappropriate stimuli, in the case of the dysthymic or phobic for example.

Furthermore as we discussed in chapter 15 other Pavlovian concepts such as cortical inhibition are involved in this theorizing to account for the differential performance over time of introverts and extraverts on tasks normally thought of as demanding vigilance. All this experimental work is summarized in the three books "Readings in Extraversion–Introversion" (Eysenck and Eysenck, 1970).

This brief outline of the theory is sufficient for our purposes because it shows first its grand scope. Like psychoanalysis, there is no aspect of human behaviour to which it is irrelevant. Long ago it was customary to criticize behaviourism on the grounds that behaviour was conceptualized in terms of stimuli and responses. It leaves out reference to the organism, a vital defect since, if we take eating as an example, the response is different depending upon when and what we last ate. Both Eysenck and Cattell have argued for many years against what this latter calls the "classical reflexological position," and Cattell in 1940 asked to substitute $R = f(O.S)$ for $R = f(S)$ where, R, O and S are parameters of response, organism and stimulus respectively. The first and second order factors of Cattell and the close approaches to second orders in Eysenck, attempt to specify the important parameters of the organism. This is particularly true of Eysenck (with N and E) and Butcher with ergs and sentiments with respect to the learning processes. Since all factorists are agreed that N and E are factors of large variance albeit under different labels it might appear that this theory approaches the ideal for a personality theory (except for omitting many other known traits) being tied to factorial observations and well established psychological processes.

A major problem with this theorizing lies in the concept of condition-ability. There is no evidence that it is a unitary concept. Thus if response A in a subject conditions quickly, does response B, C etc.? Furthermore, there is some physiological evidence which suggests that this is unlikely. Lacey's (1967) study of autonomic indices in response to stimulation found that some functions were quick to respond while others were not. For example, in one subject the PGR rather than heart rate would respond whereas in another it was breathing rate that was the sensitive index. Of course if conditionability is not unitary then Eysenck's theorizing collapses especially since eye-blink is the response that has been studied. It certainly makes nonsense of broad extrapolations to such fields as mental illness and delinquency.

Moreover, this generalized conditionability clashes with the extensive work of Cattell and Scheier (1962) showing that autonomic reflexes, e.g. the GSR, condition more readily primarily with high anxiety (not introversion) and that classroom learning rates, on the other hand, are associated with lowered anxiety. Until a factor of conditionability is clearly demonstrated the theory cannot be taken too seriously. In addition to this, however, there is the problem that the theory only deals with two factors. Now we have shown in this book that to deal with second-order factors alone is to lose a great deal of information. Indeed the depth psychometry of Vidal (1972) which deals explicitly with both first and second-order factors may prove more valuable than either group separately. This however is not all. We have also shown that although E and N are the two largest second-order factors they are not the only ones so that even at this level the theory is incomplete. Even were it correct (which is highly unlikely) it deals with only a portion of the personality variance. In addition, it omits reference to motivational factors being concerned only with the temperamental sphere.

Eysenck's theory is inadequate because it deals only with two temperamental factors. What is needed is a theory that can embrace the first and higher-order factors of both temperament and motivation.

THE MAIN PROPOSITIONS IN CATTELIAN PERSONALITY THEORY

Our main activity so far in this chapter has been to see how personality theory as developed in the last thirty years on an experimental, quantitative basis fits in with a spectrum of theories, mainly earlier and clinical in origin. This may be of scholarly interest, but more important is the way in which the theoretical structure built up by Cattell and his co-workers meets the needs of modern experiment and practice.

Although we have examined findings and conclusions in separate areas, it remains briefly to summarize what Cattellian theory means as a whole. In a survey of personality theory by Corsini (1977) some 24 "propositions" are used that state the theory in most essentials. In somewhat more condensed form that kind of approach creates a useful summary here.

1. Multivariate analysis shows a source trait structure of common and unique factors which lie at different strata levels.
2. They have the distinct modality properties assigned to ability, temperament and dynamic traits—some thirty in each modality.
3. These structures can be recognized across different age levels, where they

show a continuous development, and across different cultures.

4. These trait structures can be located equally well in any of three media of observation—behaviour rating in situ, questionnaires and objective "performance" tests.

5. A quantitative statement of trait action can be made to fit quite well in the simple form of an additive specification equation, using weighted factor scores.

6. A reasonably complete specification is not possible unless *states* are also brought in. These are found by dR and P techniques, and present about a dozen axes, such as anxiety, depression, stress, exvia, and the ergic tension levels.

7. The level of a state can be understood as the effect of modulator action by ambient situations upon a state proneness trait, L_v (for state x).

8. Evidence points to all source traits being partly genetic and partly environmentally determined in origin, although some, e.g. intelligence and surgency are largely genetic while others e.g. radicalism, ergic tension, are largely environmental in origin.

9. In the dynamic realm, with the use of objective test methods, factor analysis yields dynamic structures which have been recognized as ergs (drives) and sentiments (learned patterns from social institutions). The same structures are found by R and P techniques.

10. The behavioural specification equation recognizes the stimulus situation and the response. Every act has five signatures—a_{hijko}—corresponding to the dimensions of the *basic data relation matrix*. They are the stimulus, the person, the response act, the ambient situation and the observer. The loading term applied to a person's trait score, usually written as a behavioural index b_{hjkx} (x being the factor trait) can be split into three terms after it is initially calculated. They are c_h, a cognitive effect, e_j, an effect index, and s_k, a modulator index, expressing the ambient situation. The total situation can be expressed by a vector of c's (the perceptual quality of the stimulus), of s's (the emotional involvement action of the ambient situation), while e describes the nature of the response. This is a multiple parametric statement of each term in the basic formulation of structures, organism and response.

11. Change of the organism covers *learning*, *volution* (motivation and involution) and *somatic experience*. An appreciable knowledge now exists of the life course of various source traits though analysis needs to break it down into (in addition to volution and learning), epogenic and anopegenic components, i.e. those peculiar to living in one epoch and those general across epochs.

12. The important point of the learning component is not change in a single variable as studied in most reflexological learning theory, but change in the three vectors of the specification equation. The first is change in *traits*, responsible for building the structures we know exist, the second is

this change in the *perceptual motor* vector, and the third is the change in the *involvement* vector—the modulator indices, showing the spectrum of emotional involvements of the individual in the given situation.

13. From a different angle learning can be considered to take three forms:
   (*a*) classical conditioning (Skinner's I),
   (*b*) instrumental conditioning (Skinner's II) perhaps best called means-end learning, and
   (*c*) integration learning.
   It is the last, untouched in reflexological learning theory, that is of greatest importance to personality theory, particularly in emotional learning.

14. An *Adjustment Process Analysis* chart can be drawn up representing the "dynamic crossroads" through which any adjustment must pass. Matrix representation of paths and experience frequencies make it possible to calculate from these to personality learning generalizations.

15. The discovery of ergic and sentiment structures by the factoring of attitudes makes possible both:
   (*a*) a more analytical treatment of learning, and
   (*b*) a calculus of conflict, decision and integration.
   The former advances by permitting a quantitative, objective statement of what drive satisfactions are reinforcing a particular behaviour or symptom. It also permits quantifying the magnitude of qualification, as drive reductions, through the possibility of ergic tension measures.

16. The prediction of a decision can be made from the values in the specification equation for the two courses of action in conflict. In addition to an evaluation of the level of such *active conflict*, the dynamic calculus permits evaluation of *individual conflict* in compromise systems. It has been shown that the obverse of this conflict measure (in the total personality) forms an *integration* measure, which correlates with ego strength and freedom from clinical pathology.

17. The learnt courses of action in the individual subsidiate through sentiment sub-goal systems to the discovered ten or so ergic goals. The interest and value structures of the individual can be represented, by these stimulus response paths, in the form of a lattice—the *dynamic lattice*. The structure of the dynamic lattice can be revealed by combined use of factor analysis and manipulative experiment, using the hydraulic model. This depends on the principle that when a satisfaction path is blocked a mathematically related change in intensity will be observable in "hydraulically" related paths.

18. The control system, reducing impulsive ergic action (and therefore bringing greater social reliability) consists:
   (*i*) First of the investment in sentiments themselves, of any kind, which "drain off" ergic tension into regular discharge paths,
   (*ii*) More actively and importantly of the source trait structures called the ego (C factor), the self sentiment (Q3) and the superego (G). (These

names incidentally witness that experiment supports the clinical ego and superego patterns, though adding Q3, unknown to psychoanalysis.) The superego is an entirely independent system of dynamic demands for control actions: the self sentiment involves all attitudes centering on the self concept and is concerned with behaviour adequately designed to preserve the physical, social and conceived self. The ego is a decision mechanism the strength of which is a function of the integration measures (16 above).

19. A full evaluation of the course of conflict, integration and anxiety requires regard for the total specification equation including these three structures. A three-source formula has been given for the generation of anxiety, which is not to be regarded as an ordinary motivation source, along with ergs and sentiments, but as the ultimate debris of frustrated drives, shown at the foot of the APA (Adjustment Process Analysis) chart.

20. At a hypothetical level the U (unintegrated) and I (integrated) motivation component factors are equated with the ergic (E) and sentiment (M) terms in the total response potential of any attitude course of action. During any learning experience both the E and M terms are modulated by stimulus situations encountered, the ergic tension modulations being defined as *arousal* and the sentiment modulation as *activation*, which is a cognitive activation of an associated network. Both arousal and activation increase in this pursuit of a goal, but arousal must ultimately fall below its initial level, to produce reward if learning is to occur. The full description of mechanisms and effects in structured learning theory is, however, sufficiently complex to require referal to larger works (Cattell and Dreger, 1976).

Compared to other theories of personality which we have evaluated throughout this book, Cattellian theory has an altogether wider and more concrete foundation in structural, quantitative research. The superstructure of generalizations and findings on development and changes in ability, temperament and dynamic factors, however, is not so well supported by experiment. Much new evidence, fortunately, is coming in from real-life-setting research in clinic, school and occupational fields in which the precise instruments for measuring these structures—the 16PF, HSPQ, CPQ, MAT, SMAT, the 8 State Battery and the Anxiety scales etc.—have been used along with observations of diagnosis, therapy, school achievement and changes of personality with life events.

Such, is the outline, which needs to be filled in with further research, of the theory of personality integration developed by Cattell and his colleagues to account for the factor analytic findings that we have discussed in this book. There still remains for us to carry out a huge body of research to elucidate what at this stage are in Plato's words but the shadows on the cave. By mathematics, however, were the true forms to be apprehended and so it is in the field of personality and motivation.

TABLE 16.1

Source-Trait Index	Low-Score Description	High-Score Description
A	SIZIA Reserved, detached, critical, aloof, stiff	AFFECTIA Outgoing, warmhearted, easygoing, participating
B	LOW INTELLIGENCE Dull	HIGH INTELLIGENCE Bright
C	LOWER EGO STRENGTH At mercy of feelings, emotionally less stable, easily upset, changeable	HIGHER EGO STRENGTH Emotionally stable, mature, faces reality, calm
E	SUBMISSIVENESS Humble, mild, easily led, docile, accommodating	DOMINANCE Assertive, aggressive, competitive, stubborn
F	DESURGENCY Sober, taciturn, serious	SURGENCY Happy-go-lucky, gay, enthusiastic
G	WEAKER SUPEREGO STRENGTH Expedient, disregards rules	STRONGER SUPEREGO STRENGTH Conscientious, persistent, moralistic, staid
H	THRECTIA Shy, timid, threat-sensitive	PARMIA Venturesome, uninhibited, socially bold
I	HARRIA Tough-minded, self-reliant, realistic	PREMSIA Tender-minded, sensitive, clinging, overprotected
L	ALAXIA Trusting, accepting conditions	PROTENSION Suspicious, hard to fool
M	PRAXERNIA Practical, "down-to-earth" concerns	AUTIA Imaginative, bohemian, absent-minded

N	ARTLESSNESS Forthright, unpretentious, genuine, but socially clumsy	SHREWDNESS Astute, polished, socially aware	
O	UNTROUBLED ADEQUACY Self-assured, placid, secure, complacent, serene	GUILT PRONENESS Apprehensive, self-reproaching, insecure, worrying, troubled	
Q_1	CONSERVATISM OF TEMPERAMENT Conservative, respecting traditional ideas	RADICALISM Experimenting, liberal, free-thinking	
Q_2	GROUP ADHERENCE Group-dependent, a "joiner" and sound follower	SELF-SUFFICIENCY Self-sufficient, resourceful, prefers own decisions	
Q_3	LOW SELF-SENTIMENT INTEGRATION Undisciplined self-conflict, lax, follows own urges, careless of social rules	HIGH STRENGTH OF SELF-SENTIMENT Controlled, exacting will power, socially precise, compulsive, following self-image	
Q_4	LOW ERGIC TENSION Relaxed, tranquil, torpid, unfrustrated, composed	HIGH ERGIC TENSION Tense, frustrated, driven, overwrought	

D: *Insecure Excitability*

I bubble over with ideas of things I want to do next.

  (a) *Always*   (b) *Often*   (c) *Practically never*

The people I want never seem very interested in me.

  (a) True   (b) Uncertain   (c) *False*

J: *Coasthenia–v.–Zeppia*

I enjoy getting a group together and leading them into some activity.

  (a) True   (b) Uncertain   (c) *False*

People tell me I'm

  (a) Apt to be noisy   (b) In between   (c) *Quiet and hard to understand*

(Continued)

TABLE 16.1 (*Continued*)

K: Mature Socialization–v.–Boorishness

I prefer plays that are
    (a) Exciting   (b) In between   (c) *On socially important themes*

If I take up a new activity I like
    (a) *To learn it as*   (b) In between   (c) To read a book on it
        I go along   by an expert

P: Sanguine Casualness

I rarely let my mind stray into fantasies and make-believe.
    (a) *True*   (b) Uncertain   (c) False

I most enjoy talking with my friends about
    (a) *Local events*   (b) In between   (c) Great artists and pictures

Q_5: Group Dedication with Sensed Inadequacy

I like a project into which I can throw all my energies.
    (a) *Yes*   (b) Perhaps   (c) No

In a situation which puts sudden demands on me I feel
    (a) *No good*   (b) In between   (c) Confident of handling it

Q_6: Social Panache

I am good at inventing a clever justification when I appear in the wrong.
    (a) *Yes*   (b) Perhaps   (c) No

I have never been called a dashing and daring person.
    (a) True   (b) Uncertain   (c) *False*

Q_7: Explicit Self-Expression

I am not concerned to express my ideas at public meetings.
    (a) True   (b) Uncertain   (c) *False*

In many undertakings I am in I don't seem to get a definite idea of what to do next.
    (a) Yes   (b) Perhaps   (c) *No*

Primary Source Traits in Clinically Deviant Pathological Behaviour (Part II of $\supset$AQ)

Source-Trait Symbol	Low-Score Description (1–3)	High-Score Description (8–10)
Hd or D_1	LOW HYPOCHONDRIASIS Is happy, mind works well, does not find ill health frightening	HIGH HYPOCHONDRIASIS Shows overconcern with bodily functions, health, or disabilities
Sd or D_2	ZESTFULNESS Is contented about life and surroundings, has no death wishes	SUICIDAL DISGUST Is disgusted with life, harbours thoughts or acts of self-destruction
Bd or D_3	LOW BROODING DISCONTENT Avoids dangerous and adventurous undertakings, has little need for excitement	HIGH BROODING DISCONTENT Seeks excitement is restless, takes risks, tries new things
Ad or D_4	LOW ANXIOUS DEPRESSION Is calm in emergency, confident about surroundings, poised	HIGH ANXIOUS DEPRESSION Has disturbing dreams, is clumsy in handling things, tense, easily upset
Fd or D_5	HIGH-ENERGY EUPHORIA Shows enthusiasm for work, is energetic, sleeps soundly	LOW ENERGY, FATIGUED DEPRESSION Has feelings of weariness, worries, lacks energy to cope
Gd or D_6	LOW GUILT AND RESENTMENT Is not troubled by guilt feelings, can sleep no matter what is left undone	HIGH GUILT AND RESENTMENT Has feelings of guilt, blames self for everything that goes wrong, is critical of self

(Continued)

TABLE 16.1 (*Continued*)

Md or D_7	LOW BORED DEPRESSION Is relaxed, considerate, cheerful with people	HIGH BORED MISANTHROPIC DEPRESSION Avoids contact and involvement with people, seeks isolation, shows discomfort with people
Pa	LOW PARANOIA Is trusting, not bothered by jealousy or envy	HIGH PARANOIA Believes he is being persecuted, poisoned, controlled, spied on, mistreated
Pp	LOW PSYCHOPATHIC DEVIATION Avoids engagement in illegal acts or breaking rules, sensitive	HIGH PSYCHOPATHIC DEVIATION Has complacent attitude toward own or other's antisocial behaviour, is not hurt by criticism, likes crowds
Sc	LOW SCHIZOPHRENIA Makes realistic appraisals of self and others, shows emotional harmony and absence of regressive traits	HIGH SCHIZOPHRENIA Hears voices or sounds without apparent source outside self, retreats from reality, has uncontrolled and sudden impulses
As	LOW PSYCHASTHENIA Is not bothered by unwelcome thoughts and ideas or compulsive habits	HIGH PSYCHASTHENIA Suffers insistent, repetitive ideas and impulses to perform certain acts
Ps	LOW GENERAL PSYCHOSIS Considers self good, dependable, and smart as most others	HIGH GENERAL PSYCHOSIS Has feelings of inferiority and unworthiness, timid, loses head easily

TABLE 16.2

Primary Objective Personality Test Factors: Brief Titles Agreed Upon for
Use in Compendium

U.I. 16	Narcissistic Ego	*v.*	Secure, Disciplined Unassertiveness
U.I. 17	Inhibition-Timidity	*v.*	Trustingness
U.I. 18	Manic Smartness	*v.*	Passiveness
U.I. 19	Independence	*v.*	Subduedness
U.I. 20	Comention (Herd Conformity)	*v.*	Objectivity
U.I. 21	Exuberance	*v.*	Suppressibility
U.I. 22	Cortertia (Cortical Alertness)	*v.*	Pathemia
U.I. 23	Mobilization of Energy	*v.*	Regression
U.I. 24	Anxiety	*v.*	Adjustment
U.I. 25	Realism	*v.*	Tensinflexia (Psychotic Tendency)
U.I. 26	Narcistic Self-Sentiment	*v.*	Homespunness
U.I. 27	Sceptical Apathy	*v.*	Involvement
U.I. 28	Super Ego Asthenia	*v.*	Rough Assurance
U.I. 29	Wholehearted Responsiveness	*v.*	Lack of Will
U.I. 30	Stolidness	*v.*	Dissofrustance
U.I. 31	Wariness	*v.*	Impulsive Variability
U.I. 32	Exvia (Extraversion)	*v.*	Invia (Introversion)
U.I. 33	Dismay (Pessimism)	*v.*	Sanguine Poise
U.I. 34	Onconautia (Impracticalness)	*v.*	Practicalness
U.I. 35	Stolparsomnia (Somnolence)	*v.*	Excitation
U.I. 36	Self-Sentiment	*v.*	Weak Self-Sentiment

TABLE 16.3

Definitive Statement on Eight State Factors by Combined P- and dR-Technique

Marker by Hypothesis	Barton Chain P-Technique								Curran dR-Technique							
	Exvia	Anxiety	Depression	Arousal	Fatigue	Stress	Regression	Random	Exvia	Anxiety	Depression	Arousal	Fatigue	Stress	Regression	Guilt
Exvia																
1	80								14							−39
2	80		−25	27					28						−30	−39
3									15							−50
Anxiety																
1		29	−42		−52			59		36					29	48
2		32	46						−27	35						50
3	−48	61								22						52
Depression																
1			77						−49		03					52
2	−57	32	51	49			41		−27		18					48
3			32	−29			38			47	17			30		32
Arousal																
1				1.12			33				29	−07	−51		−58	
2				42			−61				50	02	−67		−34	
3				93								36	−25			
4		−36	40	92	−27	33						20	−70			
5				88								88				
6				1.10								73				

	1	2	3	4	5	6	7	8	9	10	11	12
Fatigue												
1		−58	41	44					89		52	25
2	47	−65	35		37				42		47	
3		−39	69	36					75			
4		−29	61	30					19			
5		−54	68	38		−26			24			
6	−31	−88	1.13	−26	42		−44	31	41			
Stress												
1		42	59		37			26	29	72		27
2		30		56						31		41
3				60						63		
Regression												
1	−49	44	35		37	−29					15	40
2	52		59	44	41			39	26		16	
3					28						34	
Guilt												
1						64						84
2								30			25	37
3						−34		38				17

Note: Decimal points omitted as in all factor loading tables. In the chain P-technique the items so far used, although they indicate the nature of the factor structure, are in two cases inescapably composite: (1) fatigue and low arousal items are mutually loaded and also loaded on regression, and (2) regression has greater breadth than the items assigned to it. It loads also some items for depression and fatigue and its items have contributions from anxiety, depression, and fatigue. The possibility is that regression is a higher-order factor contributing to both fatigue and depression.

TABLE 16.4

Strength of Motivation Factors

Name	Description
1. Alpha	conscious id
2. Beta	realized interest
3. Gamma	super ego
4. Delta	physiological id
5. Epsilon	unconscious conflict
6. Zeta 7. Eta	not identified

TABLE 16.5

Hypothesized List of Human Ergs

Goal title	Emotion
Food-seeking	Hunger
Mating	Sex
Gregariousness	Loneliness
Parental	Pity
Exploration	Curiosity
Escape to security	Fear
Self-assertion	Pride
Narcistic sex	Sensuousness
Pugnacity	Anger
Acquisitiveness	Greed
Appeal	Despair
Rest-seeking	Sleepiness
Constructiveness	Creativity
Self-abasement	Humility
Disgust	Disgust
Laughter	Amusement

Hypothesized List of Human Sentiments

S_1 *Profession*
S_2 *Parental family, home*
S_3 *Wife, sweetheart*
S_4 *The self-sentiment.* Physical and psychological self
S_5 *Superego*
S_6 *Religion.* This has emphasis on doctrine and practice, on high social and low aesthetic values

S_{15} *Theoretical–logical.* Thinking, precision
S_{16} *Philosophical-historical.* Language, civics, social–cultural, esthetic rather than economic
S_{17} Patriotic–political
S_{18} *Sedentary–social games.* Diversion, play club and pub sociability; cards

S₇ *Sports and fitness.* Games, physical activity, hunting, military activity

S₈ *Mechanical interests*

S₉ *Scientific interests.* High theoretical, low political; math.

S₁₀ *Business–economic.* Money administrative

S₁₁ *Clerical interests*

S₁₂ *Esthetic expressions*

S₁₃ *Esthetic–literary appreciation.* Drama

S₁₄ *Outdoor–manual.* Rural, nature-loving, gardening, averse to business and "cerebration"

S₁₉ *Travel-geography.* Possibly Guilford's autism here

S₂₀ *Education–school attachment*

S₂₁ *Physical–home-decoration– furnishing*

S₂₂ *Household–cooking*

S₂₃ *News–communication.* Newspaper, radio, TV

S₂₄ Clothes, self-adornment

S₂₅ Animal pets

S₂₆ Alcohol

S₂₇ Hobbies not already specified

TABLE 16.6

Differences Between Schizophrenics and Normals and Neurotics and Normals as Expected from Former Research and as Observed in the Present Study. The Factor Labels are Related to the Positive Pole, the + and − Signs of the Expected and Observed Values are Related to the Direction in Which Clinicals are Different from Controls. ns = Not Significant

Factor		Schizophrenics		Neurotics	
		Expected	Observed	Expected	Observed
U.I. 16+	Assertive Ego	−	−.05	−	−.05
U.I. 17+	Inhibition[a]	+	ns	ns	ns
U.I. 19+	Independence	−	− .05	−	− .01
U.I. 20+	Comention	ns	ns	ns	ns
U.I. 21+	Exuberance	−	−.001	−	−.01
U.I. 22+	Cortertia	ns	ns	−	ns
U.I. 23+	Mobilization of energy	−	−.001	−	−.01
U.I. 24+	Anxiety	ns	ns	+	+.05
U.I. 25+	Realism	−	−.001	ns	−.01
U.I. 28+	Asthenia	ns	ns	+	ns
U.I. 29+	Responsive- ness	ns	ns	−	ns
U.I. 30+	Somindence	−	(−)ns	ns	ns
U.I. 31+	Steadiness	ns	ns	ns	ns
U.I. 32+	Exvia	ns	−.001	−	−.05
U.I. 33+	Dismay	+	(+)ns	ns	ns

[a] From former research, schizophrenics were expected to be significantly more inhibited (U.I. 17+) than normals. Neurotics were supposed not to be different. In the present study, the differences between normals and schizophrenics respectively neurotics were not significant.

TABLE 16.7

Alphabetical List of Manifest Needs (From Murray (1938) pp. 146–7)

---

 1 n Aba = n Abasement (Abasive attitude).
 2 n Ach = n Achievement (Achievant attitude).
 3 n Aff = n Affiliation (Affiliative attitude).
 4 n Agg = n Aggression (Aggressive attitude).
 5 n Auto = n Autonomy (Autonomous attitude).
 6 n Cnt = n Counteraction (Counteractive attitude).
 7 n Def = n Deference (Deferent attitude).
 8 n Dfd = n Defendance (Defendant attitude).
 9 n Dom = n Dominance (Dominative attitude).
10 n Exh = n Exhibition (Exhibitionistic attitude).
11 n Harm = n Harmavoidance (Fearful attitude).
12 n Inf = n Infavoidance (Infavoidant attitude).
     n Inv = n Inviolacy (Inviolate attitude). This need is considered to be a
     composite of Infavoidance, Defendance and Counteraction.
13 n Nur = n Nurturance (Nurturant attitude).
14 n Ord = n Order (Orderly attitude).
15 n Play = n Play (Playful attitude).
16 n Rej = n Rejection (Rejective attitude).
     n Sec = n Seclusion (Seclusive attitude). This need has been taken as the
     opposite of Exhibition, not as a separate variable.
17 n Sen = n Sentience (Sentient attitude).
18 n Sex = n Sex (Erotic attitude).
19 n Suc = n Succorance (Succorant attitude).
     n Sup = n Superiority (Ambitious attitude). This need is considered to be
     a composite of Achievement and Recognition (see below).
20 n Und = n Understanding (Intellectual attitude).
The following needs are occasionally referred to but were not systematically
used in the present study:
n Acq = n Acquisition (Acquisitive attitude).
n Blam = n Blamavoidance (Blamavoidant attitude).
n Cog = n Cognizance (Inquiring attitude).
n Cog = n Construction (Constructive attitude).
n Exp = n Exposition (Informing attitude).
n Rec = n Recognition (Self-forwarding attitude). This was included under
     Exhibition.
n Ret = n Retention (Retentive attitude).

TABLE 16.8

McDougall's Propensities

1. To seek (and perhaps to store) food (food-seeking propensity).
2. To reject and avoid certain noxious substances (disgust propensity).
3. To court and mate (sex propensity).
4. To flee to cover in response to violent impressions that inflict or threaten pain or injury (fear propensity).
5. To explore strange places and things (curiosity propensity).
6. To feed, protect and shelter the young (protective or parental propensity).
7. To remain in company with fellows and, if isolated, to seek that company (gregarious propensity).
8. To domineer, to lead, to assert oneself over, or display oneself before, one's fellows (self-assertive propensity).
9. To defer, to obey, to follow, to submit in the presence of others who display superior powers (submissive propensity).
10. To resent and forcibly to break down any thwarting or resistance offered to the free exercise of any other tendency (anger propensity).
11. To cry aloud for assistance when our efforts are utterly baffled (appeal propensity).
12. To construct shelters and implements (constructive propensity).
13. To acquire, possess, and defend whatever is found useful or otherwise attractive (acquisitive propensity).
14. To laugh at the defects and failures of our fellow-creatures (laughter propensity).
15. To remove, or to remove oneself from, whatever produces discomfort, as by scratching or by change of position and location (comfort propensity).
16. To lie down, rest and sleep when tired (rest or sleep propensity).
17. To wander to new scenes (migratory propensity).
18. A group of very simple propensities subserving bodily needs, such as coughing, sneezing, breathing, evacuation.

Bibliography

A

Adelson, M. (1952). "A study of ergic tension patterns through the effects of water deprivation in humans." Unpub. Ph.D. Thesis. Univ. Illinois.

Adler, A. (1927). "Understanding Human Nature." New York: Chilton.

Adorno, T. W., Frenkel-Brunswick, E., Levinson, D. J., and Sanford, R. N. (1950). "The Authoritarian Personality." New York: Harper.

Allport, G. W. (1937). "Personality: A Psychological Interpretation." New York: Holt, Rinehart and Winston.

Allport, G. W., and Odbert, H. S. (1936). "Trait Names: A psycholexical study." *Psychol. Monogr.* 47, 171, 63.

Allport, G. W. and Vernon, P. E. (1933). "Studies in Expressive Movement." New York: Macmillan.

Anastasi, A. (1961). "Psychological Testing." New York: Macmillan.

Anderson, H. E. (1966). "Regression, Discriminant Analysis and a Standard Notation for Basic Statistics," pp. 153–173 *in* Cattell, R. B. (1966) Ed.

Apploy, M, H, and Trumbull, R. (Eds) 1967. "Psychological Stress: Issues in Research." New York: Appleton-Century Crafts.

Aronfreed, J. (1968). "Conduct and Conscience: The Socialization of Internalized Control over Behaviour." New York: Academic Press.

B

Bandura, A. and Huston, A. C. (1961). "Identification as a process of incidental learning." *J. Abnorm. Soc. Psychol.* 63, 311–318.

Bandura, A. and Walters, R. H. (1963). "Social Learning and Personality Development." New York: Holt, Rinehart and Winston.

Bannister, D. and Fransella, F. (1966). "A grid test of schizophrenic thought and disorder." *Brit. J. Soc. Clin. Psychol.* 5, 95.

Bargmann, R. (1953). "The statistical significance of simple structure in factor analysis." Frankfurt. Main. Hochschule Fuer Internationale Paedagogische Forschung.

Barton, K. (1973a). "The relative validities of the CTS, the EPI and the Comrey Scales as measures of second-order personality source traits by questionnaires." Advance publication No. 1: Boulder: Institute for research on morality and adjustment.

Barton, K. (1973b). "The CTS, Core Trait and State Kit." Champaign: IPAT.

Barton, K., Dielman, T. E. and Cattell, R. B. (1971). "The prediction of school grades from personality and IQ measures." *Personality* 1971, 2, 325–33.

Bateson, G., Jackson, D., Haley, J. and Weakland, J. (1956). "Towards a theory of schizophrenia." *Behav. Sci.*, 1, 251–264.

Beach, F. A. (1956). "Characteristics of Masculine Sex Drive." *In* Jones, M. R. (1956) Ed.

Beck, A. T. (1962). "Reliability of psychiatric diagnoses: a critique of systematic studies." *Amer. J. Psychiat.* 119, 210–215.

355

Beck, A. T., Ward, G. H., Mendelsson, M., Mock, J. E. and Erbaugh, J. K. (1962). "Reliability of psychiatric diagnoses II: a study of the consistency of clinical judgments and ratings." *Amer. J. Psychiat.* **119**, 351–7.

Berne, E. (1968). "Games People Play: the psychology of human relationships." Harmondsworth: Penguin.

Birnbaum, A. (1968). "Some latent trait models and their use in inferring an examinee's ability." *In* Lord and Novick (1968).

Blum, G. S. (1953). "Psycho-analytic theories of personality." New York: McGraw-Hill.

Bowers, S. K. (1973). "Situationism in Psychology: an analysis and a critique." *Psychol. Rev.* 80, 5, 307–336.

Bowlby, J. (1969). "Attachment." Vol. 1. "Attachment and Loss." London, Hogarth Press and Institute of Psychoanalysis.

Broadbent, D. E. (1971). "Decision and Stress." London: Academic Press.

Brown, R. (1965). "Social Psychology." New York: Free Press.

Bruner, J. S. and Goodman, C. (1947). "Value and need as organizing factors in perception." *J. Abnorm. Soc. Psychol.* **42**, 33–44.

Buck, J. N. (1948). "The H.T.P. Test." *J. Clin. Psychol.* **4**, 151–9.

Burdsall, C. A. and Vaughan, D. S. (1974). "A contrast of the personality structure of college students found in the questionnaire medium by items as compared to parcels." *J. Genet. Psychol.* **125**, 219–224.

Buros, O. K. (1959). "The Vth Mental Measurement Year Book." New Jersey: Gryphon Press.

Buros, O. K. (1965) (Ed.). "The VIth Mental Measurement Year Book." New Jersey: Gryphon Press.

Buros, O. K. (1972) (Ed) "VIIth Mental Measurement Year Book." New Jersey: Gryphon Press.

Burt, C. (1915). "The general and specific factors underlying the primary emotions." *Brit. Ass. Ann. Rep.* **84**, 694–6.

Burt, C. (1937). "The analysis of temperament." *Brit. J. Med. Psychol.* **17**, 158–188.

Burt, C. (1939). "The factorial analysis of emotional traits." *Charact. Temp.* **7**, 238–254, 285–299.

Burt, C. (1940). "Factors of the Mind." London: Univ of London Press.

Burt, C. (1948a). "The factorial study of temperament traits." *Brit. J. Psychol. Stat. Sect.* **1**, 178–203.

Burt, C. (1948b). "The Young Delinquent." London: Univ of London Press.

Burt, C. (1966). "The genetic determination of differences in intelligence: a study of monozygotic twins reared together and apart." *Brit. J. Psychol.* **57**, 137–153.

C

Caffelt, D. and Sweney, A. B. (1965). "Motivational dynamics of violent and non-violent criminals measured by behavioural tests." Paper: S. W. Psychol. Ass: Oklahoma.

Campbell, D. P. (1971). "Handbook for the Strong Vocational Interest Blank." Stanford: Stanford Univ Press.

Campbell, D. T. and Fiske, D. W. (1959). "Convergent and Discriminant Validation by the Multitrait-Multimethod Matrix." *Psychol. Bull,* **56**, 81–105.

Cannon, W. B. (1929). "Bodily Changes in Pain, Hunger, Fear and Rage." (2nd Edit). New York: Appleton.

Cartwright, D. (1974). "Introduction to Personality." Chicago: Rand McNally.

Cattell, R. B. (1936). "A Guide to Mental Testing." London: University of London Press.

Cattell, R. B. (1943). "Fluctuation of sentiments and attitudes as a measure of character integration and of temperament." *Amer. J. Psychol.* **56**, 195–216.

Cattell, R. B. (1944). "'Parallel proportional profiles' and other principles for determining the choice of factors by rotation." *Psychometrika*, **9**, 267–283.

Cattell, R. B. (1946). "Description and Measurement of Personality." London: Harrap.

Cattell, R. B. (1949). "r_p and other coefficients of pattern similarity." *Psychometrika* **14**, 279–298.

Cattell, R. B. (1949). "The dimensions of culture patterns by factorizations of national characters." *J. Abnorm. Soc. Psychol.* **44**, 443–469.

Cattell, R. B. (1952). "The three basic factor-analytic research designs, their inter-relations and derivatives." *In* Jackson and Messick (1967) Eds.

Cattell, R. B. (1957). "Personality and Motivation Structure and Measurement." Yonkers: World Book Co.

Cattell, R. B. (1965). "The Scientific Analysis of Personality." Harmondsworth: Penguin.

Cattell, R. B. (1966). "The Meaning and Strategic Use of Factor Analysis." *In* Cattell, R. B. (1966) Ed.

Cattell, R. B. (1966). "The Scree Test for the Number of Factors." *Multiv. Behav. Res.* **1**, 140–161.

Cattell, R. B. (1966) Edit. "Handbook of Multivariate Experimental Psychology." Chicago: Rand McNally.

Cattell, R. B. (1971) Edit. "Handbook of Modern Personality Theory." Urbana: Univ. of Illinois Press.

Cattell, R. B. (1971). "Abilities Their Structure Growth and Action." New York: Houghton Mifflin.

Cattell, R. B. (1972a). "The 16PF and basic personality structure: a reply to Eysenck." *J. of Behav. Sci.* 1972, **1**, 169–187.

Cattell, R. B. (1972b). "The nature and genesis of mood states: a theoretical model with experimental measures concerning anxiety, depression, arousal and other mood states." *In* Spielberger, C. B. (1972) Ed.

Cattell, R. B. (1973). "Personality and Mood by Questionnaire." New York: Jossey Bass.

Cattell, R. B. (1973). "Second stratum structure on a basis of pathological factors." Advance Publications No. 18. Boulder, Colo. Institute for research on morality and adjustment.

Cattell, R. B. (1973c). "The second-order structure on a broader basis of 23 primaries." Advance Publications No. 12. Boulder, Colo. Institute for research on morality and adjustment.

Cattell, R. B. (1973b). "A comparison of item and parcel factoring on four studies." Advance Publications No. 42. Boulder, Colo. Institute for research on morality and adjustment.

Cattell, R. B. (1976). "Source Trait Structure seen in Laboratory Measurement: T Data." *In Press.*

Cattell, R. B. (1977). "Personality and Learning Theory." *In Press.*

Cattell, R. B. and Beloff, H. (1960). "The H.S.P.Q." Champaign. IPAT.

Cattell, R. B. and Bjerstedt, A. (1967). "The structure of depression by factoring Q data in relation to general personality source traits." *Scand. J. Psychol.* **8**, 17–24.

Cattell, R. B. and Bolton, L. S. (1969). "What pathological dimensions lie beyond the normal dimensions of the 16PF? A comparison of M.M.P.I. and 16PF factor domains." *J. Consult. Clin. Psychol.* **33**, 18–29.

Cattell, R. B. and Bolz, C. R. (1973). Quoted by Cattell, R. B. (1973).

Cattell, R. B. and Burdsall, C. A. (1975). "The radial parcel double factoring design: a solution to the item vs. parcel controversy." *Mult. Behav. Res.* **10**, 165–169.

Cattell, R. B. and Butcher, H. J. (1968). "The Prediction of Achievement and Creativity." New York: Bobbs Merrill.

Cattell, R. B. and Cattell, A. K. S. (1955). "Factor rotation for proportional profiles: Analytical solution and an example." *Brit. J. Statis. Psychol.* **8**, 83–92.

Cattell, R. B. and Cross, P. (1952). "Comparison of the ergic and self-sentiment structures found in dynamic traits by R and P techniques." *J. Personal.* **21**, 2, 250–270.

Cattell, R. B. and Delhees, K. H. (1973). "Seven missing normal personality factors in the questionnaire primaries." *Multiv. Behav. Res.* 173–194.

Cattell, R. B. and Dielman, T. E. (1974) "The Structure of Motivational Manifestations as Measured in the Laboratory Rat: a test of motivational component theory." *Personal.* (In Press)

Cattell, R. B. and Digman, J. M. (1964). "A theory of the structure of perturbations in observer ratings and questionnaire data in personality research." *Behav. Sci.* **9**, 341–358.

Cattell, R. B. and Dickman, K. (1962). "A dynamic model of physical influences demonstrating the necessity of oblique simple structure." *Psychol. Bull.* **59**, 389–400.

Cattell, R. B. and Eber, H. W. (1954). "The IPAT Music Preference Test of Personality." Champaign: IPAT.

Cattell, R. B. and Foster, M. J. (1963). "The rotoplot program for multiple, single plane, visually-guided rotation." *Behav. Sci.* **8**, 156–165.

Cattell, R. B. and Gibbons, B. D. (1968). "Personality factor structure of the combined Guilford and Cattell personality questionnaires." *J. Pers. Soc. Psychol*, **9**, 107–120.

Cattell, R. B. and Gorsuch, R. L. (1963). "The uniqueness and significance of simple structure demonstrated by contrasting organic 'natural structure' and 'random structure' data." *Psychometrika*. **28**, 55–67.

Cattell, R. B. and Gorsuch, R. L. (1965). "The definition and measurement of national morale and morality." *J. Soc. Psychol.* **67**, 77–96.

Cattell, R. B. and Gruen, W. (1955). "The primary personality factors in 11 year-old children, by objective tests." *J. Pers.* **23**, 460–478.

Cattell, R. B. and Horn, J. (1963). "An integrated study of the factor structure of adult attitude-interest." *Genet. Psychol. Monogr.* **16**, 89–149.

Cattell, R. B. and Killian, L. R. (1967). "The pattern of objective test personality factor differences in schizophrenia and the character disorders." *J. Clin. Psychol.* **23**, 342–8.

Cattell, R. B. and Klein, T. (1974). "Inheritance of personality factors in the HSPQ." *Behav. Genet.* 3, 12–20.

Cattell, R. B. and Luborsky, L. (1947). "Personality factors in response to humour." *J. Abnorm. Soc. Psychol.* **42**, 402–421.

Cattell, R. B. and Luborsky, L. (1952). "The IPAT Humour Test of Personality." Illinois: IPAT.

Cattell, R. B. and Marshall (1973). "Supplement to the 16PF Handbook." Champaign: IPAT.

Cattell, R. B. and Muerle, J. L. (1960). "The 'Maxplane' program for factor rotation to oblique simple structure." *Educ. Psychol. Meas.* **20**, 569–590.

Cattell, R. B. and Nichols, K. E. (1972). "An improved definition, from 10 researches, of second-order personality factors on Q data (with cross-cultural checks)." *J. Soc. Psychol.* **86**, 187–203.

Cattell, R. B. and Nesselroade, J. R. (1973). "The discovery of the anxiety state pattern in Q data and its distinction in the LM model from depression, effort, stress and fatigue." *Mult. Behav. Res.*

Cattell, R. B. and Saunders, P. R. (1954). "Musical preferences and personality diagnosis 1: a factorization of 120 themes." *J. Soc. Psychol.* **39**, 3–24.

Cattell, R. B. and Scheier, I. H. (1961). "The meaning and Measurement of Neuroticism and Anxiety." New York: Ronald Press.

Cattell, R. B. and Schuerger, J. M. (1970) "Basic research foundation and construction of the HSOA battery." Champaign. IPAT Adv. Pub. No. 12.

Cattell, R. B. and Stice, G. F. (1960). "The Dimensions of Groups and their Relations to the Behaviour of Members." Champaign: IPAT.

Cattell, R. B. and Sweney, A. B. (1964). "Components measurable in manifestation of mental conflicts." *J. Aborm. Soc. Psychol.* **68**, 479–90.

Cattell, R. B. and Tatro, D. F. (1966). "The personality factors objectively measured which distinguish psychotics from normals." *Behav. Res. Therap.* **4**, 39–51.

Cattell, R. B. and Tollefson, D. L. (1966). "The IPAT Humour Test of Personality." Champaign: IPAT.

Cattell, R. B. and Vaughan, (1973). "A large sample cross-check on the factor structure of the 16PF by item and by parcel factoring." *Adv. Pub. No. 41.* Boulder, Instit. for research on morality and adjustment.

Cattell, R. B. and Warburton, E. W. (1967). "Objective Personality and Motivation Tests." Urbana: Univ. of Illinois Press.

Cattell, R. B. and Wenig, P. (1952). "Dynamic and Cognitive factors controlling misperception." *J. Aborm. Soc. Psychol.* **47**, 797–809.

Cattell, R. B., Barton, K., and Dielman, T. E. (1972). "Prediction of school achievement from motivation, personality and ability measures." *Psychol. Reports.* **30**, 35–43.

Cattell, R. B., Bolz, C. R. and Korth, B. (1973). "Behavioural types in pure bred dogs objectively determined by Taxonome." *Behav. Genet.* **3**, 205–216.

Cattell, R. B., Cattell, A. K. S. and Rhymer, R. M. (1947). "P technique demonstrated in determining psychophysiological source traits in a normal individual." *Psychometrika.* **12**, 267–288.

Cattell, R. B., Coulter, M. A. and Tsujioka, B. (1966). "The taxonometric recognition of types and functional emergents." Chapter 9 *in* Cattell, R. B. (1966) Ed.

Cattell, R. B., Schrader, R. R. and Barton, K. (1974). "The definition and measurement of anxiety as a trait and a state in the 12–17 year range.' *Brit. J. Soc. Clin. Psychol.* **13**, 173–182.

Cattell, R. B., Delhees, K. H., Tatro, D. F. and Nesselroads, J. R. (1971). "Personality structure checked in primary objective test factors for a mixed normal and psychotic sample." *Multiv. Behav. Res.* **6**, 187–214.

Cattell, R. B., Eber, H. W. and Tatsuoka, M. M. (1970). "Handbook for the sixteen personality factor questionnaire." Champaign: IPAT.

Cattell, R. B., Horn, J. and Butcher, H. J. (1962). "The dynamic structure of attitudes in adults: a description of some established factors and their measurement by the Motivation Analysis Test." *Brit. J. Psychol.* **53**, 57–69.

Cattell, R. B., Horn, J. L. and Sweney, A. B. (1970). "Motivation Analysis Test." Champaign: IPAT.

Cattell, R. B., Kawash, G. F. and De Young, G. E. (1972). "Validation of objective measures of ergic tension: response of the sex erg to visual stimulation." *J. Exp. Res. Person.* **6**, 76–83.

Cattell, R. B., Schmidt, L. R. and Bjerstedt, A. (1972). "Clinical diagnosis by the objective analytic personality batteries." *Clin. Psychol. Monogr.* **34**, 1–78.

Child, D. (1971). "Essentials of Factor Analysis." London: Holt, Rinehart.

Child, D. (1974). "Psychology for Teachers." London: Holt, Rinehart & Winston.

Clyde, D. J. (1963). "Clyde Mood Scale." Miami: Univ. of Miami.

Coan, R. W. and Cattell, R. B. (1958). "Reproducible Personality factors in middle childhood." *J. Clin. Psychol.* **14**, 339–45.

Cochrane, E. (1974). "Crime and Personality: theory and evidence." *Bull. Brit. Psychol. Soc.* **27**, 19–22.

Cofer, C. N. and Appley, M. H. (1964). "Motivation: theory and research." New York: Wiley.

Comrey, A. L. (1970). "The Comrey Personality Scales." San Diego: Educ. and Indus. Testing Service.

Comrey, A. L. (1961). "Factored homogeneous item dimensions in personality research." *Educ. Psychol. Meas.* **21**, 411–431.

Comrey, A. L. and Duffy, K. E. (1968). "Cattell and Eysenck factor scores related to Comrey personality factors." *Multiv. Behav. Res.* 379–392.

Corah, N. L., Feldman, M. J., Cohen, I. S., Green, W., Meadow, A. and Ringwall, E. A. (1958). "Social desirability as a variable in the Edwards Personal Preference Schedule." *J. Consult. Psychol.*, **22**, 70–72.

Corsini, R. J. (1977). "Current Personality theories." New York. Peacock Publications.

Court, J. H. (1965). "Anxiety among acute schizophrenics and temporal lobe patients." *Brit. J. Soc. Clin. Psychol.* **4**, 254–258.

Creighton, C. C. (1894). "A History of Epidemics in Britain." Cambridge: Cambridge Univ. Press.

Cronbach, L. J. (1946). "Response Sets and Test Validity." *Educ. Psychol. Meas.* **6**, 475–494.

Cronbach, L. J. (1950). "Further evidence on response sets and test validity." *Educ. Psychol. Meas.* **10**, 3–31.

Curran, J. P. (1968). "Dimensions of state change in Q data, and chain P technique on 20 women." Unpub. Master's Thesis. Univ. of Illinois.

Curran, J. P. and Cattell, R. B. (1974). "The Eight State Questionnaire." Champaign: IPAT.

Culpin, M. and Smith, M. (1930). "The Nervous Temperament." London: H.M.S.O.

D

Dahlstrom, W. G. and Welsh, G. S. (1960). "An MMPI Handbook." London: Oxford Univ. Press.

Dart, R. A. (1957). "The osteodontokeric culture of Australopithecus Prometheurs." Transvaal. *Mus. Mem.* 10.

Davis, C. (1966). *Quoted by* Cattell and Child (1975).

Deese, J. (1952). "The Psychology of Learning." New York: McGraw-Hill.

Delhees, K. H. and Cattell, R. B. (1971). "The dimensions of pathology: proof of their projection beyond the normal 16PF source traits." *Personal.* **2**, 149–171.

Demaree, R. G. (1972). "The Comrey Personality Scales." pp. 120–122 *in* Buros, O.K. (1972) Edit.

De Voogd, A. H. and Cattell, R. B. (1973). Research *quoted by* Cattell (1973).

De Young, G. E. (1972). "Standards of decision regarding personality factors in questionnaires: a critique of Howarth and Browne's Analysis." *Canad. J Behav. Sci.* **4**, 253–5.

De Young, G. E. and Cattell, R. B. (1973). "The effect of underfactoring upon the proportion of pseudo second-order factors in rotational resolutions." *Advance Publication, No. 44.* Boulder. Institute for research on morality and adjustment.

Dielman, T. E. and Cattell, R. B. (1974). "Child Personality Structure by Questionnaire Data in the Early Grades: a summary of seven co-ordinated studies." *Child. Develop.* (In Press)

Dielman, T. E., Barton, K. and Cattell, R. B. (1971). "The prediction of junior high school achievement from objective motivation tests." *Person.* **4**, 279–287.

Dielman, T. E., Barton, K. and Cattell, R. B. (1973). "The prediction of junior high school grades from the Culture Fair Intelligence Test and objective measures of motivation." Champaign: IPAT.

Dielman, T. E., Cattell, R. B. and Kawash, G. F. (1971). "Three studies of the manipulation of the fear erg." Adv. Pub. 14. Champaign. Laboratory of Person. and Group Anal.

Dollard, J. and Miller, N. E. (1950). "Personality and Psychotherapy." New York: McGraw-Hill.

Dollard, J., Doob, L. W., Miller, N. E., Mowrer, O. H. and Sears, R. R. (1939). "Frustration and Aggression." New Haven: Yale Univ. Press.

Dreger, R. M. (edit) (1972). "Multivariate Personality Research." Baton Rouge. Claitor Pub.

E

Edwards, A. L. (1957). "The Social Desirability Variable in Personality Research." New York: Dryden Press.

Edwards, A. L. (1959). "The Edwards Personal Preference Schedule." Revised. New York: Psych. Corp.

Edwards, A. L. (1968). "Experimental Design in Psychological Research." New York: Holt, Rinehart & Winston.

Egbert, R. L., Meeland, T. *et al.* (1954). "Preliminary summary of results on personality inventories." *Human Res. Unit. No. 2.* OCAFF. Fort. Ord.

Eibl-Eibesfeld, I. (1975). 2nd Edit. "Ethology. the biology of behaviour." London: Holt, Rinehart, & Winston.

Entwistle, N. J. (1972). "Personality and academic attainment." *Brit. J. Educ. Psychol.* **42**, 137–151.

Entwistle, N. J. and Cunningham, S. (1968). "Neuroticism and school attainment—a linear relationship?" *Brit. J. Educ. Psychol.* **38**, 123–132.

Erickson, E. H. (1950). "Childhood and Society." New York: Norton.

Eysenck, H. J. (1944). "Types of Personality—a factorial study of 700 neurotics." *J. Ment. Sci.* **90**, 851–961.

Eysenck, H. J. (1947). "Dimensions of Personality." London: Routledge.

Eysenck, H. J. (1952). "The Scientific Study of Personality." London: Routledge & Kegan Paul.

Eysenck, H. J. (1953). "Uses and Abuses of Psychology." Harmondsworth: Penguin Books.

Eysenck, H. J. (1953). "The logical basis of factor analysis." Chapter 20 *in* Jackson and Messick (1967) Ed.

Eysenck, H. J. (1954). "The Psychology of Politics." London: Routledge & Kegan Paul.

Eysenck, H. J. (1958). "The Questionnaire measurement of neuroticism and extraversion." *Rev. di Psicol.* **50**, 113–140.

Eysenck, H. J. (1959). "The Rorschach Test." *In* Buros, O.K. (1959) Edit.

Eysenck, H. J. (1961). "Handbook of Abnormal Psychology" (also 1960). New York: Basic Books.

Eysenck, H. J. (1964). "Crime and Personality." London: Routledge & Kegan Paul.

Eysenck, H. J. (1967). "The Biological Basis of Personality." Springfield: C. C. Thomas.

Eysenck, H. J. (1970). "The Structure of Human Personality," 3rd Edit. Methuen: London.

Eysenck, H. J. (1970). "Readings in Introversion Extraversion 1." London: Staples Press.

Eysenck, H. J. and Cookson, D. (1969). "Personality in primary school children: 1. ability and achievement." *Brit. J. Educ. Psychol.* **39**, 109–22.

Eysenck, H. J. and Eysenck, S. B. G. (1964). "EPI Manual." London: Univ. of London Press.
Eysenck, H. J. and Eysenck, S. B. G. (1964). "The EPI." London: Univ. of London Press.
Eysenck, H. J. and Eysenck, S. B. G. (1968b). "A factorial study of psychoticism as a dimension of personality." *Multiv. Behav. Res.*. All Clinical Special Issue. 15–31.
Eysenck, H. J. and Eysenck, S. B. G. (1969). "Personality Structure and Measurement." London: Routledge & Kegan Paul.
Eysenck, H. J. and Eysenck, S. B. G. (1975). "The EPQ." London: Univ. of London Press.
Eysenck, S. B. G. (1956). "Neurosis and Psychosis: an experimental study." *J. Ment. Sci.* **102**, 517–529.
Eysenck, S. B. G. and Eysenck, H. J. (1968). "The Measurement of Psychoticism. A study of factor stability and reliability." *Brit. J. Soc. Clin. Psychol.* **7**, 286–294.

F

Fenichel, O. (1945). "The Psychoanalytic Theory of Neurosis." New York: Norton.
Field, M. J. (1960). "Search for Security." London: Faber & Faber.
Finney, J. C. (1961). "The MMPI as a measure of character structure as revealed by factor analysis." *J. Counsell. Psychol.* **25**, 327–336.
Fisher, R. A. (1936). "Statistical Methods for Research Workers" (6th Ed.). Edinburgh: Oliver & Boyd.
Fiske, D. (1971). "The analysis of tests and test-taking situations." *In* Cattell, R. B. (Edit.) 1971.
Flugel, J. C. (1945). "Man, Morals and Society." London: Duckworth.
Freedman, A. M. and Kaplan, H. I. (1967). "Comprehensive Textbook of Psychiatry." Baltimore: Williams & Wilkins.
Freud, A. (1946). "The Ego and the Mechanisms of Defence." London: Hogarth Press and the Institute of Psychoanalysis.
Freud, S. (1905). "Three Essays on Sexuality" pp. 135–243. *In* Vol. 7 of Complete Works of S. Freud. London: Hogarth Press and Institute of Psychoanalysis.
Freud, S. (1905b). "Jokes and their relation to the unconscious." *In* Vol. 8 Standard Edition of the Complete Works of S. Freud. London: Hogarth Press and Institute of Psychoanalysis.
Freud, S. (1927). "The future of an illusion." *In* Standard Edition of the Complete Psychological Works of S. Freud. Vol. 21. 3.
Freud, S. (1928). "Dostoyevsky." Vol. 21 of Standard Edition of Complete Works of S. Freud. London: Hogarth Press and Institute of Psychoanalysis.
Freud, S. (1933). "New Introductory Lectures in Psychoanalysis." *In* Vol. 22 of the Standard Edition of the Works of S. Freud. London: Hogarth Press and Institute of Psychoanalysis.
Freud, S. (1940). "An Outline of Psychoanalysis." *In* Vol. 23, of Standard Edition of Works of S. Freud. London: Hogarth Press and Institute of Psychoanalysis.
Fromm, E. (1949). "Man for Himself." London: Routledge & Kegan Paul.
Fromm, E. (1974). "The Anatomy of Human Destructiveness." London: Jon. Cape.
Furneaux, W. A. (1957). "Report to Imperial College of Science and Technology."

G

Gagné, R. M. (1965). "Psychological Principles in System Development." New York: Holt, Rinehart & Winston.

Gale, A. M. (1973). "Individual Differences: studies in extraversion and the E.E.G." *In* Kline, P. (Edit) (1973).

Gaudy, E., Wagg, P. and Spielberger, C. D. (1975). "Validation of the state-trait distinction in anxiety research." *Mult. Behav. Res.*, **10**, 331–334.

Ghiselli, E. E. (1966). "The validity of occupational aptitude tests." New York: Wiley.

Gilmer, B. V. H. (1966). "Industrial Psychology." New York: McGraw-Hill.

Glass, D. C. (1967) Ed. "Neurophysiology and Emotion." New York: Rockfeller Univ. Press.

Glueck, E. and Glueck, S. (1950). "Unravelling Juvenile Delinquency." New York: Commonwealth Fund.

Gordon, E. W. (1970). "Problems in the determination of educability in populations with different characteristics." *In* Hellmuth, J. (1970) Ed.

Gorsuch, R. L. and Cattell, R. B. (1967). "Second stratum personality factors defined in the questionnaire realm by the 16PF." *Multiv. Behav. Res.* **2**, 211–223.

Grossman, S. P. (1967). "A textbook of Physiological Psychology." New York. Wiley.

Grygier, T. G. (1961). "The Dynamic Personality Inventory." Windsor, N.F.E.R.

Grygier, T. G. (1970). "Manual to the Dynamic Personality Inventory." Windsor. N.F.E.R.

Guilford, J. P. (1940). "An inventory of factors STDCR." Beverley Hills: Sheridan Supply Co.

Guilford, J. P. (1956). "Psychometric Methods" (2nd Edit.) New York: McGraw-Hill.

Guilford, J. P. (1959). "Three faces of intellect." *Amer. Psychol.* **14**, 469–479.

Guilford, J. P. (1959). "Personality." New York: McGraw-Hill.

Guilford, J. P. (1967). "The Nature of Human Intelligence." New York: McGraw-Hill.

Guilford, J. P. (1975). "Factors and Factors of Personality." *Psychol. Bull.* **82**, 803–814.

Guilford, J. P. and Guilford, R. B. (1934). "An analysis of the factors in a typical test of introversion-extraversion." *J. Abnorm. Soc. Psychol.* **28**, 377–399.

Guilford, J. P. and Guilford, R. B. (1936). "Personality factors, S, E and M, and their measurement." *J. Psychol.* **2**, 109–127.

Guilford, J. P. and Guilford, R. B. (1939a). "Personality factors, D, R, T and A." *J. Abnorm. Soc. Psychol.* **34**, 21–6.

Guilford, J. P. and Guilford, R. G. (1939b). "Personality factors, N and G D." *J. Abnorm. Soc. Psychol.* **34**, 239–248.

Guilford, J. P. and Martin, H. G. (1943). "An Inventory of Factors GAMIN." Beverley Hills: Sheridan Supply Co.

Guilford, J. P. and Martin, H. G. (1943). "The Guilford-Martin Personnel Inventory." Beverley Hills: Sheridan Supply Co.

Guilford, J. P. and Zimmerman, W. S. (1949). "The Guilford–Zimmerman Temperament Survey: Manual of Instructions and Interpretations." Beverley Hills: Sheridan.

Guilford, J. P. and Zimmerman, W. S. (1956). "Fourteen dimensions of temperament." *Psychol. Monogr.* **70**, 10, 1–26.

Gulliksen, H. and Gulliksen, D. P. (1972). "Attitudes of different groups towards work, aims, goals and activities." *Multiv. Behav. Res. Monogr.* 3.

Guttman, L. (1954). "Some necessary conditions for common factor analysis." *Psychometrika*, **19**, 149–61.

Guttman, L. (1954). "A new approach to factor analysis: the Radex." *In* Lazarsfeld, P. F. (Ed.) (1954).

Guttman, L. (1957). "Empirical verification of the Radex structure of mental abilities and personality traits." *Educ. Psychol. Meas.* **17**, 391–407.

Guttman, L. (1955). "A generalized simplex for factor analysis." *Psychometrika*, **20**, 173–192.

Guttman, L. (1966). "Order analysis of correlation matrices." Chapter 14 *in* Cattell, R. B. (1966).

H

Hall, C. S. and Lindzey, G. (1957). "Theories of Personality." New York: Wiley.

Halpern, G. (1965). "Relative Contributions of Motivator and Hygiene Factors to Overall Job Satisfactions." APA Chicago Paper.

Hamilton, V. (1970). "Non-cognitive factors in University students' performance." *Brit. J. Psychol.* **61**, 229–241.

Hampson, S. and Kline, P. (1976). "The G index in the study of criminals." In press. *Brit. J. Criminol.*

Harman, H. H. (1964). "Modern Factor Analysis." Chicago: Univ. of Chicago Press.

Hathaway, S. R. and McKinley, J. C. (1951). "The Minnesota Multiphasic Personality Inventory Manual (Revised.") New York: The Psychological Corp.

Haverland, E. M. (1954). "The application of an analytical solution for proportional profiles rotation to a problem and to the drive structure in rats." Unpub. Ph.D. Thesis, Univ. Illinois.

Heim, A. W., Watts, K. P. and Simmonds, V. (1970). "AH4, AH5 and AH6 Tests." Windsor: N.F.E.R.

Heim, A. W., Watts, K. P. and Simmonds, V. (1969). "Brook Reaction Test." Windsor: N.F.E.R.

Hellmuth, J. (1970) (Ed.). "Disadvantaged Child." Vol. 3. "Compensatory Education: A National Debate." New York: Brunner–Mazel.

Hendrickson, A. E. and White, P. O. (1964). "Promax: a quick method of rotation to oblique simple structure." *Brit. J. Stat. Psychol.* **17**, 65–70.

Herzberg, F. (1966). "Work and the Nature of Man." London: Staples Press.

Herzberg, F., Mausner, B. and Snyderman, B. (1959). "The Motivation to Work." New York: Wiley & Sons.

Holland, J. L. (1965). "Vocational Preference Inventory." 6th Version. Palo Alto: Consulting Psychologists Press.

Holland, J. L. (1966). "The Psychology of Vocational Choice." Waltham, Mass. Blaisdell.

Holland, J. L. and Whitney, D. R. (1968). "Changes in the Vocational Plans of College Students: Orderly or Random?" *ACT. Res. Rep.* **25**, 1–44.

Holland, J. L. Whitney, D. R., Cole, N. S. and Richards, J. M. (1969). "An empirical occupational classification derived from a theory of personality and intended for practice and research." *Act. Res. Rep.* **29**, 1–22.

Holley, J. W. (1973). "The Rorschach." *In* Kline, P. (Ed.) (1973).

Holley, J. W. and Guilford, J. P. (1964). "A note on the G index of agreement." *Educ. Psychol. Meas.* **24**, 749–53.

Holtzman, W. H. (1968). "Holtzman Inkblot Technique." *In* Rabin A. I. (Ed.) (1968).

Honess, T. and Kline, P. (1974a). "Extraversion, Neuroticism and academic performance in Uganda." *Brit. J. Educ. Psychol.* 74–5.

Honess, T. and Kline, P. (1974b). "The use of the EPI and the JEPI with a student population in Uganda." *Brit. J. Soc. Clin. Psychol.* **13**, 96–8.

Horn, J. L. (1966). "Motivation and dynamic calculus concepts from multivariate experiment" *in* Cattell, R. B. (1966) Edit.

Horney, K. (1939). "New Ways in Psychoanalysis." New York: Norton.

Horst, P. (1966). "An overview of the essentials of multivariate analysis methods" pp. 129–152, *in* Cattell, R. B. (1966) Edit.

Hotelling, H. (1936). "Relations between two sets of variates." *Biometrika* **28**, 321–377.

Howarth, E. and Browne, J. A. (1971a). "Investigation of personality factors in a Canadian context. 1. Marker structure in personality questionnaire items." *Canad. J. Behav. Sci.* **3**, 161–173.

Howarth, E. and Browne, J. A. (1971b). "An item factor analysis of the 16PF questionnaire." *Person. Internat. J.* **2**, 117–139.

Howells, J. G. and Lickorish, J. R. (1962). "The Family Relations Indicator." Edinburgh: Oliver & Boyd.

Hudson, L. (1966). "Contrary Imaginations." Methuen: London.

Hull, C. L. (1943). "Principles of Behaviour." New York: Appleton-Century Crofts.

Hundal, P. S. (1970) "Achievement motivation of fast and slow progressing entre preneurs measured by projective techniques" pp. 173 179, *in* Rorschach Proceedings VII. Berne: Hans Huber.

Hundal, P. S., Sudhakar, Y. P. and Sidhu, K. (1972). "Factor analytical study of measures of Anxiety, Intelligence and Academic Achievement." *J. Psychol. Res.* **16**, 28–34.

Hundleby, J. (1973). "The measurement of personality by objective tests." *In* Kline, P. (Edit.) (1973).

Hundleby, J., Pawlik, K. and Cattell, R. B. (1965). "Personality Factors in Objective Test Devices." San Diego: Knapp.

Hunt, J. M., Ewing, T. N., LaForge, R. and Gilbert, W. M. (1959). "An integrated approach to research on therapeutic counselling with samples of results." *J. Counsel. Psychol.* **6**, 46–54.

Hurley, J. R. and Cattell, R. B. (1962). "The Procrustes program: producing direct rotation to test a hypothesized factor structure." *Behav. Sci.* **7**, 258–262.

I

Isaacson, R. L., Douglas, R. J., Lubar, J. F. and Schmaltz, L. W. (1971). "A Primer of Physiological Psychology." New York: Harper & Row.

J

Jackson, D. N. (1967). "Personality Research Form." New York: Research Psychologists Press.

Jackson, D. N. and Messick, S. (1967). (Eds.) "Problems in Human Assessment." New York: McGraw-Hill.

Janet, P. (1903). "Les Obsessions et la Psychasthenie." Paris: Alcan.

Jones, M. R. (1956) Ed. "Nebraska Symposium on Motivation." Lincoln: Univ. of Nebraska Press.

Joynson, R. B. (1974). "Psychology and Common Sense." London: Routledge & Kegan Paul.

Jung, C. G. (1918). "Studies in Word Association." London: Heinemann.

Jung, C. G. (1923). "Psychological Types." New York: Harcourt Brace.

Jung, C. G. (1940). "The Integration of the Personality." London: Kegan Paul.

K

Kaiser, H. F. (1968). "The variance criterion for analytic rotation in factor analysis." *Psychometrika*, **23**, 187–200.

Kardiner, A. (1945). "The Psychological Frontiers of Society." New York: Columbia University Press.

Karson, S. (1960). "Validating clinical judgements with the 16PF test." *J. Clin. Psychol.* **16**, 394–397.

Kelly, G. A. (1955). "The Psychology of Personal Constructs." New York: Norton.

Kimble, G. A. (1961). "Hilgard & Marquis' Conditioning and Learning." New York: Appleton, Century Crofts.

Kline, P. (1966). "Extraversion, Neuroticism and academic performance among Ghanaian University students." *Brit. J. Educ. Psychol.* **36**, 93–4.

Kline, P. (1967). "Obsessional traits and emotional instability in a normal population." *Brit. J. Med. Psychol.* **40**, 193–197.

Kline, P. (1967b). "The use of Cattell's 16PF Test and Eysenck's EPI with a literate population in Ghana." *Brit. J. Soc. Clin. Psychol.* **6**, 97–107.

Kline, P. (1968a). "The validity of the Dynamic Personality Inventory." *Brit. J. Med. Psychol.* **41**, 307–311.

Kline, P. (1968b). "An investigation of the Freudian Concept of the anal character." Unpub. Ph.D. Thesis. Univ. Manchester.

Kline, P. (1969). "The Anal Character: a cross-cultural study in Ghana." *Brit. J. Soc. Clin. Psychol.* **8**, 201–210.

Kline, P. (1969b). "The reliability of the Brook Reaction Test." *Brit. J. Soc. Clin. Psychol.* **8**, 83–4.

Kline, P. (1970b). "The validity of the Brook Reaction Test." *Brit. J. Soc. Clin. Psychol.* **9**, 42–5.

Kline, P. (1971). "Ai3Q Test." Windsor: N.F.E.R.

Kline, P. (1971). "Experimental manual to Ai3Q." Windsor: N.F.E.R.

Kline, P. (1972). "Fact and Fantasy in Freudian Theory." London: Methuen.

Kline, P. (1973). (Ed.) "New Approaches in Psychological Measurement." Chichester: Wiley.

Kline, P. (1973b). "The IPAT Music Preference Test of Personality in Great Britain." *Brit. J. Proj. Psychol.* **18**, 27–8.

Kline, P. (1973c). "Assessment in Psychodynamic Psychology." *In* Kline, P. (1973) Edit.

Kline, P. (1975). "The Psychology of Vocational Guidance." London: Batsford.

Kline, P. (1976). "Cross-Cultural Studies and Freudian Theory." *In* Warren, N. (1976).

Kline, P. and Gale, A. M. (1971). "Extraversion, neuroticism and performance in a psychology examination." *Brit. J. Educ. Psychol.* **41**, 90–3.

Kline, P. and Grindley, J. (1974). "A 28-day case-study with the MAT." *J. Mult. Exp. Person. Clin. Psychol.* **1**, 13–32.

Kline, P. and Knowles, A. (In prep.) "The personality of creative artists."

Kline, P. and Thomas, M. (1971). "The Brook Reaction Test as a measure of temperament with children of 13 and 14 years." *Brit. J. Educ. Psychol.* **41**, 317–321.

Kline, P. and Thomas, M. (1972). "The Brook Reaction Test and the Rothwell-Miller Interest Blank." *Occup. Psychol.* **46**, 31–34.

Knapp. R. R. (1961). "Objective Personality Tests and sociometric correlates of sick bay visits." *J. App. Psychol.* **45**, 104–110.

Kohlberg, L. (1969). "Stages in the Development of Moral Thought and Action." New York: Holt, Rinehart and Winston.

Kragh, U. (1955). "The Actual Genetic Model of Perception Personality." Lund: Gleerup.

Kragh, U. and Smith, G. (1970). "Percept Genetic Analysis." Lund: Gleerup.

Kretschmer, E. (1925). "Physique and Character." London: Routledge & Kegan Paul.

Krout, M. H. and Krout, T. J. (1954). "Measuring personality in developmental terms." *Genet. Psychol. Mongr.* **50**, 289–335.

Krug, S. (1970). Research *quoted by* Cattell, R. B. (1973).

Krug, S. (1971). "An examination of experimentally induced changes in ergic tension levels." Unpub. Ph.D. Thesis. Univ. Illinois.

Kuder, G. F. (1970). "The Kuder Occupational Interest Survey." Chicago: Science Research Associates.

L

Lacey, J. I. (1967). "Somatic Response Patterning and stress: some revisions of activation theory." *In* Appley & Turnbull (1967).

Lack, D. (1943). "The Life of the Robin." London: H. F. & G. Witherby.

Laing, R. D. (1960). "The Divided Self." London: Tavistock.

Lawlis, G. F. (1971). "Motivational factors affecting employment stability." *J. Soc. Psychol.* **84**, 215–225.

Lazarsfeld, P. F. (1950). "The logical and mathematical foundation of latent structure analysis." *In* Stoufer, S. et al (1950).

Lazarsfeld, P. F. (1954). Ed. "Mathematical thinking in the social sciences." Glencoe: Illinois Free Press.

Levonian, E. (1961). "Personality Measurement with items selected from the 16PF questionnaire." *Educ. Psychol. Meas.* **21**, 937 946.

Levy, D. M. (1934). "Experiments on the sucking reflex and social behaviour in dogs." *Amer. J. Orthopsychiat.* **4**, 203 24.

Levy, P. (1973). "On the relation between test theory and psychology." *In* Kline, P. (1973) Edit.

Lord, F. M. and Novick, M. R. (1968). "Statistical Theories of Mental Test Scores." New York: Addison-Wesley.

Lorenz, K. (1966). "On Aggression." London: Methuen.

Luborsky, L. and Cattell, R. B. (1947). "The validation of personality factors in humour." *J. Pers.* **15**, 283–91.

Lykken, D. T. (1972). "The Clyde Mood Scale," pp. 55–6 *in* Buros (1972) Edit.

M

McClelland, D. C., Atkinson, J. W., Clark, R. A. and Lowell, E. L. (1953). "The Achievement Motive." New York. Appleton-Century Crofts.

McClelland, D. C. (1961). "The Achieving Society." Princeton: Van Nostrand.

McDougall, W. (1908). "An Introduction to Social Psychology." London: Methuen.

McDougall, W. (1926). "Outline of Abnormal Psychology." New York: Scribner.

McDougall, W. (1932). "Energies of Men." London: Methuen.

McQuaid, J. (1970). "A personality profile of delinquent boys in Scottish Approved Schools." *Brit. J. Criminol.* **10**, 147–57.

McQueen, J. B. (1966). "Some methods for classification and analysis of multivariate observations." *Paper* 196. Univ. California: W. Management Science Institute.

Madan, V. (1967). "The relation of neuroticism and extraversion to intelligence and educational attainment at different age levels." Ph.D. Thesis. Univ. of Punjab, Chandigarh.

Mahrer, A. R. (1970) (Edit.) "New Approaches to Personality Classification." New York: Columbia Univ. Press.

May, D. R. (1971). "Psychiatric syndrome classifications checked by taxonome and discriminant functions on the clinical analysis questionnaire." Unpub. Ph.D. Thesis. Univ. of Illinois.

May, J. M. and Sweney, A. B. (1965). "Personality and Motivational changes observed in the treatment of psychotic patients." *Paper:* S. W. Psychol. Assoc.: Oklahoma.

Mayer, J. (1955). "Regulation of energy intake and the body weight: the glucostatic theory and the lipostatic hypothesis." *Amals N.Y. Acad. Sci.* **63**, 15–43.

Mayer-Gross, W., Slater, E. and Roth, M. (1967). "Clinical Psychiatry." London: Cassell.

Meehl, P. E. (1954). "Clinical vs Statistical Prediction." Minnesota: Univ. Minnesota Press.

Mehlman, B. (1952). "The reliability of psychiatric diagnoses." *J. Abnorm. Soc. Psychol.* **47**, 577–8.

Miller, R. B. (1965). "Task Description and Analysis." Chapter 6 *in* Gagné (1965).

Miller, R. B. (1966). "Human factors in Systems." *In* Gilmer, B. V. H. (1966).

Mischel, W. (1968). "Personality and Assessment." New York: Wiley.

Mischel, W. (1971). "Introduction to Personality." New York: Holt, Rhinehart & Winston.

Mischel, W. (1973). "Towards a Cognitive Social Learning reconceptualization of Personality." *Psychol. Rev.* Vol. 80, **4**, 252–83.

Morgan, C. T. (1943). "Physiological Psychology." New York: McGraw-Hill.

Mowrer, O. H. (1950). "Learning Theory and Personality Dynamics." New York: Ronald.

Murray, H. A. (1938). "Explorations in Personality." New York: Oxford Univ. Press.

N

Nesselroade, J. R. (1973). *Quoted by* Cattell, R. B. (1973).

Nesselroade, J. R. and Bates, P. B. (1975). "Higher-order factor convergence and divergence of two distinct personality systems: Cattell's H.S.P.Q. and Jackson's P.R.F.." *Mult. Behav. Res.* **10**, 387–408.

Nesselroade, J. R. and Cable, D. (1974). "Sometimes it's O.K. to factor difference scores—the reparation of state and trait anxiety." *Multiv. Behav. Res.* **9**, 273–82.

Nichols, K. E. (1973). "Collation of second and third order studies of personality structure in the high school period." *Advance Publication No. 55.* Boulder: Institute for Research on Morality and Adjustment.

Nowlis, V. and Green, R. F. (1957). "The experimental analysis of mood." Brussels: Proc. 15. *Internat. Congress of Psychol.*

O

Oakley, C. A. et al (1937). "Handbook of Vocational Guidance." London: Univ. of London Press.

Orme, J. E. (1965). "The relationship of obsessional traits to general emotional instability." *Brit. J. Med. Psychol.* 38, p. 269.

Ornstein, R. E. (1975). "The Psychology of Consciousness." London: Jonathan Cape.

P

Pasamanick, B., Dinitz, S. and Lefton, M. (1959). "Psychiatric orientation and its relation to diagnosis and treatment in a mental hospital." *Amer. J. Psychiat.* **116**, 127–32.

Pawlik, K. and Cattell, R. B. (1964). "Third order factors in Objective Personality tests." *Brit. J. Psychol.* **55**, 1–18.

Pervin, L. A. (1975). "Personality: Theory, Assessment and Research." New York: Wiley.

Pierson, G. R. and Kelly, R. F. (1963). "Anxiety, extraversion and personality idiosyncrasy in delinquency." *J. Psychol.* **56**, 441–5.

Pierson, G. R., Cattell, R. B. and Pierce, J. (1966). "A demonstration by the HSPQ of the nature of personality changes produced by institutionalization of delinquents." *J. Soc. Psychol.* **70**, 229–239.

Pinzka, C. and Saunders, D. R. (1954). "Analytic rotation to simple structure II: extension to an oblique rotation." *Res. Bull.* RB-54-3. Princeton: E.T.S.

Popper, K. (1959). "The Logic of Scientific Discovery." New York: Basic Books.

R

Rubin, A. I. (1968) Ed. "Projective Techniques in Personality Assessment." New York: Springer.

Rao, C. R. (1952). "Advanced Statistical Methods in Biometric Research." New York: Wiley.

Reich, W. (1945). "Character Analysis." New York: Orgone Institute.

Rickels, K., Cattell, R. B., Macafee, A. and Hesbacher, P. (1965). "Drug response and important external events in the patient's life." *Dis. Nerv. Syst.* **26**, 782–6.

Rodger, A. (1952). "The Seven-Point Plan." Paper No. 1. London: N.I.I.P.

Rokeach, M. (1960). "The Open and Closed Mind." New York: Basic Books.

Rorschach, H. (1921). "Psychodiagnostics." Berne: Hans Huber.

Rosenthal, R. (1964). "Experimenter outcome-orientation and the results of the psychological experiment." *Psychol. Bull.* **61**, 405–12.

Rosenzweig, S. (1951). "Idiodynamics in personality theory with special reference to projective methods." *Psychol. Rev.* **58**, 213–223.

Royce, J. R. (1963). "Factors as Theoretical Constructs." Chapter 24, *in* Messick and Jackson (1967) Eds.

S

Sanford, N. (1963). "Personality: its place in psychology." *In* Koch, S. (Ed.) "Psychology: a study of a science." Vol. 5, pp. 488–592. New York: McGraw Hill.

Sankar, D. V. S. (1969). "Schizophrenia: Current Concepts and Research." New York: PJD Publications.

Sarason, I. G. (1972) 2nd Edit. "Personality: an objective approach." London: Wiley.

Sarason, S. B., Davidson, K. S., Lighthall, F. F., Waite, R. R. and Ruebush K B., (1960). "Anxiety in Elementary School Children." New York: Wiley.

Savage, R. D. (1966). "Personality factors in academic attainment in junior school children." *Brit. J. Educ. Psychol.* **36**, 91–4.

Schachter, S. (1967). "Cognitive Effects on Bodily Functioning Studies of Obesity and Eating." *In* Glass, C. P. (Ed.) (1967).

Schmidt, H. O. and Fonda, C. P. (1956). "The reliability of psychiatric diagnosis: a new look." *J. Abnorm. Soc. Psychol.* **52**, 262–7.

Schmidt, L. R. (1972). "Differential Diagnosis mit Hilfe Objectiver Personlichkeitstests." *Diagnostica*.

Schneider, K. (1958). "Psychopathic Personalities." London: Cassel.

Schonell, F. J. (1944). "Backwardness in the Basic Subjects." Edinburgh: Oliver & Boyd.

Schuerger, J. M. and Cattell, R. B. (1971). "The High-School Objective Analytic Test Battery." Champaign: I.P.A.T.

Schwartz, P. (1959). "Attitudes of Middle Management Personnel." Pittsburgh: American Institute for Research.

Sells, S. B. (1972). "The Dynamic Personality Inventory." *In* Buros, O. K. (1965) Ed.

Semeonoff, B. (1973). "New Developments on Projective Testing." *In* Kline, P. (1973) Edit.

Sheldon, W. H. and Stevens, S. S. (1942). "The Varieties of Temperament." New York: Harper & Row.

Skelton, J. J. (1968). "The Vocational Application of an Objective Test of Motivation." Report 4/68, Psycho. Res.-Unit, Autralian Military Forces.

Skinner, B. F. (1953). "Science and Human Behaviour." New York: Macmillan.

Slukin, W. (1974). "Imprinting Reconsidered." *Bull. Brit. Psychol. Soc.* **27**, 447–51.

Smith, P. C., Kendall, L. M. and Huslin, C. L. (1969). "Measurement of Satisfaction in Work and Retirement." Chicago: Rand McNally.

Smith, W. G. (1966). "A model for Psychiatric diagnosis." *Arch. Gen. Psychiat.* **14**, 521–9.

Snedecor, G. W. (1956). "Statistical Methods" (5th Ed.) Ames: Iowa State College Press.

Spearman, C. (1927). "The Abilities of Man." London: Macmillan.

Spielberger, C. B. (1972) Ed. "Anxiety: Current Trends in Theory and Research." New York: Academic Press.

Spielberger, C. B., Gorsuch, D. L. and Lushene, R. E. (1970). "Manual for the Strate-Trait Anxiety Inventory." Palo Alto: Consulting Psychologists' Press.

Stafford-Clark, D. (1963). "Psychiatry Today." Harmondsworth: Penguin.

Stagner, R. R., Lawson, E. D. and Moffit, J. W. (1955). "The Krout Personal Preference Scale: a factor analytic study." *J. Clin. Psychol.* **11**, 103–113.

Stott, P. H. and Sykes, E. G. (1956). "Bristol Social Adjustment Guides." London: Univ. of London Press.

Stoufer, S. et al (1950). "Studies on social psychology in World War II. Vol 4. Measurement and Prediction." Princeton, N.J.: Princeton Univ. Press.

Stringer, P. (1967). "A comparison of the self-images of art and architecture students." *Stud. Art. Ed.* **9**, 33–49.

Stringer, P. (1970). "A note on the factorial structure of the Dynamic Personality Inventory." *Brit. J. Med. Psychol.* **43**, 95–103.

Strong, E. K. (1943). "Vocational Interests of Men and Women." Stanford: Univ. Press.

Strong, E. K., Campbell, D. P., Berdie, R. E. and Clark, K. E. (1971). "Strong Vocational Interest Blank." Stanford: Stanford Univ. Press.

Szasz, T. S. (1961). "The Myth of Mental Illness." London: Secker & Warburg.

T

Tatro, D. F. (1967). "The interpretation of objectively measured personality factors in terms of clinical data and concepts." Unpub. Ph.D. Thesis: Urbana: Univ. of Illinois.

Tatsuoka, M. M. and Cattell, R. B. (1970). "Linear equations for estimating a person's occupational adjustment based on information on occupational profiles." *Brit. J. Educ. Psychol.* **40**, 324–334.

Tatsuoka, M. M. (1971). "Multivariate Analysis." London: Wiley.

Teitlebaum, E. and Stellar, P. (1954). "Recovery from the failure to eat produced by hypothalamic lesions." Sic. 120, 894–895.

Thompson, R. F. (1967). "Foundations of Physiological Psychology." New York: Harper Internat.

Thurstone, L. L. (1938). "Primary Mental Abilities." Chicago: Univ. of Chicago Press.

Thurstone, L. L. (1947). "Multiple factor analysis. A Development and Expansion of the Vectors of the Mind." Chicago: Univ. Chicago Press.

Thurstone, L. L. and Chave, E. J. (1929). "The Measurement of Attitude." Chicago: Univ. Chicago Press.

Tinbergen, N. (1951). "The Study of Instinct." Oxford: Oxford Univ. Press.

Tinbergen, N. (1953). "The Herring Gull's World." London: Collins.

Tolman, E. C. (1932). "Purposive Behaviour in Animals and Men." New York: Appleton-Century.

Tsujioka, B. and Cattell, R. B. (1965). "A cross-cultural comparison of second-stratum questionnaire personality factor structures in America and Japan." *J. Soc. Psychol.* **65**, 205–219.

Tsushima, T. (1960). "Notes on trends and problems of psychotherapy in Japan." *Psychologix*, **1**, 231–236.

Tucker, L. R. (1955). "The objective definition of simple structure in linear factor analysis." *Psychom.* **20**, 209–225.

V

Van Egeren, L. F. (1963). "Experimental determination by P technique of functional unities of depression and other psychological states." Unpub. Master's Thesis. Univ. Illinois.

Van De Geer, J. P. (1971). "Introduction to Multivariate Analysis for the Social Sciences." San Francisco: Freeman.

Vaughan, D. (1974). "On the technical standards of ten representative factor analyses purporting to decide personality theories." *J. Behav. Sci.*

Vernon, P. E. (1961). "The Structure of Human Abilities." London: Univ. of London Press.

Vernon, P. E. (1964). "Personality Assessment." London: Methuen.

Vernon, P. E. and Parry, J. B. (1949). "Personnel Selection in the British Forces." London: Univ. of London Press.

Vidal, A. (1972). "BG8 Diagnostic Psychologique a compte vendu programme sur ordinquteur." Paris: Centre de Psychologie Appliquee.

W

Warburton, F. W. (1968). "The Structure of Personality Factors." *Unpub. Ms.* Univ. of Manchester.

Warburton, F. W. (1968b). "The relationship between personality factors and scholastic attainment." *Unpub. Ms.* Univ. of Manchester, Manchester.

Warburton, F. W. (1972). "The relationship between personality factors and scholastic attainment." Chapter 14 *in* Dreger, R. M. (1972).

Warburton, F. W., Butcher, H. J. and Forrest, G. M. (1963). "Predicting student performance in a university department of Education." *Brit. J. Educ. Psychol.* **33**, 68–79.

Warren, N. (Edit.) (1976). "Progress in Cross-Cultural Psychology." London: Academic Press.

Webb, E. (1915). "Character and Intelligence." *Brit. J. Psychol. Monogr. Supp* 1, 3.

Wenig, P. (1952). "The relative roles of naive, artistic, cognitive and press compatability misperception and ego defence operations in tests of misperception." Unpub. Master's Thesis. Urbana: Univ. Illinois.

Wiggins, J. S. (1968). "Personality Structure." *Ann. Rev. Psychol.* **19**, 293–330.

Williams, P. A., Kirk, B. A. and Frank, A. C. (1968). "New Men's SVIB: a comparison with the old." *J. Counsel. Psychol.* 287–294.

Witkin, H. A. (1962). "Psychological Differentiation: Studies of Development." New York: Wiley.

Author Index

Subject Index

A

Ai3Q, 90, 107, 308
Abilities, 299
  Guilford's model, 27, 49
Ability distribution, 298, 303
Academic performance
  motivation, 282–285
  personality, 274–282
Accident proneness, 116, 304
Acquiescence, 38, 85, 95
Adjustment process chart (A.P.A.
  chart), 269–271, 284, 287
Analysis of variance, 10, 262
Anxiety, 121–122, 148, 213, 218, 222,
  223–224, 250, 253, 264, 270–271,
  275, 277, 280, 289, 338
Attitudes, 136, 165, 317
  measurement, 165–166

B

Balloon blowing test, 40, 128
Bargmann's test, 18, 103
Behaviour change, 232–233
Behavioural indices, 231
Behavioural specification equation,
  160, 194, 231, 268–269, 301, 303,
  304–307
Beta weights, 12, 302, 303
Bloated specific, 27, 49, 97, 101, 108,
  117
Body-build, 112, 326–328
Brook Reaction Test, 183, 204–206

C

CAQ, 55–57, 63, 102, 246, 254–258,
  261, 328

CPQ, 46, 50, 51, 52, 62, 275
C3MAT, 175, 186, 189
Canonical analysis (correlation), 12
Central state and trait kit, 224
Chiasm, 270
Circumplex, 22
Cluster analysis, 22, 33
Cold pressor test, 115
Communalities, 26, 29, 80, 103, 325
Comrey's factors, 86
Confactor rotation, 17, 19, 261
Conditioning, 162–163
Content analysis, 32
Constants file, 304
Creativity, 114, 117
Criminality, 259–260, 267, 311
Criterion keying, 54, 203–204, 258, 304
Cross-cultural studies, 170, 315
Cross-validation, 81
Cultural change, 126
Cultural differences, 170, 274, 277,
  280, 281, 315–316
Culture dimensions, 316
Cursive miniature situations test, 136

D

DPI, 27, 86–90, 106–108, 145, 308
Deliberate distortion, 36, 126
Delinquency, 259–260, 325
Depth psychologies, 323–325
Dichotomous variables, 32, 55, 85, 318
Discriminant function analysis, 12, 262
Distraction test, 41
Drives, 76, 108, 138, 144, 163, 176, 200,
  230
Dynamic calculus, 200–203